JOHN SEED

FOREWORD BY
KATHERINE STANEK

DISRUPTED REALISM

PAINTINGS FOR A
DISTRACTED
WORLD

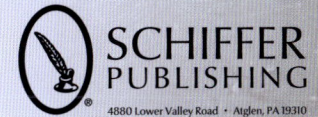

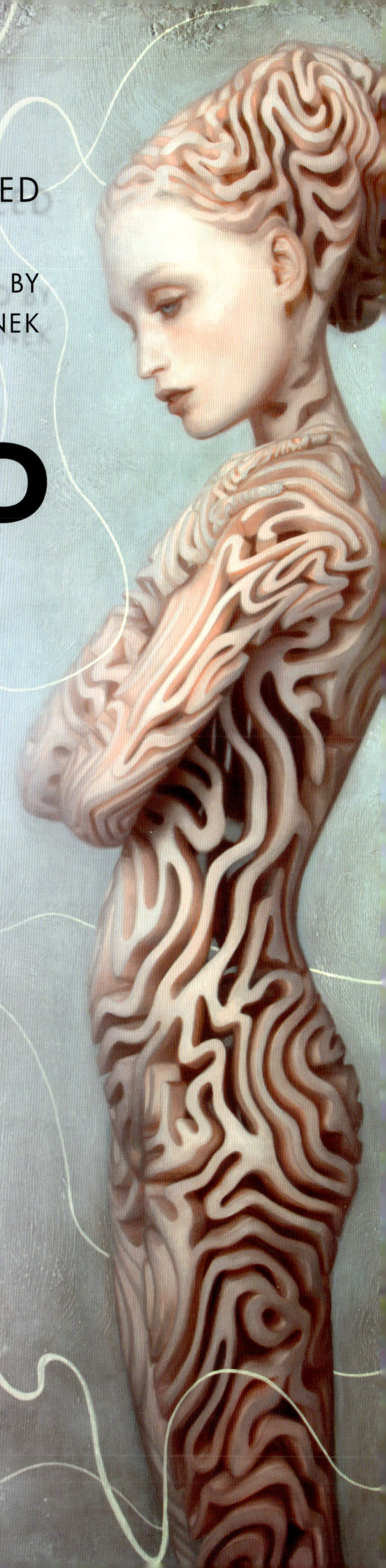

SCHIFFER
PUBLISHING
4880 Lower Valley Road · Atglen, PA 19310

Other Schiffer Books on Related Subjects:

50 Contemporary Women Artists: Groundbreaking Contemporary Art from 1960 to Now, ed. by John Gosslee and Heather Zises, foreword by Elizabeth Sackler, ISBN 978-0-7643-5653-7

Scott Fraser: Selected Works, Timothy J. Standring, William H. Gerdts, Robert C. Jackson, ISBN 978-0-7643-5398-7

Encaustic Art in the Twenty-First Century, Anne Lee & E. Ashley Rooney, foreword by Kim Bernard, afterword by Ellen Koment, ISBN 978-0-7643-5023-8

Designed by Molly Shields
Type set in Verlag/ZapfEllipt BT
Front jacket: Daniel Bilodeau. *Solace*, 2018. Oil on paper on board: 8.75 x 5.75 inches.
Back jacket: Mia Bergeron. *Sanctuary*, 2016. Oil on panel: 13.5 × 20 inches.
Title page: Dorian Vallejo. *Passages*, 2016. Oil on panel: 24 × 36 inches. (Detail)

ISBN: 978-0-7643-5801-2
Printed in China
7 6 5 4

Published by Schiffer Publishing, Ltd.
4880 Lower Valley Road
Atglen, PA 19310
Phone: (610) 593-1777; Fax: (610) 593-2002
E-mail: Info@schifferbooks.com
Web: www.schifferbooks.com

For our complete selection of fine books on this and related subjects, please visit our website at www.schifferbooks.com. You may also write for a free catalog.

Schiffer Publishing's titles are available at special discounts for bulk purchases for sales promotions or premiums. Special editions, including personalized covers, corporate imprints, and excerpts, can be created in large quantities for special needs. For more information, contact the publisher.

We are always looking for people to write books on new and related subjects. If you have an idea for a book, please contact us at proposals@schifferbooks.com.

Opposite: Radu Belcin. *Learning to Fly 2*, 2015. Oil on linen: 56 × 45 inches.

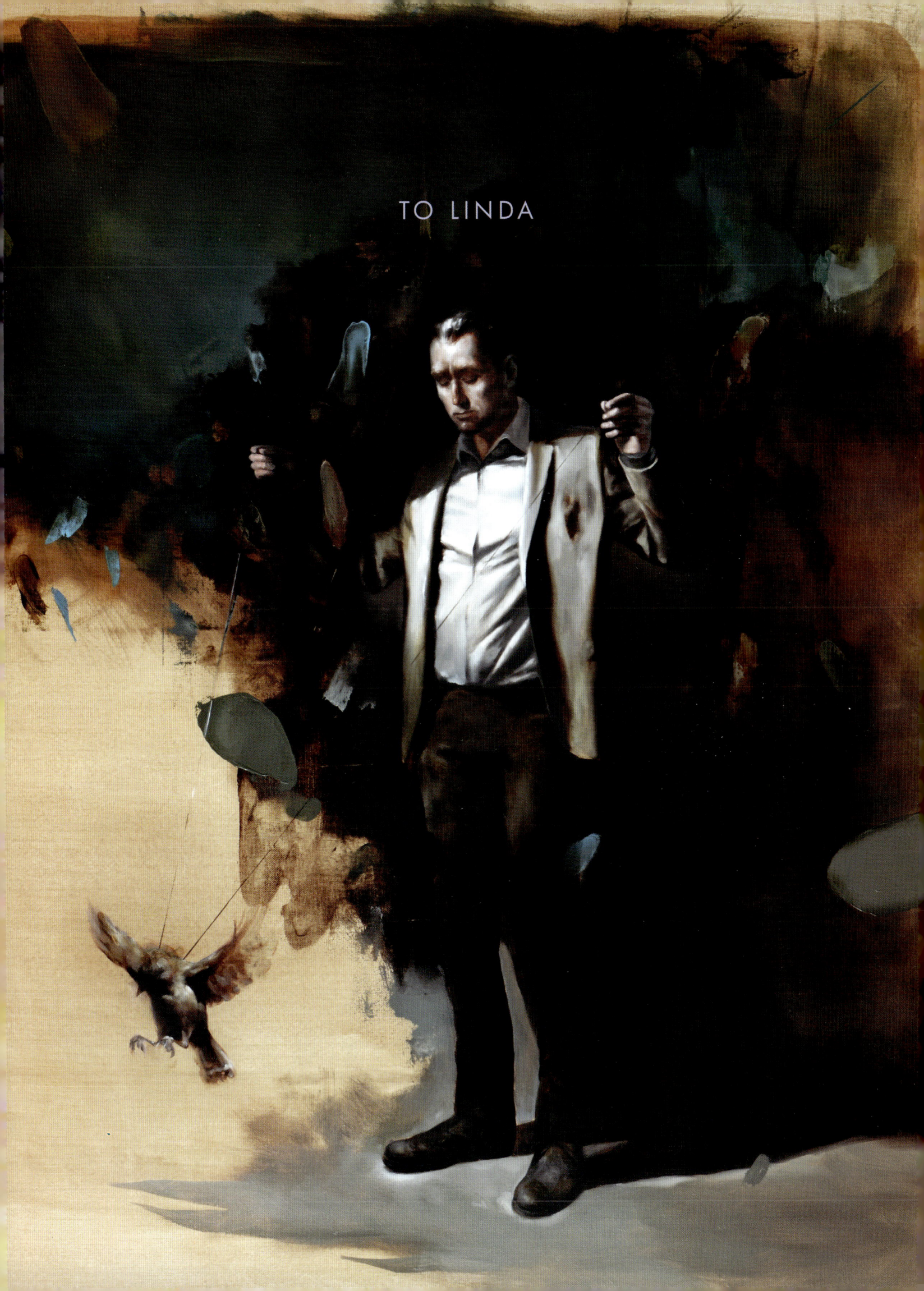

TO LINDA

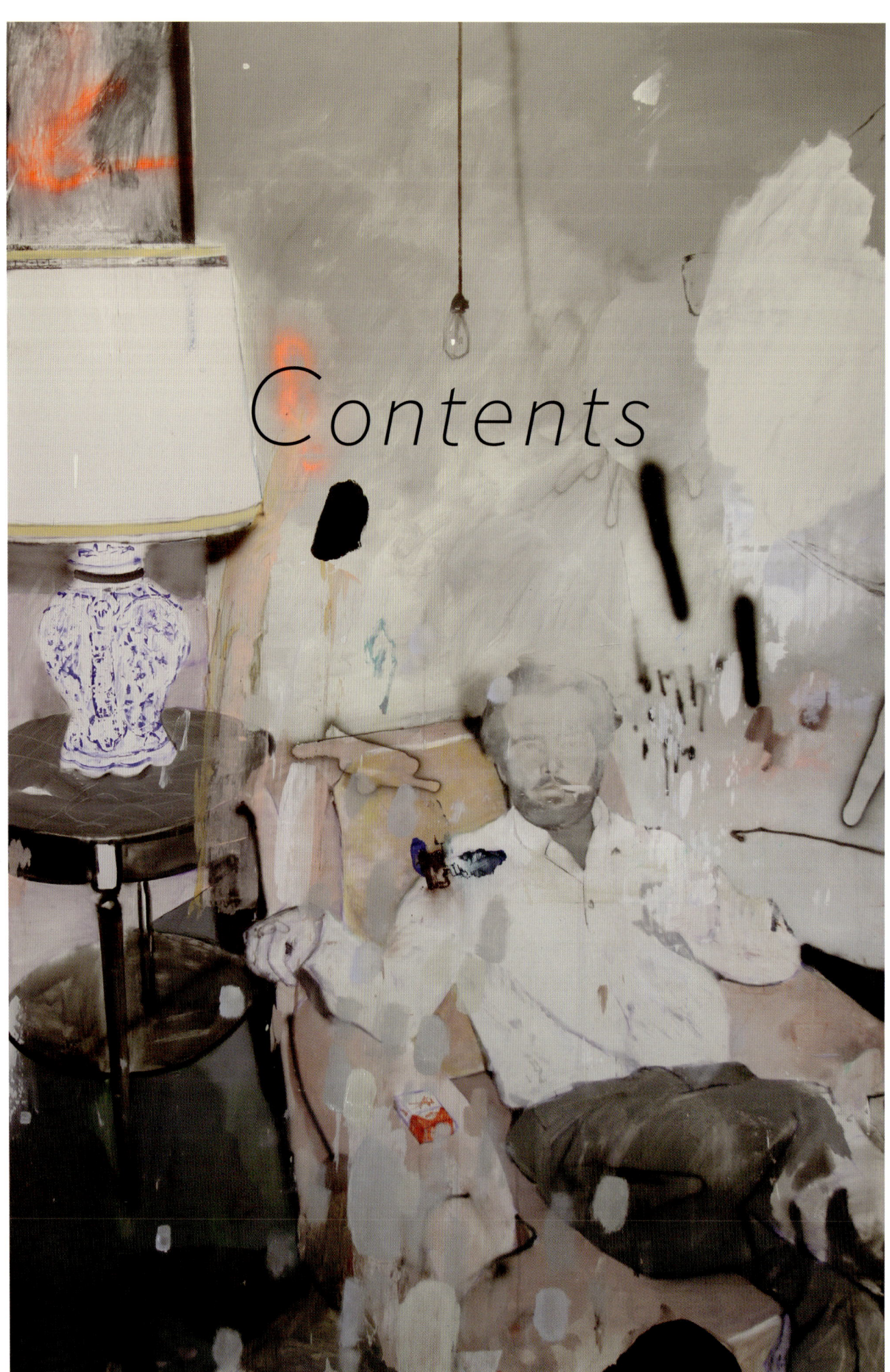

Contents

Opposite: Lou Ros. *Hijack*, 2015. Acrylic oil and pastel on canvas: 77 × 51 inches.

Foreword

KATHERINE STANEK

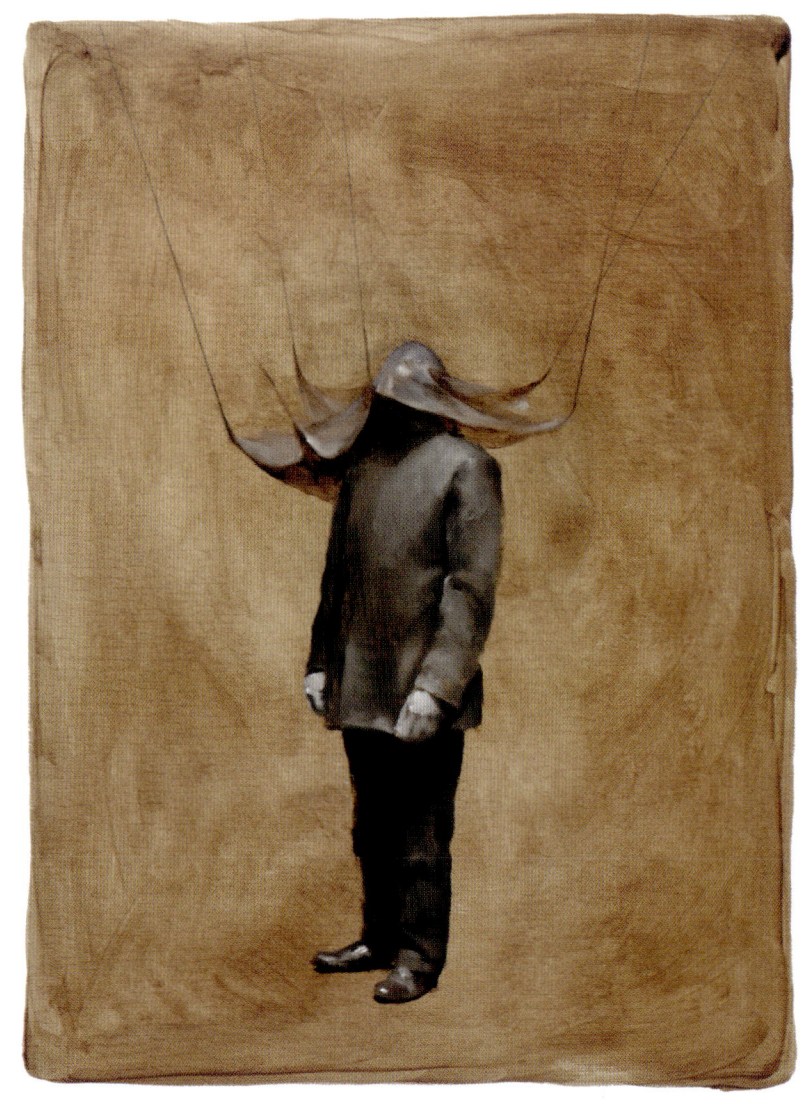

An art movement of substance and longevity can be neither calculated nor contrived; rather, it arises organically, often during periods of significant social and cultural change. "Disrupted realism" is no exception. In my view, it is a movement that begins with awareness that all things are interconnected.

Every era witnesses emergence of groundbreaking technologies that transform how society functions by influencing ways in which people interact with one another and with the world. Handheld devices alter our attention span and redefine our visual experience. There is so much pictorial competition, we believe we must scroll through multiple images incessantly just to sustain what we perceive is required to remain connected to our world. The eye doesn't have time to settle and the brain doesn't have time to process what the eye has just seen before we are on to the next image. The amount of information is overwhelming. It leaves little time to invest in a singular moment or engage with a complex individual, resulting in what can be described as a disruption of reality.

The role of a traditional art gallery, also significantly affected by modern technologies and devices, has been changing as well. Galleries around the world are faced with a difficult choice of in-depth restructuring or retiring. Intimate in-the-flesh experience of fine art is being replaced with perusing digital galleries' impersonal Rolodex in cyberspace. High-quality artwork is being overlooked in favor of flashy trends and superficial gimmicks, as once-successful artists producing meaningful work are struggling to find desirable exhibition opportunities and move out of increasingly expensive metropolitan areas. Philadelphia, for one, is experiencing such an exodus of great artists who have studied, taught, worked, and exhibited in this city, including some painters featured in this book.

With technology ranking undisputably high among far-reaching agents of change, it comes as no surprise that "disrupted realism" has taken root in the current era. What is unusual is for this international movement in painting to make its premier appearance in an exhibition at a small, sculptor-owned fine art gallery in Philadelphia within the first two years of its existence.

As a working artist in the times of change we've all been witnessing, I too was faced with a decision either to move with the tide or to attempt to alter its direction. I created Stanek Gallery with the intention of reinventing the gallery experience by bringing its focus back to quality and depth of the fine art I was to exhibit within its walls. Ability to recognize attributes of great art produced by an authentic creator is paramount to attaining this objective. The guiding principle of Stanek Gallery's selection process is that artwork, to be of the highest quality, must unequivocally possess originality,

content, and craft. That is certainly true for the work presented in an exhibition of disrupted realism.

Paintings in this book represent immense skill acquired through arduous study and discipline grounded in a profound search for meaning. An individual artist's imagery is influenced by his or her unique experiences that in turn shape his or her specific artistic process. Consequently, no work is alike and each offers a very personal take on disruption. These artists respond viscerally to the world around them, presenting us with recognizable fragments of the human figure rendered in a way that does not allow the eye the time to settle. The viewer finds himself following the painter all around the surface, between layers, in and out of pictorial space. Figures exist in different planes, disappearing and reappearing, fragmented, overlapping, moving. Unpredictability is woven in with familiar uneasiness that is accurately captured to resonate with all of us living in this particular moment of technologically and socially disrupted time, a period that will ultimately take its place in history.

I have counted many of these artists among my colleagues for years and have always been an avid admirer of their work. However, not until John Seed wrote a blog about a group of highly skilled painters challenging the traditional concept of realism did I make the connection between their work and my own observations about worldwide changes I was witnessing, particularly in the art world. Seed's blog initiated a cross-continental dialogue with influential Philadelphia-based artists at its heart, making it clear that there was a need for an exhibition bringing these artists together in Philadelphia and hosted by none other than the Stanek Gallery, which had only just opened its doors at that time. Collaborative engagement with curators and emphasis on showcasing important artists being the gallery's modus operandi since its inception had further removed any possible doubts about our young team taking on a project of such far-reaching significance.

In January 2018, an exhibition titled *Disrupted Realism* debuted at the Stanek Gallery in Philadelphia's Old City as a collaborative effort among John Seed, the Stanek Gallery team, and a group of extraordinarily talented contemporary artists with a unique but shared vision.

Influence of these artists continues two years later as the movement they pioneered evolves. Remarkable skill and perceptiveness exhibited in their work means it has the legs to keep going. Not knowing where the movement is ultimately headed but being there to tell its story is what I find most exciting as I witness history being made before my very eyes at a small Philadelphia gallery, whose objective was and continues to be recognition and appreciation of great art created by great artists.

Opposite: Radu Belcin. *Stories #10,* 2017. Oil on paper: 16 × 12 inches.

Preface

My career as an art writer came about because the internet was disrupting print journalism. Getting into art writing at a time when newspapers were shrinking at first seemed ill fated but soon turned out to be perfectly timed. Disruption was my friend.

In early 2010 I contacted my local newspaper, the *Riverside Press Enterprise*, and asked if they needed an art critic. The answer was "yes": the editor liked my sample piece and gave me an assignment to review a local exhibition. I visited the show, turned in my review, and waited for the editor's response. It came to me a week later, via email, along with a revised draft. The content had been gutted. Any higher-level vocabulary and art terminology had been removed and my text—now bearing a "cute" title with a pun—had been reduced to a series of easily digested bullet points. The editor clearly felt that his local readers didn't need or want substantial, opinionated art writing. I told him to keep the $50 fee and remove my name from the piece.

As it turns out, writing for a newspaper would have been a dead end: by 2012, newspapers had become America's fifth-fastest-declining industry. My journalism career would have been over had I not complained on Facebook about what had happened. "You should contact Peter Frank," a friend advised. "He is going to be writing about art for the new *HuffingtonPost* Arts page." I followed that advice and sent Peter a writing sample. My first blog, "Picasso's Recession-Proof Harem," was published on May 13, 2010. As my piece was shared, discussed, and disseminated my eyes were being opened to the power of blogging, a truly revolutionary form of publishing.

As a blogger for the first major web-based newspaper—the *HuffingtonPost*—I was at the leading edge of change. Traditional print-based journalism, challenged by blogging and social media, was being forever transformed as smaller newspapers went out of business while larger newspapers shrank and struggled. Art and music critics were often the first to go when

layoffs came. Since I was writing for free as part of a new vanguard of volunteer bloggers—teaching paid my bills—I was able to focus on my craft. When friends asked me why I wrote for free, I explained that it felt liberating, which was true. I was soon posting roughly one blog each week and quickly came to understand just what made blogging so dynamic.

Newspaper art critics had traditionally dealt with a set of constraints: topics were preapproved or assigned by an editor, length was limited by column inches, and the use of photos was limited. As a blogger, I faced none of these roadblocks. The *Huffpost* allowed me to write about any artist or topic that interested me. My editor Kimberly Brooks, a painter herself, shared and supported my interests. On top of that I could write blogs of varying lengths and could include slideshows of as many images as I wished. Formats were also flexible: I could post reviews, interviews, commentaries, or even satires. I had stumbled into a revolution in art writing and publishing.

One great advantage of blogging is that it attracts communities of readers with similar interests. The editor of the *Press-Enterprise* had been correct: most of his local readers likely had little interest in art. The *HuffingtonPost*, in contrast, was attracting scores of readers from all over the world who would gravitate to the topics they cared about most. I now had what bloggers call a "platform," an enviable situation.

My blogs soon attracted hundreds and even thousands of page views: one that was featured on the front page of the *HuffPost* attracted a million views in twenty-four hours. But even more important than page views—which can be deceptive—was the fact that my blog was building a community of engaged readers. Every time I blogged I made new friends and a few frenemies as I responded to comments and took part in the discussions that each blog generated on social media.

This remarkable situation gave me an opportunity to do something that I felt had not been done widely or well before, which was to write about representational painters. I started

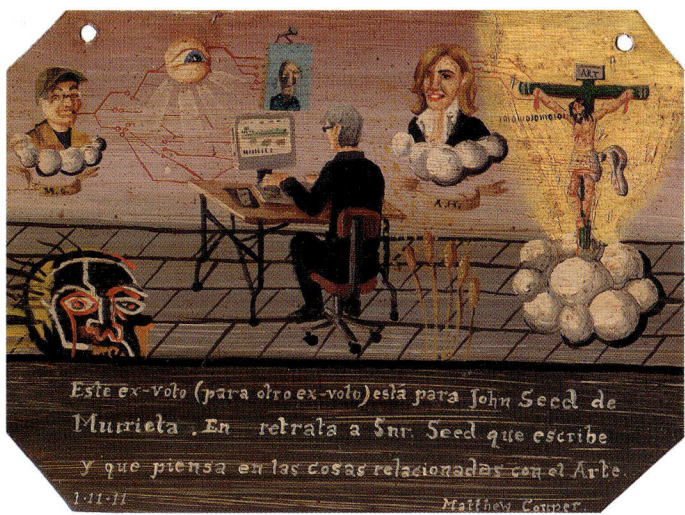

by writing about California artists whom I knew personally and whose work I had watched develop. This led to contacts—via Facebook and later Instagram—with other leading representational painters across the US and also in Europe. Because it did not seem appropriate to review shows I could not see in person, I often contacted artists whose work I had seen only on the web and asked them if I could interview them. This seemed like a great way to get the word out about artists without playing the role of a critic, who needed access to the work to render judgment. Eventually I interviewed 114 artists, gaining insights into their work as I went.

My audience, which increasingly consisted of artists, grew into a kind of support network.

After five years of blogging I found myself with a kind of overview that I could never have obtained writing for a newspaper: my beat was the blogosphere. I was seeing the work of new and exciting artists almost every day, observing trends as they unfolded and watching communities form. All of this happened with tremendous immediacy. I could see the work of an artist for the first time over my morning coffee, email them an interview request, edit that piece that evening, and have it posted within twenty-four hours.

Blogging allowed my writing—and my art interests—to coalesce and become distinctive. I was noticing more and more paintings by representational artists that had drifted away from the norms of traditional realism. I became interested in artists who were reconfiguring what they saw around them through a process of perception, breaking down recognizable forms and rendering them subjectively. Their styles of painting were tremendously varied and individualistic: something that I responded to. Like me, the artists I met via the internet were enlarging their social circles, feasting on the fast-changing buffet of images and ideas just as I was and forming into overlapping social circles.

When painter F. Scott Hess pointed out to me that many current representational paintings had an element of what he called "discombobulation"—a kind of visual disorientation often related to capturing time or motion—he got my attention. Scott had seen something that I needed to understand and explore through research and writing. Stimulated by Scott's observation, I searched for artists whose works had similar qualities. About a year later, in September 2016, I posted a blog titled "Interrupted Images: Discombobulation in Painting Is Definitely a Thing," describing what I had found and identifying a few key artists, including Alex Kanevsky and Ann Gale. Writing that blog and discussing it with my friends as it was shared on social media helped convince me that I was on to something.

Vanessa Werring, the manager of the Stanek Gallery in Philadelphia, apparently felt the same way. Vanessa, whom I had never met, read the blog and told Katherine Stanek, the owner of the gallery, "This would make a great show." Katherine agreed, and after a series of emails and phone discussions an exhibition was scheduled. Alex Kanevsky—who lives in Philadelphia and was featured in the show—also took part in some of the discussions, and his input convinced me that *Disrupted Realism* was the best and most appropriate title. The idea of disruption struck a chord, and sixteen artists—including eleven whose works appear in this book—were invited to exhibit. I posted my final blog for the *HuffingtonPost*, and six months later, in January 2018, *Disrupted Realism* opened at the Stanek Gallery.

The way that writing took me toward and into the future—with a blog stimulating a conversation that led to a show chronicling an important set of developments—was remarkable. In many ways, being able to recognize and write about disrupted realism was the culmination of my career as a blogger. It pleases me immensely that while the exhibition was on view at the Stanek Gallery, Meghan Schaffer, a representative of Schiffer Publishing, visited and realized that the show deserved to be a book. It is worth noting that all the artists in this book, which provides an expanded view of the themes found in the original exhibition, came to my attention via the internet and social media. This book would not have come to be without the World Wide Web.

Although blogging created the connections and social energy that brought this book into existence, I am well aware of the limits of words. In the pages that follow—which include short interviews with each artist—you will be introduced to works of art that I think say quite a bit about the time we live in. The works themselves are the reason for the book and deserve to be stared at and savored. It will be up to you to decide what you see in them and what you feel about them, but I doubt you will be disappointed.

"Disrupted realism" isn't a single style, but rather a gathering of individual styles. The best attempts of talented artists to find poetry, humanity, and meaning in the events of their lives are represented in these works. The paintings contained in this book—when viewed with an open heart and open mind—will provide you with powerful realizations about modern life and also some space to dream in.

I am in awe of these artists and feel honored to present their individual visions.

John Seed
Cambria, California
johnseed@gmail.com
www.johnseed.com

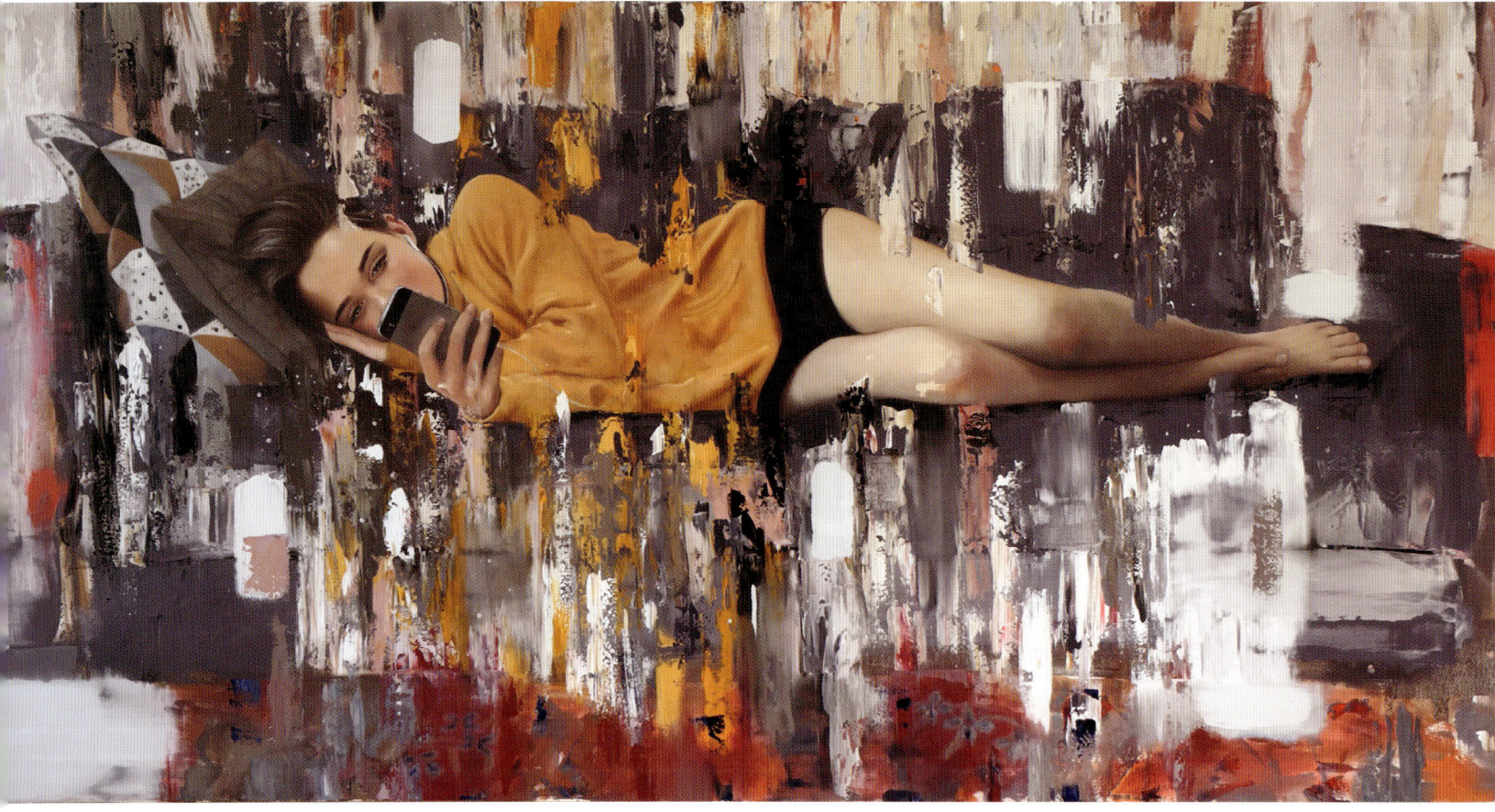

Meredith Marsone. *Lost Generation*, 2018. Oil
on canvas: 70.8 × 35.4 inches.

Acknowledgments

This book would never have come to be without the innovations, inspiration, and guidance provided by the following individuals:

Arianna Huffington, Kimberly Brooks, and Kathleen Massara, all formerly of the *HuffingtonPost*
Hrag Vartanian of Hyperallergic.com
Didi Menendez of Poets and Artists
Katherine Stanek and Vanessa Werring of the Stanek Gallery, Philadelphia
Lisa Chadwick, Melanie Ross, and Ian Gill of Dolby Chadwick Gallery, San Francisco
Meghan Schaffer and Sandra Korinchak of Schiffer Publishing

The following institutions and organizations have supported my progress as an arts professional:

Mount San Jacinto College
Laguna College of Art and Design
The Representational Art Conference (TRAC) sponsored by California Lutheran University
The Sam Francis Foundation

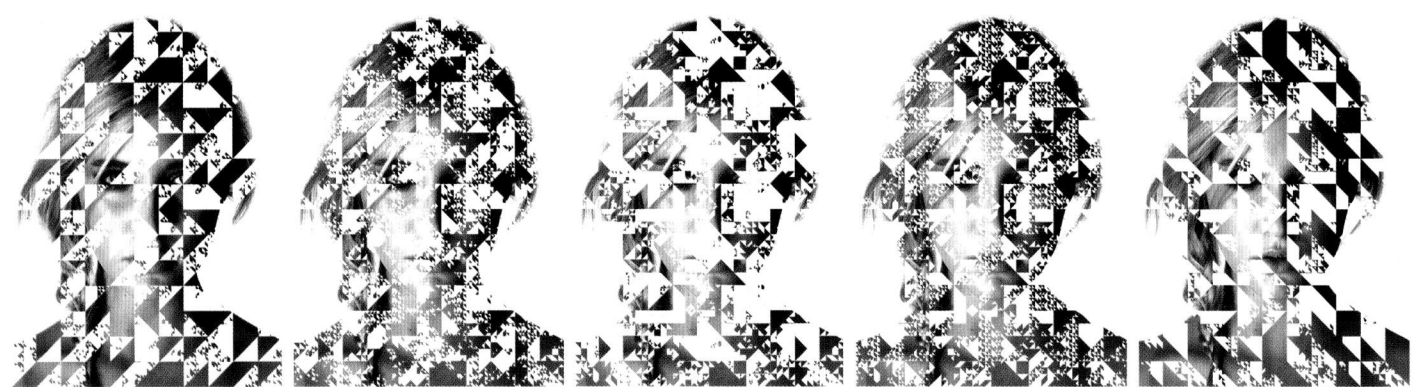

Introduction

FINDING CLARITY

Six months ago my family and I moved to the central coast of California. After more than thirty years of living in Southern California's "Inland Empire"—where the heat and traffic were becoming unbearable—living in a small coastal town feels like a dream. My wife and I now take our morning walk on bluffs overlooking the ocean: we used to follow bland sidewalk rimmed by tract houses and parked cars. As we stroll, we breathe in the cool sea air, admire the crashing waves, and catch glimpses of leaping dolphins and the occasional tummy-slapping otter. It's a routine that offers a sense of respite, one that takes us away from life's concerns.

The trail we take is sprinkled with wooden benches, including one next to the ocean that looks out over a spectacular rock formation. On one recent morning we glanced toward this favorite bench—hoping it might be empty—but it was occupied: by a couple staring at their phones. Yes, with a jaw-dropping view vista straight ahead, they chose to check their Facebook. I wanted to feel superior, but that would have been hypocritical. The truth is that I have done the same thing.

Few among us are strong enough to resist the tantalizing flow of images and information that is prying us away from what previous generations called "reality." Nature, other people, and great paintings in museums still interest us, but smartphones are giving them some serious competition. We are the most distracted society in the history of the world. Television, which so many media-age Savonarolas warned us would be the end of culture, was just a warm-up for this whatever-you-want-on-demand tsunami of personalized content.

We now live in an "attention economy," where there is always some kind of distraction at our fingertips. While stuck in traffic—and there is a lot of that—we can turn to digital devices that break up the monotony with satellite radio, playlists, and podcasts. Boredom has been vanquished, and that may not be a good thing. If you have a smartphone, Twitter, Facebook, and Instagram are always in your pocket. Yes, the screens we stare at can show us things of really high quality—if you have the patience to be selective—but the same screen that shows you a well-made movie is also a trapdoor hovering just above the quicksand of never-ending content. This scenario is changing our lives and affecting the art of our times.

The availability of endless stimulation via the digital world is relatively new. The energies and interruptions of actual life endure. In addition to the dramas we view on screens, our real, actual lives—the parts that aren't digital—alternate between the mundane, the profound, and the tragic. While reading the interviews of artists submitted for this book, I was struck by the mentions of challenging and life-changing events that have reshaped their lives and works.

Aiden Kringen's life was forever changed when he was struck in the head by a foul ball at Dodger Stadium, Justin Bower decided to get his MFA in painting after being stabbed, and Zack Zdrale has grappled with the issues caused by a brain tumor. The spaces and subjects of Alyssa Monk's paintings were profoundly transformed after the experience of watching her mother succumb to cancer, and Meredith Marsone has struggled with depression.

Ryan Bradley. *Untitled (Fabienne Series, 1-5)*, 2015.
Pastel on Arches paper: 122.5 × 18 inches.

Given the intense mix of events and images that come through our minds—from real life and from screens—is it any wonder that modern reality can be hard to grasp? Is there still any peace to be found anywhere? How can you find the time and space to steer your mind toward the people, causes, and questions that really matter? Just where—one wonders—can clarity be found? My feeling is that painters, especially gifted ones, are asking themselves those questions in the studio. When that is the case, searching for answers becomes a central motivation.

Painting is a form of meditation. It is a solitary activity best done in quiet—or maybe to some favorite music—that generates an alternative universe. In contemporary painting, those universes reflect ideas, images, and impulses gleaned from the artist's life, sometimes placed there consciously, sometimes unconsciously. If you think about the long tradition of realism in Western art, the "alternative universes" that emerged in paint were filled first with religious and mythological scenes and then later with real people and their surroundings.

Since the advent of mechanical image-making—with its rapid takeover of the traditional domains of realism—artists have had the opportunity to make their work more subjective. The vanguard styles of the modern era became possible because of the subjectivity that emanated from the central question of Paul Cézanne's work: "Is this what I see?" In the current phenomenon of disrupted realism, the process of seeing tends to overlap with perception, which leads to another kind of question: "What am I feeling?" This engagement with the subjectivity of feeling is something that is meant to be shared between the artist and his audience, as Joshua Meyer explains: "I want someone who approaches the painting to feel what it is like to make a painting, and to feel the struggle to understand and to see the world."

Yes, "straight" realism—meaning art made with an undeviating and strict allegiance to what the eye sees—is still valid, possible, and, in skilled hands, masterful and moving. I think of realism as being like opera: when real talent is involved it is transcendent, but when talent and skill are lacking it can be embarrassing or worse.

I also try to remember that even the strictest realism is inherently abstract—it's just paint on canvas, creating illusions, right?—and realist painters who don't balance their drive for clarity with at least a hint of ambiguity will make dull work.

For these reasons and others, realism is hard to learn and even harder to master. Forty years ago there were only a handful of schools and teachers that even bothered to pass on the necessary information and skills, which were considered passé. I can't tell you how many times I have heard representational artists from my generation say "I had to teach myself" or "There was only one professor at the college I attended who actually understood perspective, but he was an alcoholic who was shunned by the other faculty."

Still, something was happening. A handful of newly founded institutions—including the New York Academy of Art (founded in 1982) and the Florence Academy (founded in 1991)—went against the grain and offered programs that revived the foundational skills needed by realist artists. Several established schools, including the Pennsylvania Academy of Fine Art and the Slade School in London, had notable faculty members who extended and expanded the possibilities of figurative and representational painting. It took some time, but

the graduates of these schools (and a few others) fanned out to become teachers themselves or to open ateliers, and a new generation of skilled painters took shape. There are, it appears, thousands of artists in the West who are very much capable of painting convincingly in a realist fashion. And yes, there are many thousands more in Asia and eastern Europe (where realism never experienced quite the same decline in status).

All of this brings me closer to the real topic of this essay, which is disrupted realism. And the elephant-in-the-room question is this: If you are a painter who has the chops, why not just *be* a realist? There isn't one answer to this question. In fact, there are as many answers as there are disrupted realists. As it turns out, "disrupted realism" isn't a style—these days the idea of a well-defined style is perhaps as outdated as a newspaper in a driveway—but rather a phenomenon. What I kept noticing as a blogger was a growing cadre of well-trained artists who were doing something to exit the cul-de-sac of realism and explore the winding roads of hybridity.

The various impulses toward disruption—and I'm using that word broadly and flexibly—were as individual as the artists themselves, but there did seem to be some level of shared conviction that the tradition of realism needed to flex in order to be more in tune with modern life. Dorian Vallejo, for example, says that his evolution was "not necessarily to disrupt anything I hold dear, but in order to genuinely ascertain whether I might add another way of sharing what I understand as the human experience." When I look at the variety of individual approaches that I consider disrupted realism, I am struck by the tension between the artist's need to make singular work and their universal and humanistic aspirations. It is as if they are responding to anthropologist Margaret Mead's sage advice: "Always remember that you are absolutely unique. Just like everyone else."

The experiences of contemporary artists are diffuse and diverse. They encompass, and reframe, every kind of experience. What I have come to realize is that the diverse forms of disrupted realism have to do with everything in each artist's life: the real, the remembered, the digital, the imagined, and the dreamed, all filtered through the artist's perceptions. Trying to argue that the works in this book can be anything tighter than loose frameworks is a losing argument. Respecting the richness, individuality, and hybridity they represent makes much more sense.

Is there a single conviction that these artists share? You would have to ask them, but I will toss this out: they believe that painting is a way of moving toward life's center at a time when our atomized culture keeps dragging us all toward its edges. To put it another way, when our senses are sated, our souls still need the nourishment of art.

As you consider and look over the six groups of artists and themes that follow, I hope you see some connections. The themes are not meant to be exclusive or definite but are there to offer a way to enter a series of works and discern connections. As you look over the groupings, I hope you will be arguing with me in your mind, avidly noting the inevitable overlaps and contradictions that will unfold. I have decided that "disrupted realism" is a flexible enough label for a wide range of approaches. Whether you agree or disagree I hope you will respect and admire the art and artists gathered between the covers of this book. Each individual artist has demonstrated a commitment to extending the language of realism—and of art—in a remarkable way.

What Is Disrupted Realism?

Disrupted realism is a term that describes works of art made by artists who have deviated from the norms of realism. These deviations, which may involve one or more formal elements—such as line, form, and color—are made intentionally, often through improvisation, to serve expressive purposes. By "disrupting" and expanding the tradition of realism, artists may suggest time, memory, and individual experience or refer to digital, photographic, or cinematic sources. It is a subjective approach to painting that favors perception over seeing and embraces subjectivity.

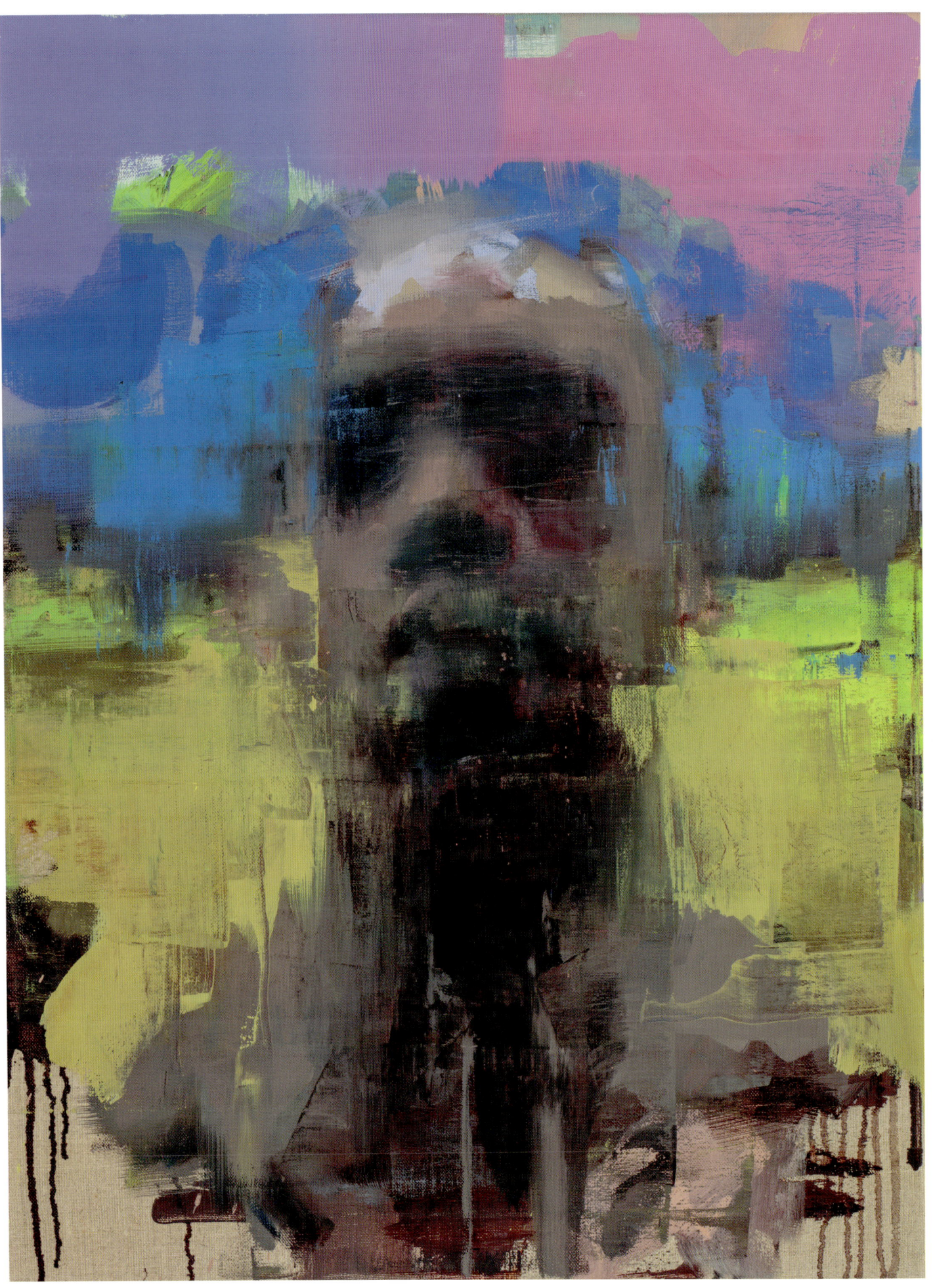

Toward Abstraction

*If traditional realism means painting
what's there, emulating reality, then I'm
trying to run away from that—
nonforcefully—at any cost. This deviation
begins with abstraction, with fragments
both real and imagined, and the realist
elements kind of hover over and between
the landscapes of chaos and color that
peek through wherever I leave a void.*

—Jerome Lagarrigue

In the past, abstraction and realism have often seemed to be in opposition, incapable of reconciliation. Over time, and through the efforts of modern artists, including those of the Bay Area Figurative movement, these approaches have interwoven, creating new hybrids. These artists take advantage of the flexibility and sensuality of paint, adding subjectivity and mystery to their works. By interrupting the reality of their subjects with painterly improvisations, these artists create new personal languages and worlds.

VALERIO D'OSPINA

ALEX KANEVSKY

JEROME LAGARRIGUE

J. LOUIS

ALEX MERRITT

NICK RUNGE

KAI SAMUELS-DAVIS

Jerome Lagarrigue. *Untitled*, 2017.
Oil on linen: 16 × 24 inches.

VALERIO D'OSPINA

Lives and Works in: Philadelphia
Education: BA and MFA in painting, Accademia
di Belle Arti di Firenze, Italy
Selected Collections: Museo Arte Contemporanea Sicilia,
SK Hynix, McGraw-Hill Education
Representation: Stanek Gallery, Philadelphia

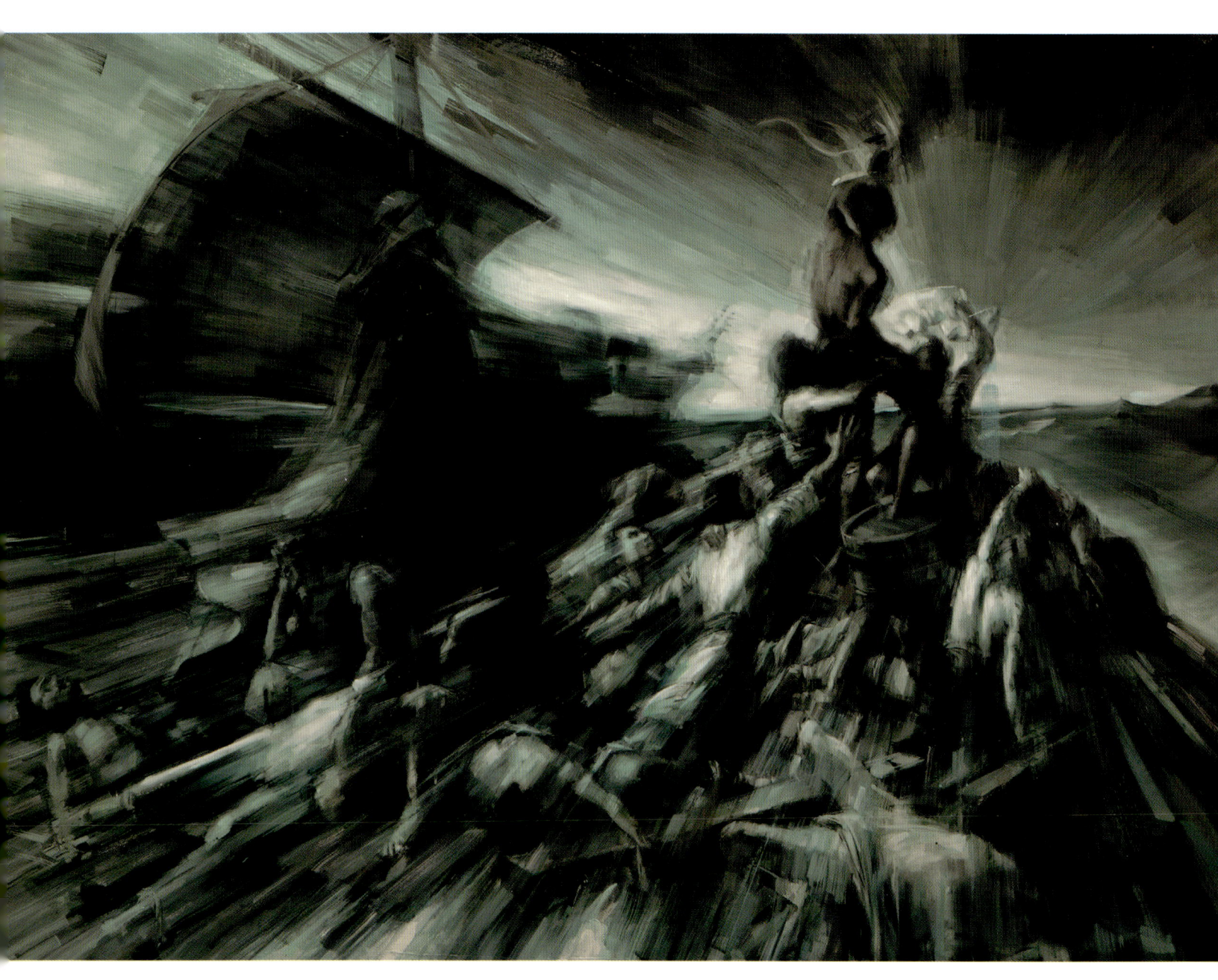

*I try to endow my large oil paintings with
dramatic movement and a life of their own.*

How and why does your work disrupt or deviate from traditional realism?

My painting process is not premeditated; the velocity of my brushstrokes has to ignite a conflict with what my rational thought would do. Immediately before giving my brain time to process which color to use and how to define shapes and values, my hand has already marked the canvas with a series of gestural and abstract strokes. These marks will eventually merge together in the eyes of the observer, forming an apparent realistic image at a certain distance that will disrupt as the observer moves closer to the painting. In this sense, my work is never finished until the perception of the observer comes into play to complete it. Each individual has a different way of perceiving the work, so the final image they interpret is always personal.

I paint memories of things and not the things themselves. I see my memories as undefined blurred images, in which only the details that are most relevant to me are vaguely defined.

How has your work evolved and developed over time?

The development of my work over time has happened quite naturally and in concurrence with the development of my taste, knowledge, interests, and the need of new forms of expression. Often, these changes have been determined by moving to different subjects and themes. I make the conscious choice of certain subjects, not only out of aesthetic pleasure but also to put myself in a sort of discomfort. I tend to gravitate toward images that will challenge my stability, seeking to create something ridiculously complex with a lot of moving and undefined parts. It is almost as if I am in constant competition with my abilities, trying to reach new levels with each painting and never settling for satisfactory.

What are some of the influences that have shaped your work?

There are many things and millions of people that inspire me. Almost anything can influence my work: reading a book, watching a movie, taking a walk, going for a bike ride, or just navigating the web can potentially all be things that give me the urge to paint.

I've also been influenced by my own fears, exorcised by painting them: for example, my aerial cityscapes series in relation to my fear of heights. Other sources of inspiration are places, people, and scenarios that are strictly related to my memories. In this way, almost all of my work could be considered autobiographical.

Mention something interesting about your life or background.

I was born and raised in Italy and studied for seven years at the first academy of fine art in the world—the Florence Academy, founded in 1563. I now live in Philadelphia, which is home to the first academy of fine art in the US—the Philadelphia Academy of Fine Arts, founded in 1805.

My wife, Victoria, is an associate gallery director, and we named our son after a very special pigment: Viridian.

Valerio D'Ospina. *Hopeless (B.I. after Géricault),* 2014.
Oil on canvas: 75 × 54 inches.

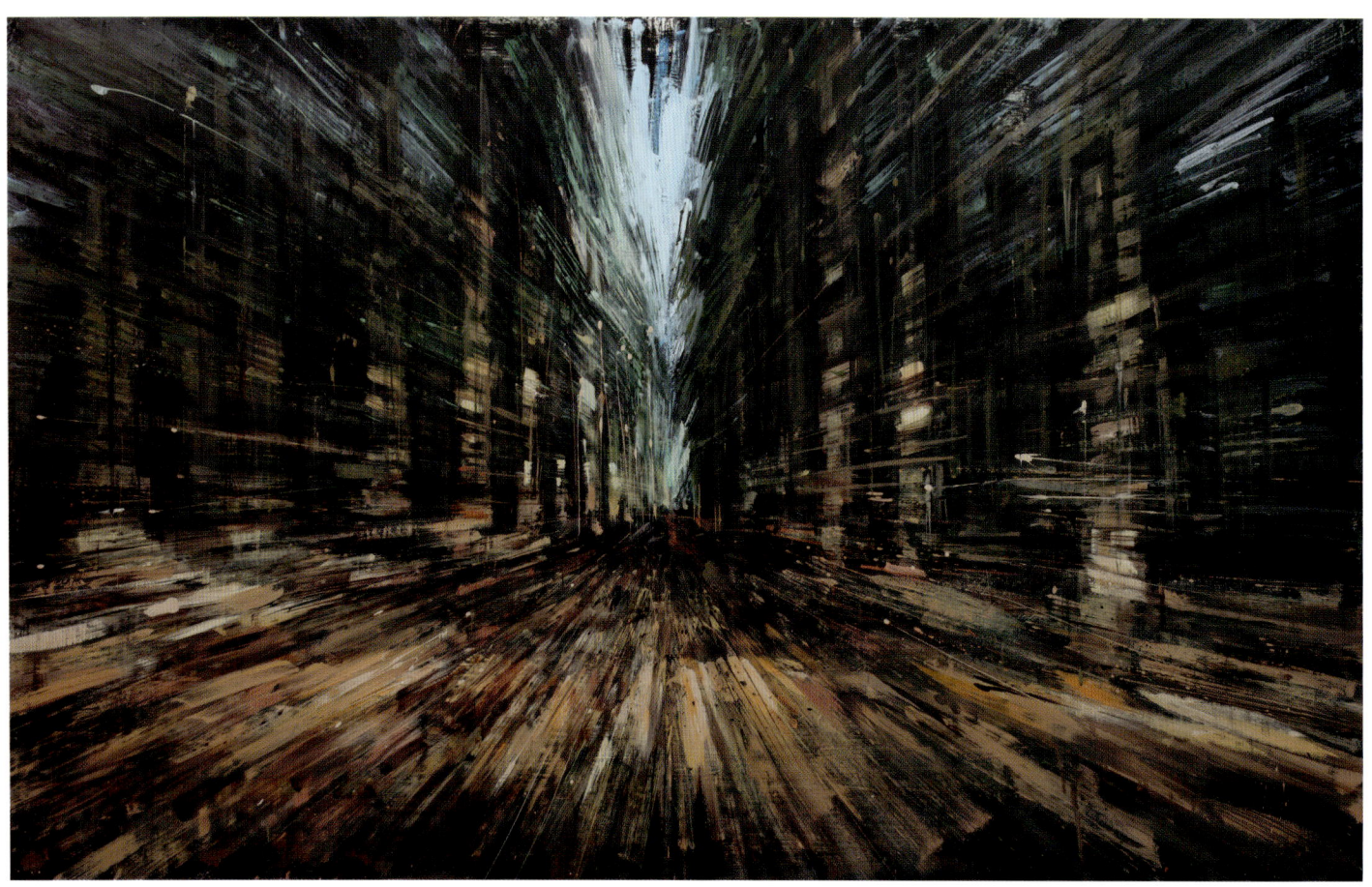

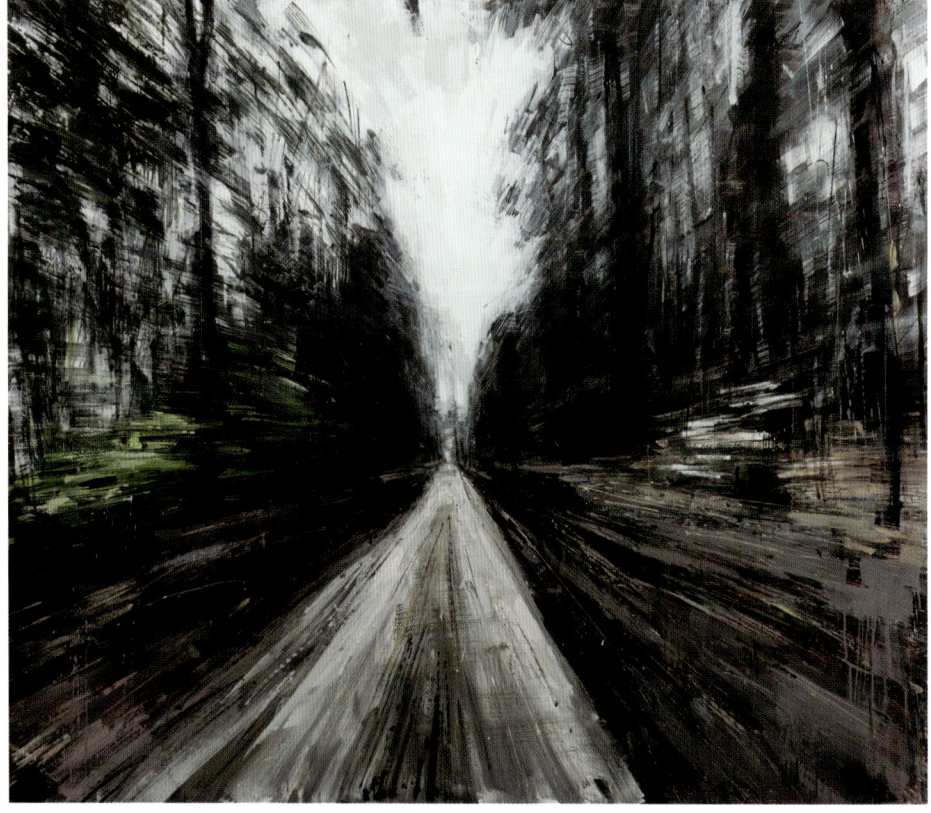

Valerio D'Ospina. *Biking in White's Woods #2,* 2016. Oil on panel: 48 × 30 inches.

Valerio D'Ospina. *Biking in White's Woods,* 2016. Oil on panel: 48 × 41 inches.

Opposite: Valerio D'Ospina. *Falling for You (The Bride),* 2018. Oil on panel: 32 × 48 inches.

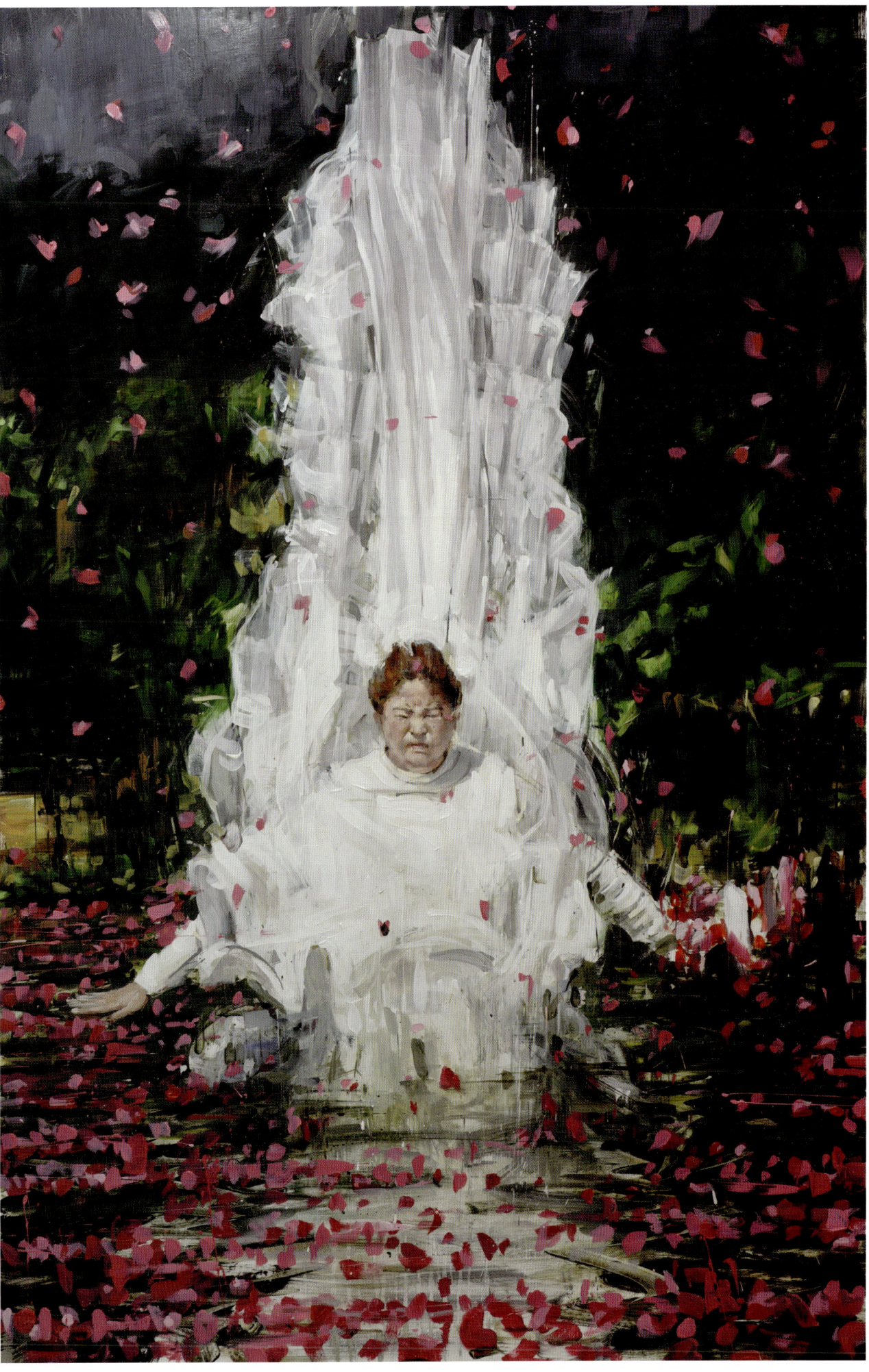

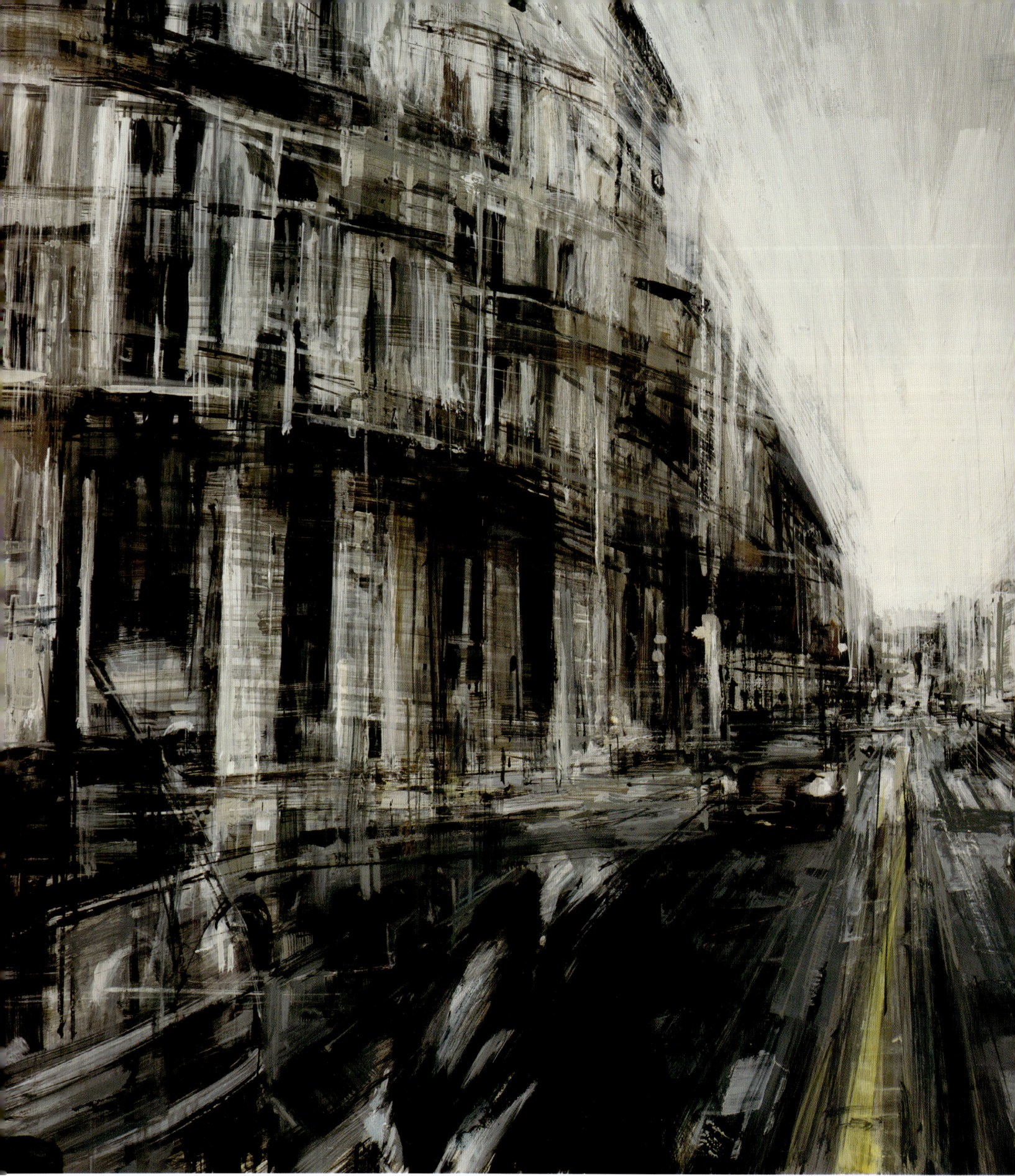

Valerio D'Ospina. *Rush Hour,* 2015.
Oil on panel: 31 × 17 inches.

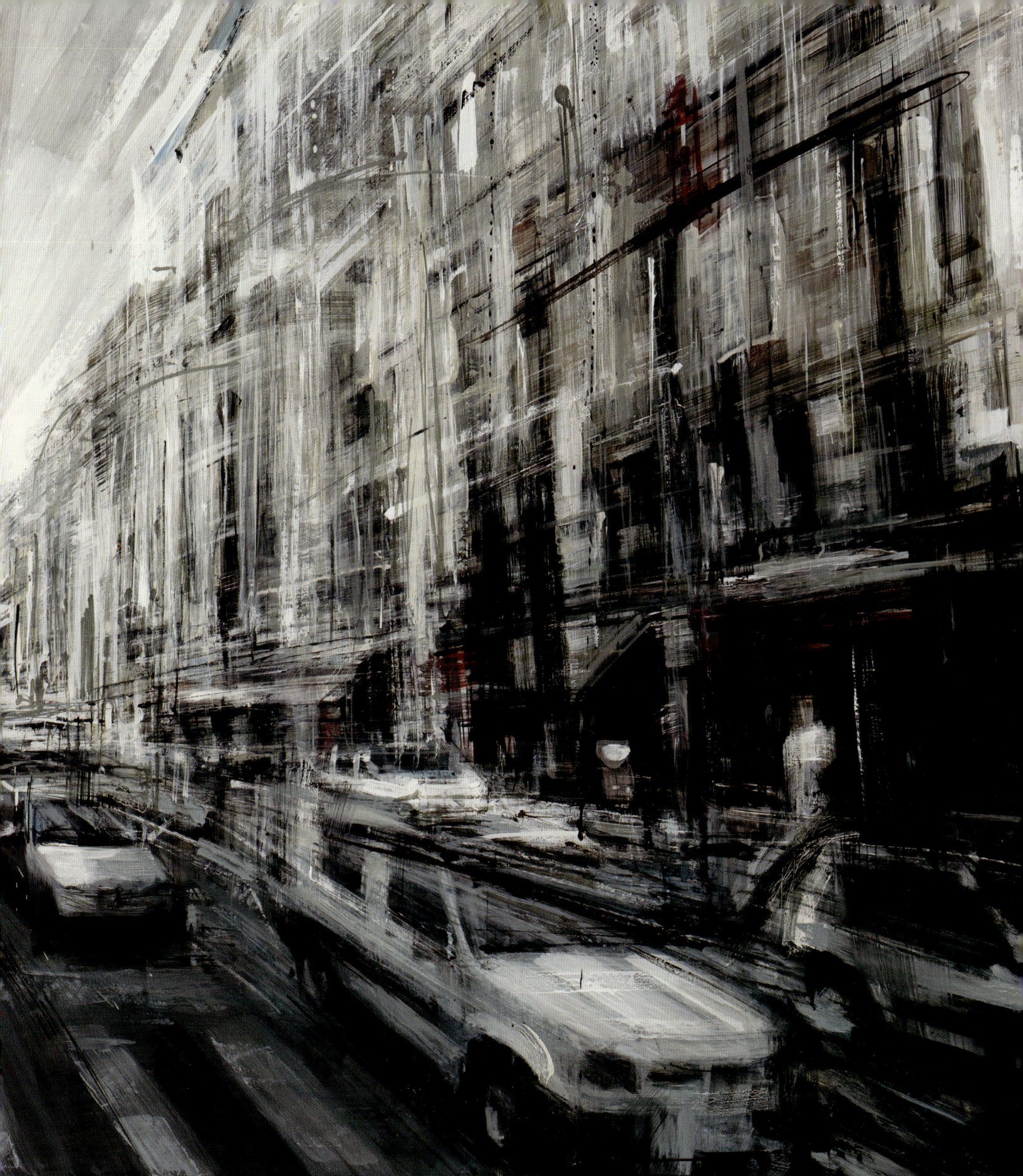

ALEX KANEVSKY

Lives and Works in: Philadelphia
Education: Vilnius University (Lithuania),
Philadelphia Academy of Fine Arts
Selected Collections: Achenbach Collection, Fine Arts Museums
of San Francisco; de Young Museum, San Francisco
Representation: Dolby Chadwick Gallery, San Francisco

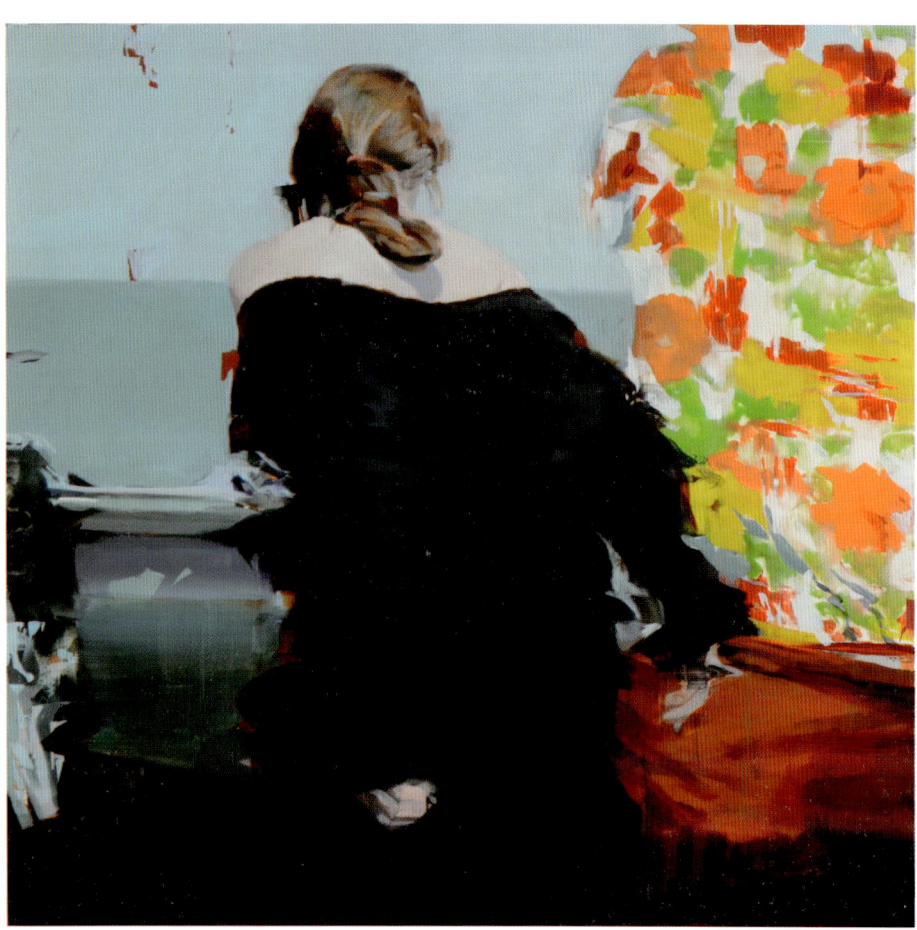

If painting is a form of language, an artist attempts to create a language—foreign to all but himself—and then say a few things in that language in such a way that would make them clear to anybody who listens, even if the language remains foreign to them.

If I have a need to comment on my own painting, then I will have failed as an artist. Everything that I wanted to say is already in my work. Any additional words from me would dilute the impact and confound the meaning. I believe that paintings function where words fail, and prefer it that my paintings have this opportunity.

Alex Kanevsky. *Unstable Equilibrium,* 2018.
Oil on panel: 34.75 × 36 inches.

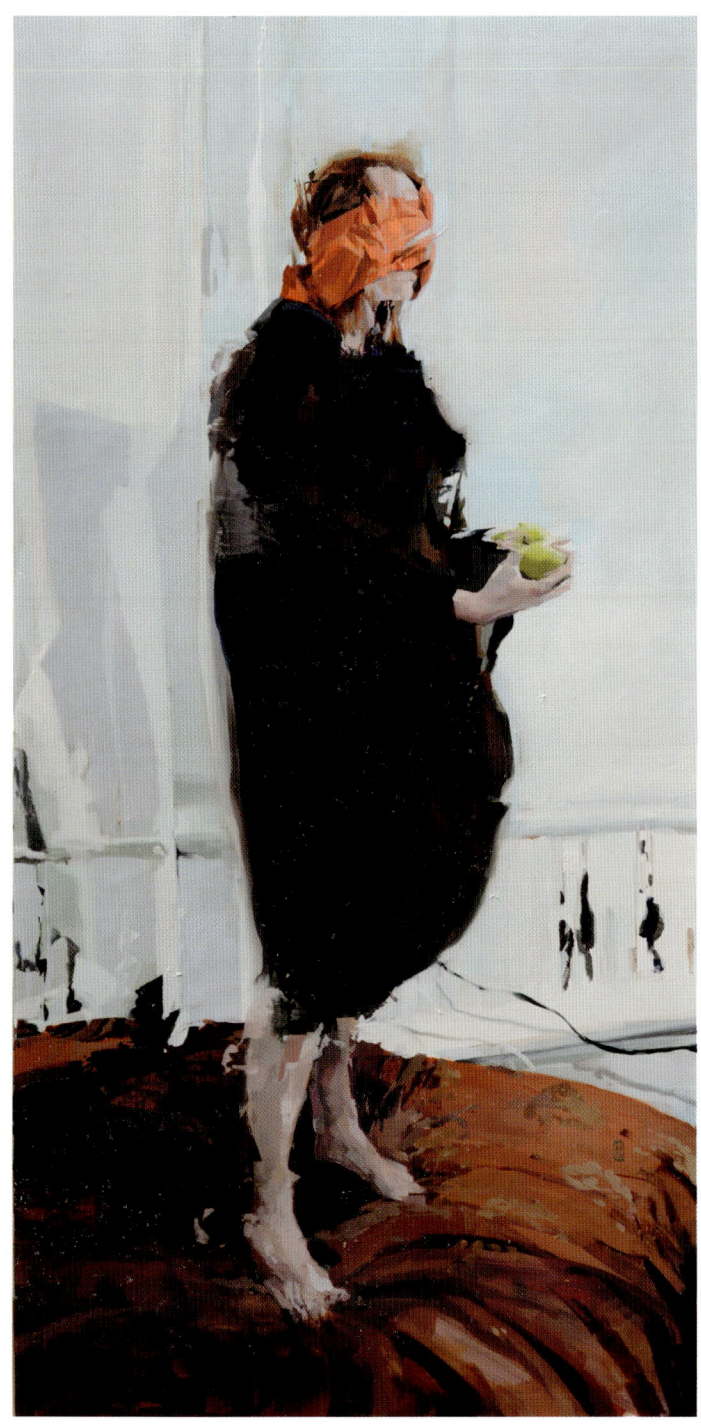

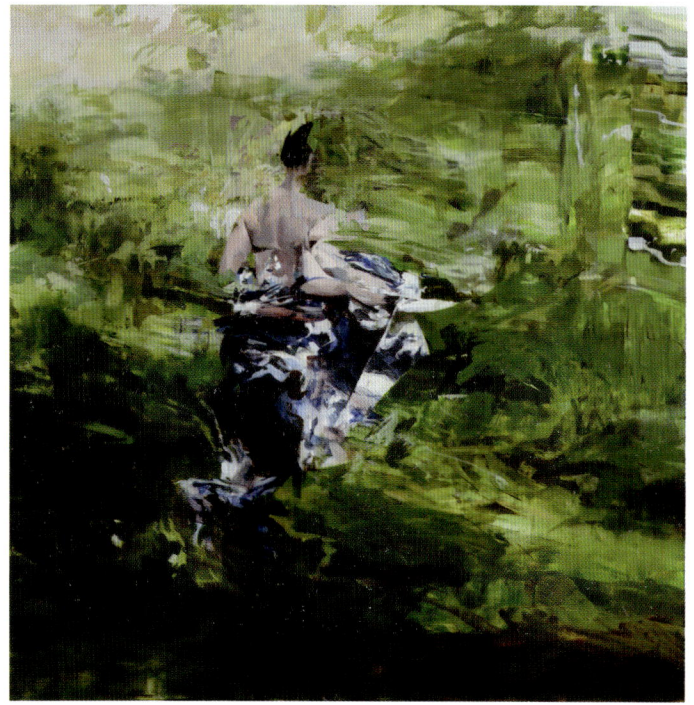

My paintings are, as one observer put it, a form of glossolalia: a clear and passionate speech by a fully involved participant in a language nobody knows.

Alex Kanevsky. *S.B. with Apple,* 2018.
Oil on panel: 48 × 24 inches.

Alex Kanevsky. *Fin de Siècle,* 2018.
Oil on panel: 36 × 36 inches.

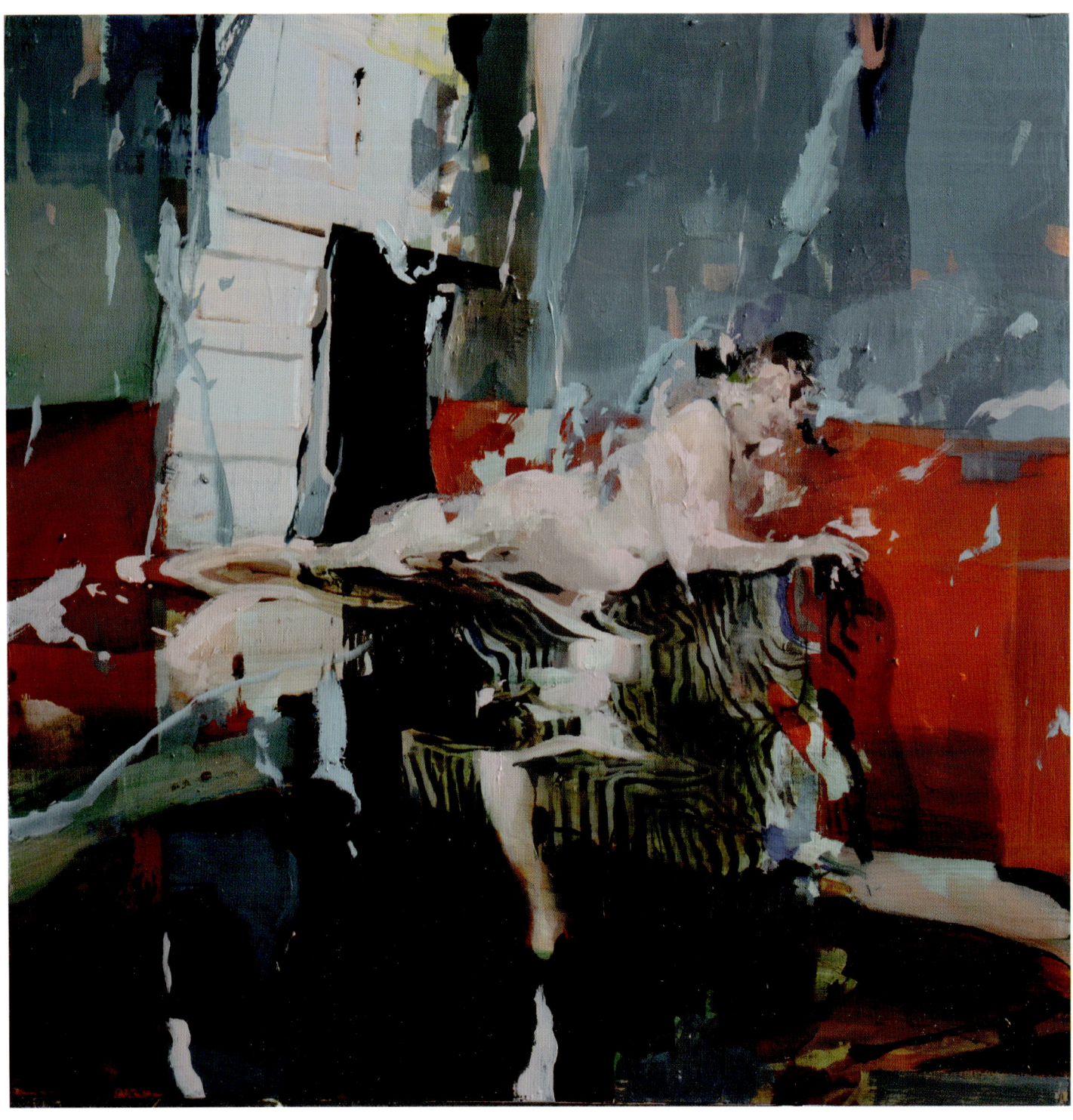

Alex Kanevsky. *R.L. Dancing*, 2018.
Oil on panel: 18 × 18 inches.

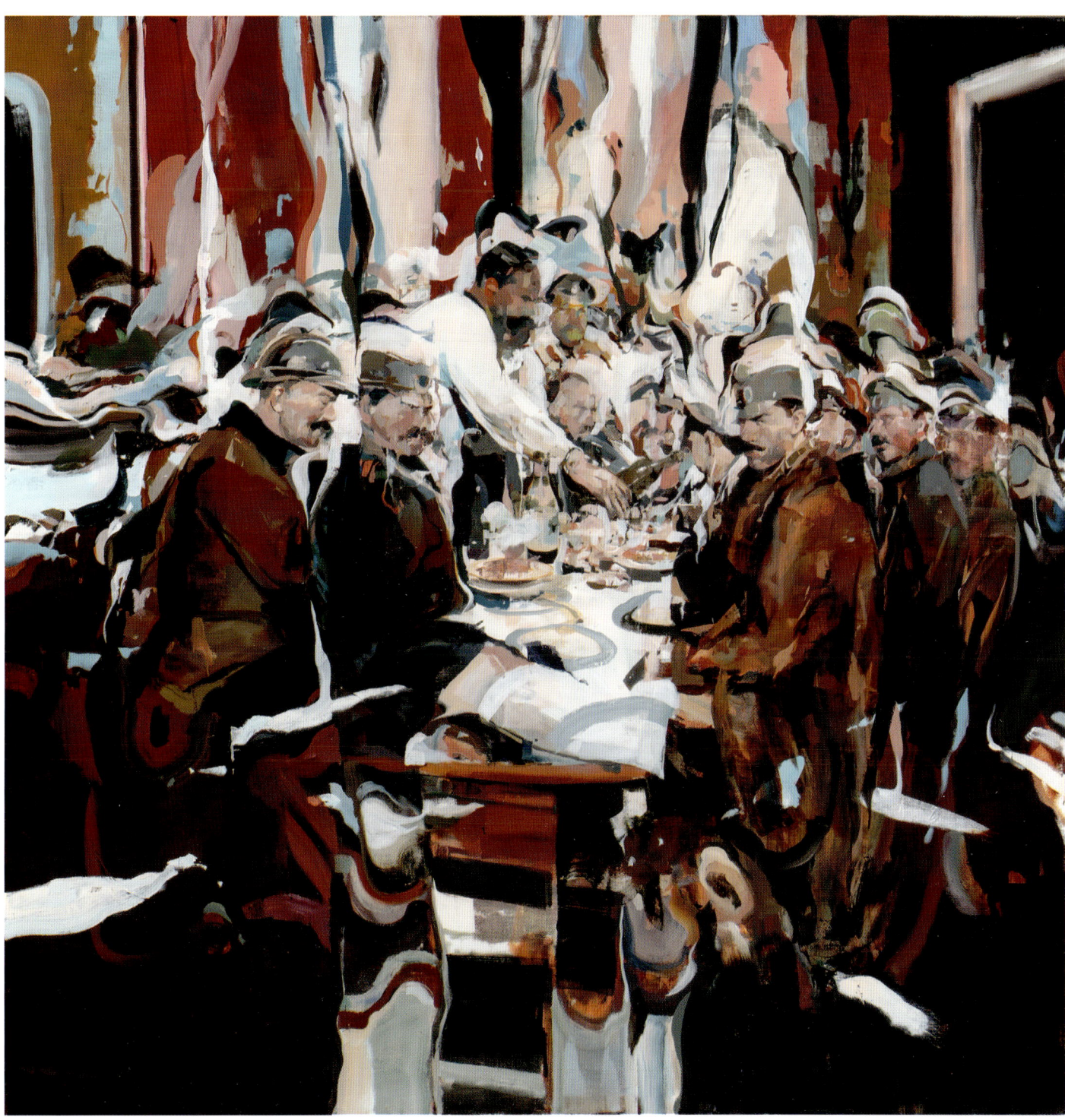

Alex Kanevsky. *Dinner on a Battlefield,* 2018.
Oil on wood: 66 × 66 inches.

JEROME LAGARRIGUE

Lives and Works in: Brooklyn, New York
Education: BFA, Rhode Island School of Design
Selected Collections: Peggy Cooper Cafritz,
George Lucas, Swizz Beatz
Representation: Galerie Olivier Waltman, Paris

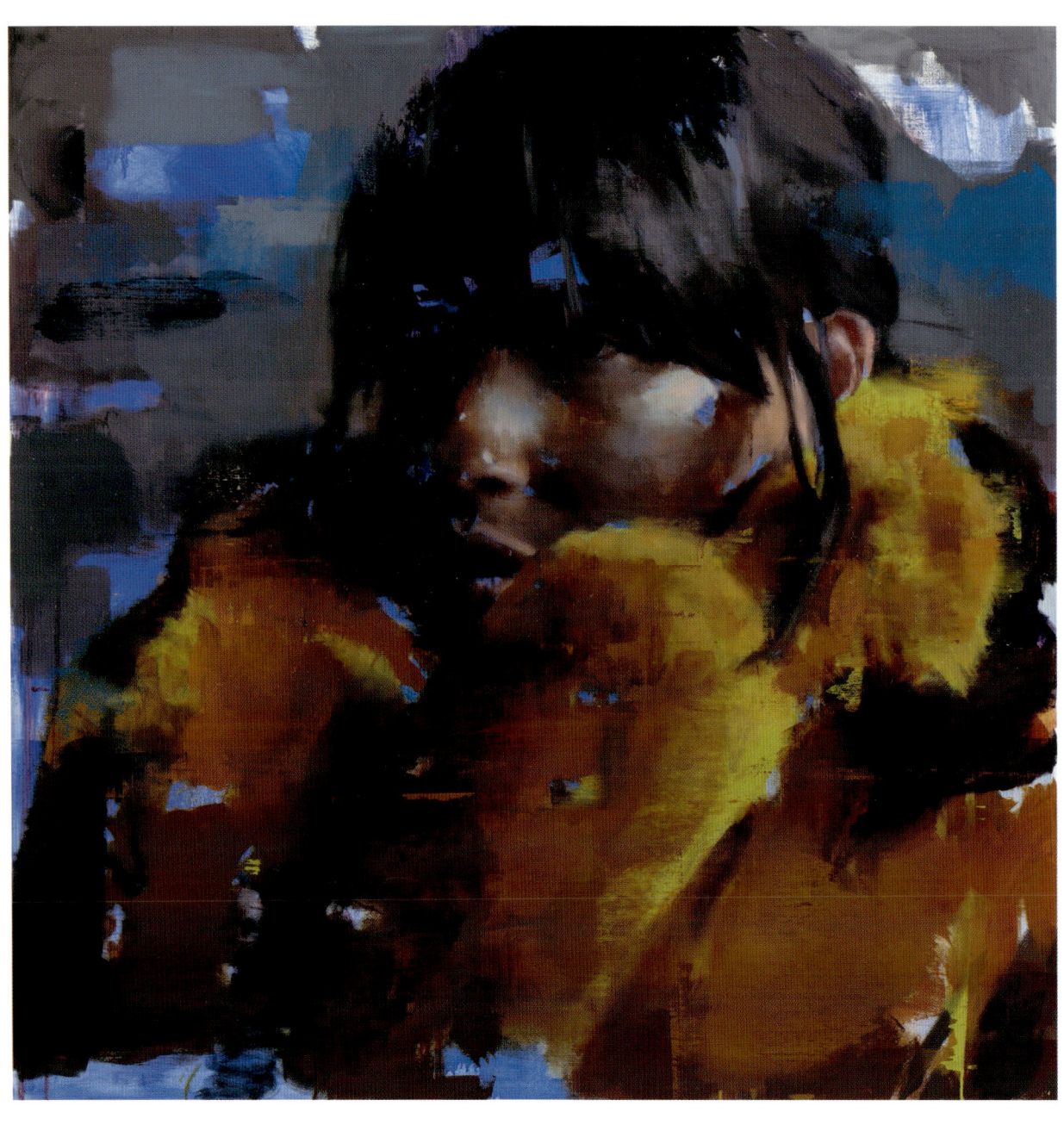

I paint people in a state of engagement with me—or with one another—in a context of my own invention that explores the unspoken, the unseen, and the unknown.

How and why does your work disrupt or deviate from traditional realism?

If traditional realism means painting what's there, emulating reality, then I'm trying to run away from that—gradually—at any cost. This deviation begins with abstraction, with fragments both real and imagined, and the realist elements kind of hover over and between the landscapes of chaos and color that peek through wherever I leave a void. I'm intentionally obscuring the canvas as I paint—kind of like painting through fog—allowing the realist elements to collide with or partially drown out the abstract ones in the same way that, for example, a melody might be punctuated by dissonance or feedback, or compression artifacts appear in a glitchy video stream. This disruption of realism with abstraction is what excites me the most because it's unpredictable, even unreliable, and it's there that I hope viewers will find themselves most compelled to engage with the work.

How has your work evolved and developed over time?

I started out doing graffiti, then went to art school and learned illustration, which finally led to painting. The goal was always to sustain myself with my painting. I honed my skills, put in the time doing commissions, but in my own work there has always been a clear progression toward abstraction, a loosening of brushstrokes and energy. More recently, the work has become more personal, focusing on family, tradition, race: there is a lot of looking inward. It's instinctive and emotional, and a bit terrifying, but it's also liberating because there is no right or wrong.

What are some of the influences that have shaped your work?

Bacon, Freud, Coltrane, Kubrick, Giacometti, Basquiat, Goya, Velásquez, nonrepresentational sculpture, and tribal art. I suppose that the unifying thread is a radical acceptance of and simultaneous revolt against human nature, a certain fearlessness in confronting its dark sides. Roman ruins intrigue and inspire me, just as partial documents or torn photos do: I'm fascinated by things that tell a story but are missing some key elements of it. The voids are full of suggestion, like the shadows in a Rembrandt painting. I'm drawn to the emptiness where something was or should be, and a lot of my work involves letting my imagination fill it in.

Mention something interesting about your life and background.

These days I love observing the way old people move. Their rhythms are encoded with habits, rituals, and a sense of purposefulness. Also, the stare of an old dog really speaks to me.

Jerome Lagarrigue. *Thais with Fur,* 2018.
Oil on linen: 59 × 59 inches.

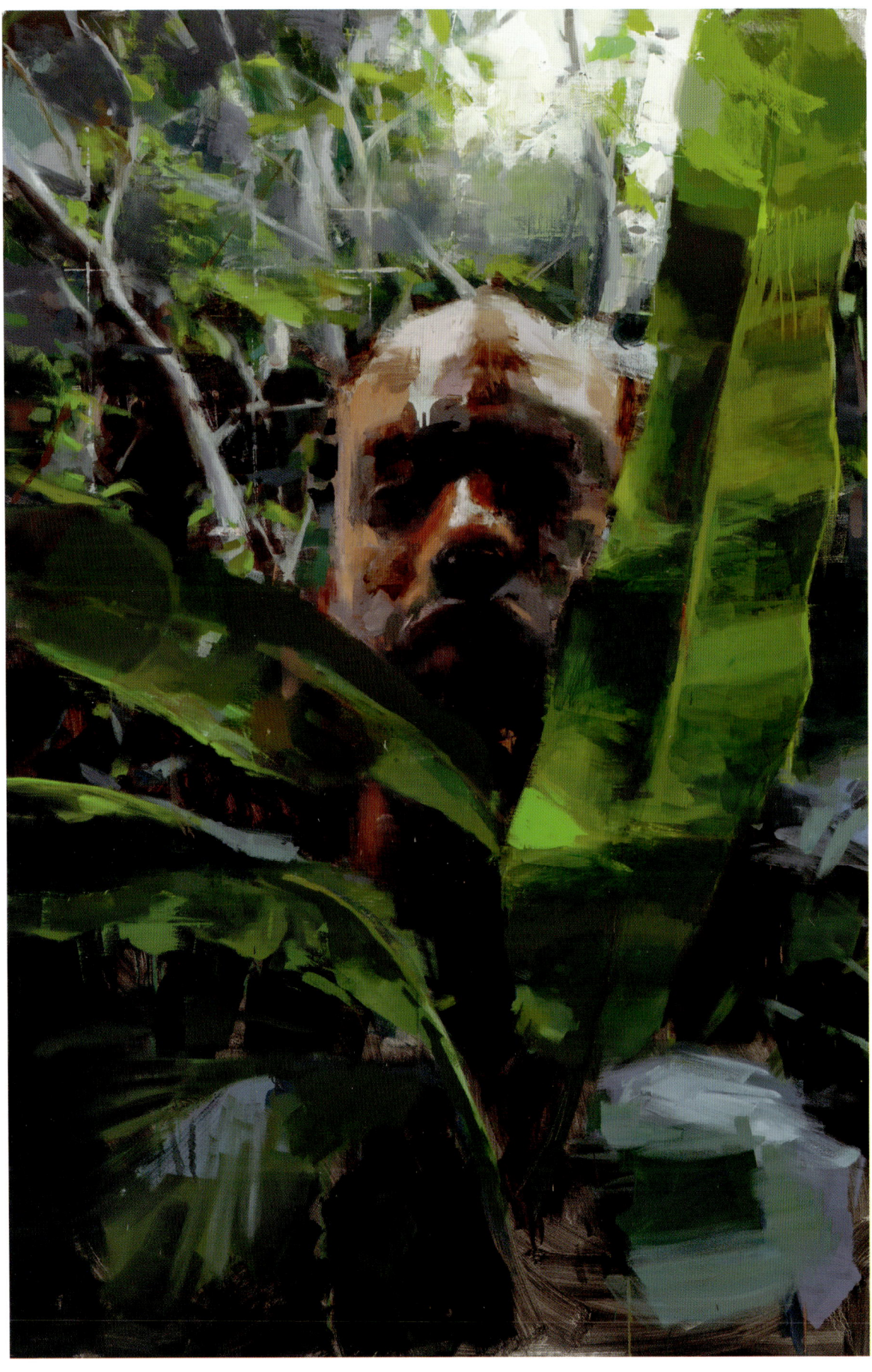

Jerome Lagarrigue. *In the Middle of the Jungle*, 2017. Oil on linen: 72 × 54 inches.

Opposite, top: Jerome Lagarrigue. *Le Cri*, 2014. Oil on linen: 79 × 79 inches.

Opposite, bottom: Jerome Lagarrigue. *Amadou at Night*, 2017. Oil on linen: 16 × 24 inches.

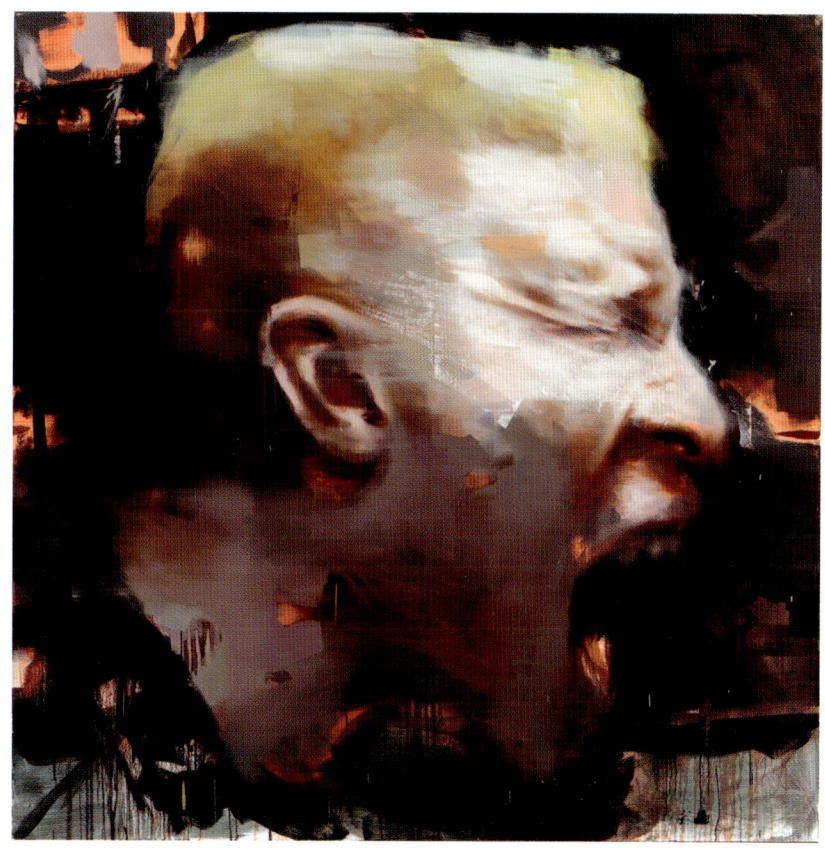

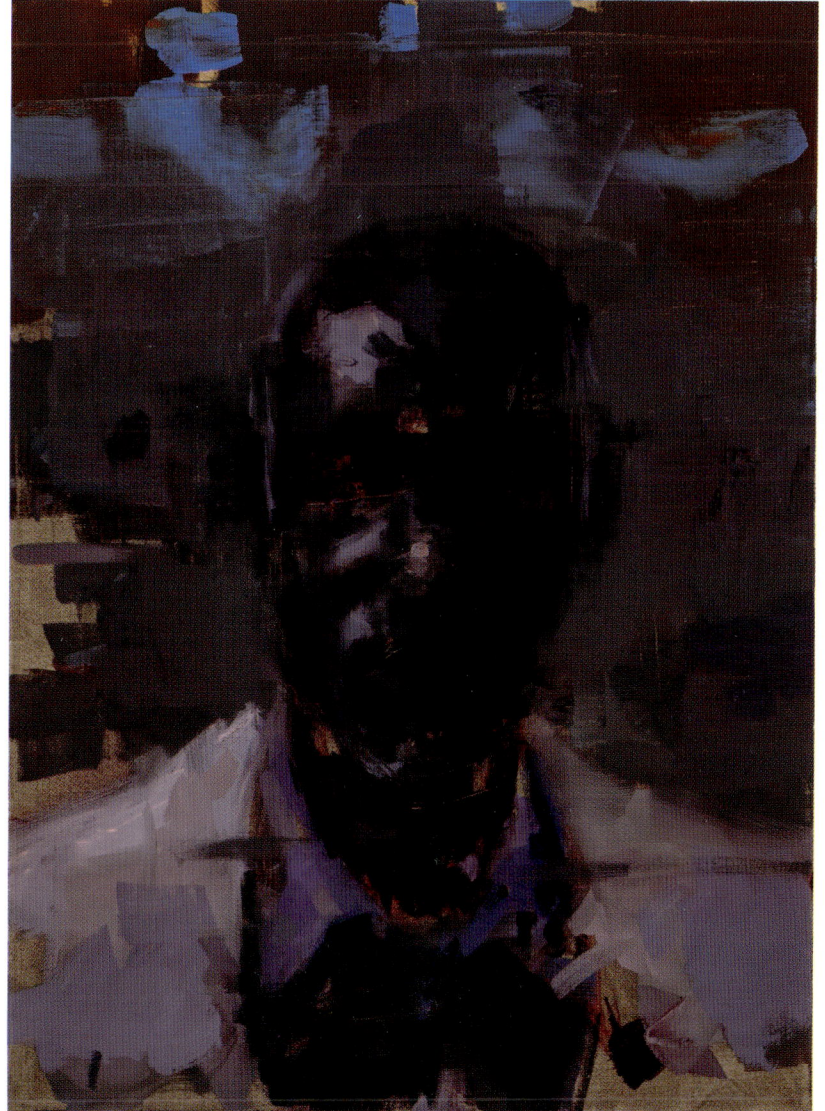

J. LOUIS

Lives and Works in: New York
Education: Savannah College of Art and Design (SCAD)
Selected Collections: SCAD
Representation: Arcadia Contemporary, Pasadena, California

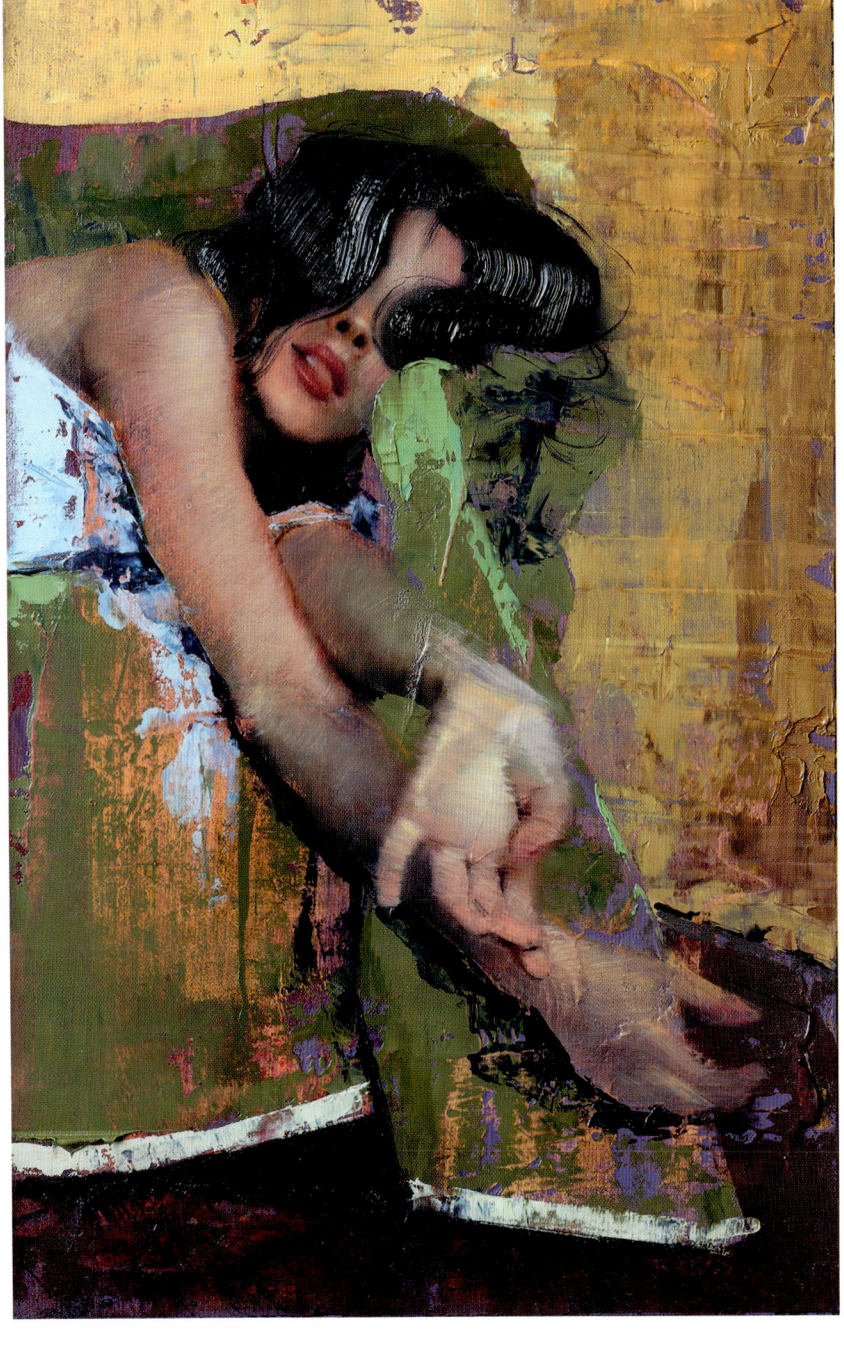

I create work that strikes the viewer intensely at first glance through the compositional presentation, unorthodox color, and texture exploration and then slowly reveals graceful feminine depictions in its softness and sensual touches to provide an exceptional, fresh viewing experience.

J. Louis. *Relapse,* 2018.
Oil on linen mounted on a cradled panel:
15 × 23 inches.

How and why does your work disrupt or deviate from traditional realism?

I paint using color and texture that surrounds the figures, which I feel creates an instant emotional interaction and experience between the viewer and the work of art. When I paint in this style, I highlight the figure and achieve a heightened sense of emotional dialogue. The choices I make with color and texture are meant to transcend time and not associate with any specific place or era. I strive to encourage my viewers to focus on their own personal connection to my subjects during their visual experience. I accomplish this raw emotional relationship through the use of form, color, and texture that goes outside the boundaries of expected traditional realism and into a fresh, contemporary, figurative art experience.

How has your work evolved and developed over time?

My work has gradually changed over time, as I've been able to rid myself of unnecessary elements in my images. My ability to edit particular elements has developed, and the details, the ones I felt were very important in the beginning, became less significant. The emotional content portrayed by my figures has become increasingly complex while the space they occupy on the canvas has receded in visual importance. Over the past years, I've been able to focus on depicting each individual figure's intense emotion. I work very hard to portray each specific emotion by choosing smaller, subtle elements in the painting to provide focus while eliminating other unnecessary details. I accomplish my final edit by following my instincts until I feel the emotion is represented properly and tells a complete story.

What are some of the influences that have shaped your work?

My aesthetic style, my love of color and shape, and my love of line drawing started while studying industrial design at Savannah College of Art & Design. I was fortunate to share thinking space with exceptionally creative people and was allowed time to explore shape, color, and varied design elements in the industrial design program. At SCAD, I was able to draw inspiration and collect ideas from collaborating with clothing designers, industrial designers, photographers, illustrators, and sculptors. I was surrounded by inspiring and driven individuals, but the thing I learned best through my creative relationships was how to apply the use of material and storytelling directly to my work. I found that by constantly pushing myself to explore new materials and interpreting traditional materials in innovative ways, I could support the storyline within my works.

Another influence, in addition to my time at SCAD, was my foreign travel and the hundreds of hours I enjoyed in museums around the world. I have been inspired by firsthand views of the greatest works of art in many countries. I found a great connection with the works of Gustav Klimt, Egon Schiele, and Antonio Mancini. Like these great master painters, I attempt to dive deep into the psyche of my subject while exploring the impact of composition and material exploration for the viewer's experience.

I am currently influenced by the grace and empowerment of women, and I am exploring the many facets of the feminine gaze and how this affects the viewer experience. This has been brought about by my relationship with my incredible wife. She's rocked my world, and I want to share her strength and the strength of other empowered women through my work.

Mention something interesting about your life and background.

I grew up the son of a military officer and moved many times during my childhood. The one constant was my passion for soccer. Prior to finding my passion for painting, I was passionate about soccer, and I trained as a goalkeeper in the US Olympic Developmental pool. This early commitment to sports provided me with the opportunity to play soccer on a full-ride scholarship for the Savannah College of Art & Design and study industrial design. I made the decision to become a full-time fine artist before I even graduated college and left my soccer cleats behind.

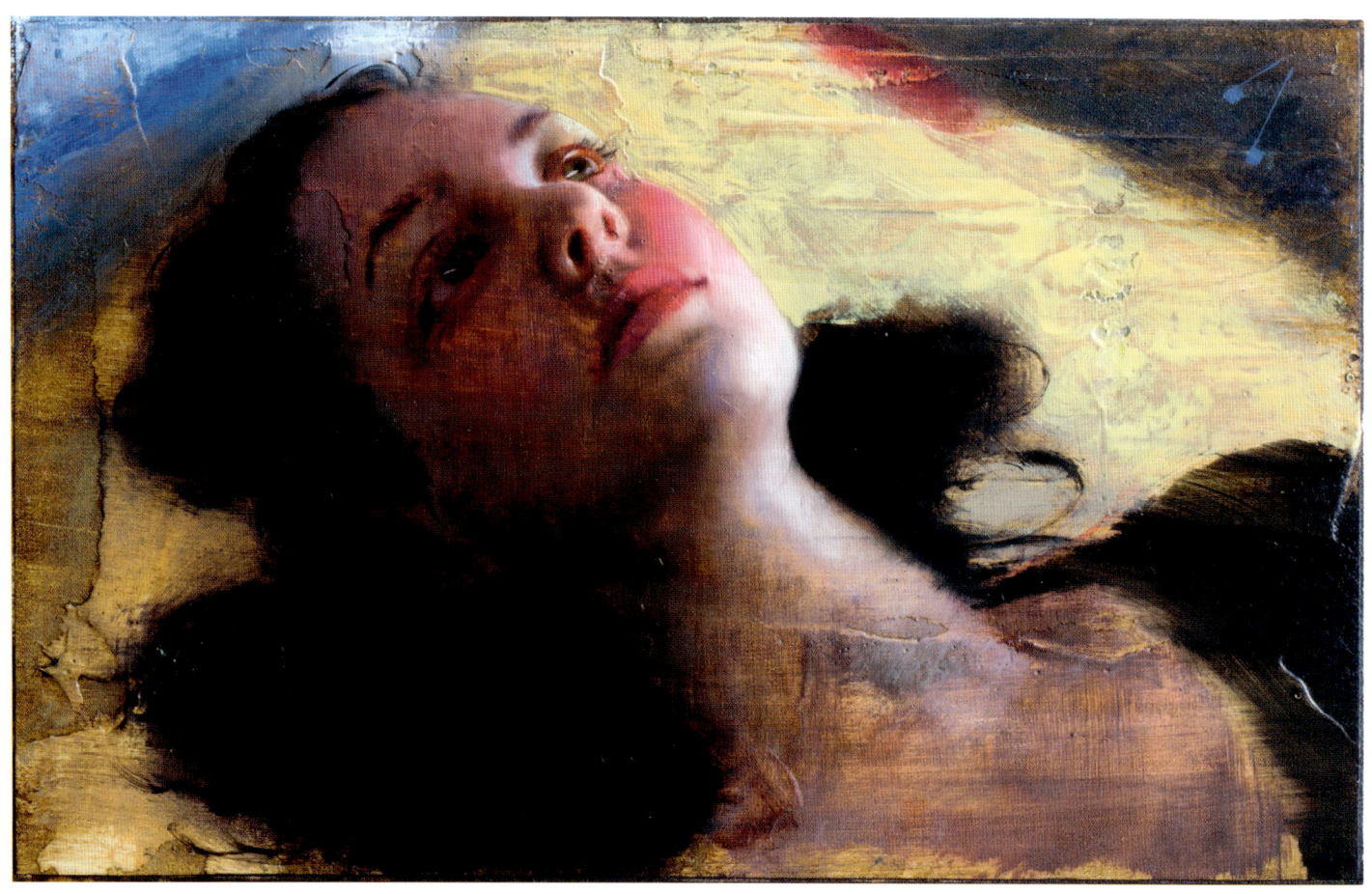

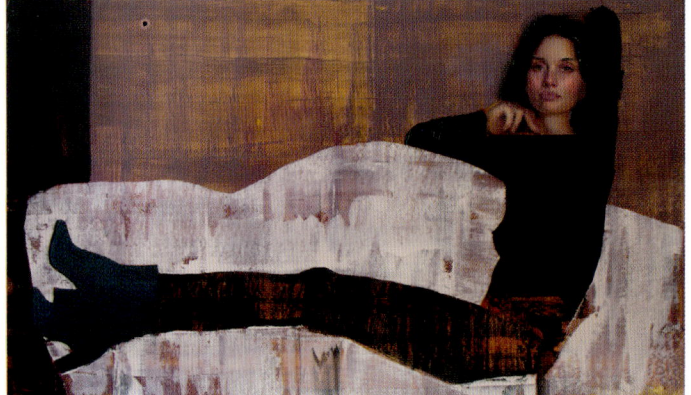

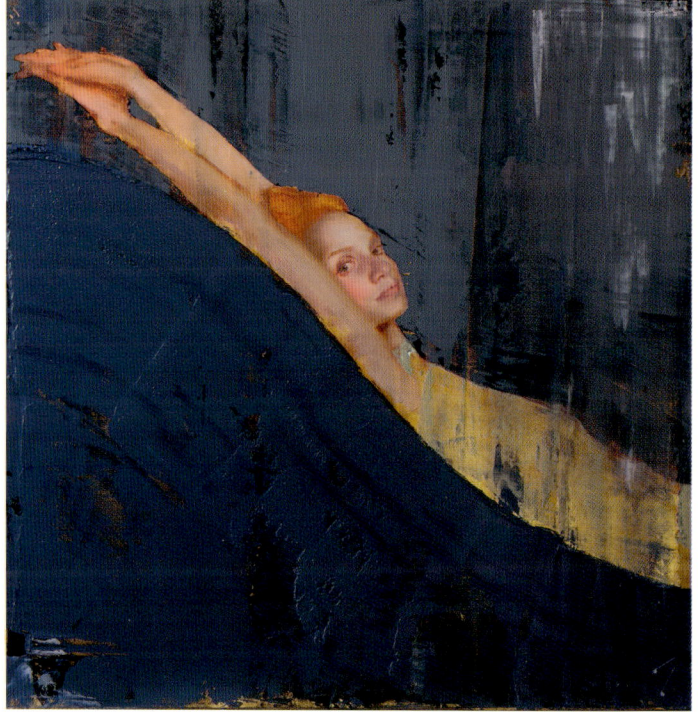

Top: J. Louis. *Chicago*, 2018.
Oil on linen mounted on a cradled panel:
11 × 21 inches.

J. Louis. *Disposition XII*, 2017.
Oil on linen mounted on a cradled panel:
41 × 73 inches.

J. Louis. *Tsunami*, 2017.
Oil on linen mounted on a cradled panel:
48 × 48 inches.

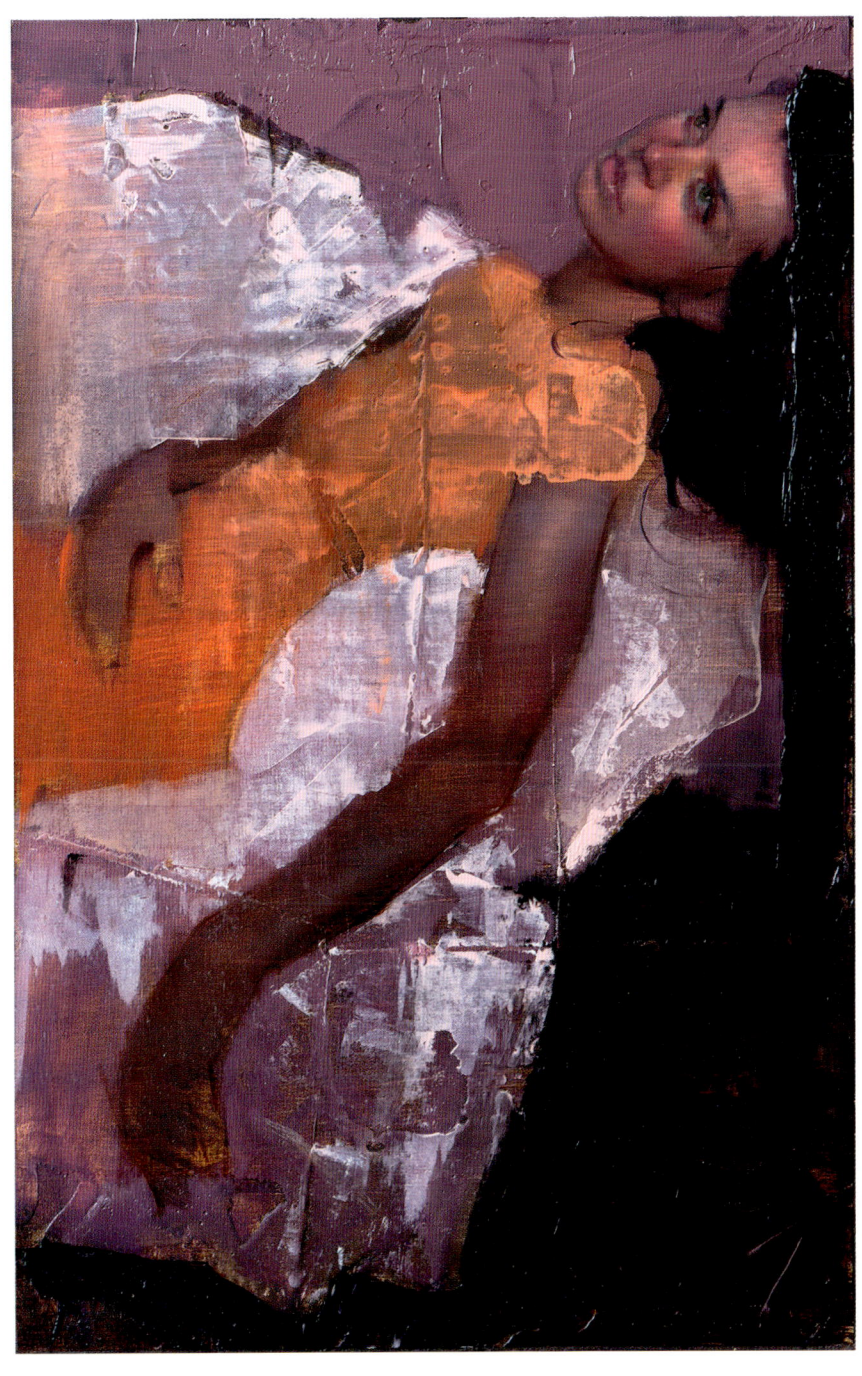

J. Louis. *Orange Dress*, 2018.
Oil on linen mounted on a cradled panel:
13 × 21 inches.

ALEX
MERRITT

Lives and Works in: New York / Jersey City, New Jersey
Education: BA, MICA; MFA, New York Academy of Art
Representation: Booth Gallery, New York

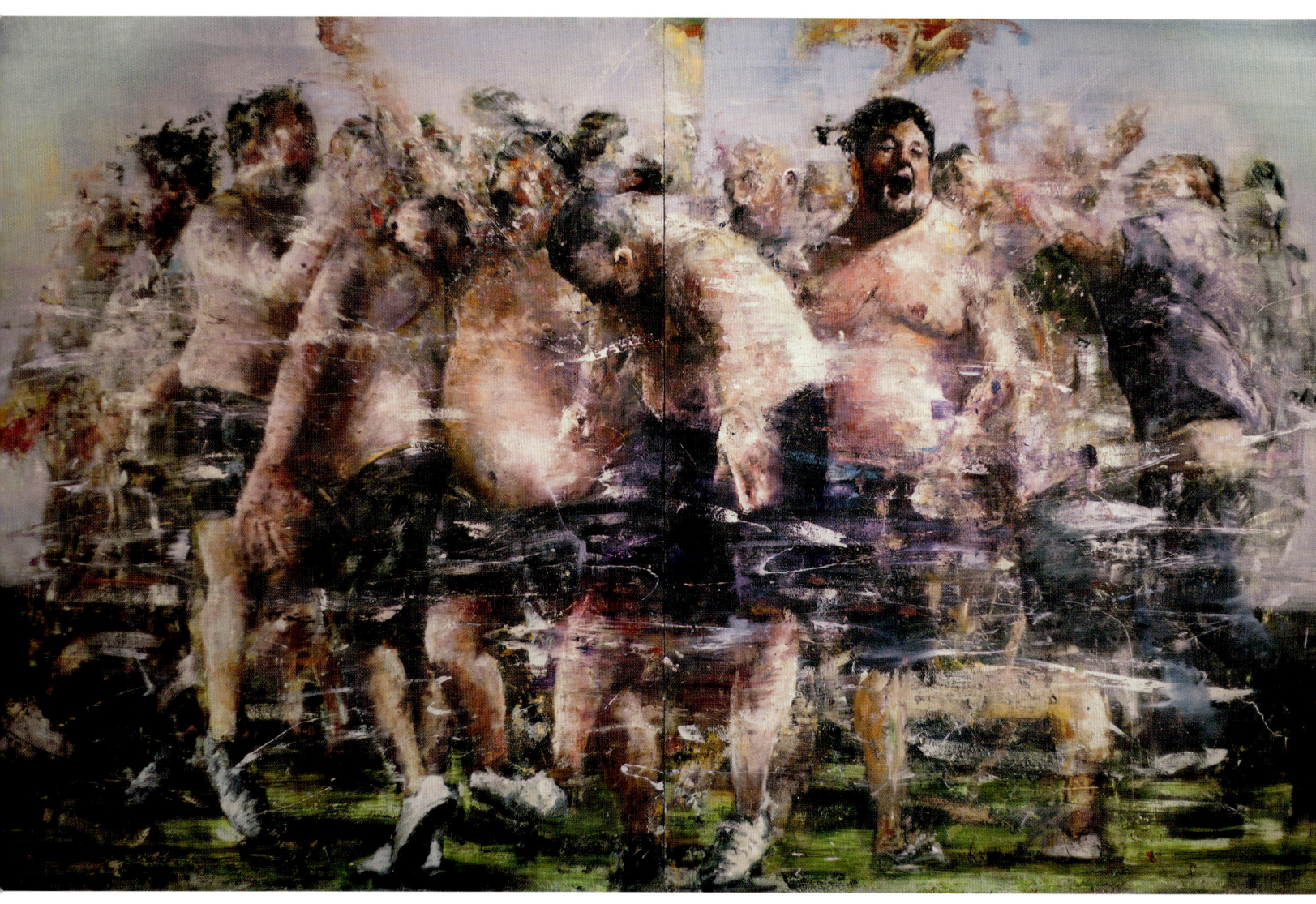

Alex Merritt. *Grand Mal,* 2017.
Oil on linen: 100 × 160 inches.

My paintings want to be felt before they are understood.

How and why does your work disrupt or deviate from traditional realism?

Traditional realist painting prioritizes the faithful representation of truth in nature, whereas my work seeks to disrupt visual truth by filtering it through an emotional lens. I desire to inspire a feeling so overwhelmingly intense that it creates a reality without the literal representation of any reality familiar to the human eye. The scenes I create are constructed primarily by the quiet observation of memory, rather than visual reference. I do this as an attempt to engage my viewer in the immediacy of a flashback: a fragmented memory. These paintings are the physical expression of my struggle between the constant search for clarity and the concurrent negation of that clarity during the process; like an unfolding dream that is simultaneously collapsing in on itself.

How has your work evolved and developed over time?

In the early stages of my career, my paintings always began with a final image in mind, and I worked toward its completion with a definite goal. However, over the years, my focus has shifted. The visual representation of an image is now secondary to the feeling that I want to inspire. Although I still begin paintings with an idea in mind, my approach is more open ended. I trust the painting to take a life of its own through the process of its creation, welcoming divergences from any preconceived ideas, thereby allowing the final image to gradually and organically reveal itself to me.

What are some of the influences that have shaped your work?

Artists who inspire me and have changed the way that I look at and think about art tend to be artists who confront the darker side of things. Paintings like *Nights Watch* by Rembrandt and *Two Stags Fighting* by Courbet (to name only a few) are permanently stamped in my mind, continuously influencing my every brushstroke. Paintings like *The Slave Ship* by Turner and Goya's Black Paintings have forever changed the way I prioritize representation of emotion over realistic or anatomical correctness. Painters like Cecily Brown, Francis Bacon, Chaim Soutine, artists whose work functions on the gut level, have had a significant influence on my decision to free myself from traditional realism and trust my instincts.

Mention something interesting about your life and background.

My introduction to painting came through graffiti, street art, skateboarding, and constant trips to the National Gallery in Washington, DC. Although I had made some art when I was younger, I did not begin painting seriously or receive any formal training until I was thirty. So when I started painting, I was using spray paint outdoors, yet trying to emulate artists like Rembrandt.

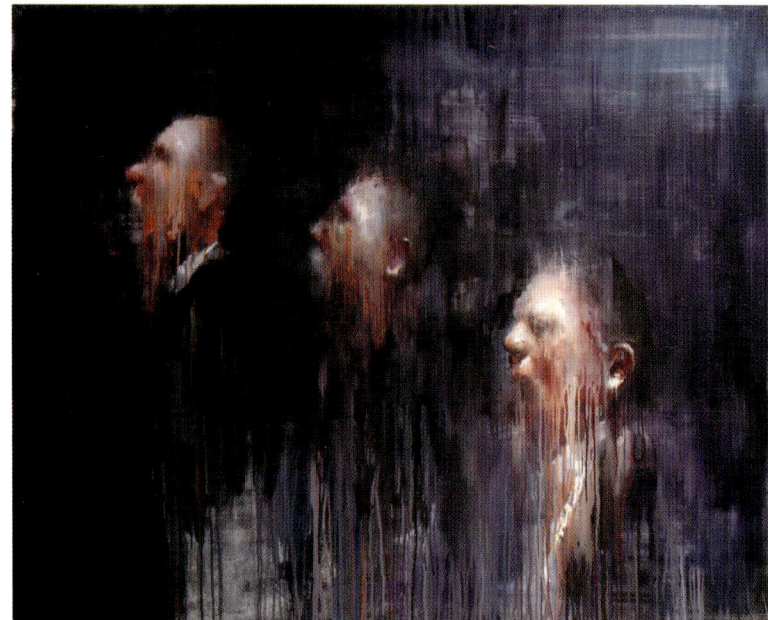
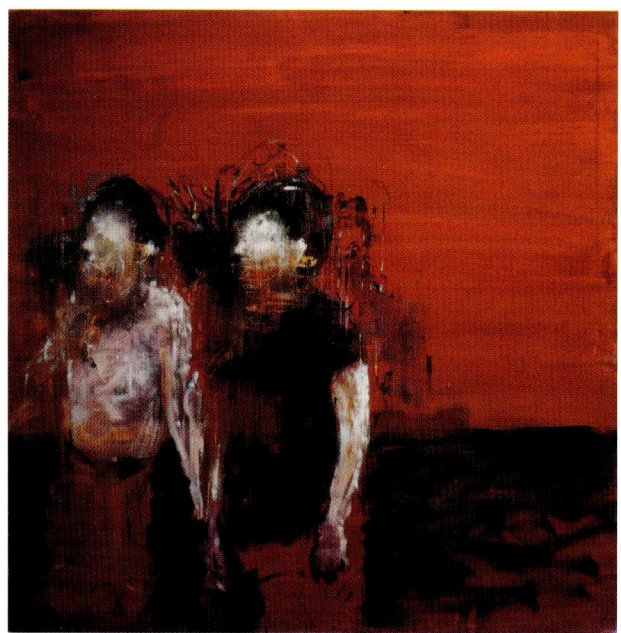

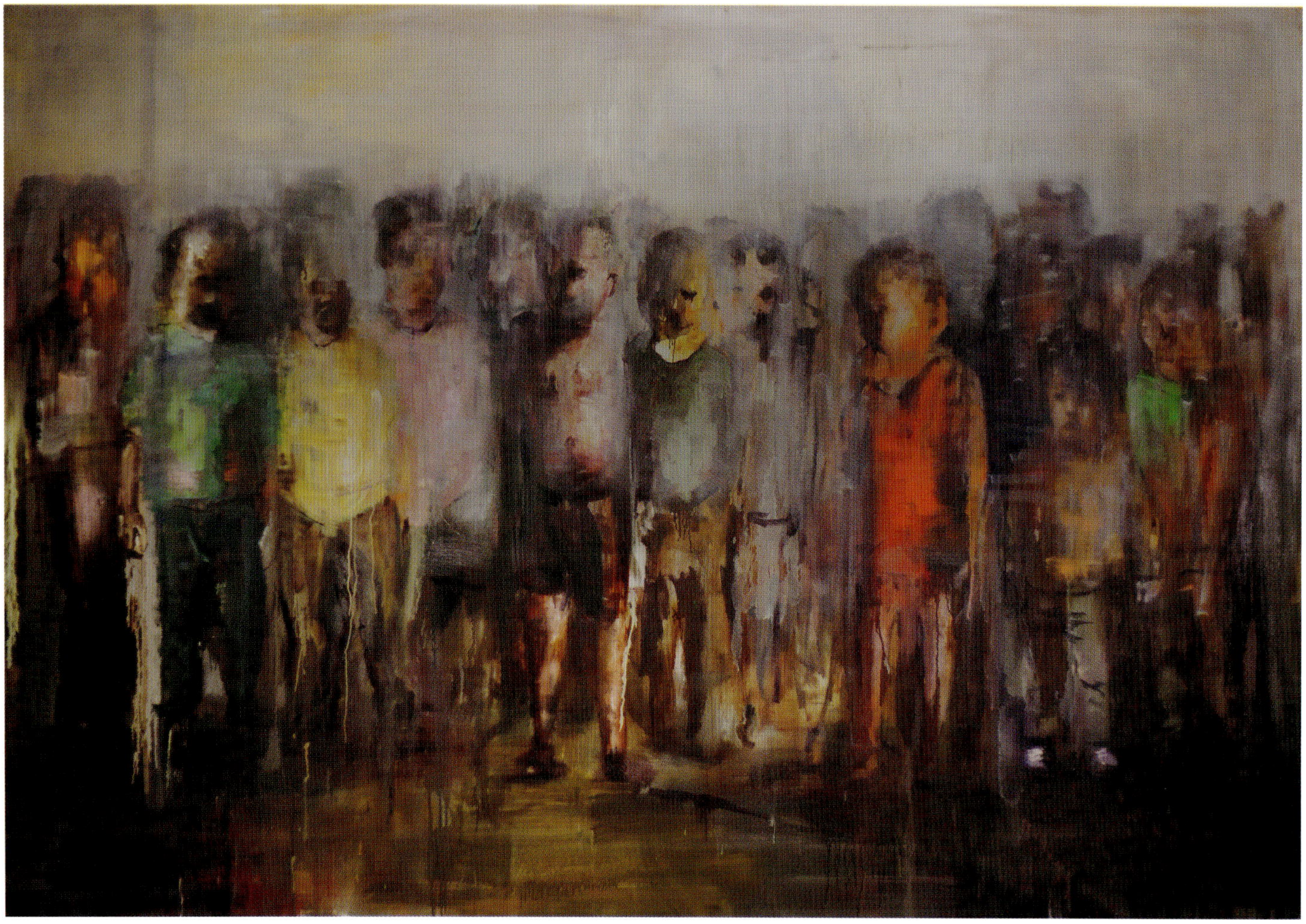

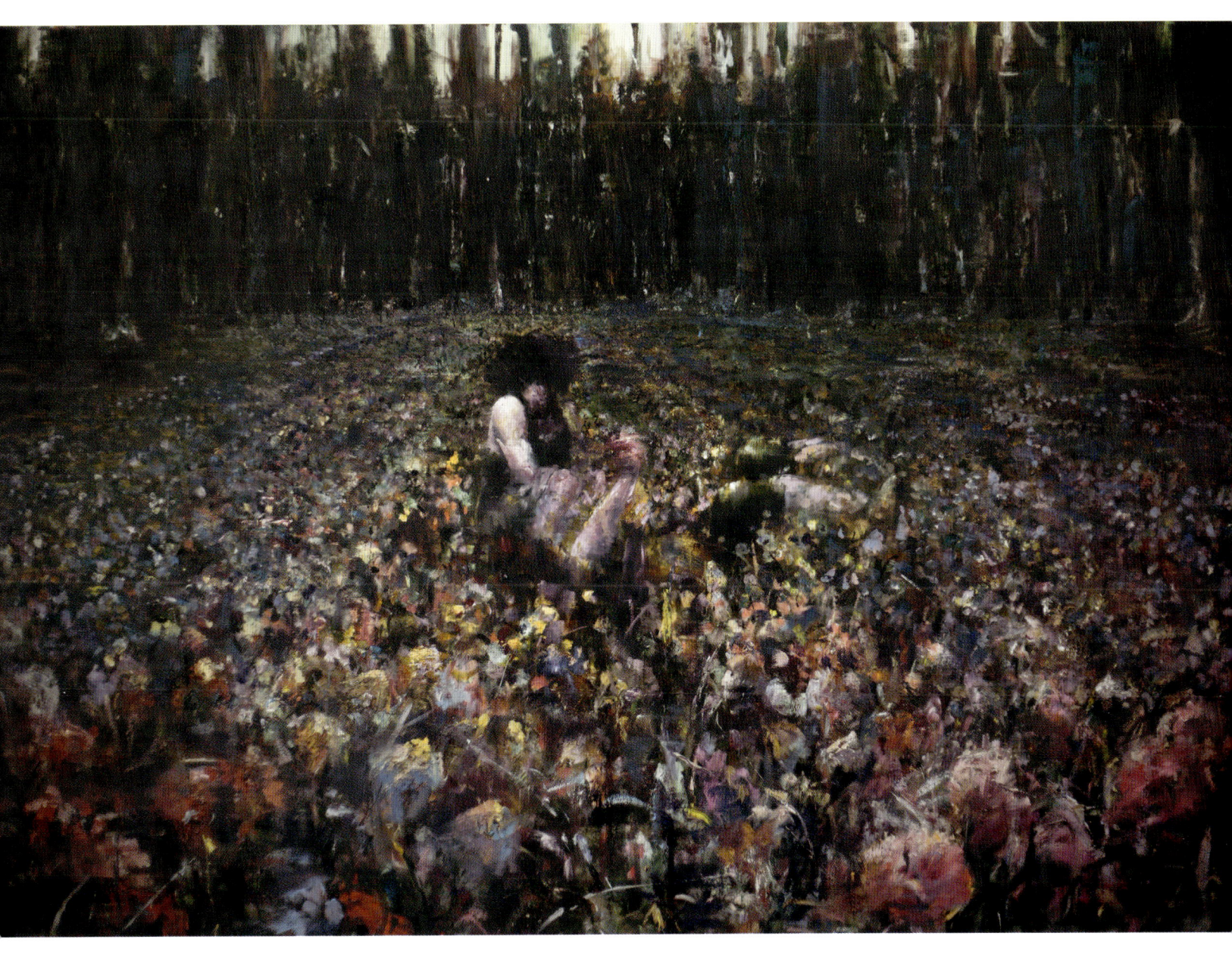

Alex Merritt. *Delirium*, 2018.
Oil on linen: 80 × 120 inches.

NICK RUNGE

Lives and Works in: Los Angeles
Education: Front Range Community College, Colorado
Representation: Abend Gallery, Denver, Colorado

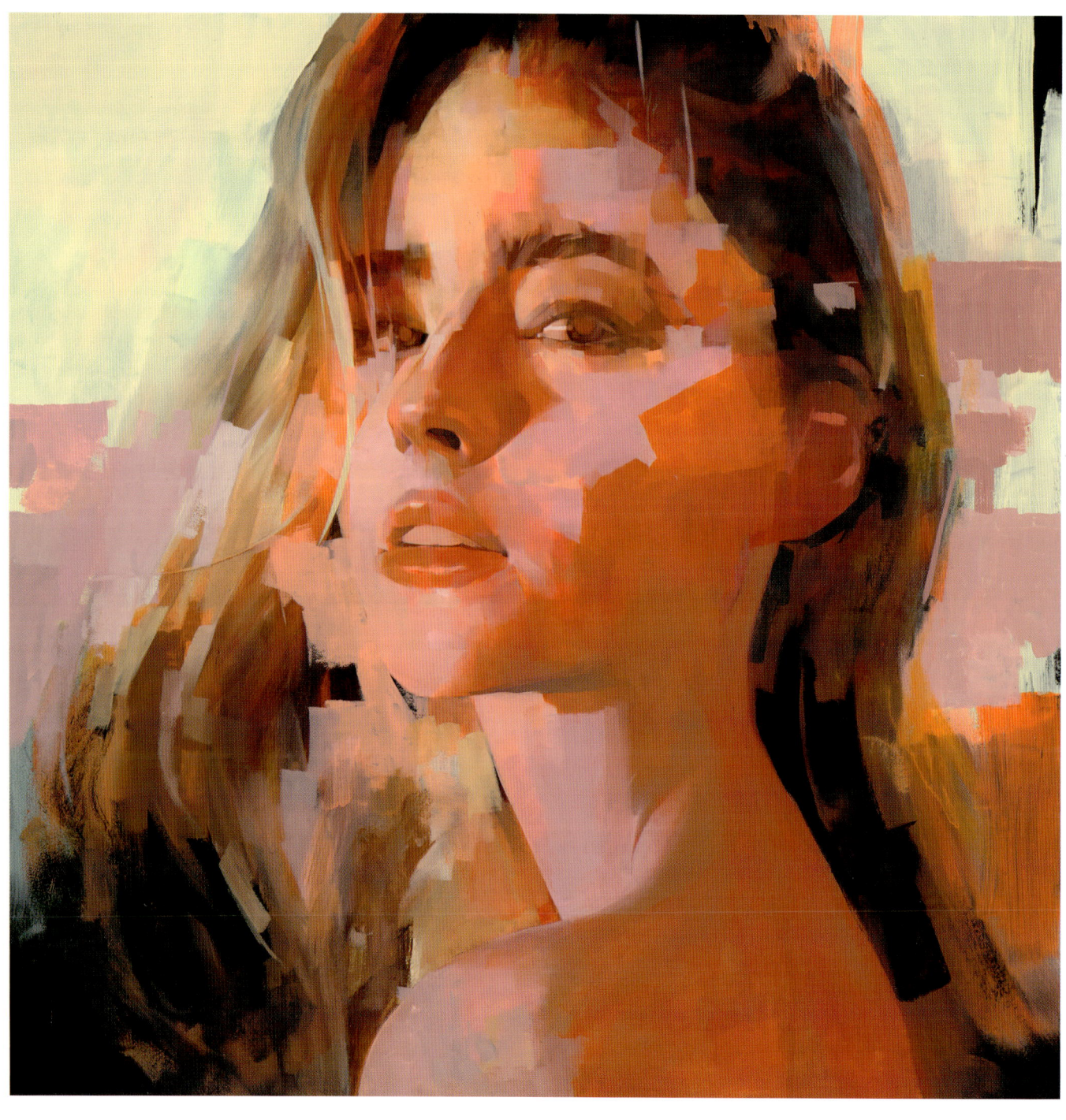

I paint what I can't see.

How and why does your work disrupt or deviate from traditional realism?

At first glance, my work might seem to make a mess of realism. Hopefully though, it draws the viewer in with certain color choices and abstract elements to help shape something real in their mind. I want to create the same interest toward a disrupted face or figure that a person might have toward a traditional portrait. Capturing something accurately with exact value and local color is certainly very different from building up the values and form with imagined, saturated colors and broken shapes, but the impact can be the same if the art is intriguing. I want the disruption to make someone "feel" instead of "think."

How has your work evolved and developed over time?

My worked has changed quite drastically over the last few years. I worked as an illustrator from 2004 to 2015, and my time was completely dedicated to the client. I could feel my own intuition and ideas beginning to fade away over time, with one project overlapping the next, so I chose to step away from illustration and focus on personal work full time. As far as the paintings themselves, my older work was done with acrylics and colored pencils, in a very tight, controlled style. My fine art is made with either watercolor or oil. I try to focus less on the subject matter and more on composition and color.

What are some of the influences that have shaped your work?

Both of my parents are artists. My mother worked as a graphic designer for many years, and my father is a painter who taught college art while I was growing up. My brother Alex is a talented artist, and our home as kids was a very creative atmosphere, which still influences me today when I draw or paint. As far as painters who have influenced me, some of the first were N. C. Wyeth, Andrew Wyeth, Degas, Rembrandt, Caravaggio, and Sorolla, as well as Klimt, Van Gogh, Dali, and Picasso. Later some were Nicolai Fechin, Euan Uglow, and illustrators like Dean Cornwell, J. C. Leyendecker, and Drew Struzan. These days, some of my main influences are Nicolas Uribe, Jenny Saville, Phil Hale, Benjamin Bjorklund, Aaron Westerberg, Justin Hopkins, Daniel Segrove, Emilio Villalba, and Felicia Forte.

Mention something interesting about your life and background.

My first interest is art but I'm also a drummer and have studied filmmaking, photography, and acting. I'm very curious about storytelling in general, whether it's in cinema or music. I keep my painting separate but I'd very much like to pursue some kind of film, short film, or story one day. I don't know how interesting that is, but it's something I don't mention a lot.

Nick Runge. *Light of Day*, 2017.
Oil on canvas: 36 × 36 inches.

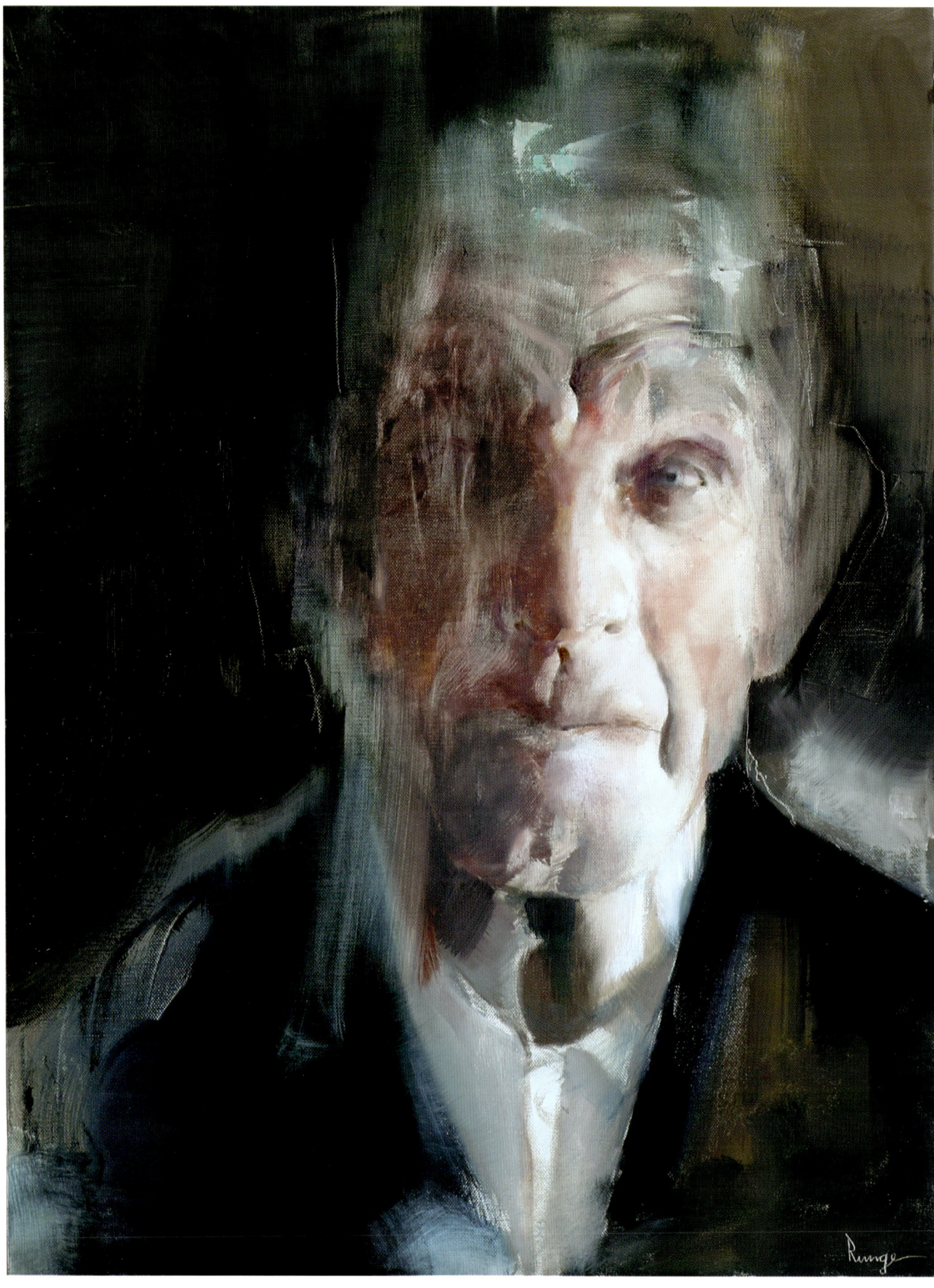

Nick Runge. *Bus Driver*, 2016.
Oil on canvas: 18 × 24 inches.

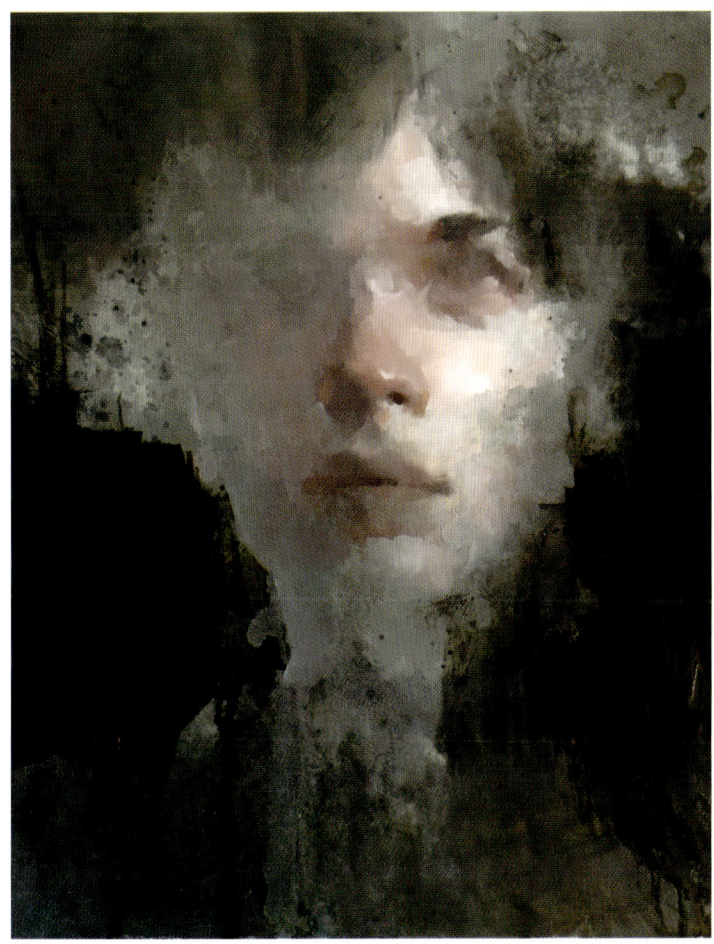

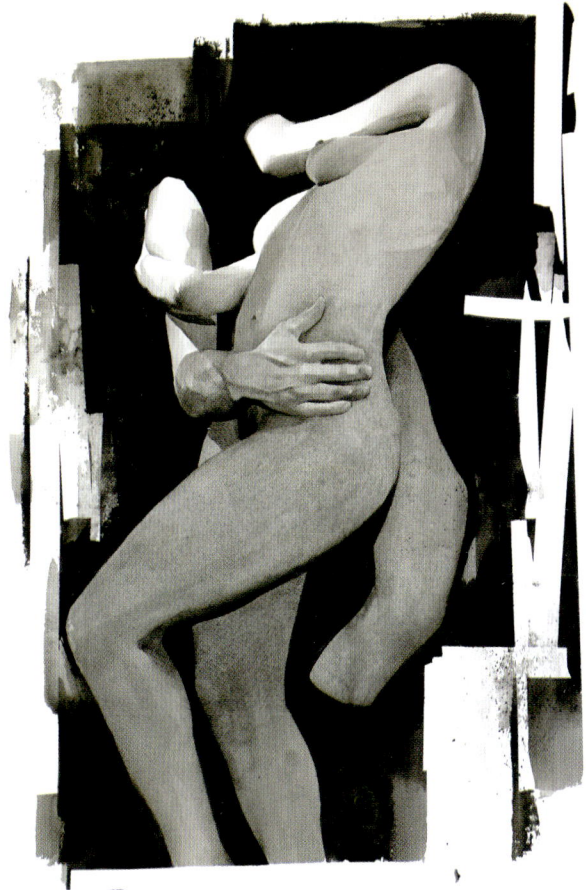

Nick Runge. *Resonance,* 2017.
Oil on wood panel: 18 × 24 inches.

Nick Runge. *Vestige,* 2017.
Watercolor on Arches cold press: 22 × 15 inches.

Overleaf: Nick Runge. *The Coast,* 2017.
Oil on wood panel: 24 × 36 inches.

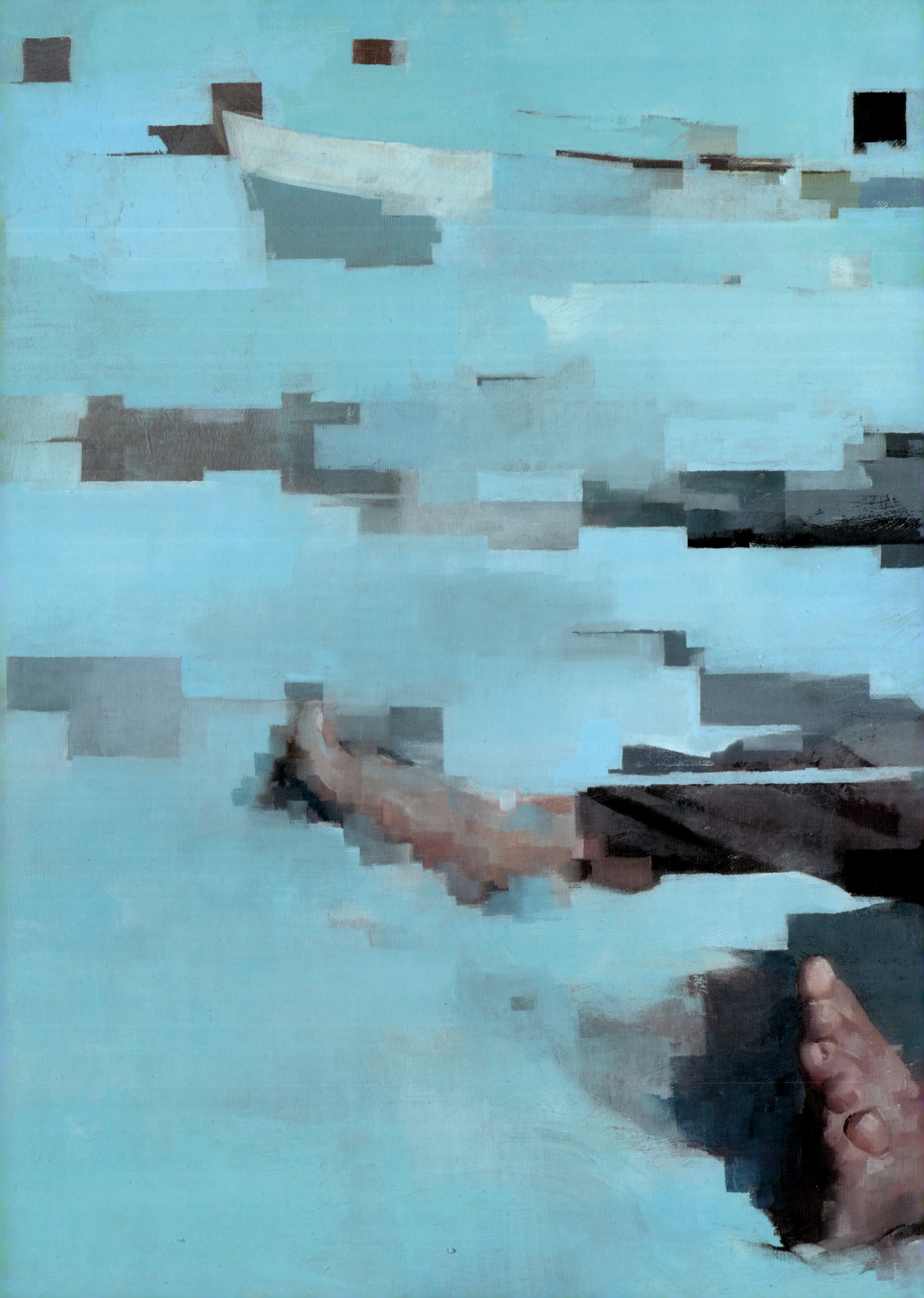

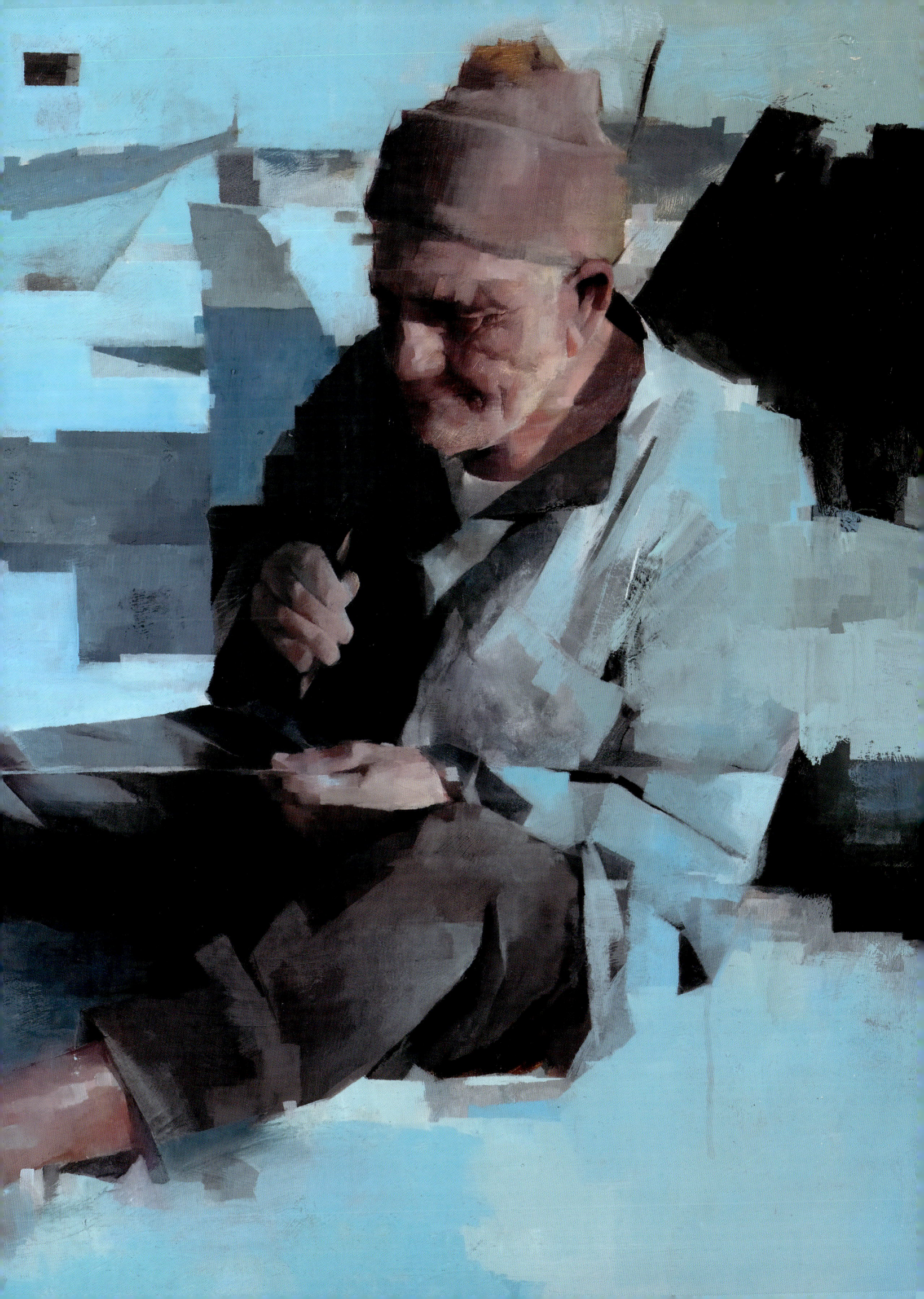

KAI SAMUELS-DAVIS

Lives and Works in: Inverness, California
Education: BFA, SUNY Purchase, New York; MFA,
Art Center College of Design, California
Representation: Dolby Chadwick Gallery, San Francisco

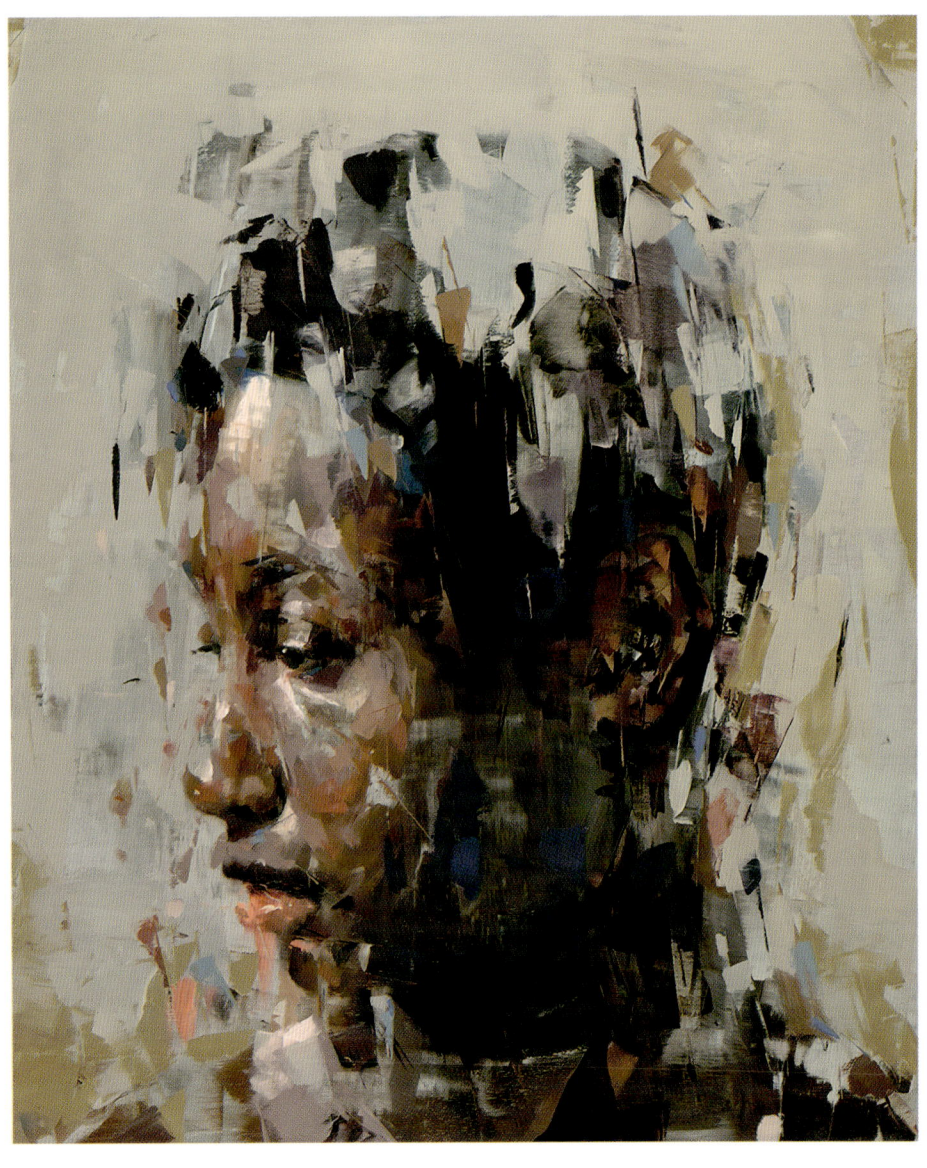

I paint mostly portraits—abstracted just enough to reveal the emotions present—with texture and marks that invite a closer exploration.

Kai Samuels-Davis. *The Question*, 2016.
Oil on panel: 36 × 30 inches.

How and why does your work disrupt or deviate from traditional realism?

While my work has always been anchored in representation, I try not to focus on depicting specific individuals. I like the subjects of my paintings to act as a vessel to evoke emotions, memories, and connections. I don't want to know who the person is (which is why I use found photographs as references), so that the viewer can determine that for themselves. Over time each piece takes on a life of its own, and that's usually when it's finished.

I use a combination of brushes, paint sticks, and scrapers to apply layer upon layer of paint, highlighting history, texture, and abstraction. Most of the tools I use help me relinquish control so that structures and spaces become fragmented or blurred to bring focus to the emotional content rather than the source material.

How has your work evolved and developed over time?

My paintings have always shifted between being rendered and expressive, with the goal being the happy place in between. I tend to go through five-year cycles in the studio, which combine to form an ongoing narrative of whatever is going on in my head and life. Each body of work starts fresh and rough, reaches a peak where the paintings feel perfect and balanced, and then inevitably I try and fail to re-create that feeling. I tighten up, I overthink things, the work becomes too polished, and then I need to shake my head and regroup. I think this process (though not deliberate) keeps the work moving in a forward progression.

What are some of the influences that have shaped your work?

I've always been drawn to figures and portraits when making art; going back to grade school and especially by the time I was fifteen or so, it was all faces and bodies. They've evolved slowly and organically over the past few decades to where they are now, and they'll keep evolving. Each one feeds off the last, so I think they influence each other. I glean inspiration wherever I can, but when I'm painting it's more of an unconscious process. I don't have specific ideas or references in my head. It's just me, paint, and a panel (with loud music in the background and a beer within arm's reach).

Mention something interesting about your life and background.

I had a rough time growing up (stealing, drugs, depression, bullied, family issues, yada yada). I retreated into myself and out came art, so I think the only interesting thing about me is my work—other than that I'm a pretty boring person. I spend time with my amazing wife and daughter, cook, drink wine, take care of the house, go to the beach, normal stuff. Mostly I just feel lucky to have gone from a lost crazy person to a mildly crazy person with a career, family, and home.

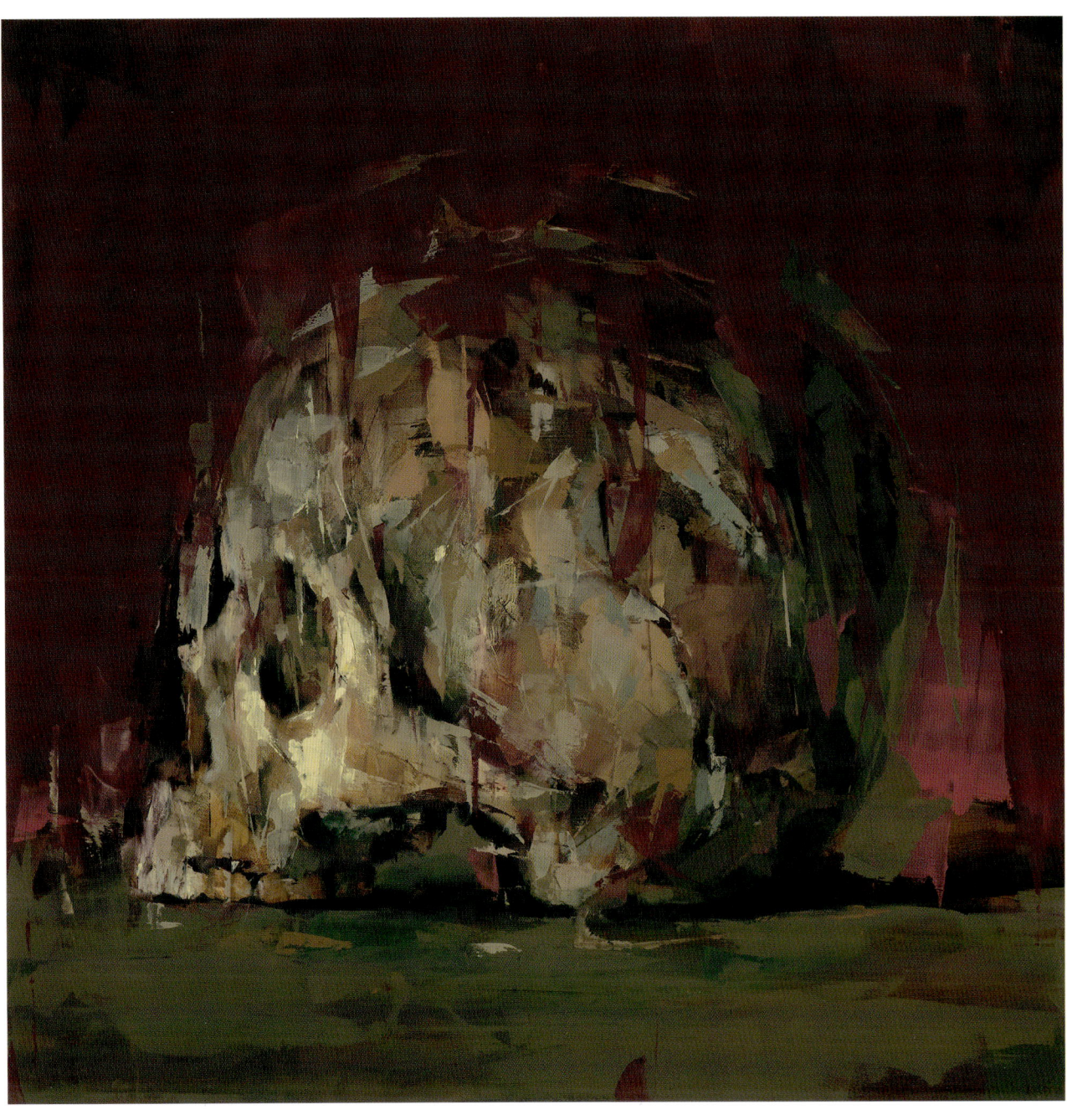

Kai Samuels-Davis. *The End*, 2017.
Oil on panel: 24 × 24 inches.

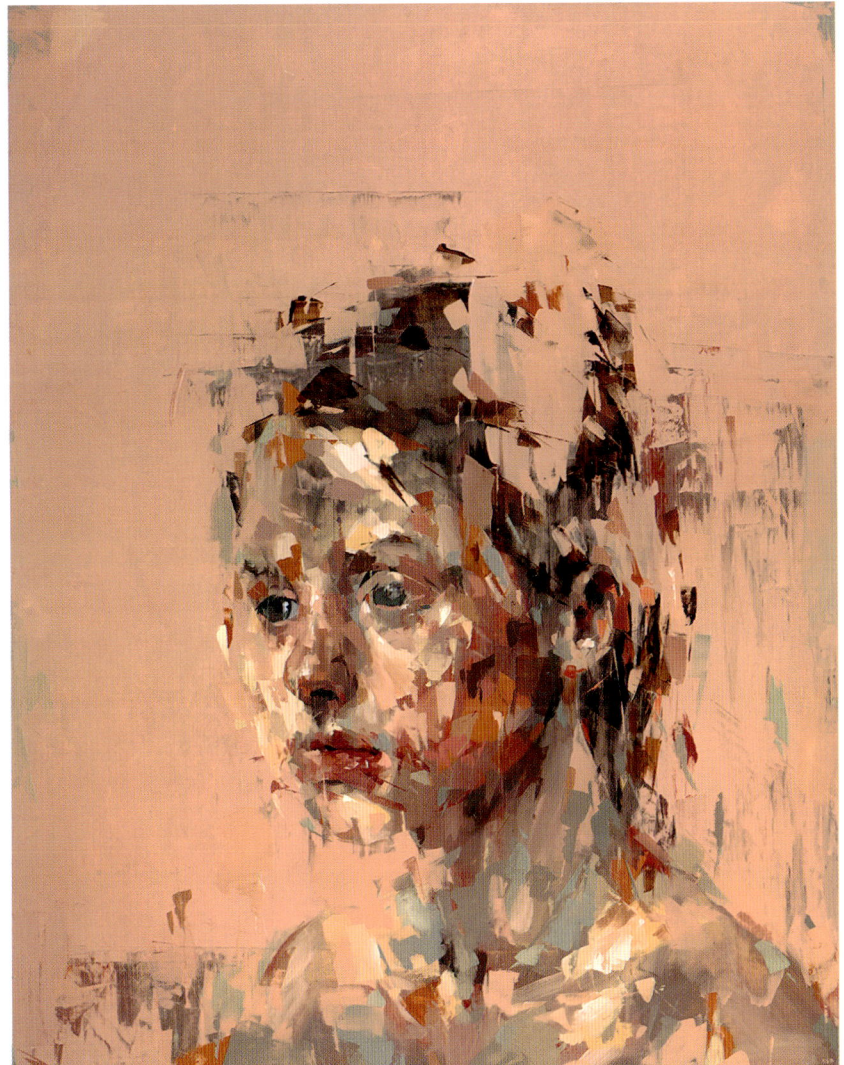

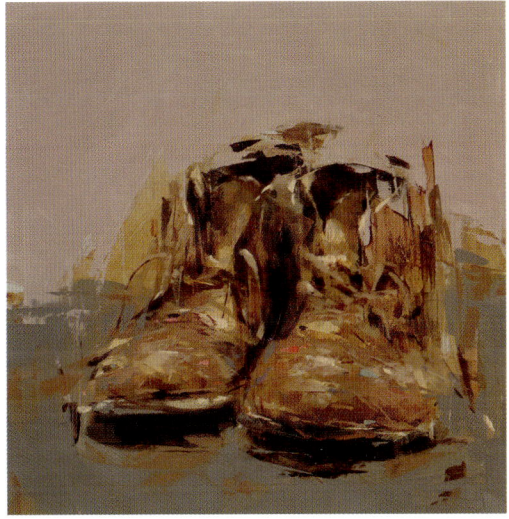

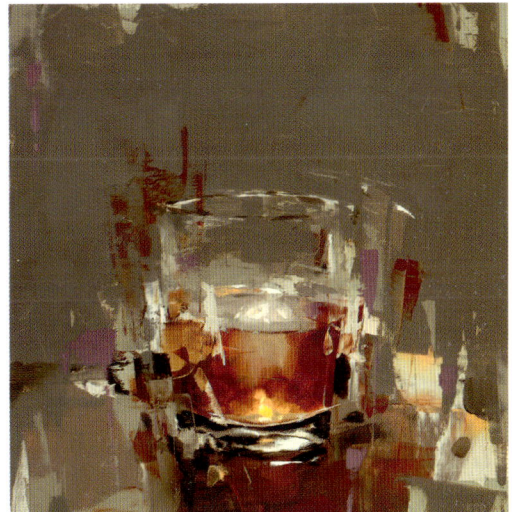

Kai Samuels-Davis. *Borrowed Eyes*, 2016.
Oil on panel: 60 × 48 inches.

Kai Samuels-Davis. *The Traveled II*, 2018.
Oil on panel: 18 × 18 inches.

Kai Samuels-Davis. *The Vessel IV*, 2016.
Oil on panel: 12 × 12 inches.

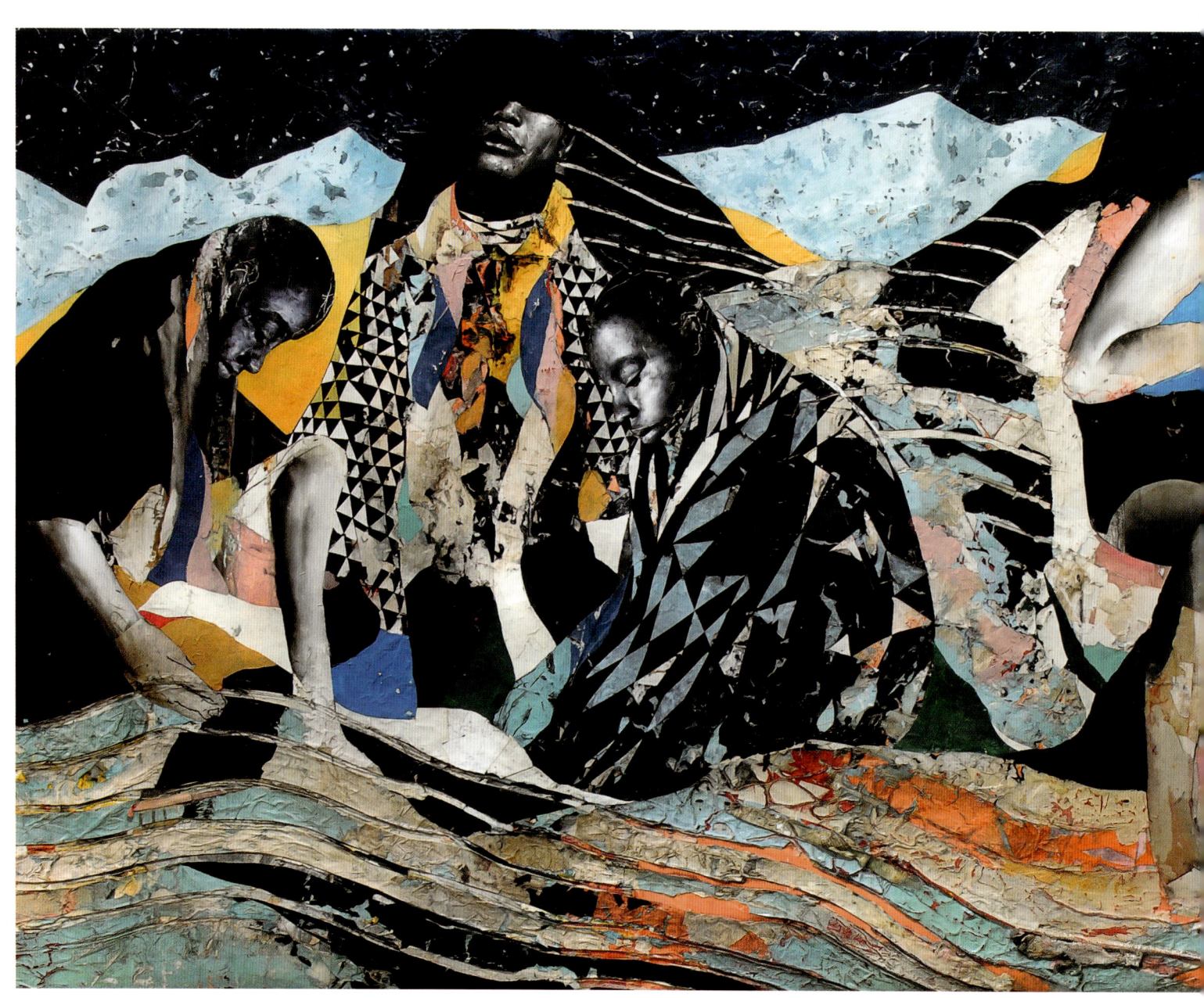

Disrupted Bodies

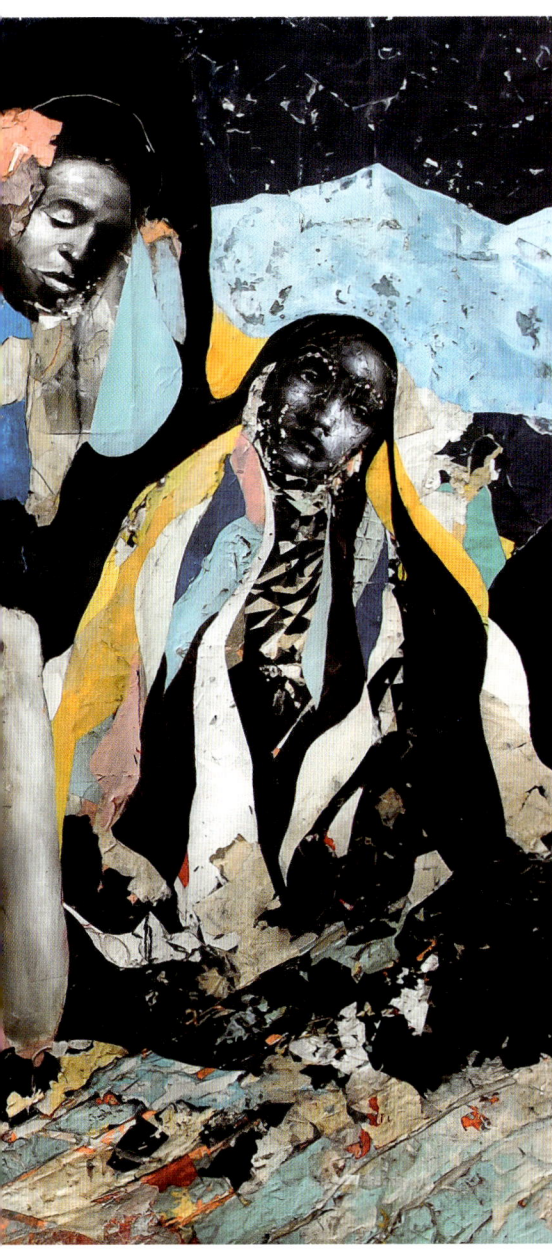

I want a loss of clarity, and an obscuring of definition and category, while still creating an image that has the capability to punch you in the face: something that still feels human.

—Paul Cristina

The human body—art's greatest and most enduring subject—was often distorted and even rearranged by modern artists. In disrupted realism, the body continues to be revised, often in ways that suggest how it is perceived and felt (as opposed to simply seen). Made up of glances—as in Ann Gale's work—or seemingly pierced by imagery in Justin Bower's, the body's fragility and susceptibility to outside forces stands out and demands reconsideration. It is as if seeing the body now involves a series of probing questions rather than simple recognition.

Paul Cristina. *Our Own New Rituals,* 2018.
Charcoal, acrylic, oil, and paper on canvas:
49 × 89 inches.

JUSTIN BOWER

PAUL CRISTINA

ANN GALE

KIRSTINE REINER HANSEN

WYATT MILLS

JUSTIN BOWER

Lives and Works in: Santa Ana, California
Education: Claremont Graduate University
Selected Collections: Eugenio Lopez,
the Weisman Collection, Carlos Slim
Representation: Unix Gallery, New York

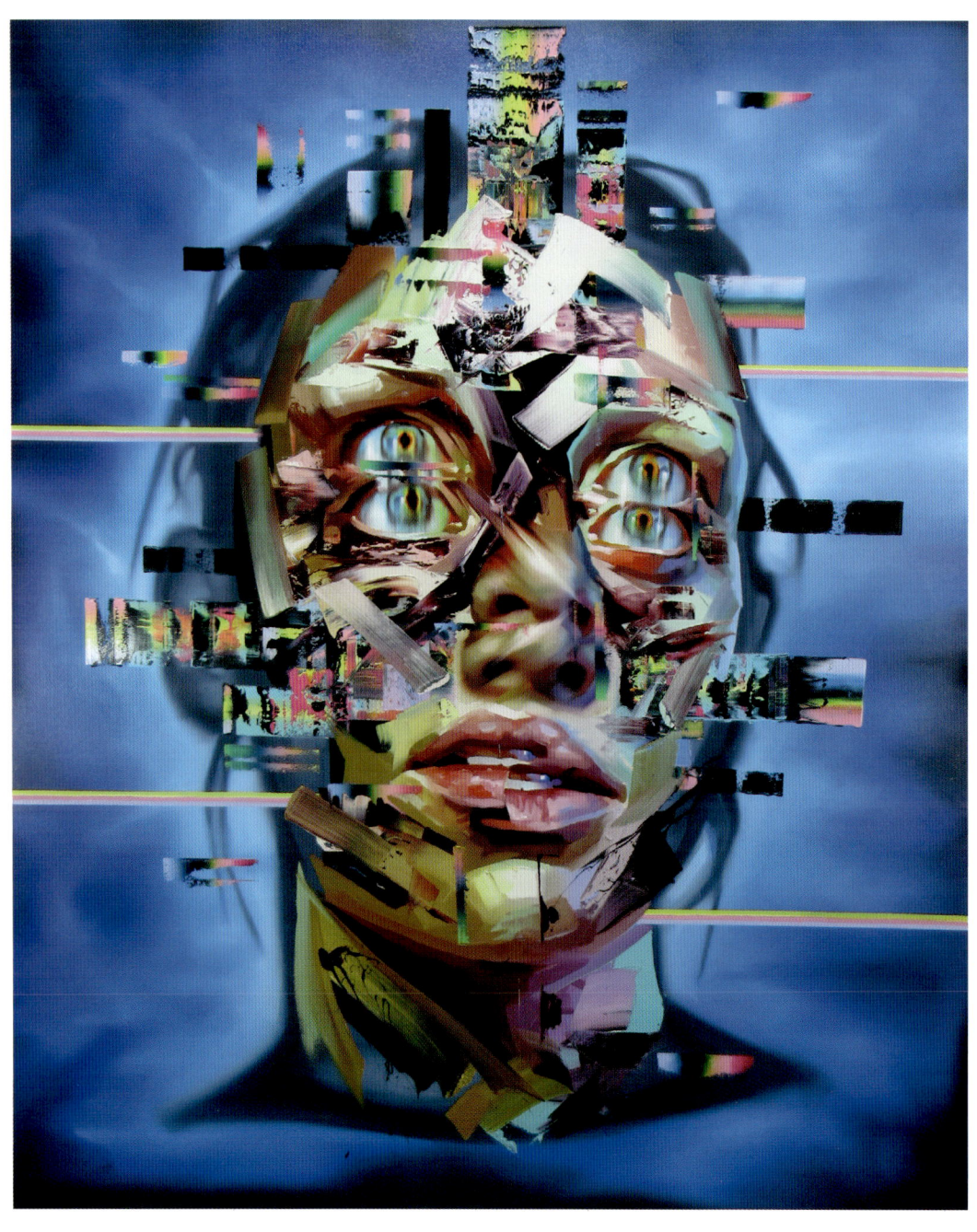

*My aim is to make images that
resonate today and that could only be
made in this era.*

**How and why does your work disrupt
or deviate from traditional realism?**

I paint my subjects as destabilized, fractured post-humans in a nexus of interlocking spatial systems. My paintings problematize how we define ourselves in this digital and virtual age while suggesting the impossibility of grasping such a slippery notion. I use paint as an instrument of dissection and inquiry rather than a traditional rendered closed system. Flesh acts as a complex veneer, functioning as a biological boundary from externalized technologies; all the while the viewer realizes that the same externalized technologies are always already inside the subject. While holding several positions at once, this ultimately creates an open system, an incomplete subject becoming and degrading, not knowing where the outside starts and the internal ends. The boundaries of the traditional subject are now leaking into my concept of subjectivity.

**How has your work evolved and
developed over time?**

I have entered into a religious zone in some of my genuflection series, swapping a stabilized notion of faith with a somewhat myopic faith in future technology. I have also begun to place the full figure in the frame, questioning what does the human figure look like in this context.

**What are some of the influences
that have shaped your work?**

I am studying the many different ways we define ourselves, and in many ways there is an overlap in concept with Cyberpunk; the films of Aronofsky, Kubrick, and Tarkovsky; film noir; science journals, etc., but I am doing it within the rich history of painting. Picasso didn't necessarily have Einstein's theory of relativity in mind when he created cubism, but there was an overlapping of ideas between completely different endeavors.

**Mention something interesting
about your life or background.**

I was stabbed, then I decided to go to grad school.

Justin Bower. *The Magician,* 2015.
Oil on canvas: 6 × 5 feet.

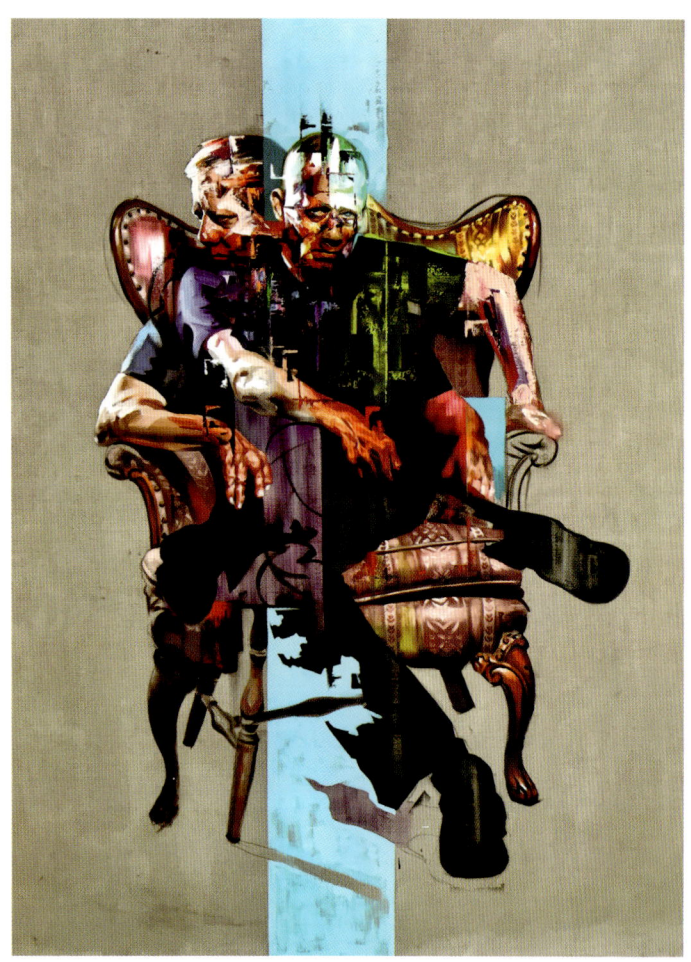

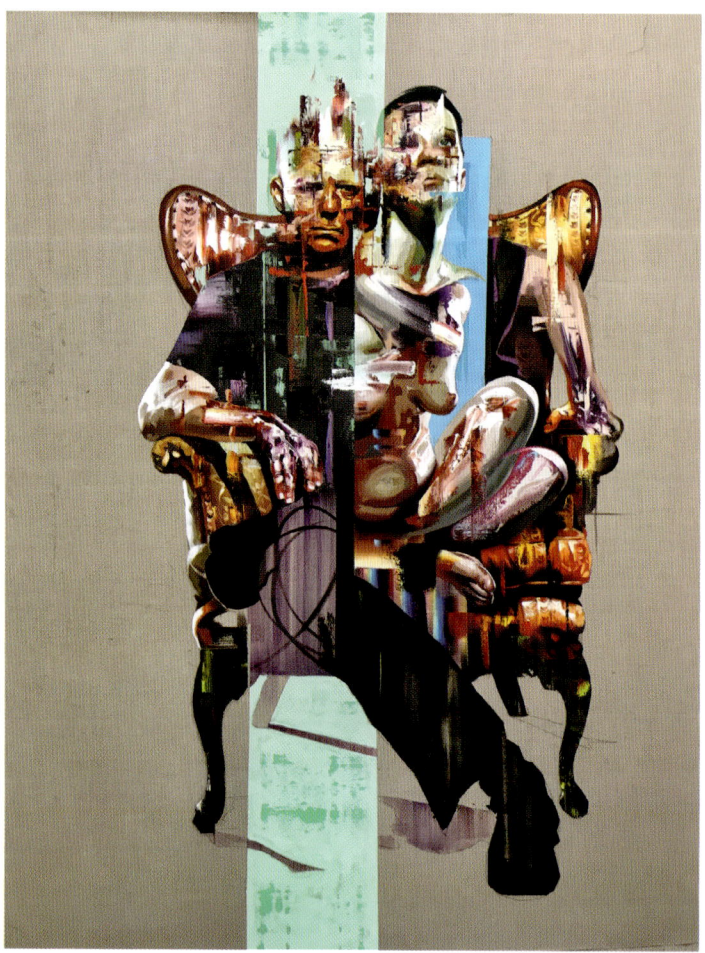

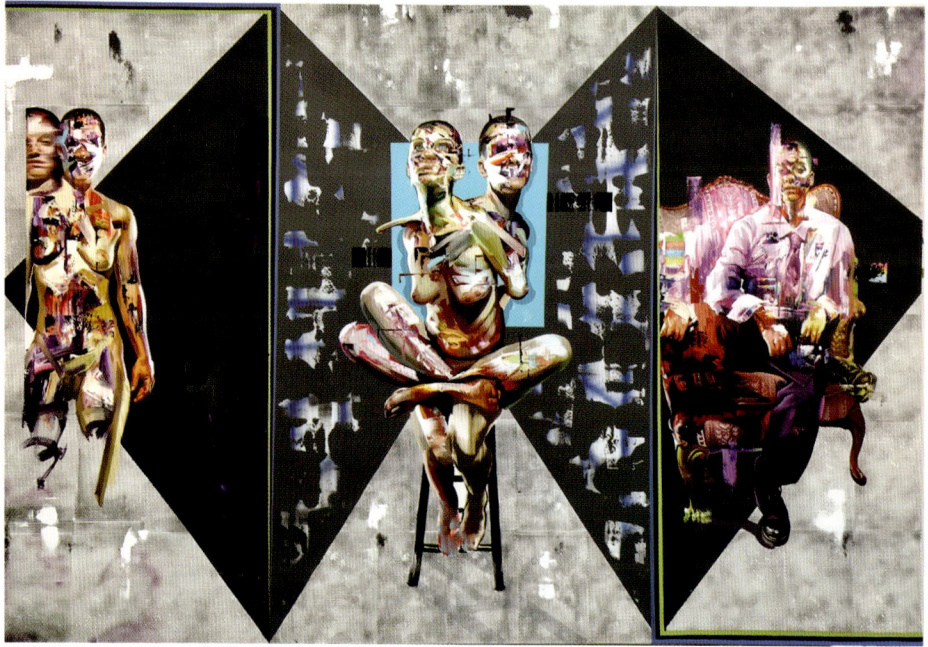

Top left: Justin Bower. *Untitled (Subject Study 1)*, 2018. Oil on linen: 7 × 6 feet.

Top right: Justin Bower. *Untitled (Subject Study 2)*, 2018. Oil on linen: 7 × 6 feet.

Justin Bower. *Colossus Id* (triptych), 2018. Oil on canvas: 9 × 12 feet.

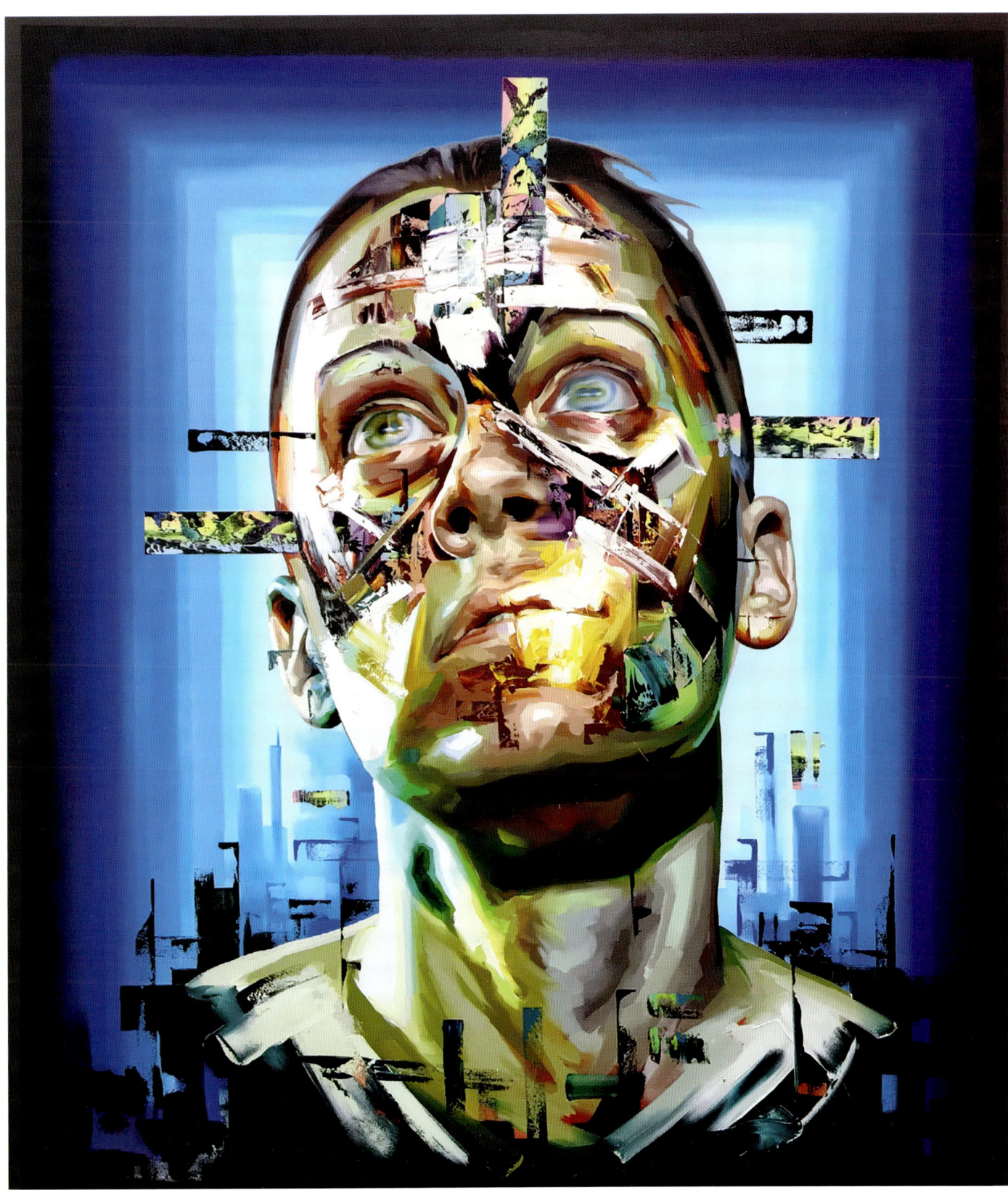

Justin Bower. *Son Stroke 6,* 2018.
Oil on canvas: 7 × 6 feet.

PAUL
CRISTINA

Lives and Works in: Charleston, South Carolina
Representation: Booth Gallery, New York

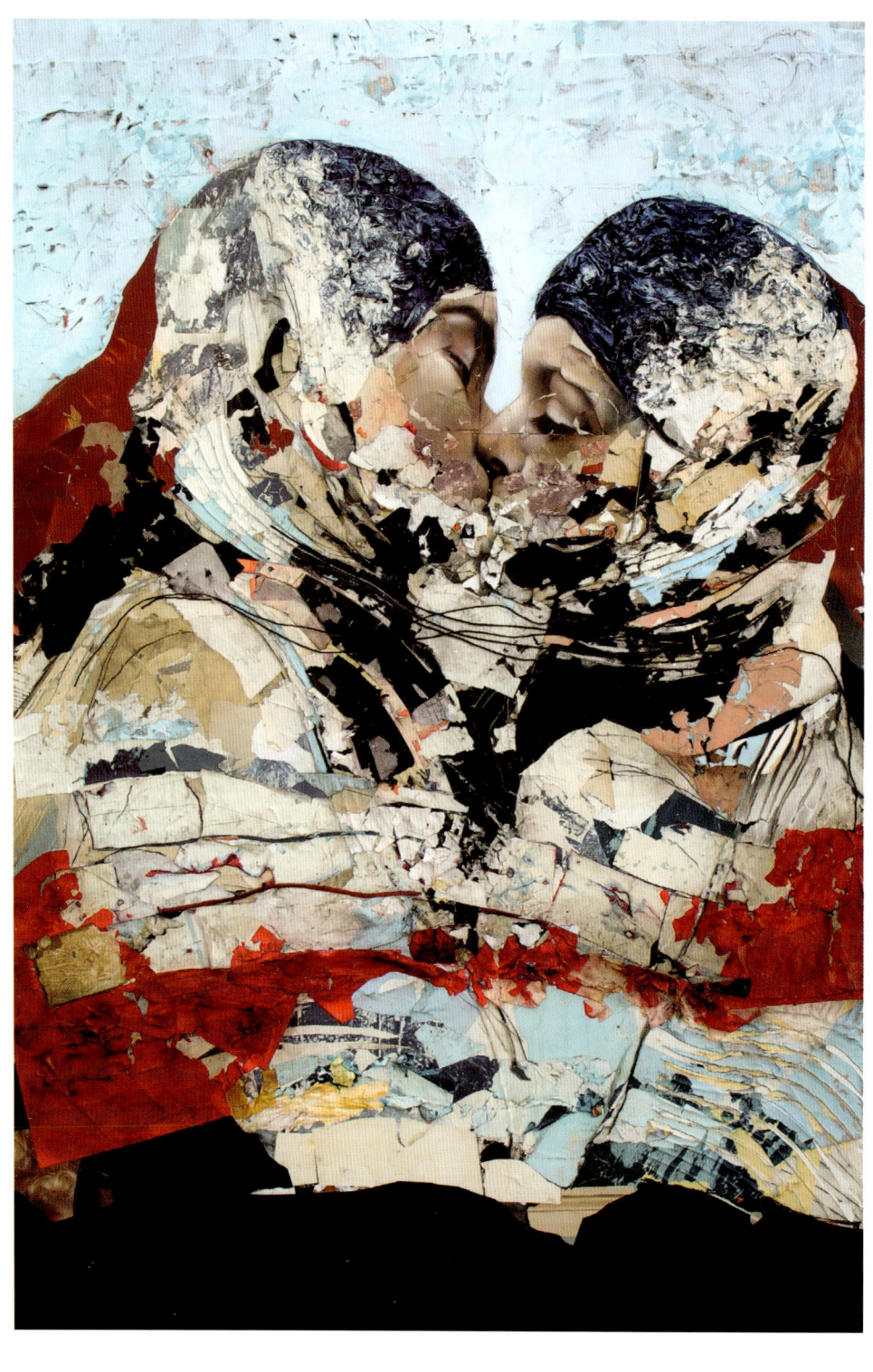

*I want my work to deliver an experience
that is unavoidably human: something that
make us think, feel, and ask questions.*

**How and why does your work disrupt
or deviate from traditional realism?**

I don't like being spoon-fed answers and descriptions in regard to visual art, film, music, etc. I like the unknown and ambiguous spaces of life, especially those related to human behavior and psychology. I suppose I want the work to reflect that line of thinking. I don't want things to be straightforward and easy to digest. I want a loss of clarity, and an obscuring of definition and category, while still creating an image that has the capability to punch you in the face: something that still feels human. I like asking questions, and I want others to ask questions when looking at art, as opposed to simply existing in familiar territories that have already been explored.

**How has your work evolved and
developed over time?**

Through consistent and dedicated studio practice, ideas grow and mature over time and new discoveries are made. My pieces evolve through trial and error, and I began to allow these so-called mistake layers to remain visible and contribute to the finished state of the piece. Some of the pieces can be read from back to front, and you get a sense of its development through time. I became interested in an archeological approach to building a painting: building up, digging, cutting, tearing down, and rediscovering. This fascination has allowed the work to become more layered and dimensional.

**What are some of the influences
that have shaped your work?**

Looking at other artists' work, talking with other artists, artist lectures, reading books, learning art history, looking, looking, and then more looking. Asking questions to myself and to others.

**Mention something interesting
about your life or background.**

I worked as a paramedic for six years from 2010 to 2016, prior to shifting my focus and my life toward making art. I'm self-taught in fine art. I experimented with drugs at a very early age and got expelled from Catholic school.

Paul Cristina. *Modern Lovers,* 2018.
Charcoal, acrylic, oil, and paper on canvas:
68 × 44 inches.

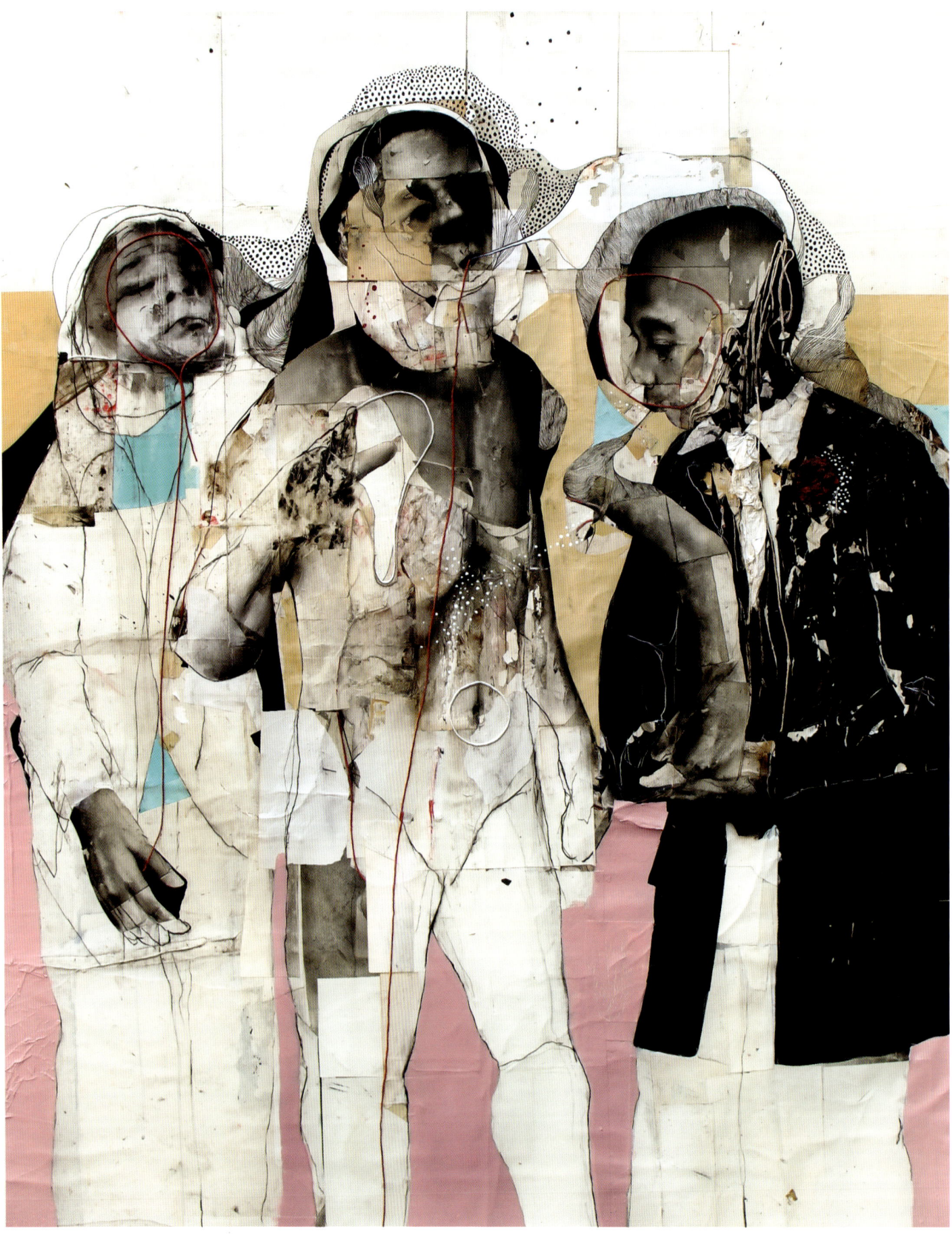

Paul Cristina. *How to Play Jazz in Hell,* 2018. Charcoal, acrylic, oil on paper on canvas: 51 × 47 inches.

Opposite, top: Paul Cristina. *We Were Never Told the Truth about the Dying of the Sun,* 2017. Charcoal, acrylic, oil on paper on canvas: 36 × 36 inches.

Opposite, bottom: Paul Cristina. *Until Nothing Comes,* 2017. Charcoal, acrylic, oil on paper on canvas: 40 × 30 inches.

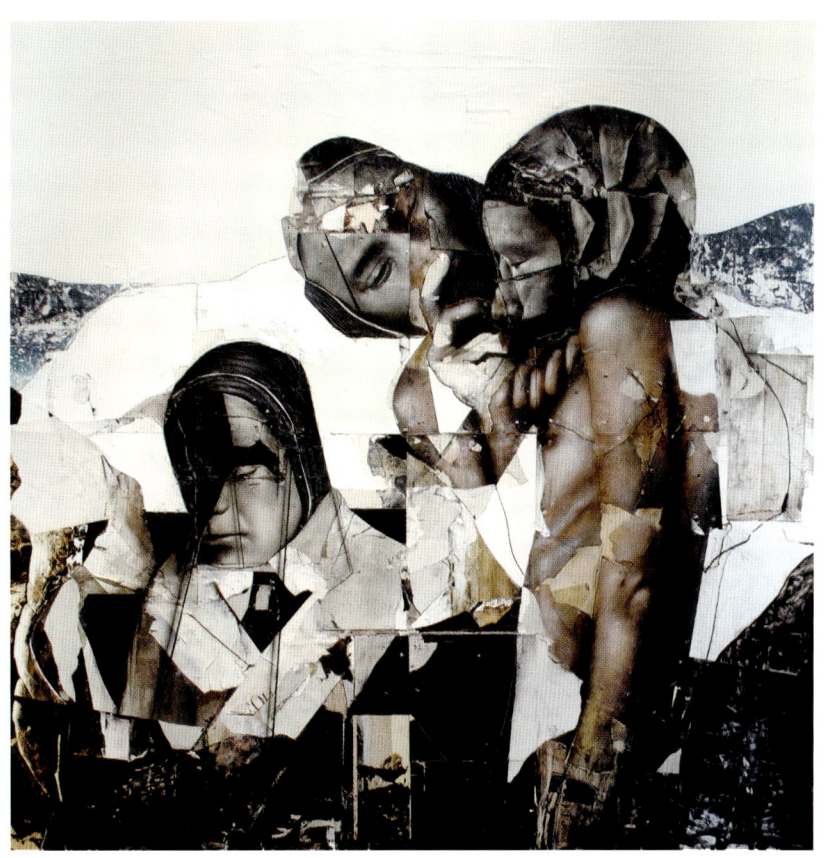

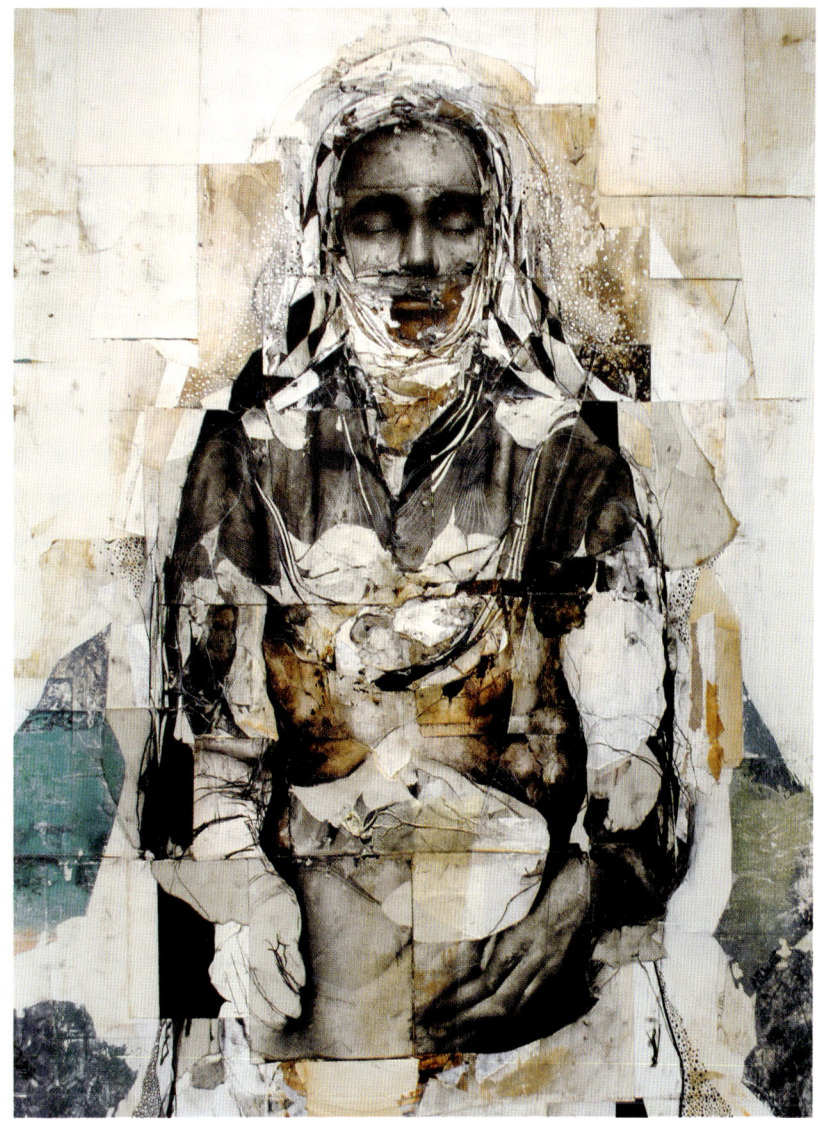

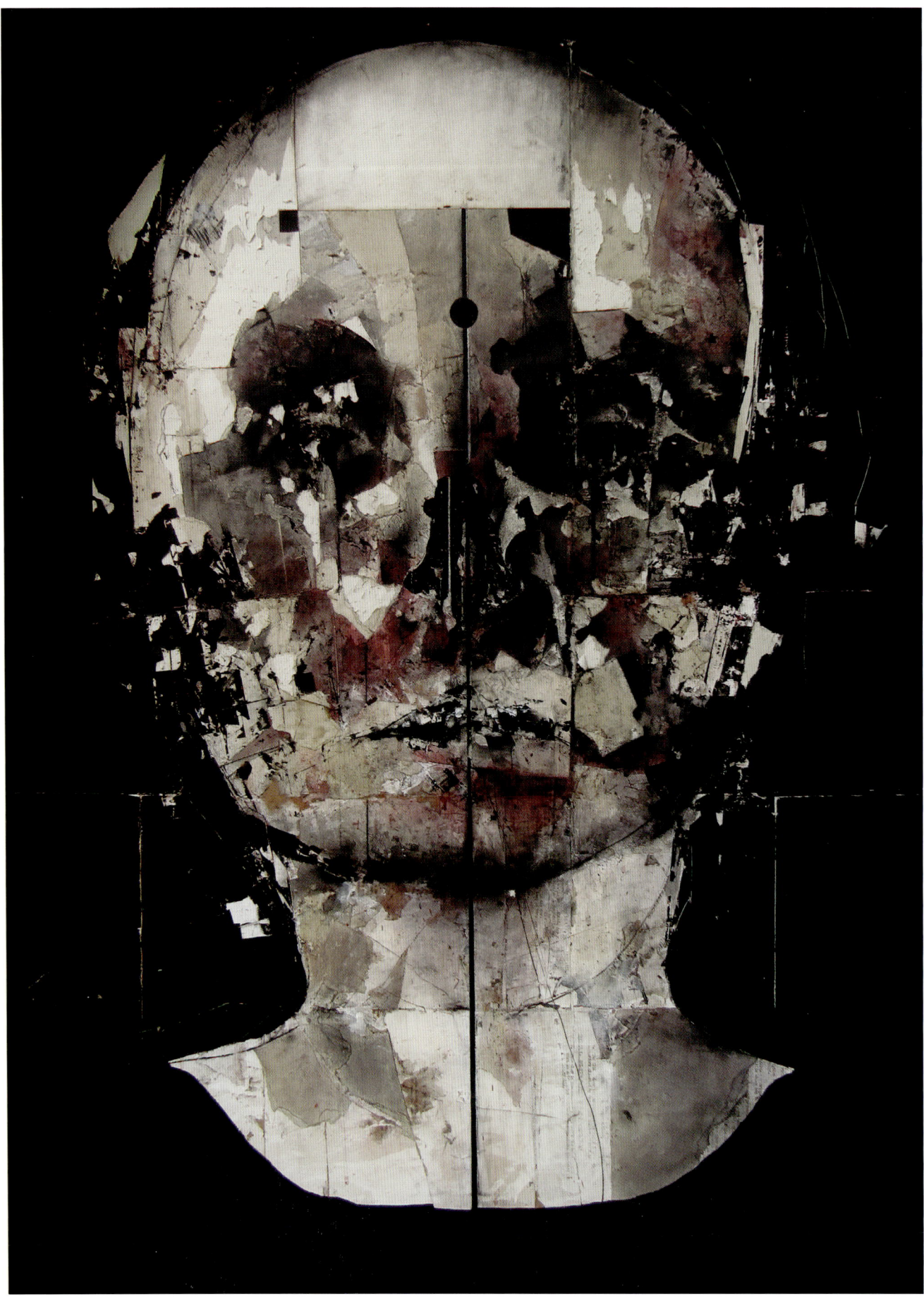

Paul Cristina. *The Body in Morose Endeavors
while Awaiting the Rite of Interment,* 2016.
Charcoal and acrylic on paper on wood panel:
50 × 36 inches.

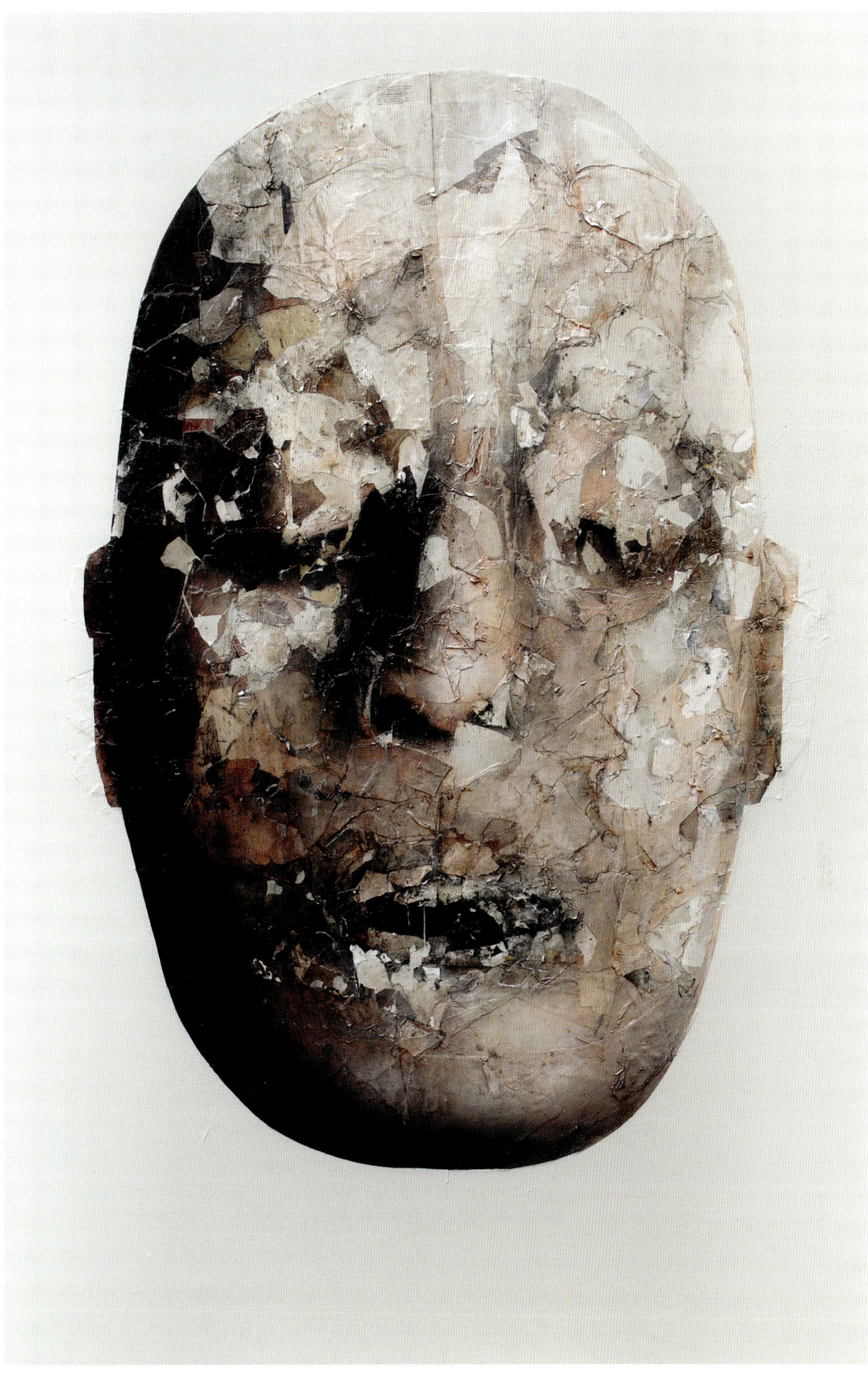

Paul Cristina. *For Ritual Purposes that are to
Carry Us Beyond the Limitations of Flesh*, 2016.
Charcoal, acrylic, collage on paper on canvas:
72 × 48 inches.

ANN GALE

Lives and Works in: Seattle, Washington
Education: BFA, Rhode Island College; MFA,
Yale University School of Art
Collections: National Academy of Art, New York;
Tucson Museum of Art; Portland Art Museum
Representation: Dolby Chadwick Gallery, San Francisco

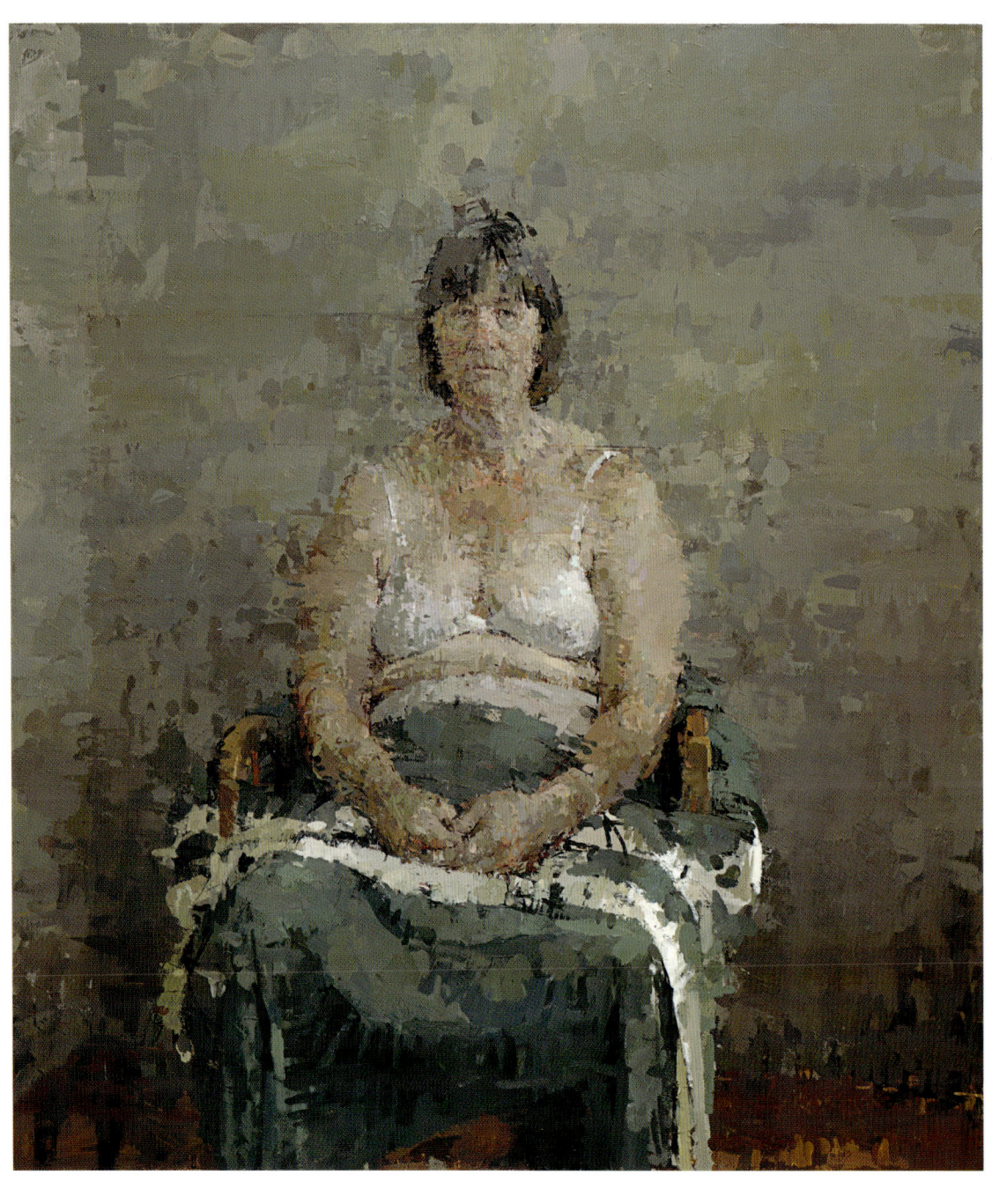

My portraits—made of accumulated marks—focus on the psychological presence of the figure.

How and why does your work disrupt or deviate from traditional realism?

Though I'm urgently measuring and trying to be accurate to my observation, this does not develop detail or focus. I'll often observe and track color relationships as they move through the figure and context. Throughout the process of the work, every alteration of color, distance, or proportion changes my point of view, remeasures our proximity, and indicates a slightly different relationship. While there is a precision to the measuring, tracking the changing light and gesture often breaks the image of the figure. The image exists as an intricate composite of observations, revealing the fragile and momentary nature of perception.

How has your work evolved and developed over time?

Though I have continued to be very interested in the figure and perception, I'm looking for the expression more in the changing context of light and form, over time.

What are some of the influences that have shaped your work?

Traveling and living in places with extreme seasonal changes has helped me experience how differently light feels and behaves.

My teachers were willing to share what they saw and experienced in paintings.

I have seen so many great paintings by Giorgio Morandi, Johannes Vermeer, Vincent van Gogh, Edouard Vuillard, Rembrandt van Rijn, Alberto Giacometti, Lucian Freud, Euan Uglow, Patrick George, William Bailey, Andrew Forge, Howard Hodgkin, Catherine Murphy, Sylvia Plimack Mangold, Alice Neel, Antonio Lopez Garcia . . .

This list could be very long and would be quite different tomorrow.

Mention something interesting about your life or background.

My mother is an artist and my daughter is an artist. We live very far away from each other but sometimes draw and paint together in the summer.

Ann Gale. *Babs with Ribbons*, 2008.
Oil on Masonite: 14 × 11 inches.

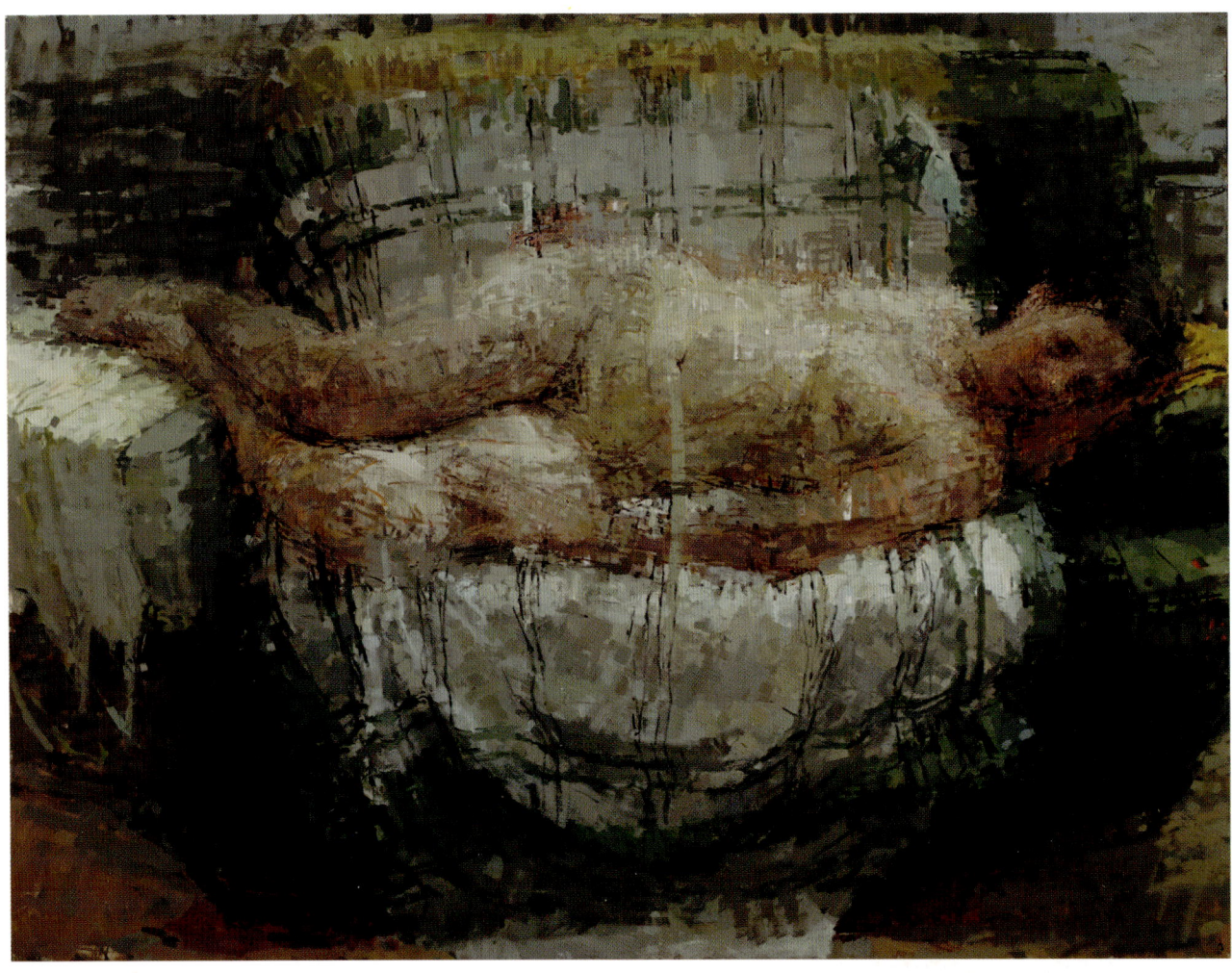

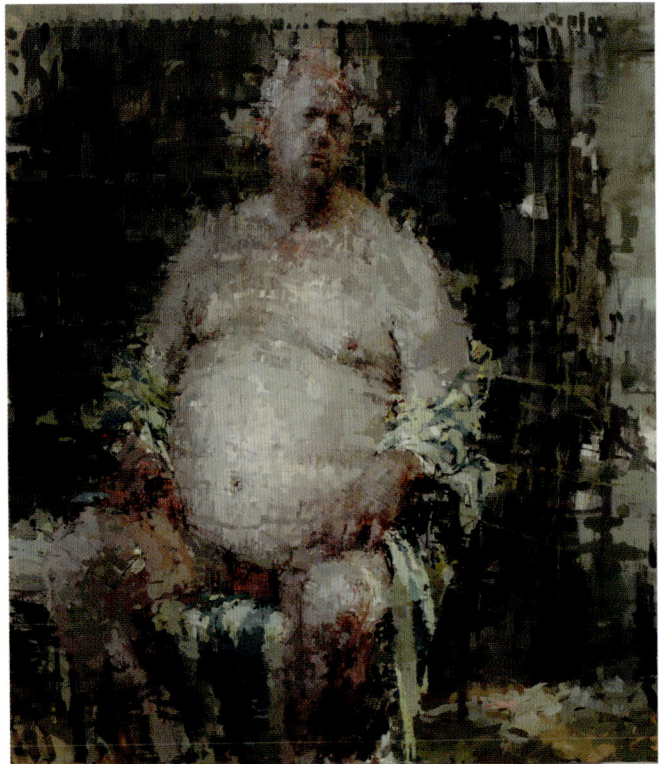

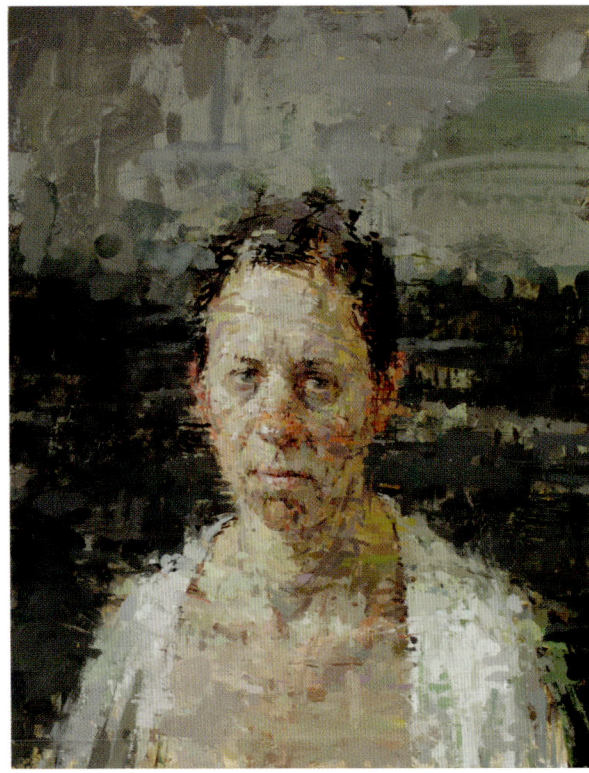

Ann Gale. *Shawna in Lines*, 2016.
Oil on canvas: 58 × 44 inches.

Ann Gale. *Peter with Striped Kimono*, 2014.
Oil on canvas: 50 × 44 inches.

Ann Gale. *Rachel with White Robe*, 2014.
Oil on Masonite: 14 × 11 inches.

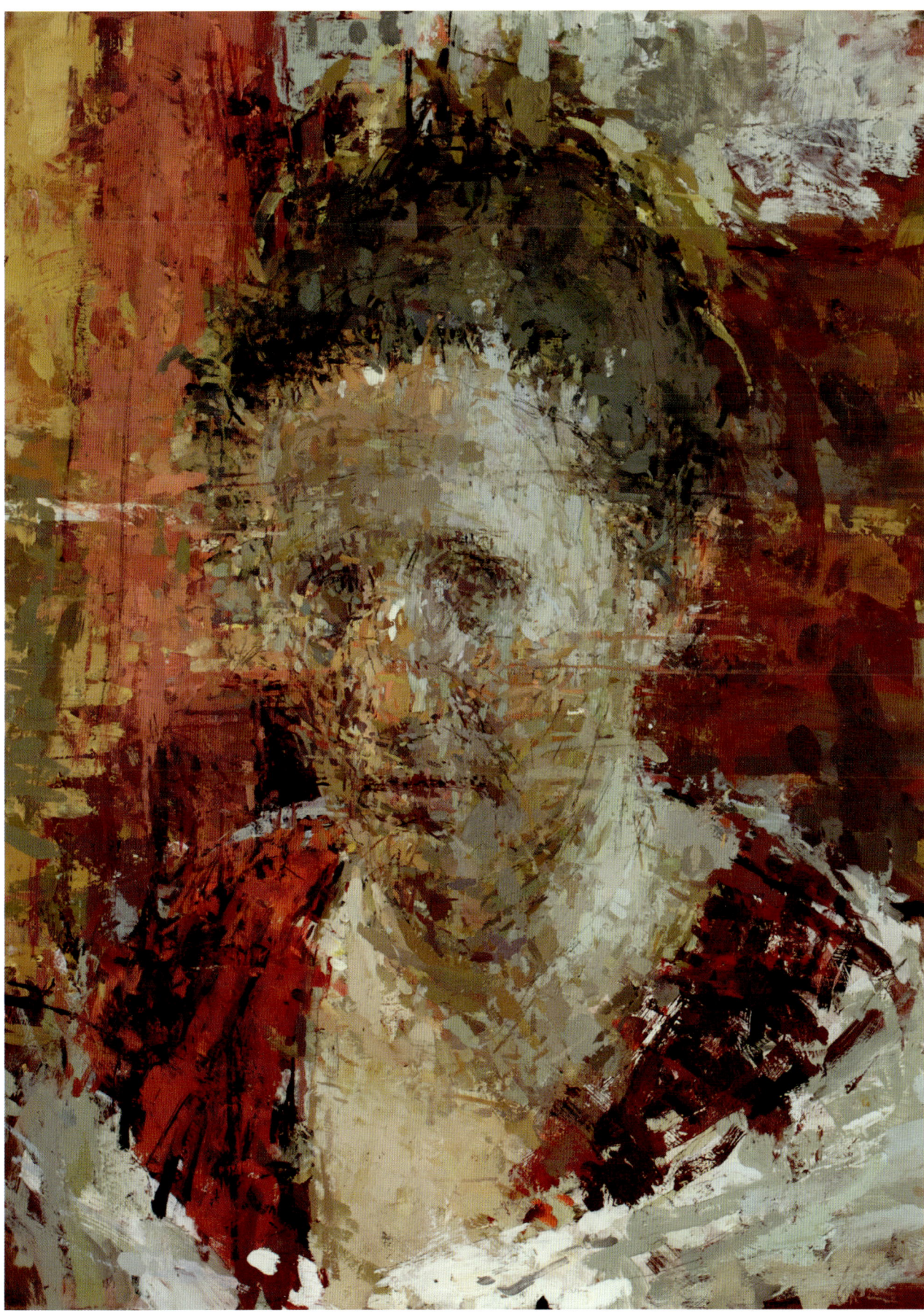

Ann Gale. *Shannon in Red,* 2015.
Oil on copper: 12 × 9 inches.

KIRSTINE
REINER HANSEN

Lives and Works in: Berlin

Education: BA in graphic design & illustration,
the Kolding School of Design, Denmark

Selected Collections: CEO of Uber Technologies Inc., owner of
the Peninsula Hotels, authors Claire Tomalin and Michael Frayn

Representation: Jack Fischer Gallery, San Francisco

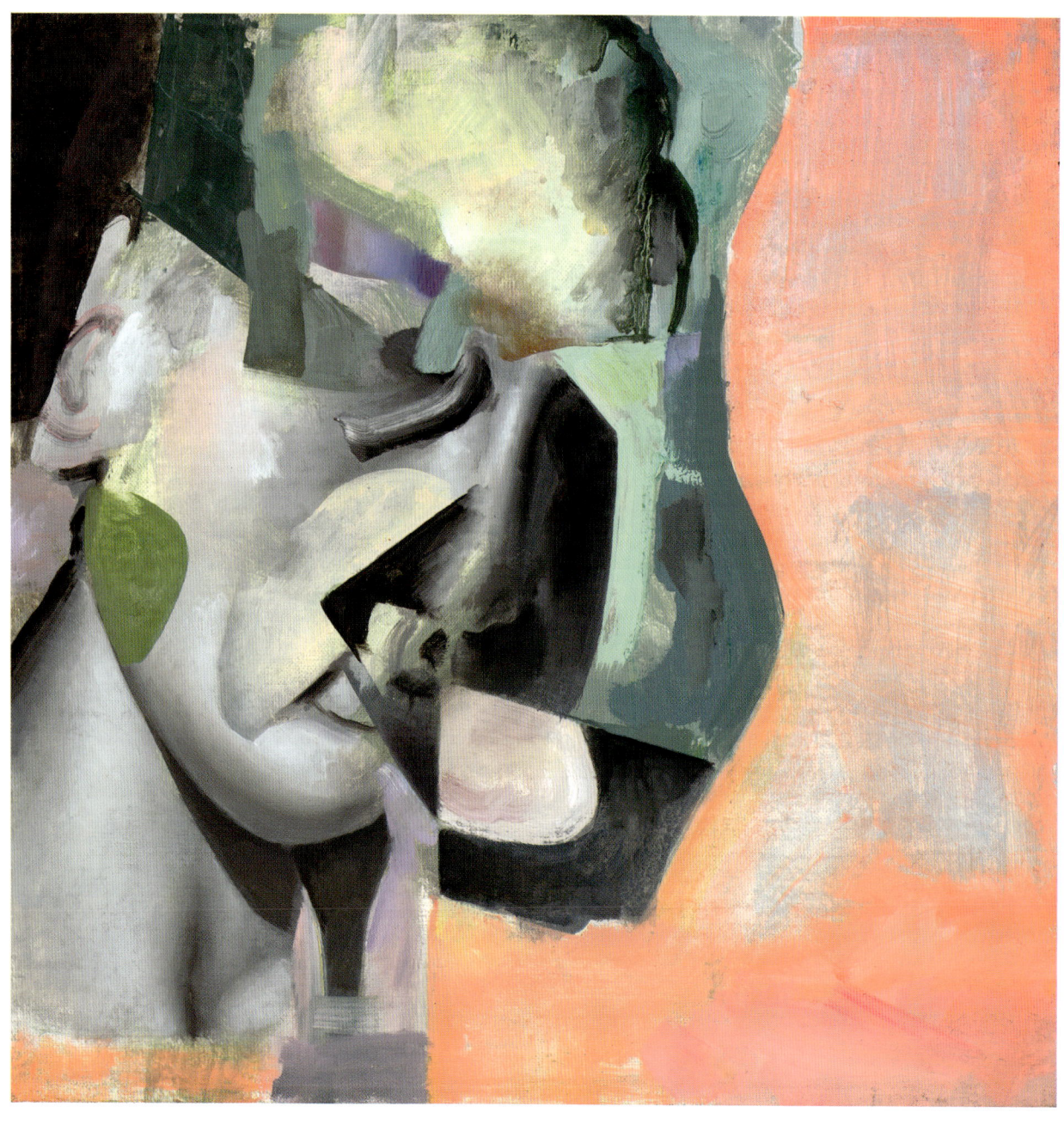

*I paint distorted but glamorous beings
struggling to exist in impossible spaces.*

How and why does your work disrupt or deviate from traditional realism?

I am interested in incorporating painting styles that are polar opposites within the same painting, and in the process of making them work together in beautiful disharmony. I handle the paint in different ways; for example, thick and expressive, clumsy accidental strokes paired with more sensitive paint handling, glazes, and realistic depictions. I approach the painting process as a sort of intuitive puzzle, where one clue leads to the next, rather than having it all laid out beforehand. Experimentation with collaged compositions almost always precedes the painting, as I find collage to be the best method of creating the desired disruption of the realistic imagery. They are used solely to look at while painting. This means that part of the painting is still observational, while other parts are experimental.

How has your work evolved and developed over time?

Early on I was drawn to expressive painters like De Kooning and Van Gogh. Being self-taught, my early classical realist work started as a sort of exercise, as I felt I needed to master oil-painting techniques to the fullest before loosening up. After being immersed in every aspect of Renaissance painting for years and with great enthusiasm, the work naturally evolved into something more experimental. The work I do now allows me to sample and appropriate different art forms that I've been preoccupied with in the past: collage, Photoshop techniques, modernism, photo realism, and Renaissance painting methods.

What are some of the influences that have shaped your work?

As a child it was beaten into us that the modernists were the true artists. In my twenties I discovered Renaissance and baroque painters: Rembrandt became a massive influence. For a while I literally used a Rembrandt book as a manual next to the easel. While living in the UK, the School of London artists were very influential, particularly Auerbach and Bacon. San Francisco opened me up to the Bay Area Figurative artists, and while living in New York I got to explore a wealth of conceptual art. I admire contemporary painters like Chantal Joffe, Dana Schutz, Andrew Ghenie, and David Salle.

Mention something interesting about your life or background.

I've worked as a designer, sculptor, ghost painter, and art teacher. I am Danish, but because I've been able to call many different countries "home," with the upheaval that brings, I would consider myself a nomad of sorts, and I think this kind of fragmented life has informed my work.

Kirstine Reiner Hansen. *Percolate*, 2018.
Oil on linen: 12 × 12 inches.

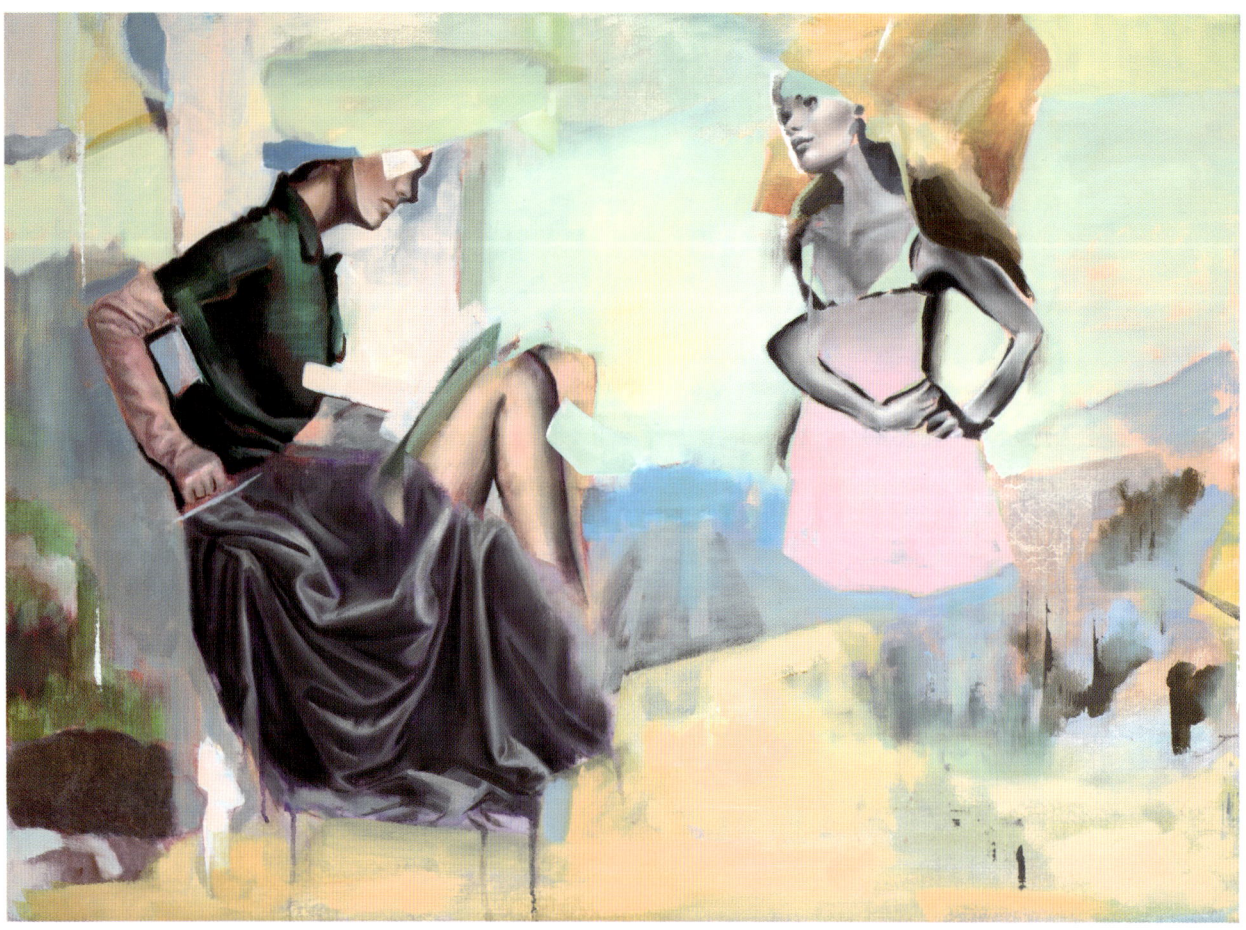

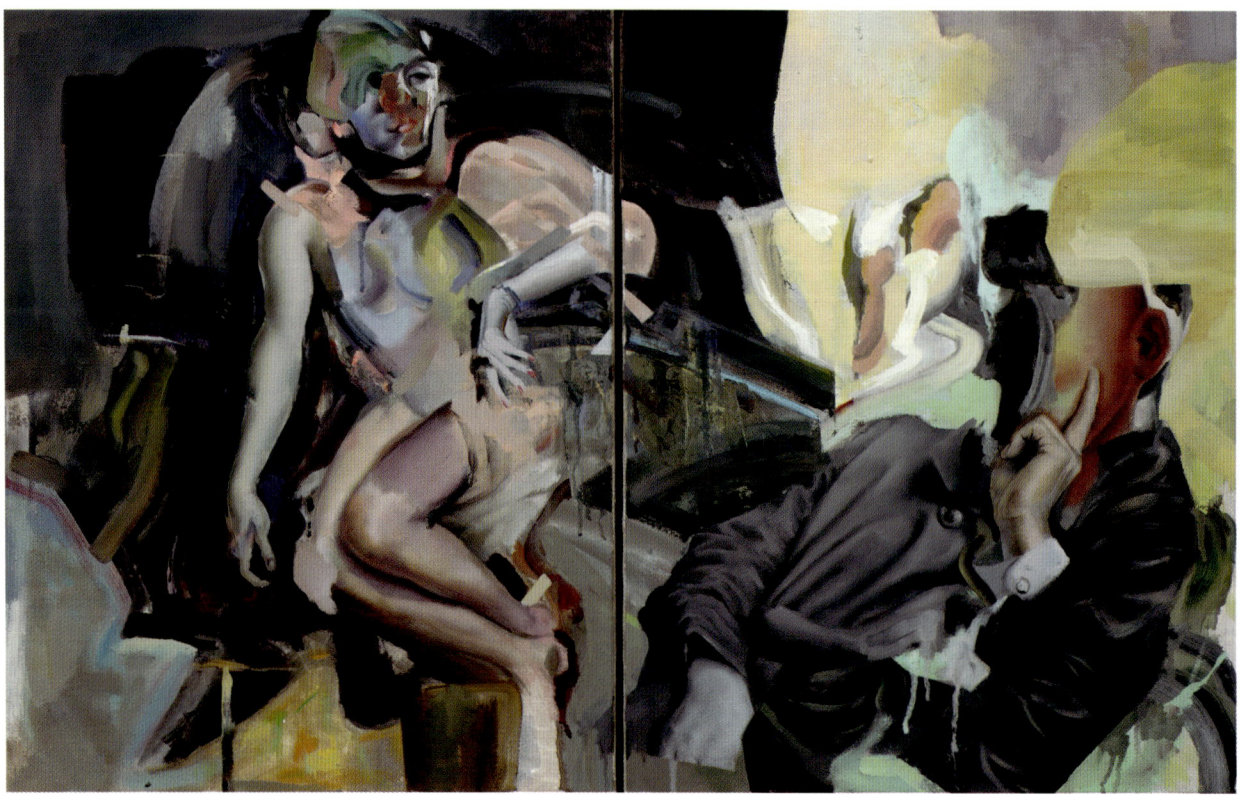

Kirstine Reiner Hansen. *Twinset 6*, 2018.
Oil on linen: 20 × 28 inches.

Kirstine Reiner Hansen. *Ego Sunset* (diptych), 2018.
Oil on linen: 20 × 32 inches.

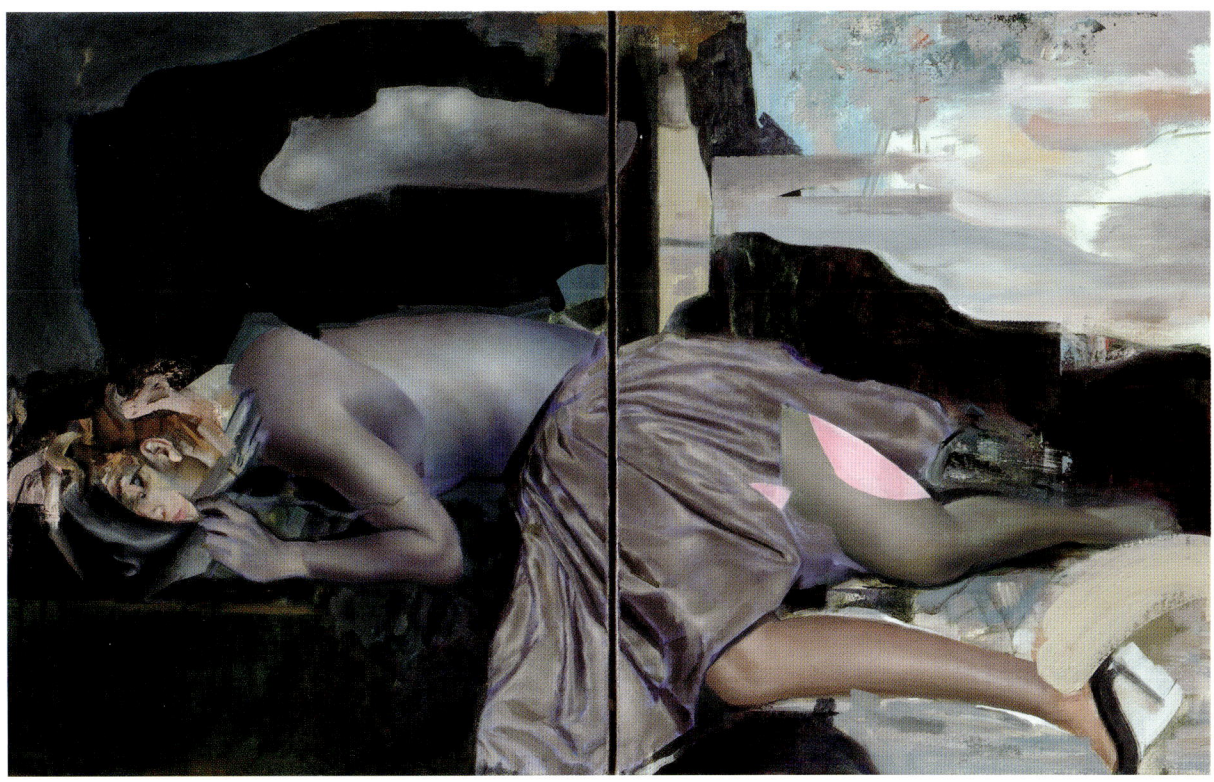

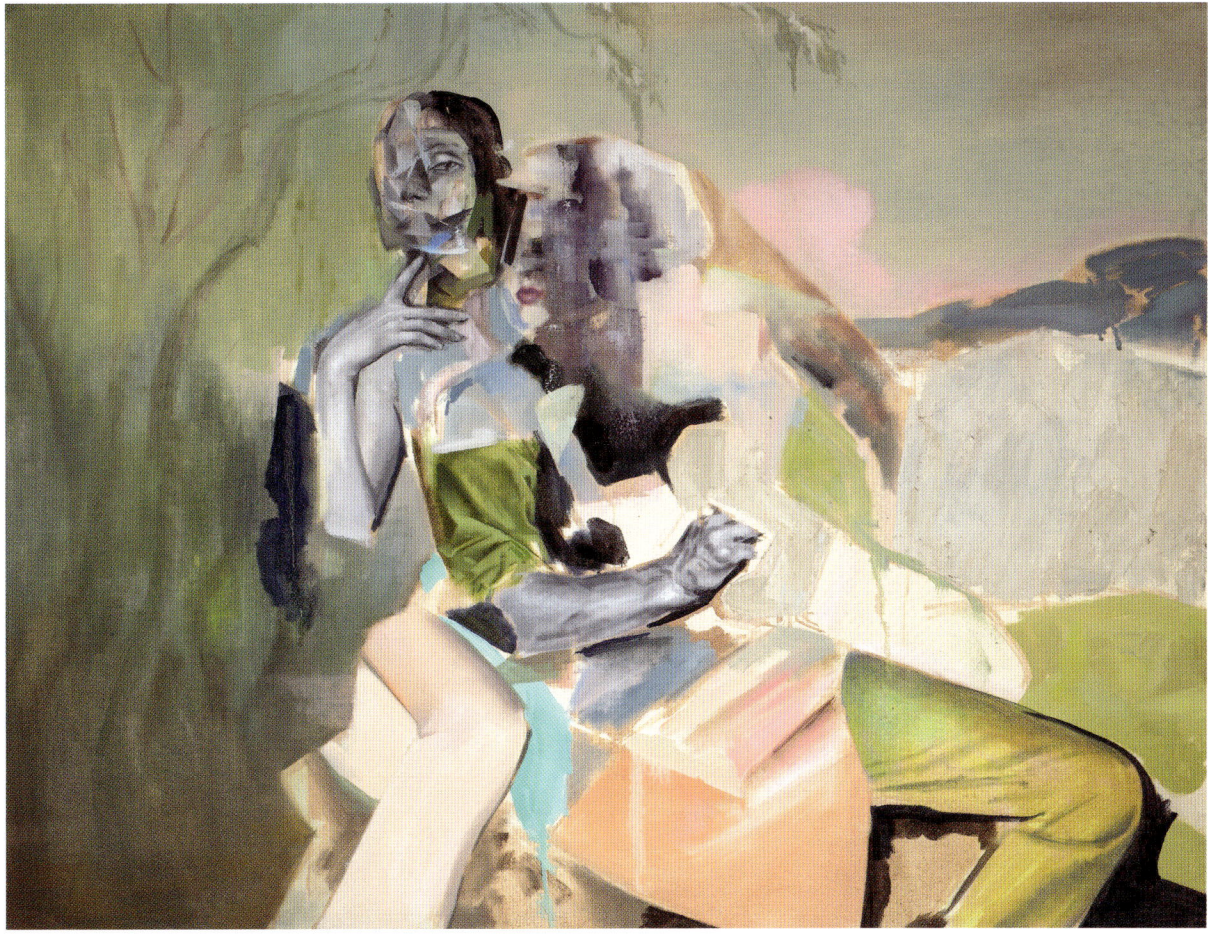

Kirstine Reiner Hansen. *Borderspace* (diptych), 2017.
Oil on linen: 20 × 32 inches.

Kirstine Reiner Hansen. *Twinset 5*, 2018.
Oil on canvas: 30 × 40 inches.

WYATT MILLS

Lives and Works in: Los Angeles
Education: BFA School of Visual Arts, New York
Collections: Private collections in New York,
Los Angeles, and Miami
Representation: Mugello Gallery, Los Angeles

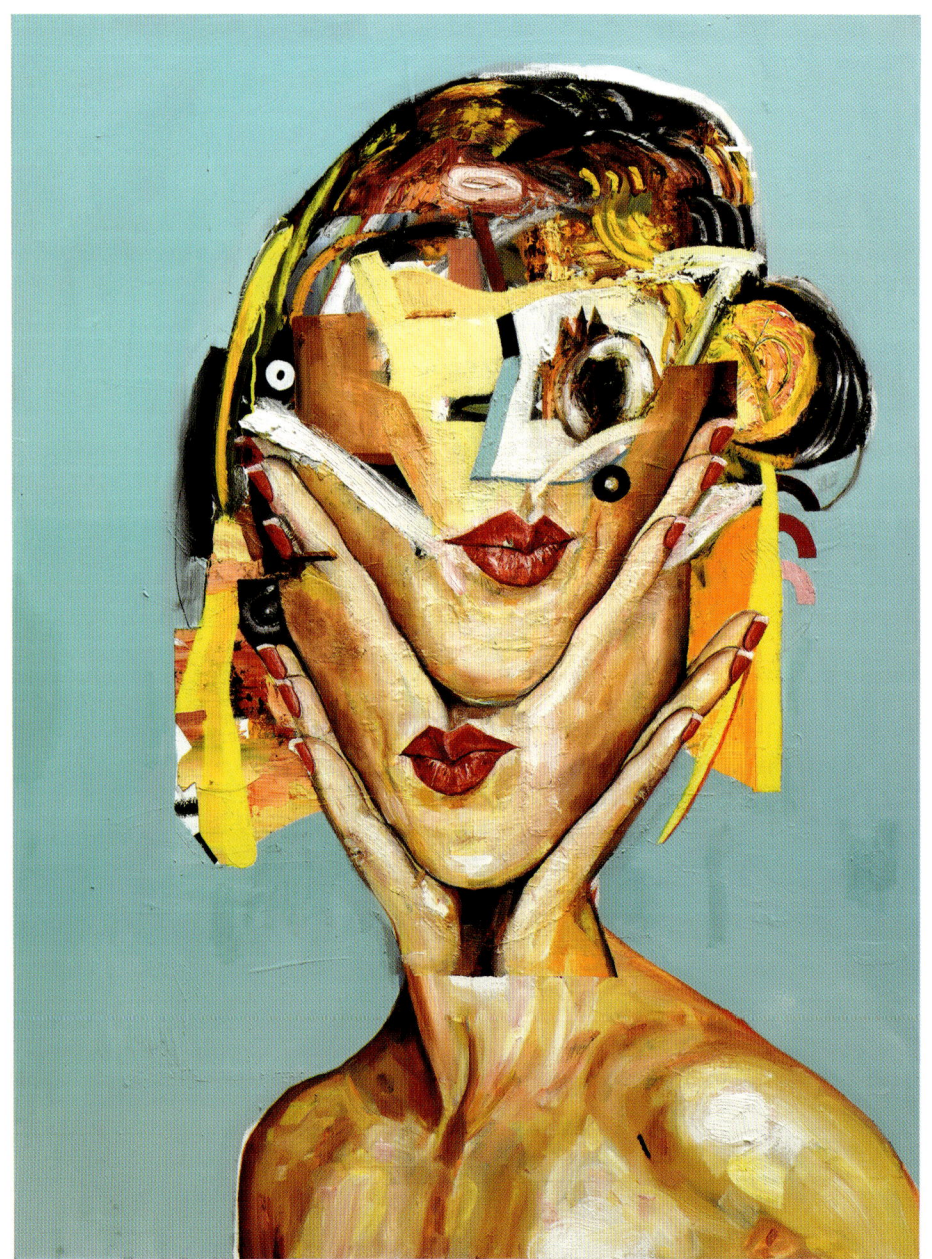

My ruler broke.

How and why does your work disrupt or deviate from traditional realism?

I joined a painting class starting at age ten because I liked a girl who was in it; that led to years of learning traditional techniques.

Then, when I was around twenty, I was working on a really bad painting. It was really stiff and nothing about it was working, but I had spent so much time on it. I finally got so frustrated one night that I turned off the lights, tossed it on the ground, and started frisbeeing paint at it, poured random oil mediums over it, stabbed it with a palette knife a few times, and went to a bar.

The next day when I came back, there was this really interesting thing on the ground; it even had these skin-like wrinkle textures everywhere from the AC blowing on the drying liquids. Ever since then I've tried to add an element of surprise to my process, whether it's using new materials, substituting brushes with fingernails / random objects, or incorporating other mediums like silk screening, or cutting apart two paintings and joining them. I enjoy inviting spontaneity into the situation and finding opportunity in the wreckage of an image. It's much more playful and rewarding to me than a fully linear process.

How has your work evolved and developed over time?

I have spent so much time experimenting with different techniques, trying new mediums mixed with paint, and inviting an abundance of randomness into my process. After years of doing this, the bar for random gets set higher and higher, and all of the previously random things become little tools and tricks in your visual vocabulary. To avoid telling the same story over and over, I force myself to take more risks, some calculated and some blind—but it's always to learn and reinvent. I'm still in the same stormy sea, but I keep finding more driftwood and upgrading my boat.

What are some of the influences that have shaped your work?

When I was eighteen my visual diet pretty much consisted of *MAD Magazine*, *Twilight Zone*, and campy horror films. I loved artists like Ralph Steadman for his wild use of lines, and Lucien Freud's texture and ephemeral application of paint. I then slowly discovered artists like Otto Dix, Max Ernst, and George Grosz—which led to my obsession with German expressionism and films like *Dr. Caligari*.

Now I get ideas from anywhere: daily interactions, a picture of a beatdown laundromat in my neighborhood, or a strange place in the internet. I like people watching. I also have reference banks of endless photos I've taken of places and friends that can be inspiring to revisit. I'm always blown away by heavy-hitting painters like Philip Guston, Francis Bacon, and Willem De Kooning, but I also really admire painters with a softer touch like Marlene Dumas.

Mention something interesting about your life and background.

I recently lived and worked in Berlin for two years. I worked in a studio located in an old Stasi prison in Lichtenberg during this time.

Wyatt Mills. *Flirt*, 2018.
Oil on canvas: 36 × 48 inches.

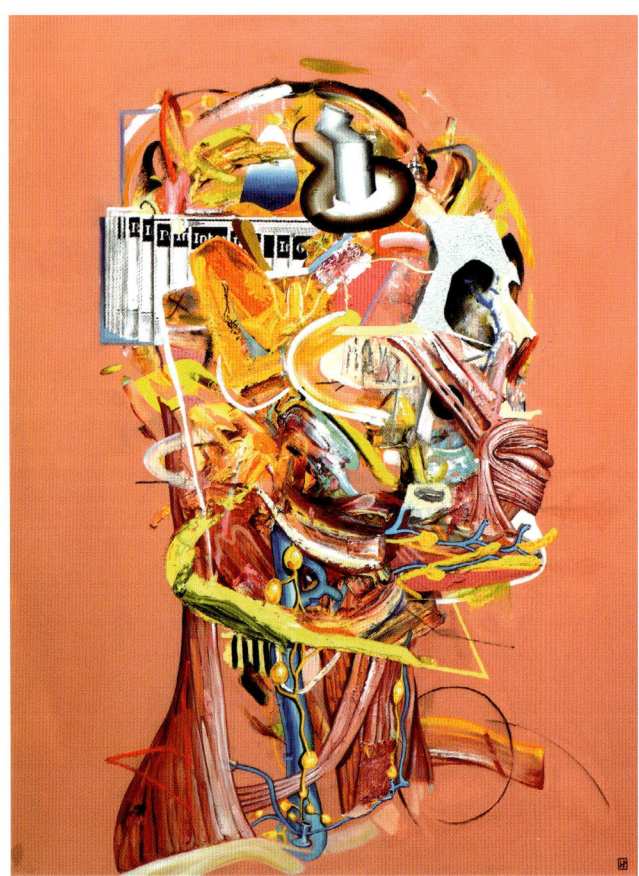

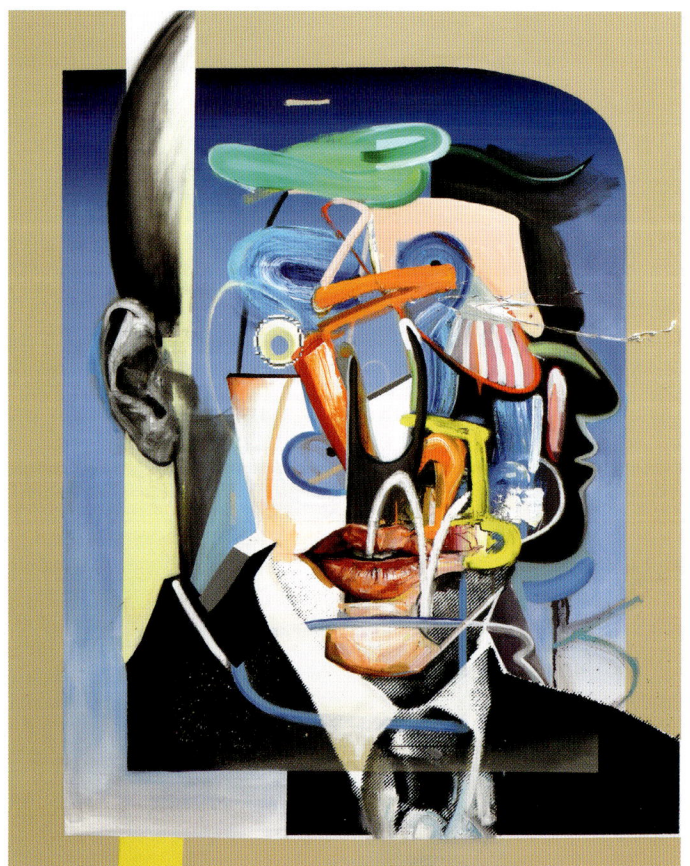

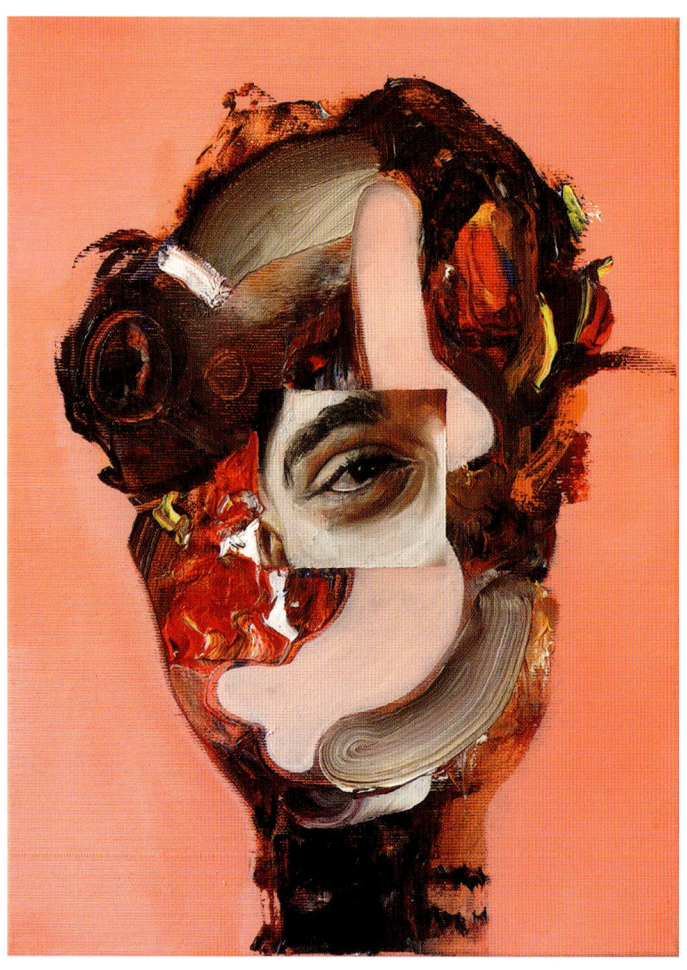

Wyatt Mills. *Internal Dialogue,* 2018.
Oil on canvas: 74 × 54 inches.

Wyatt Mills. *Nobody,* 2018.
Oil silkscreen and mixed media on canvas:
48 × 60 inches.

Wyatt Mills. *Vivian,* 2018.
Oil silkscreen and mixed media on canvas:
36 × 48 inches.

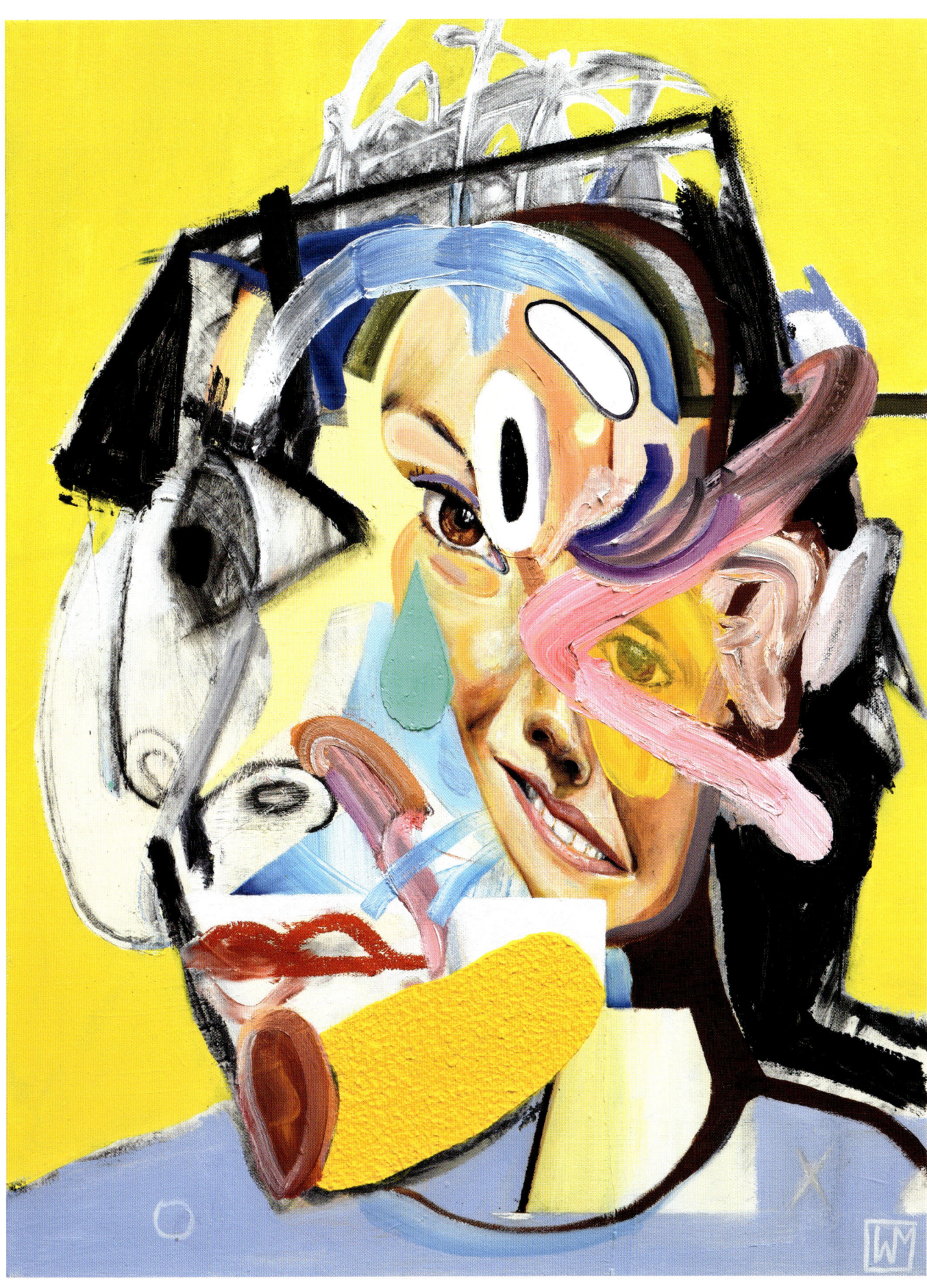

Wyatt Mills. *Untitled*, 2018.
Oil on canvas: 18 × 24 inches.

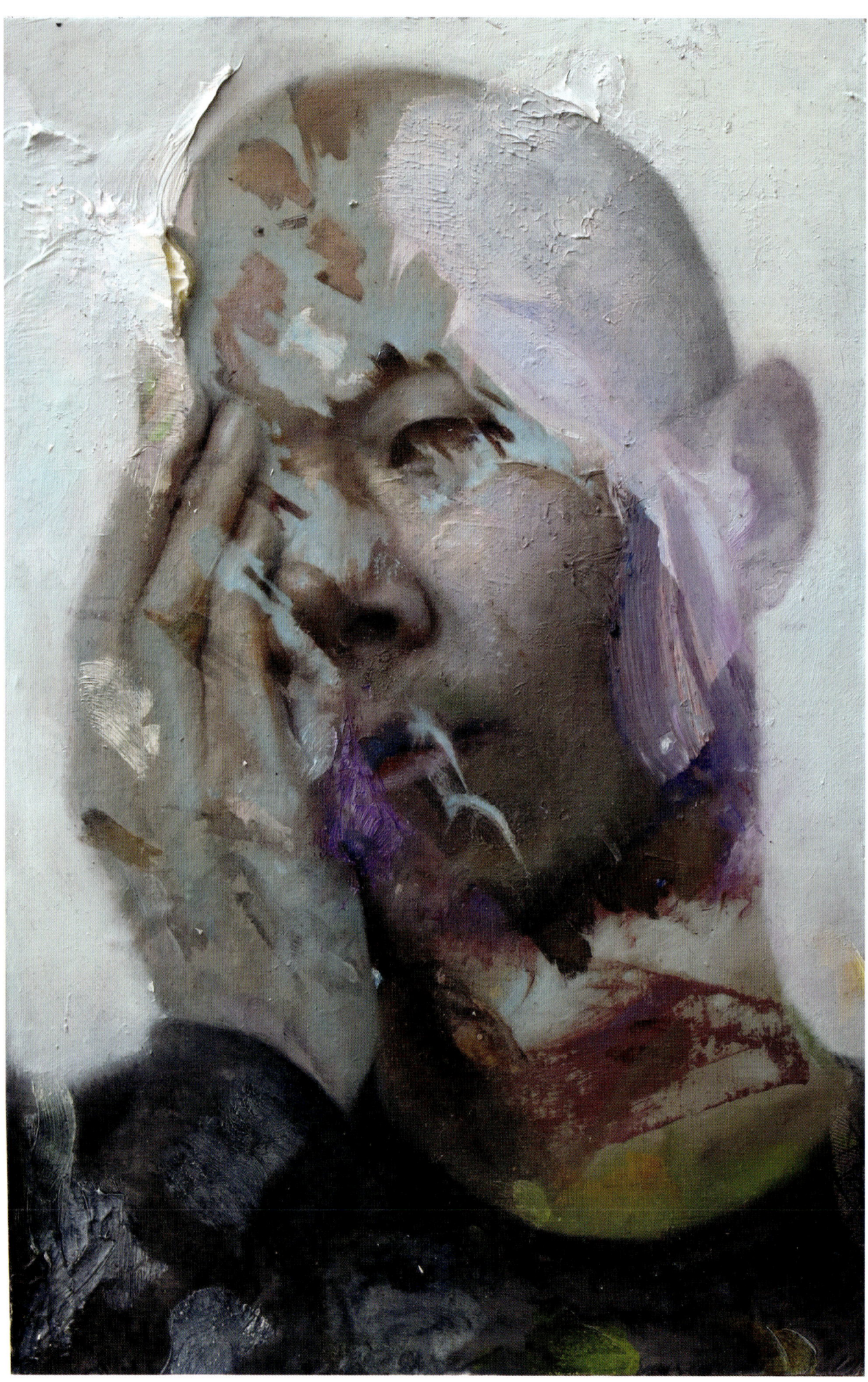

Emotions and Identities

*As a material narrative forms in each work,
the developing image generates questions
about human identity. I become conscious that
I am creating a portrait of a person shaped by
their culture, time, family, and country; a
likeness painted in detail and specificity.*

—Daniel Bilodeau

Constructing an artistic identity—a parallel process to "finding oneself" amid the flux of modern values—is an ongoing task. The process of painting inevitably opens up personal situations and emotions and in turn offers them to viewers as a gift that invites understanding. Painting images of the self or of others and going beyond mere appearances—disrupting the obvious—opens up the possibility of imagery that deals with psychological and emotional narratives. From them can come profound empathy and a sense of connection between the artist and viewer.

Daniel Bilodeau. *Solace*, 2018.
Oil on paper on board: 8.75 × 5.75 inches.

DANIEL BILODEAU

SANTIAGO GALEAS

ANNE HARRIS

JEAN-PAUL MALLOZZI

MEREDITH MARSONE

JOHN WENTZ

ZACK ZDRALE

DANIEL BILODEAU

Lives and Works in: New York
Education: BFA, Ringling College of Art and Design;
MFA, the New York Academy of Art
Selected Collections: Citadelle Museum, New York Law
School, the University of Virginia
Representation: Thinkspace Gallery, Los Angeles

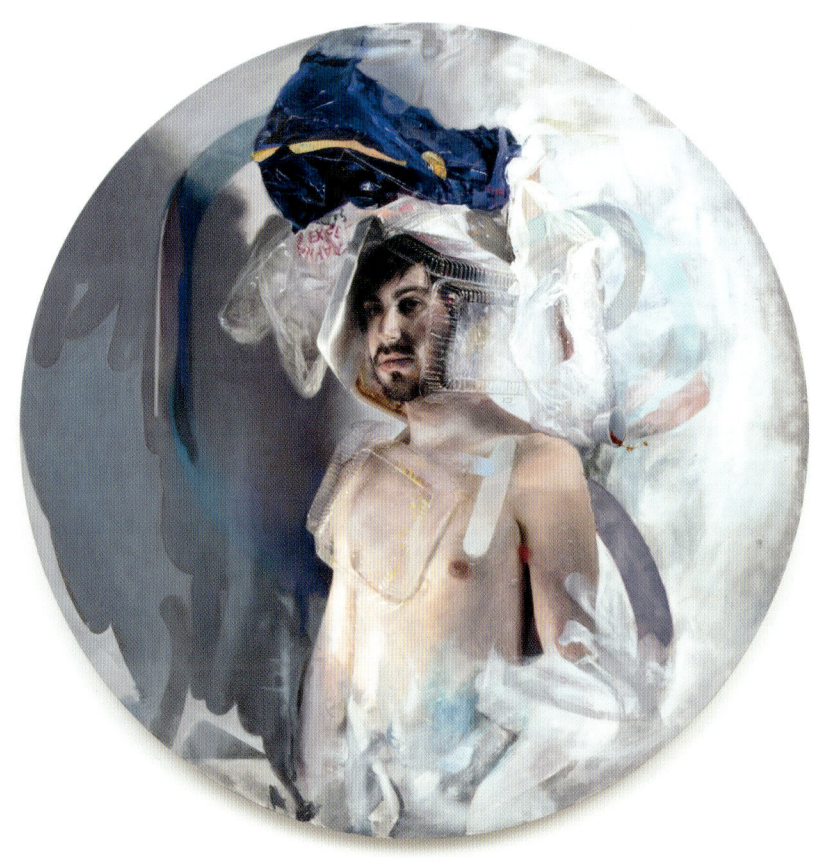

I think of my work as a place where I can allow the polarities of painting to come out and play in unison.

Daniel Bilodeau. *Consumed,* 2016.
Encaustic and oil on circular panel: 44 inches
in diameter.

How and why does your work disrupt or deviate from traditional realism?

First I'd say that a love of the medium and a love for color and design are central to my process. What the works are "about" is based in the pure satisfaction I derive from the act of creating art. Realism is just a tool to make the dance of painting subtler by calling on me to observe the visual world closely. Painting is a dance—an interplay between soft and hard, open and closed, muted and saturated, light and dark—and the natural extension of these dichotomies into smooth versus textured, illusory versus abstract, and deliberate versus spontaneous.

As a material narrative forms in each work, the developing image generates questions about human identity. I become conscious that I am creating a portrait of a person shaped by their culture, time, family, and country; a likeness painted in detail and specificity. The closed passages of realism give way to abstraction, suggesting the shifting psychological variations of selfhood. As I progress, gravity, liquidity, and the addition of new forms will change the work. If I can set nature's forces in motion with little interference, the result seems to speak of the ineffable—adding the ultimate attribute of the self.

How has your work evolved and developed over time?

My early works allowed me to experiment with color theory and achieving a reality effect. Today my focus involves combining that education with the abstraction and design I love in a unified whole. It's an exercise in artistic range as I attempt to portray the selfhood of an individual and the way that all of the tributaries that feed into a sense of self can come together and be deeply felt.

I practice meditation—which helps quiet down the chatter in my mind—so that I can feel cleared out and receptive to and perceptive of whatever may be present in my art. After meditation I feel poised as an observer and can feel astonishment; the certain perfection of things just as they are. My works—in form and function—speak to both our educated, rational sides and our direct and childlike sides. This tension between the inner sublime and the absolute world of symbols is what I think of as the joy of painting.

What are some of the influences that have shaped your work?

A pivotal moment in my development came when my fifth-grade teacher took us to the Montreal Museum of Fine Arts to see a Marc Chagall retrospective. As a child I could relate to the freedom with color and the lack of concern for anatomical accuracy. I could see that these works—on display in hallowed halls—were moving and important. After passing through the exhibition, we entered a room full of paper and art supplies and were told, essentially, "Now it's your turn." In that moment I could draw new parallels and felt a sense of empowerment.

The painters of the Dutch golden age have given me ideas about temperature modulation and composition. I admire and have tried to absorb the fresh and life-affirming quality in the works of modernists such as Matisse and Picasso. I have studied the painted passages in contemporary works by Anselm Kiefer, Gerhard Richter, and Adrian Ghenie. I also like Francis Bacon, Cecily Brown, Cy Twombly, and Edgar Degas.

Mention something interesting about your life or background.

Crucial moments in my life and art have included studying at the museums of Italy and France for a summer, living as a monk at a Zen monastery for another summer, and taking part in a blood ceremony with the chief of the Yaqui native tribe. No one was significantly injured.

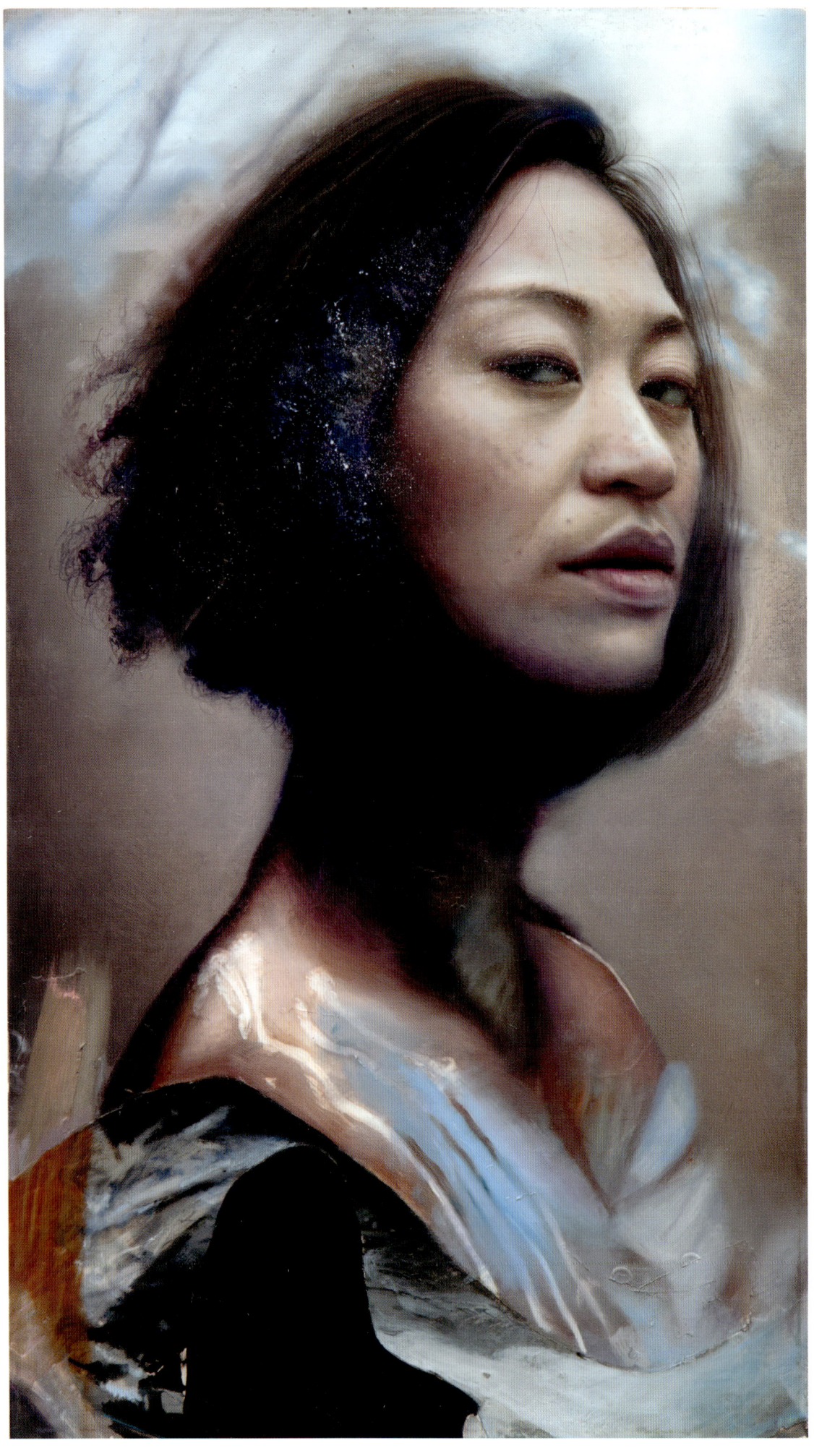

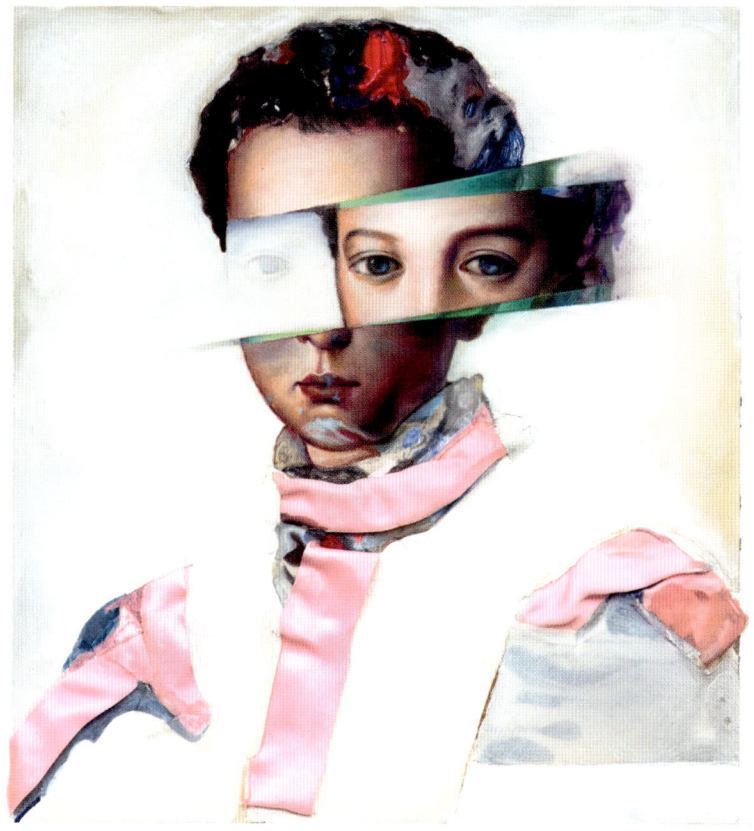

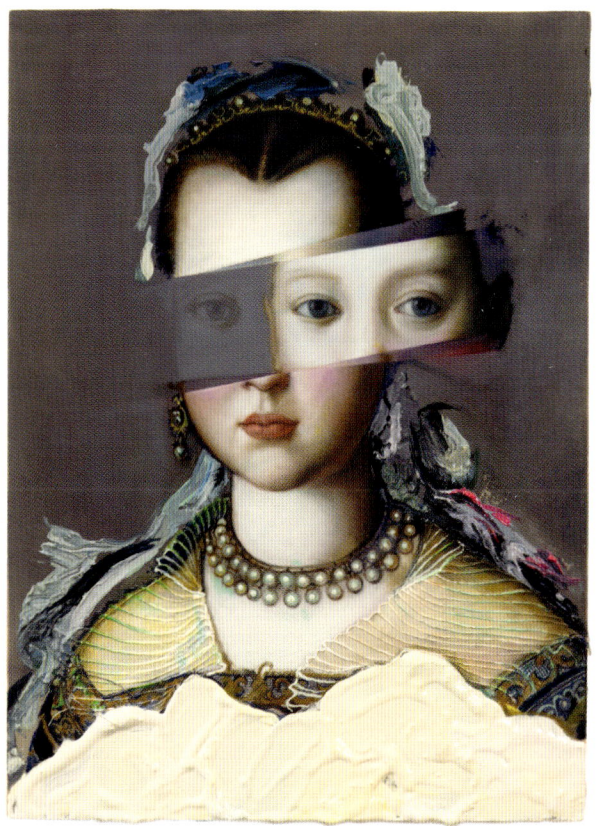

Opposite: Daniel Bilodeau. *Cool Like That*, 2017.
Oil on board: 16 × 9.5 inches.

Daniel Bilodeau. *Portrait of a Boy*, 2016.
Acrylic, oil, and ribbon on board: 12 × 12 inches.

Daniel Bilodeau. *Ritratto di Maria de' Medici
after Bronzino*, 2016.
Oil and string on paper mounted on board:
12 × 9 inches.

SANTIAGO GALEAS

Lives and Works in: Philadelphia

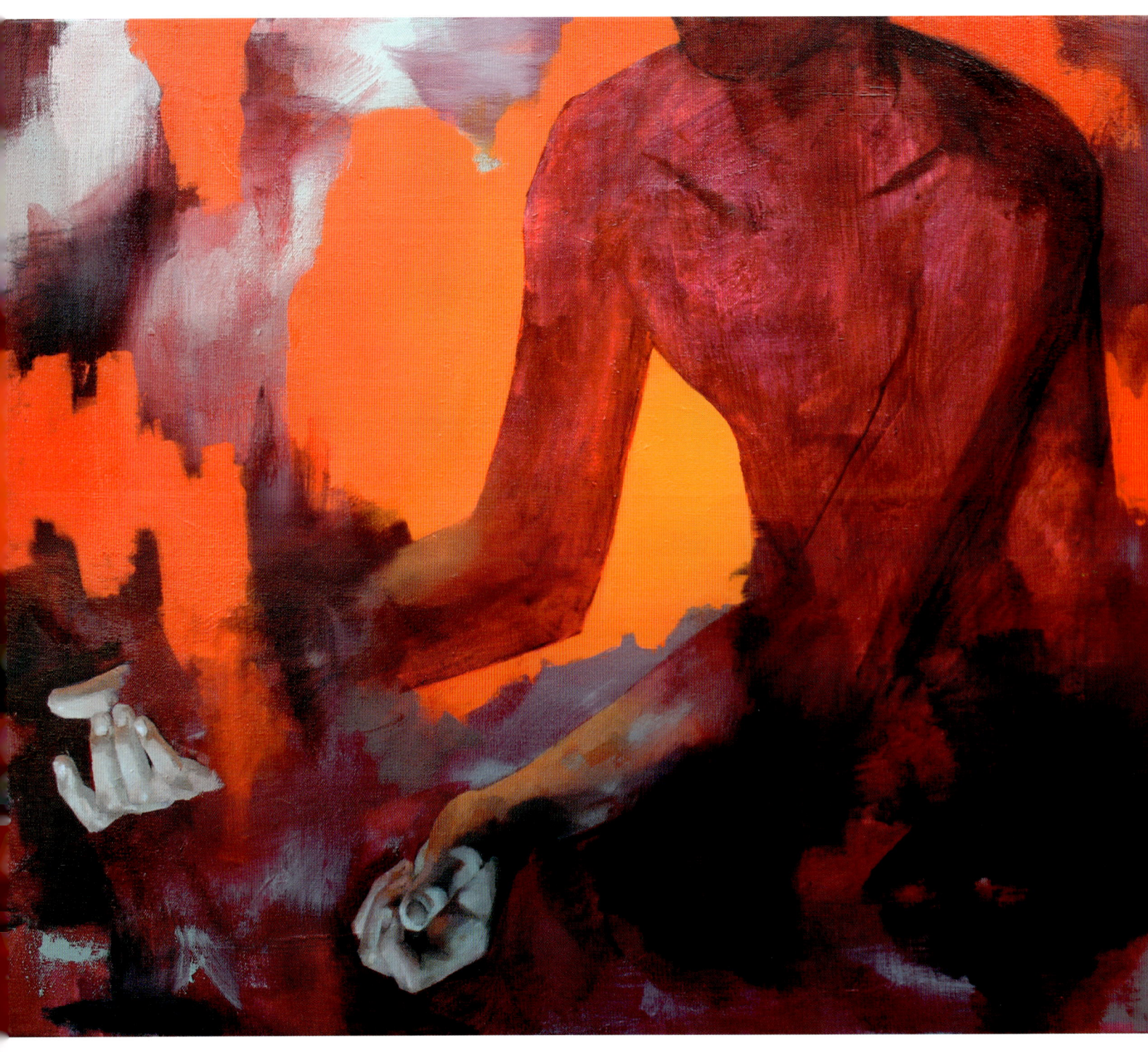

Santiago Galeas. *Supination*, 2016.
Oil on canvas: 24 × 30 inches.

I try to paint my subjects with all of
the strength they encompass.

How and why does your work disrupt or deviate from traditional realism?

I don't think what I do is very different from what most other contemporary figurative painters do: I mix traditional figure painting with nonlocal color and abstract elements. I'm absolutely following in the footsteps of artists that I admire, but I think the subject matter is the driving force for me. I'm coming from a very specific place as a figurative painter. I studied painting because I love working with faces, portraits, people; but on a more conceptual level, I feel a social responsibility to use this medium to capture the images of as many minority groups as possible, specifically from communities that I represent. Traditional realism has deep roots in European ideologies, while abstraction—specifically abstract expressionism—was established in the US. I think painters who enjoy both styles naturally fall into this category.

How has your work evolved and developed over time?

Up until the 2016 US elections I had been making very subtle work. They were about an underlying dialogue between masculine and feminine energy and color association. I always worked exclusively with people of color to help "close the gap," but I think my work was quiet about what it was saying. Now the sociopolitical climate seems more tumultuous than ever. Just as Americans are radicalizing in either direction, I feel myself and my work following suit. Being queer wasn't something I focused on before, but now I feel emboldened to make my work as loud as possible. Through the canon of art history, people of color and queer-identifying people haven't been a huge part of the conversation, specifically in figurative art. It's everything for me to ensure that these populations are represented.

What are some of the influences that have shaped your work?

Aside from the election, I recently went on a residency in Ecuador, TrueQué Residencia Artística. It commemorated the twentieth anniversary of the decriminalization of homosexuality, and it involved a lot more research and writing than I'd anticipated! We met people who survived protest after protest, seeing their loved ones killed by civilians and law enforcement alike. Hearing everything and speaking with them was incredibly emotional. So lately I've been thinking a lot about "queer ancestry": those who paved the path for queer people in the Americas. Trans women in particular were always on the front line and the first to suffer for it. In terms of literature, *Borderlands / La Frontera: The New Mestiza* by Gloria Anzaldúa has been huge in shaping my direction.

Mention something interesting about your life or background.

I'm a child of immigrants, first generation. I consider myself very American. My mother is from South America, my father is from Central America, and I was born in North America. My mother was in school to become a nun before she met my dad in an English class in DC. Naturally, I had a very Catholic upbringing. I catch myself always going back to a little Catholic imagery here and there.

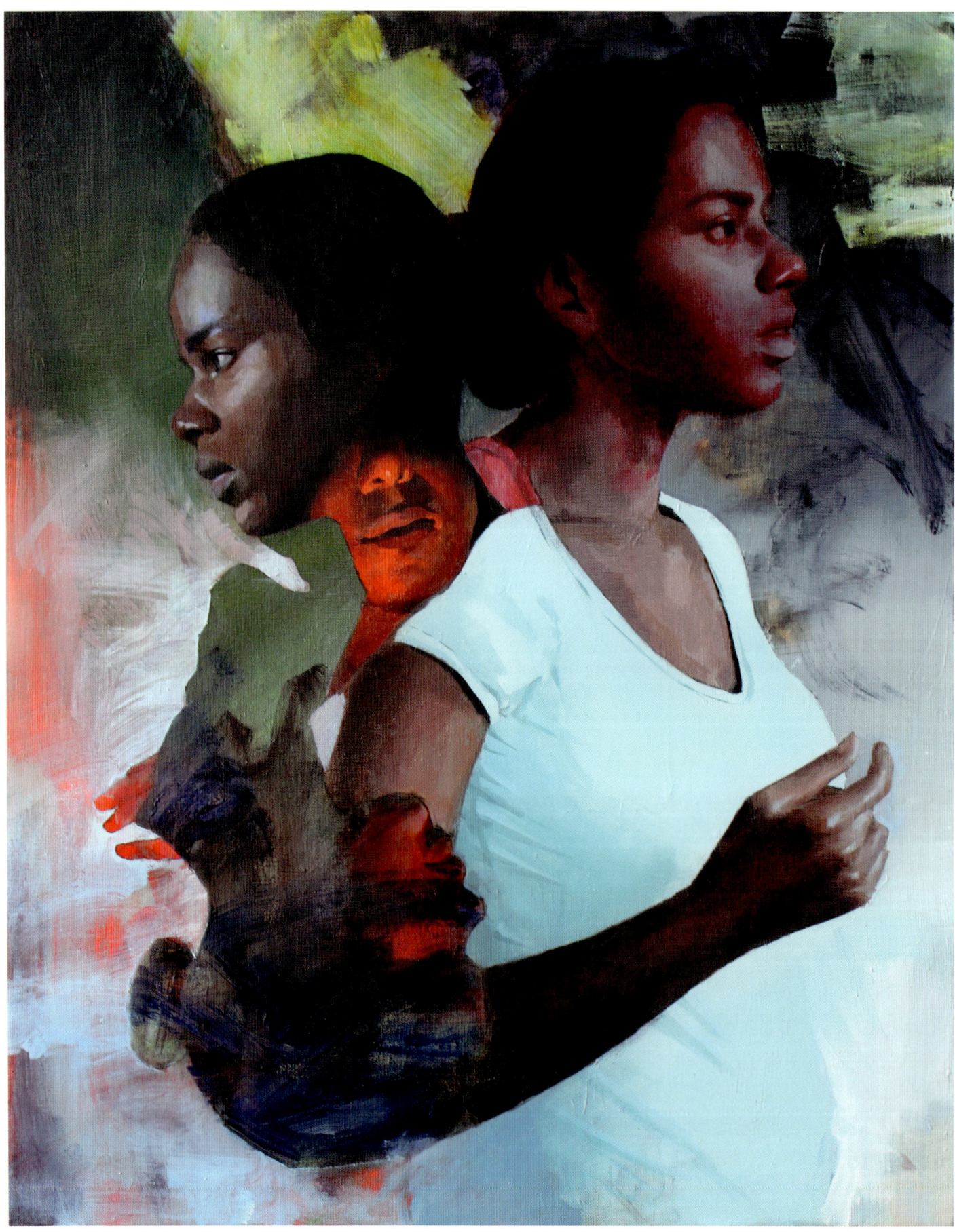

Santiago Galeas. *Unraveler,* 2016.
Oil on canvas: 30 × 24 inches.

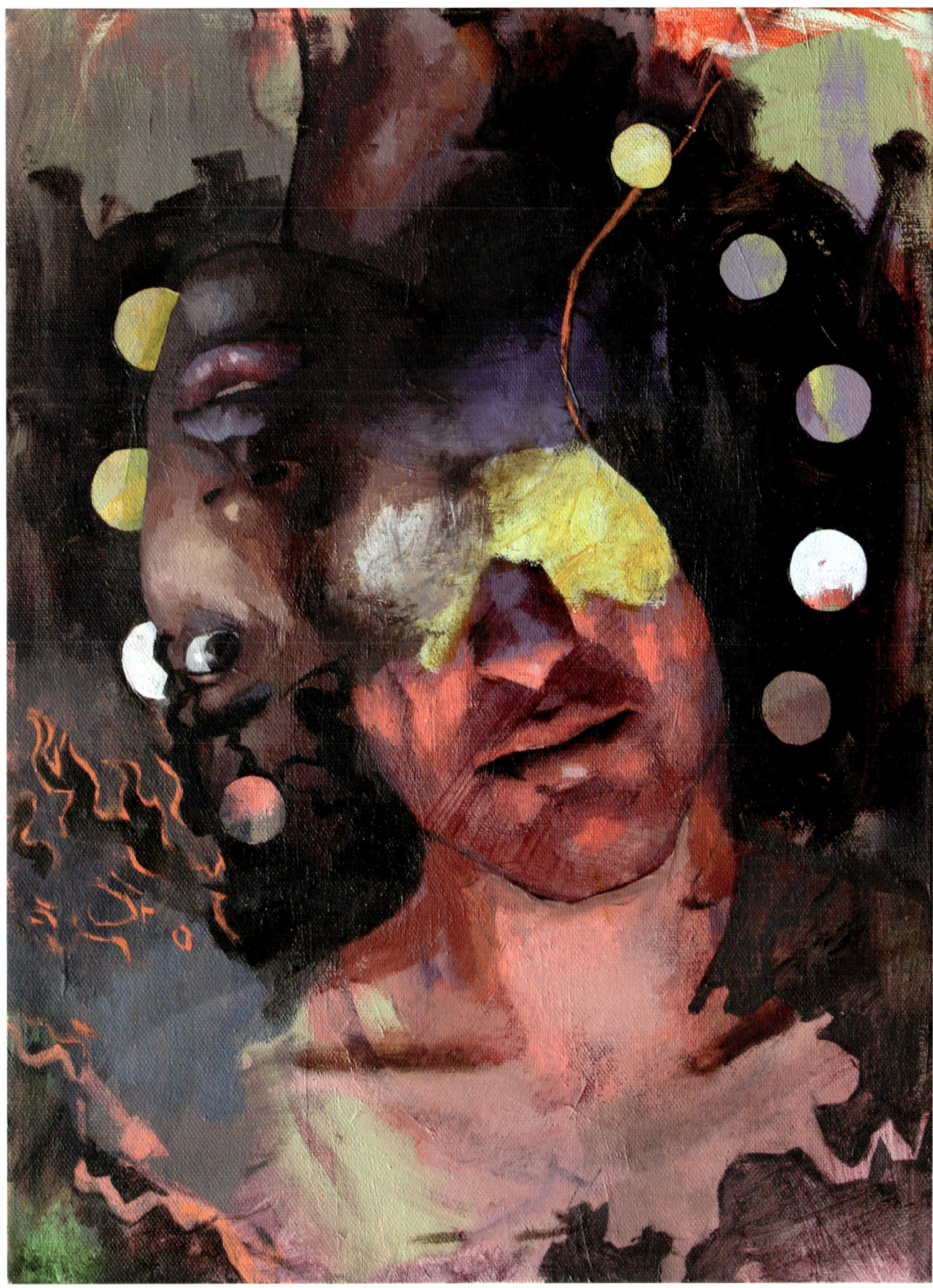

Santiago Galeas. *Vidas Pasadas,* 2017.
Oil on canvas: 16 × 12 inches.

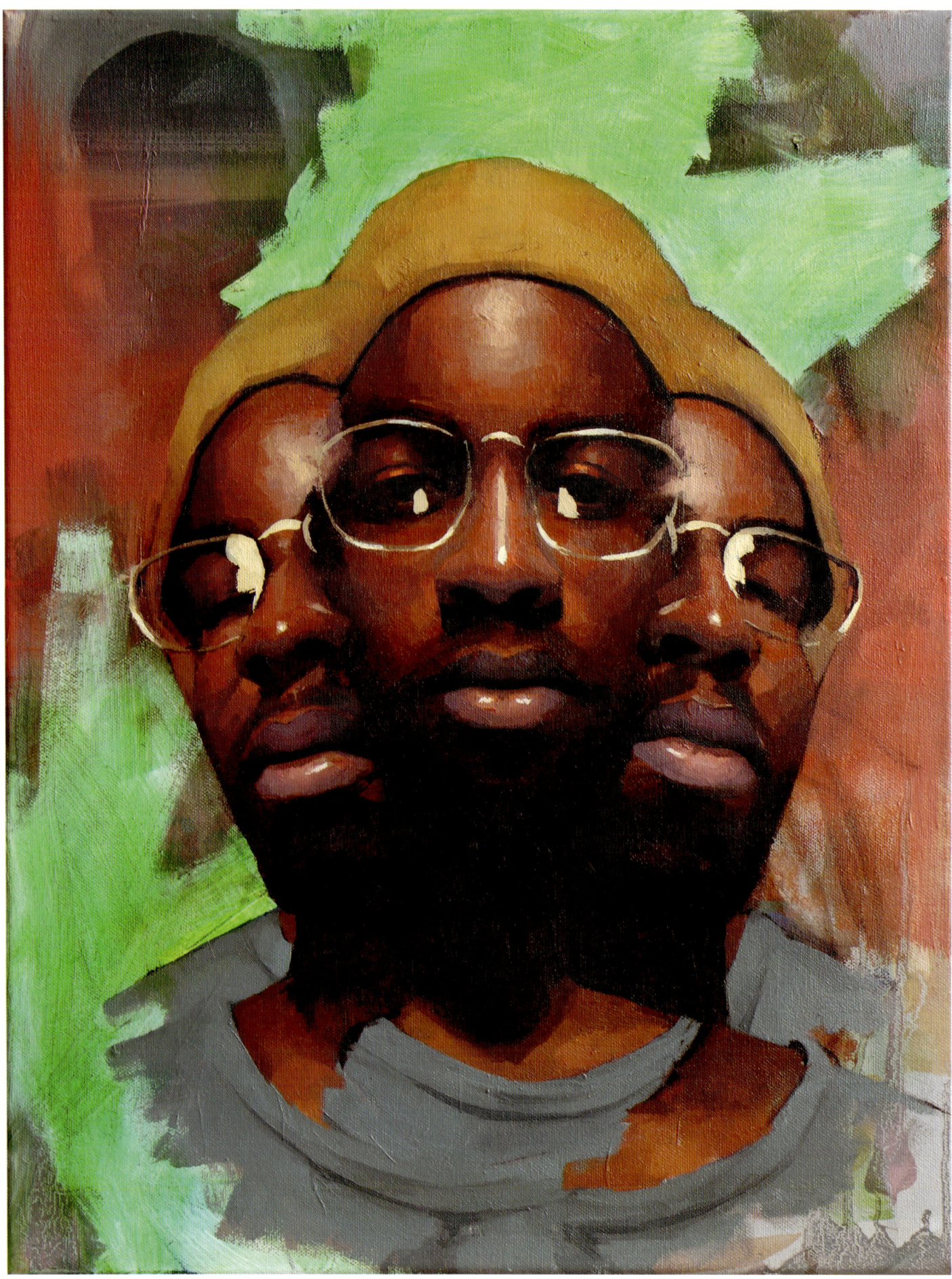

Santiago Galeas. *Victorious*, 2017.
Oil on canvas: 18 × 14 inches.

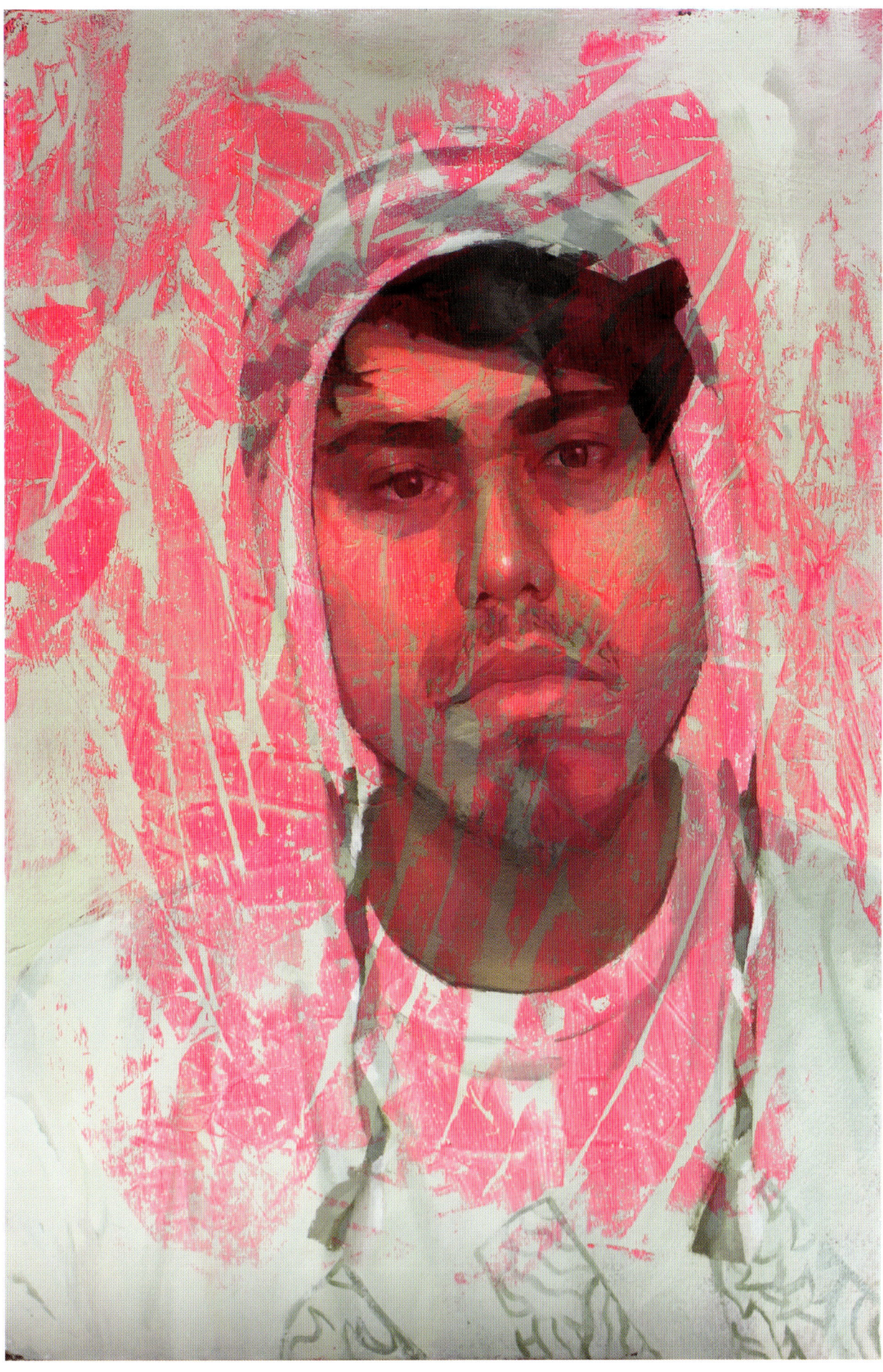

Santiago Galeas. *Self Portrait at 26,* 2018.
Oil on board: 18 × 12 inches.

ANNE HARRIS

Lives and Works in: Riverside, Illinois
Education: BFA, Washington University; MFA, Yale School of Art
Selected Collections: Fogg Museum (Harvard), New York
Public Library, Portland Museum of Art
Representation: Alexandre Gallery, New York

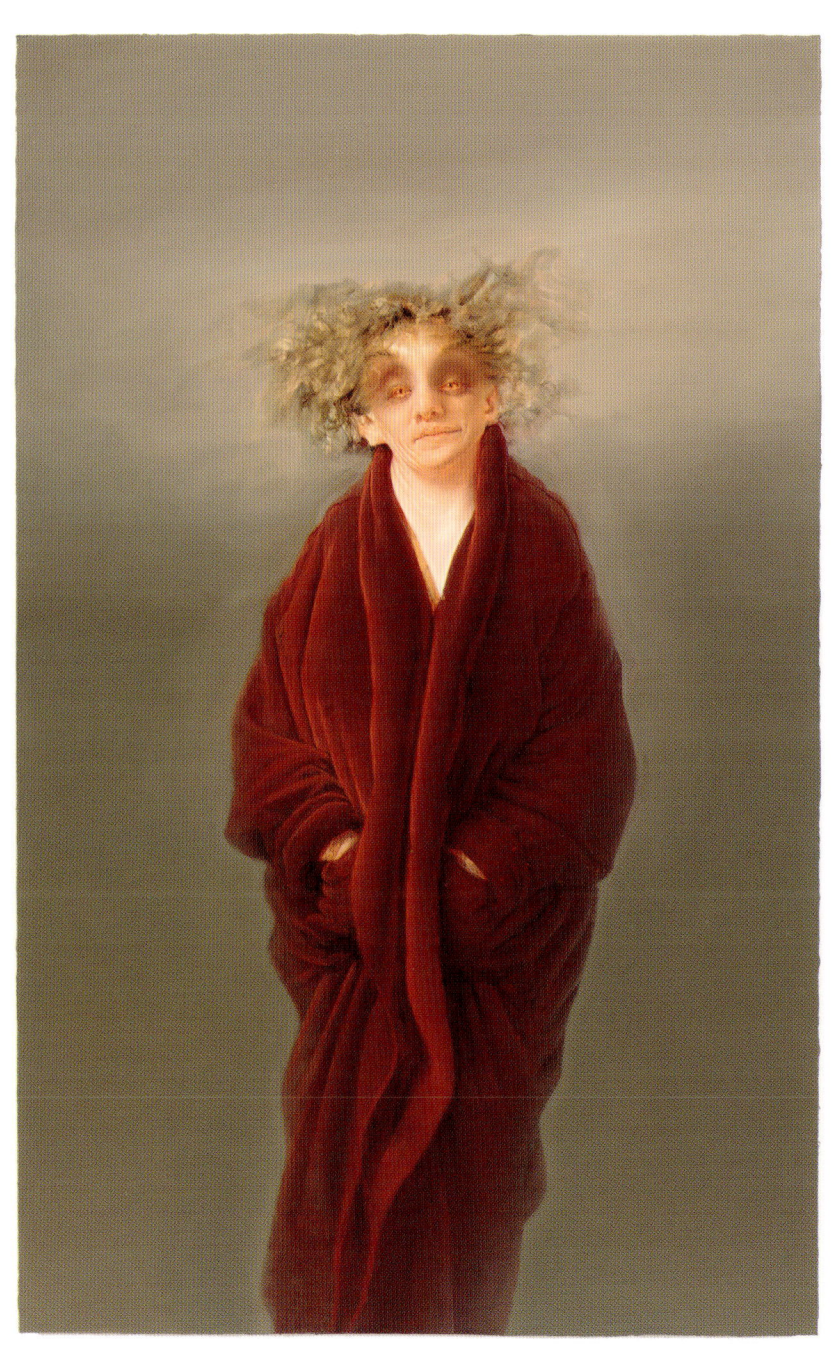

*I've been painting and drawing the same
freaky self-portrait for thirty years.*

How and why does your work disrupt or deviate from traditional realism?

I can't even engage with the term "traditional realism." Painting is fiction. Invention. That's what interests me. I do, however, love illusion.

How has your work evolved and developed over time?

Hopefully, it's gotten subtler.

What are some of the influences that have shaped your work?

I love to read. I read everything from cereal boxes to Tolstoy. I've been looking at Rembrandt since I was five: my mother bought a heavy coffee-table book that I pored over. I'm mesmerized by beautiful faces, the kind that are so unique they become strange. I look at a broad range of art. Again, I'm looking to be mesmerized.

Mention something interesting about your life or background.

My dad was a surgeon and a veteran who became a peace activist. My mom went back to school in the '70s to become an architect. We moved a lot when I was a kid and finally landed in eastern Kentucky—the Appalachian foothills—where I went to high school. We moved there because Dad wanted to work in a clinic that needed a surgeon.

So, I grew up in a liberal, educated, socially active household. I'm lucky in that. I also was very shy as a kid, and all that moving was awful. Now, I'm married to a photographer. We have one son, who is twenty-three. Two dogs, two cats, my studio is behind my house. I teach at the School of the Art Institute of Chicago. I don't assume any of this is interesting to anyone but me.

Anne Harris. *Portrait (Red Robe)*, 2012.
Oil on linen: 52 × 33 inches.

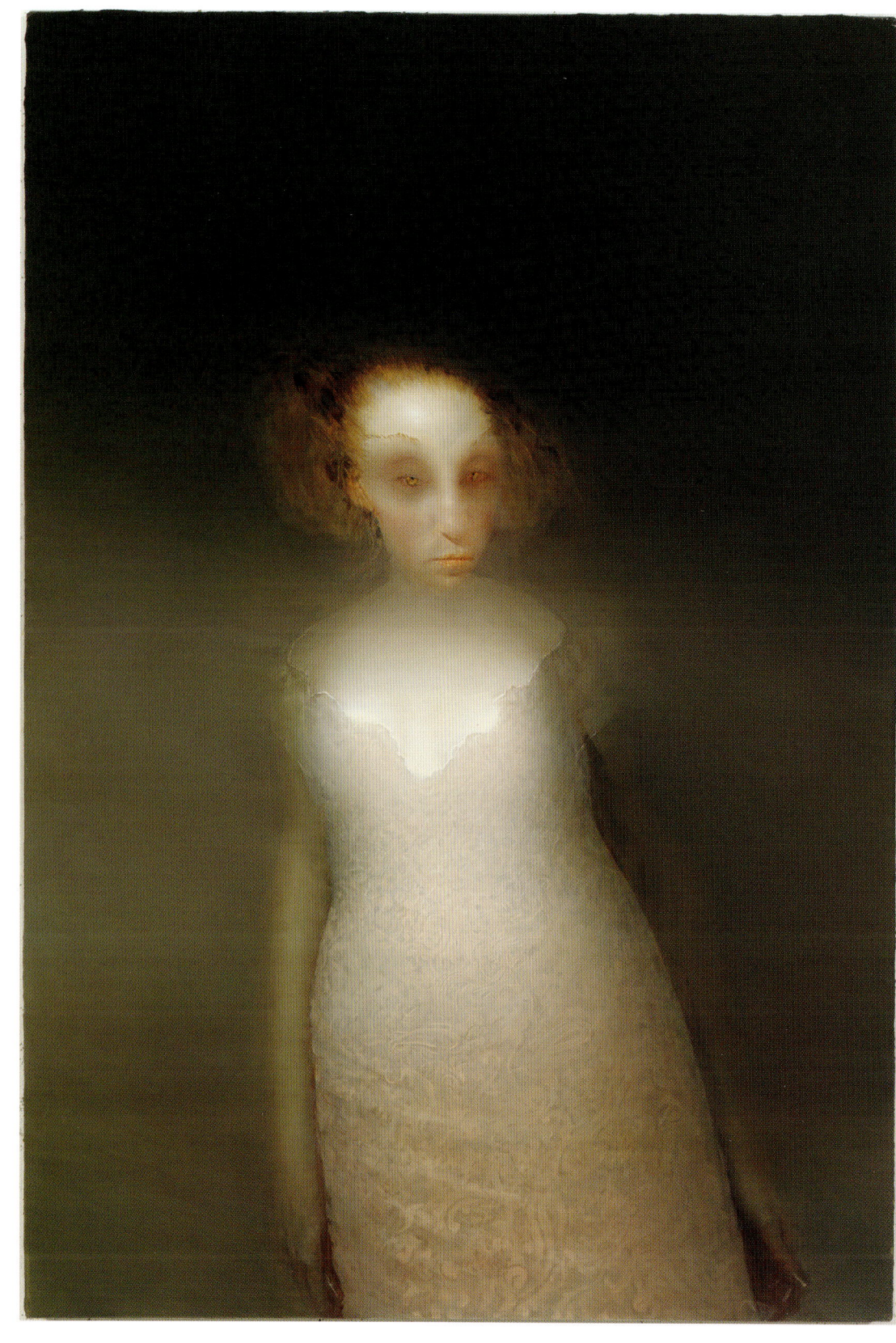

Anne Harris. *Portrait (Pink)*, 2010.
Oil on linen: 44 × 30 inches.

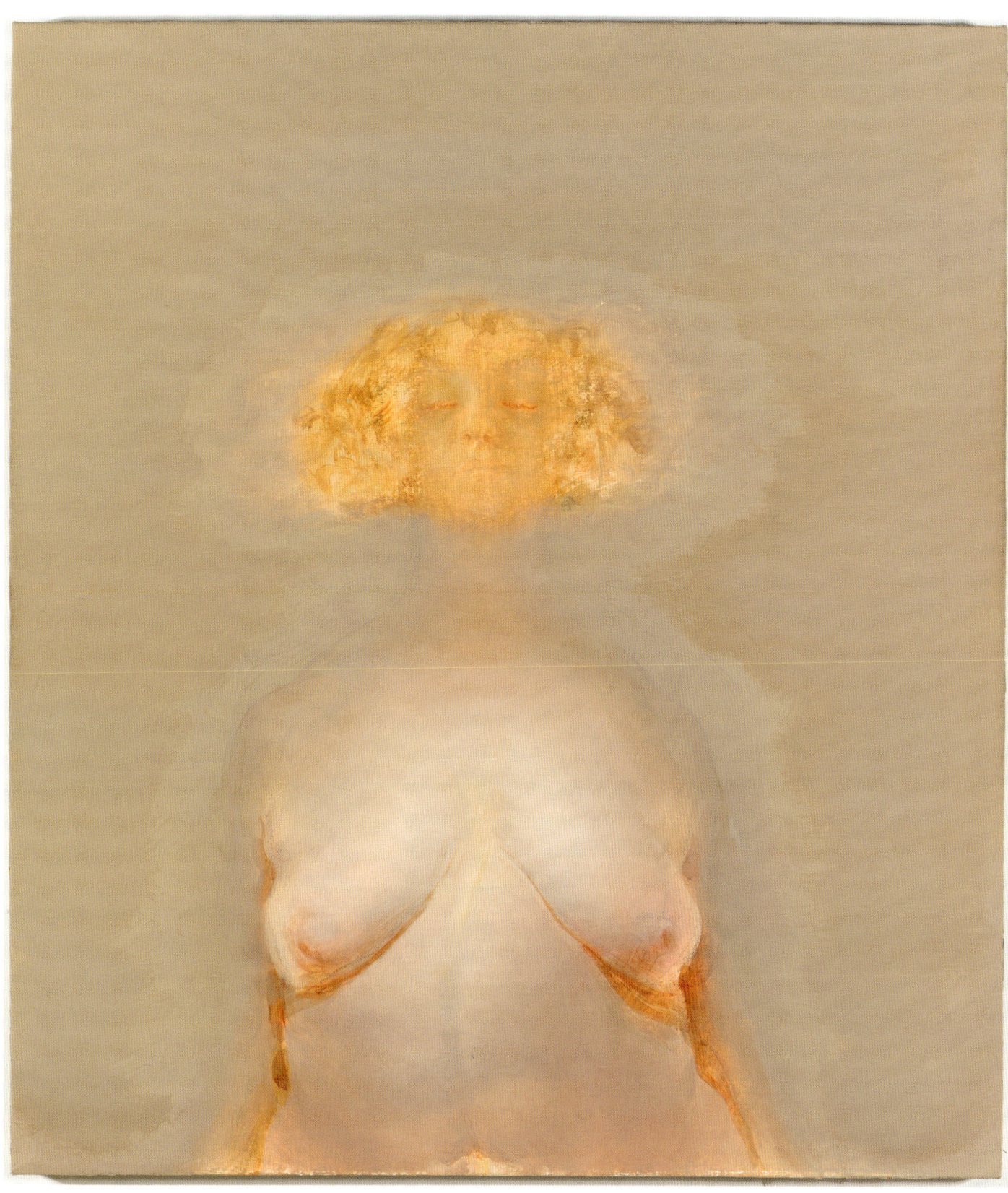

Anne Harris. *Invisible (Blonde),* 2012.
Oil on linen: 33 × 30 inches.

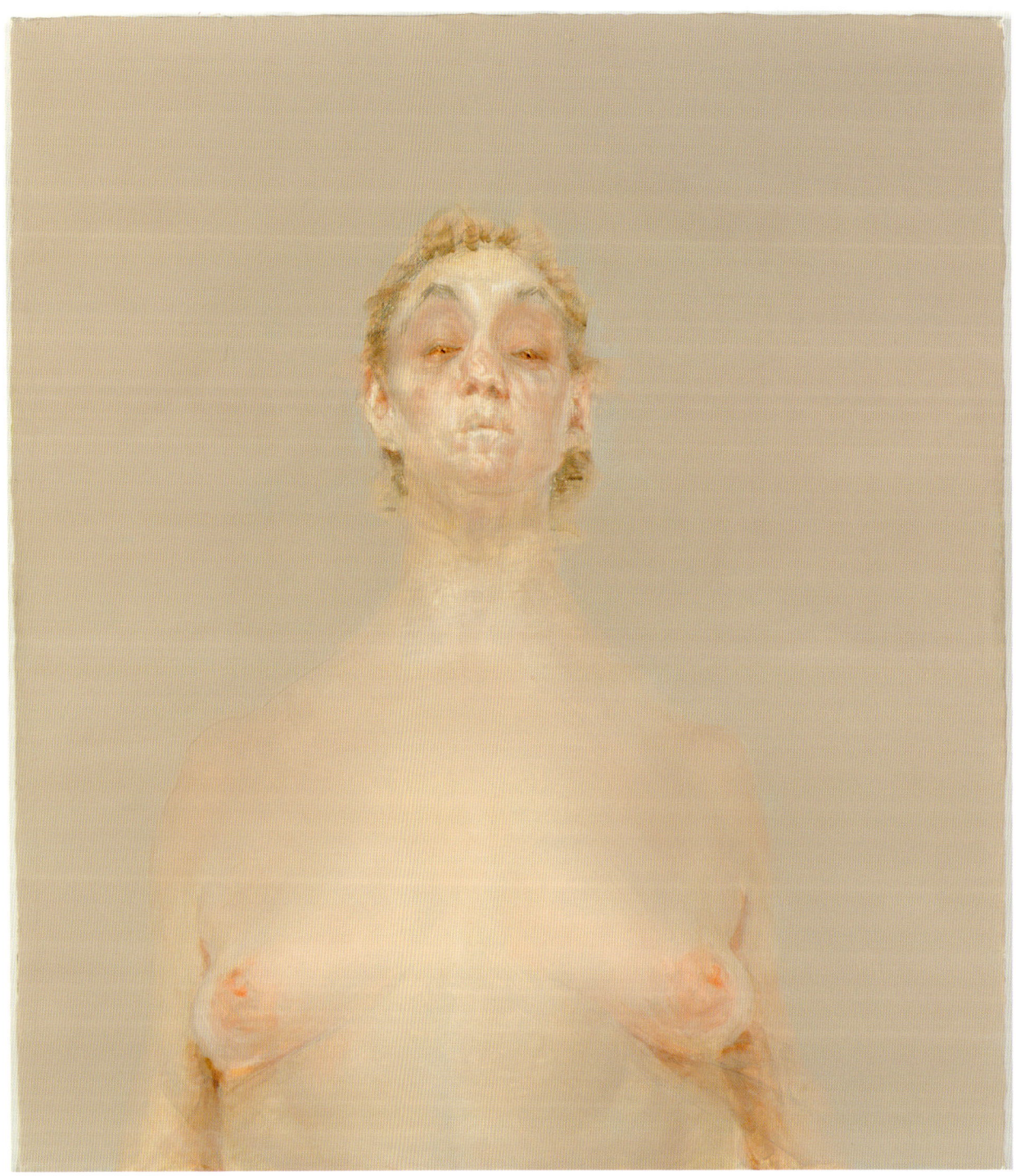

Anne Harris. *Invisible (Cropped)*, 2012.
Oil on linen, 27 × 24 inches.

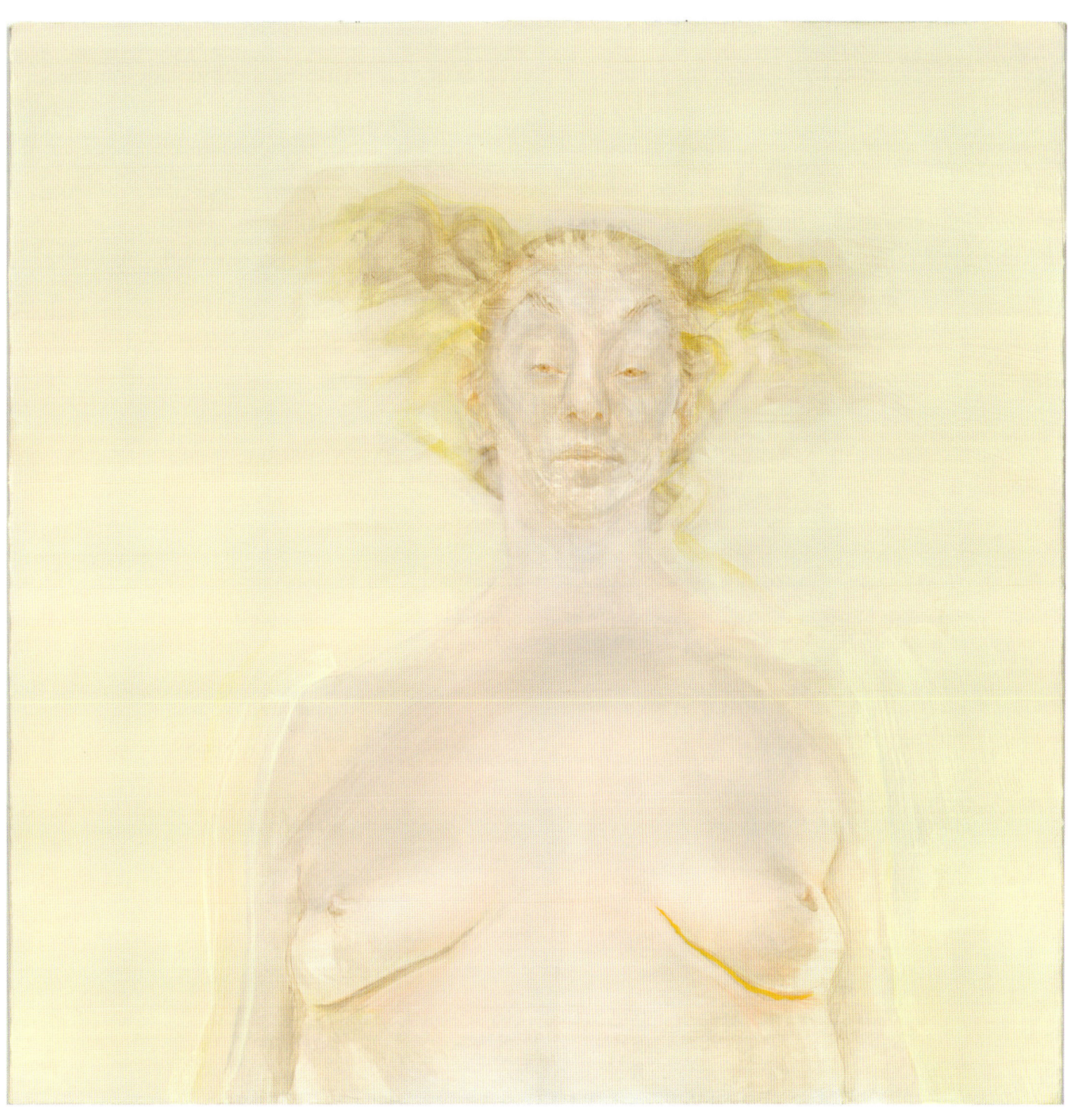

Anne Harris. *Invisible (Yellow),* 2013.
Oil on linen: 26 × 26 inches.

JEAN-PAUL MALLOZZI

Lives and Works in: Miami, Florida

Education: Rhode Island School of Design

Selected Collections: Anne Hathaway & Adam Shulman,
Brendan Mullinix, Ken Stone

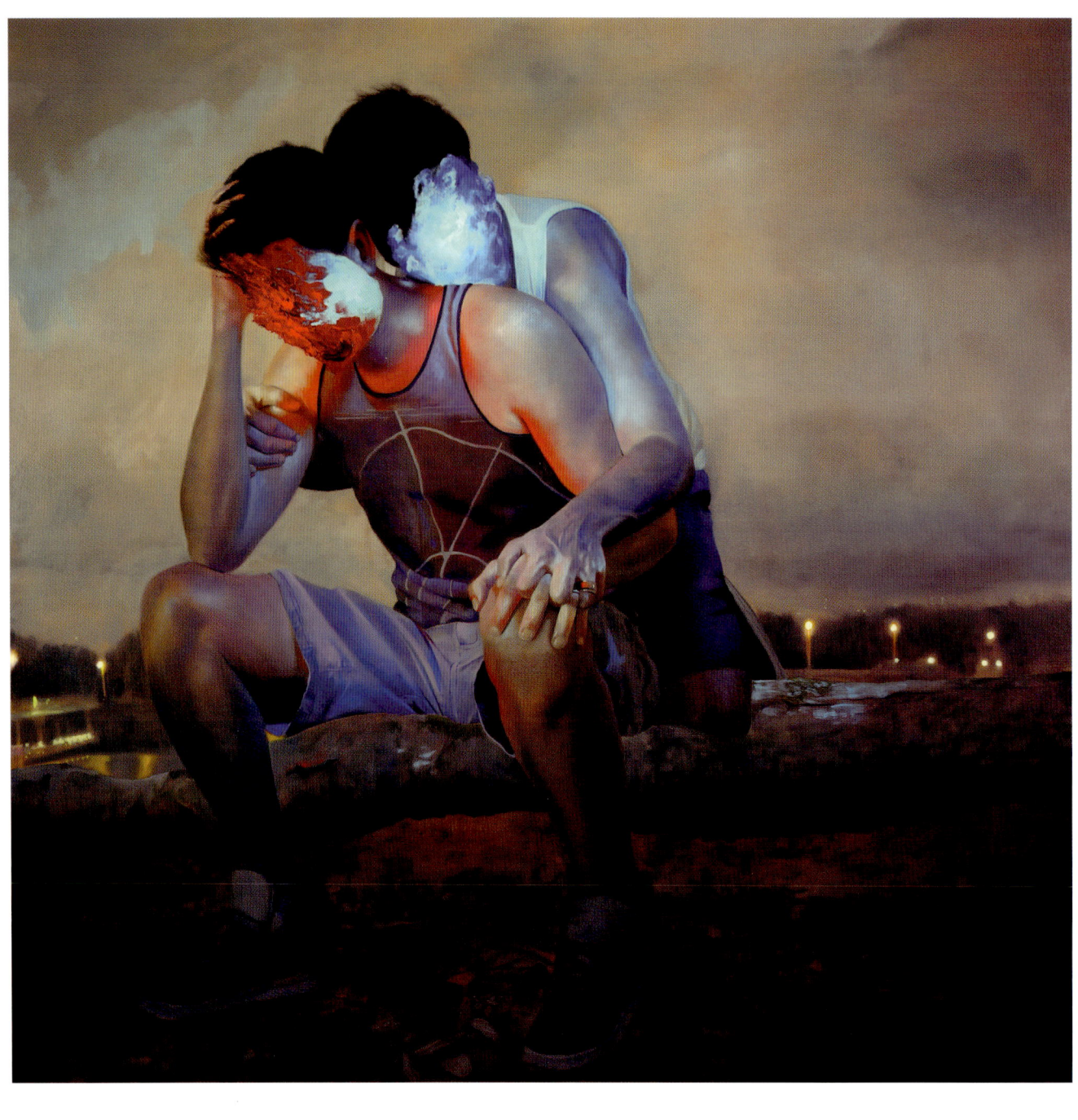

My work strives to be honest about masculinity, sexuality, and identity.

How and why does your work disrupt or deviate from traditional realism?

I explore my fascination with the human condition and the inherent, nuanced complexities of personal relationships, specifically intimate male relationships, which are often hypersexualized and informed by society's rigid and conflicting constructs of masculinity, sexuality, and identity. These concepts are layered using attention to delicately rendered details in paint that emphasize the ebb and flow of these intimate relationships and their ever-changing emotional states.

I wanted to create a reflective atmosphere in which these human relationships play out and challenge the male gaze, thereby revealing other possibilities for performing and seeing "masculinity." The incorporation of color fields across the faces enhances, and also obscures, the subjects' internalized emotional states without the need for facial cues.

How has your work evolved and developed over time?

It started off with kids rendered in graphite and broke into painting with mature adults. I also took a self-imposed break after I was done with my current series.

What are some of the influences that have shaped your work?

My love for narratives from video games, comic books, and my fascination with classical paintings as a kid.

Mention something interesting about your life and background.

I'm the first generation born in this country, the son of immigrant parents. My mom came from Cuba and my dad from Italy. Both cultural influences bring storytelling to the forefront because my parents were so nostalgic about what they missed from their own countries.

Jean-Paul Mallozzi. *Calm Down,* 2016.
Oil on canvas: 60 × 60 inches.

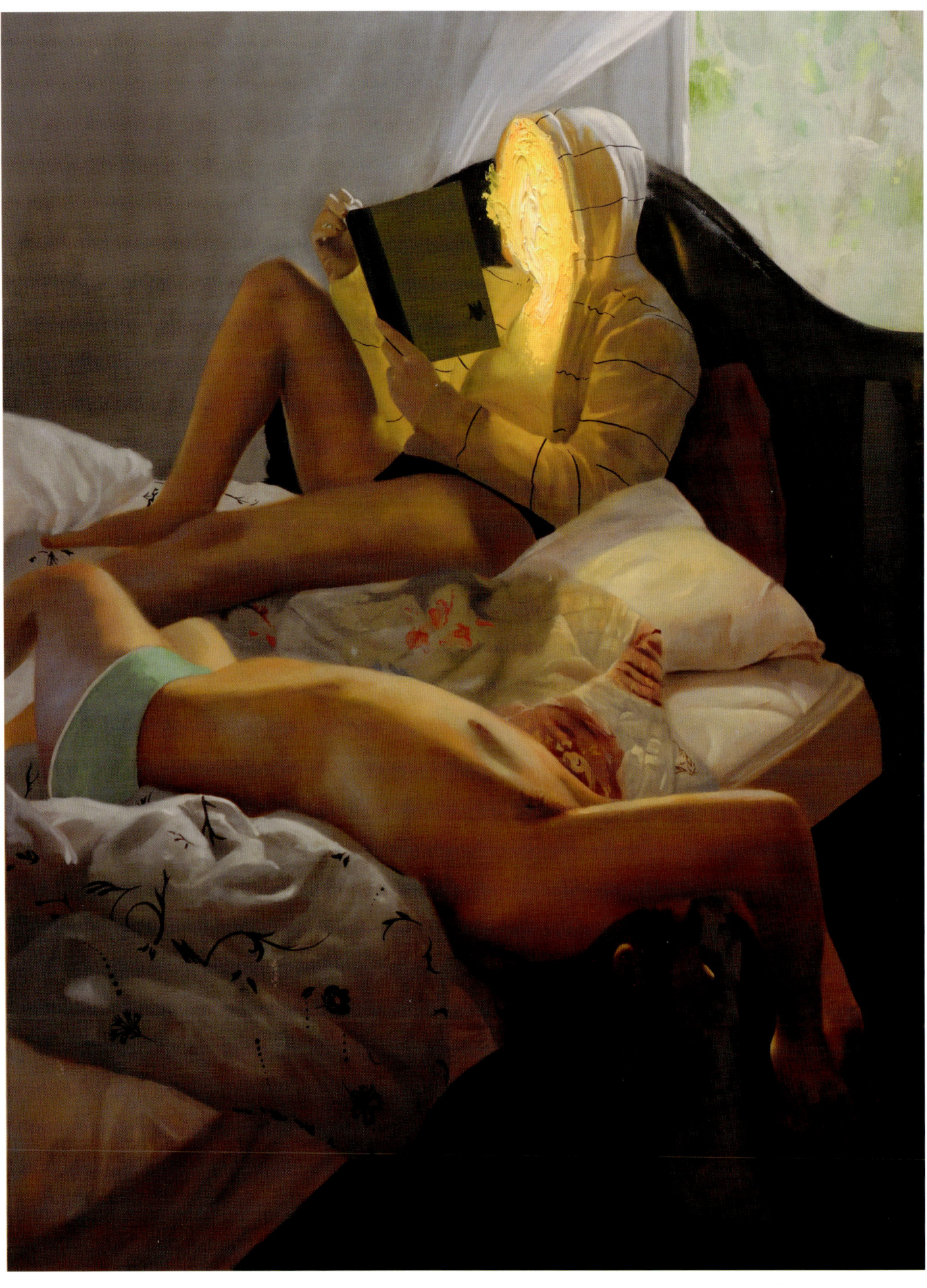

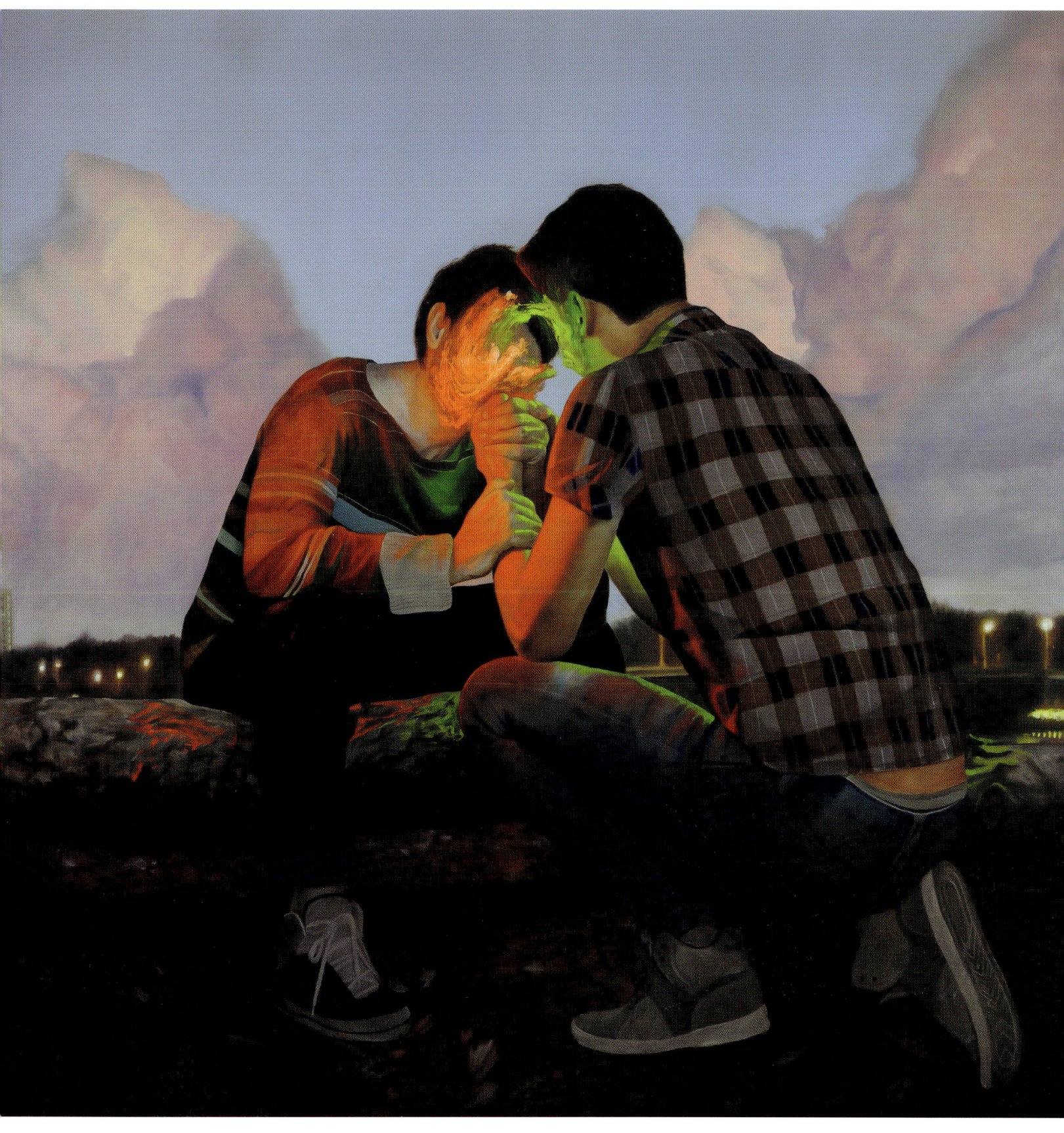

Jean-Paul Mallozzi. *Cat and Maus*, 2016.
Oil on canvas: 48 × 36 inches.

Jean-Paul Mallozzi. *Now Get Up*, 2016.
Oil on canvas: 60 × 60 inches.

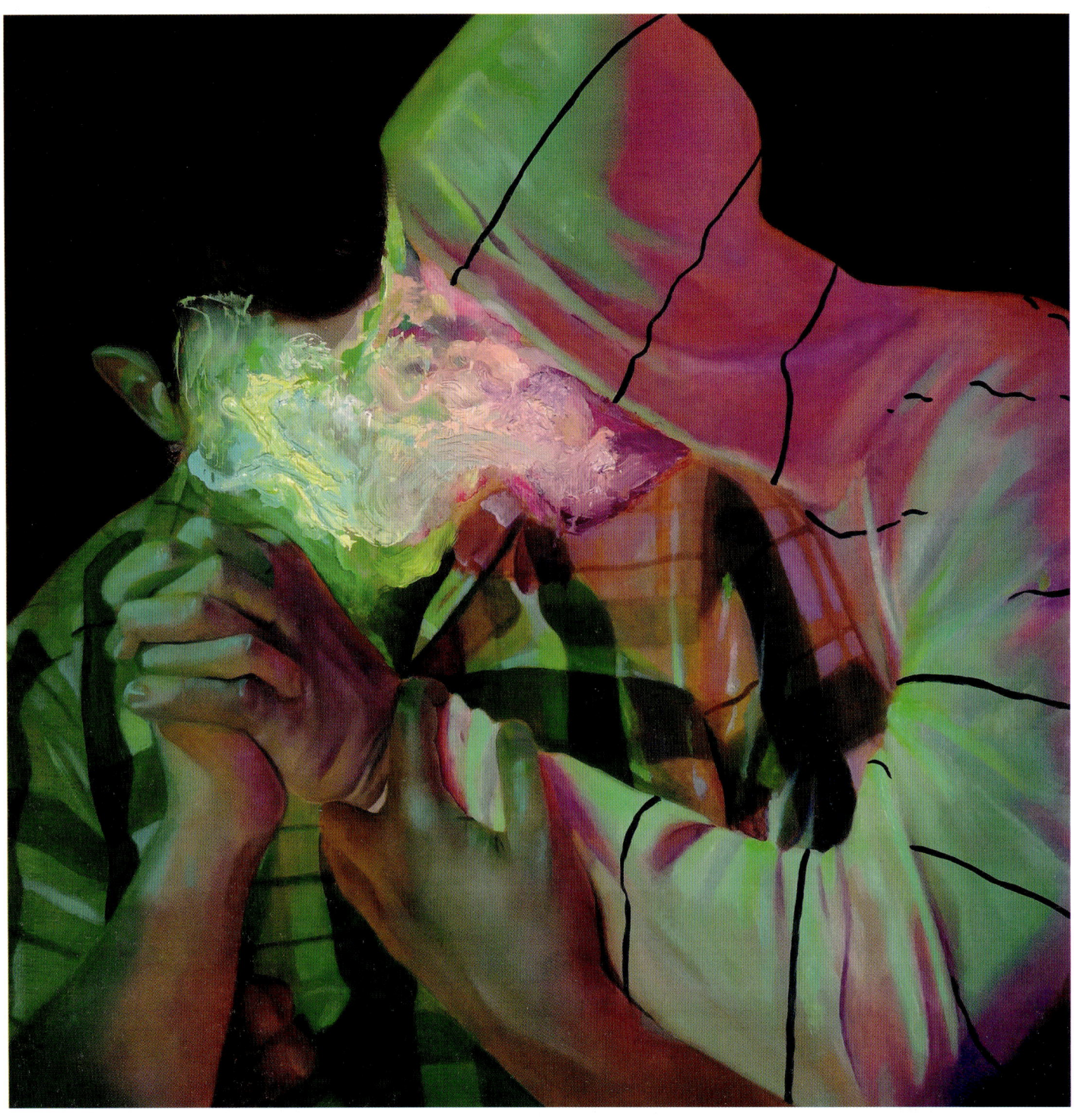

Jean-Paul Mallozzi. *Reconcile,* 2016.
Oil on cradled wood panel: 16 × 16 inches.

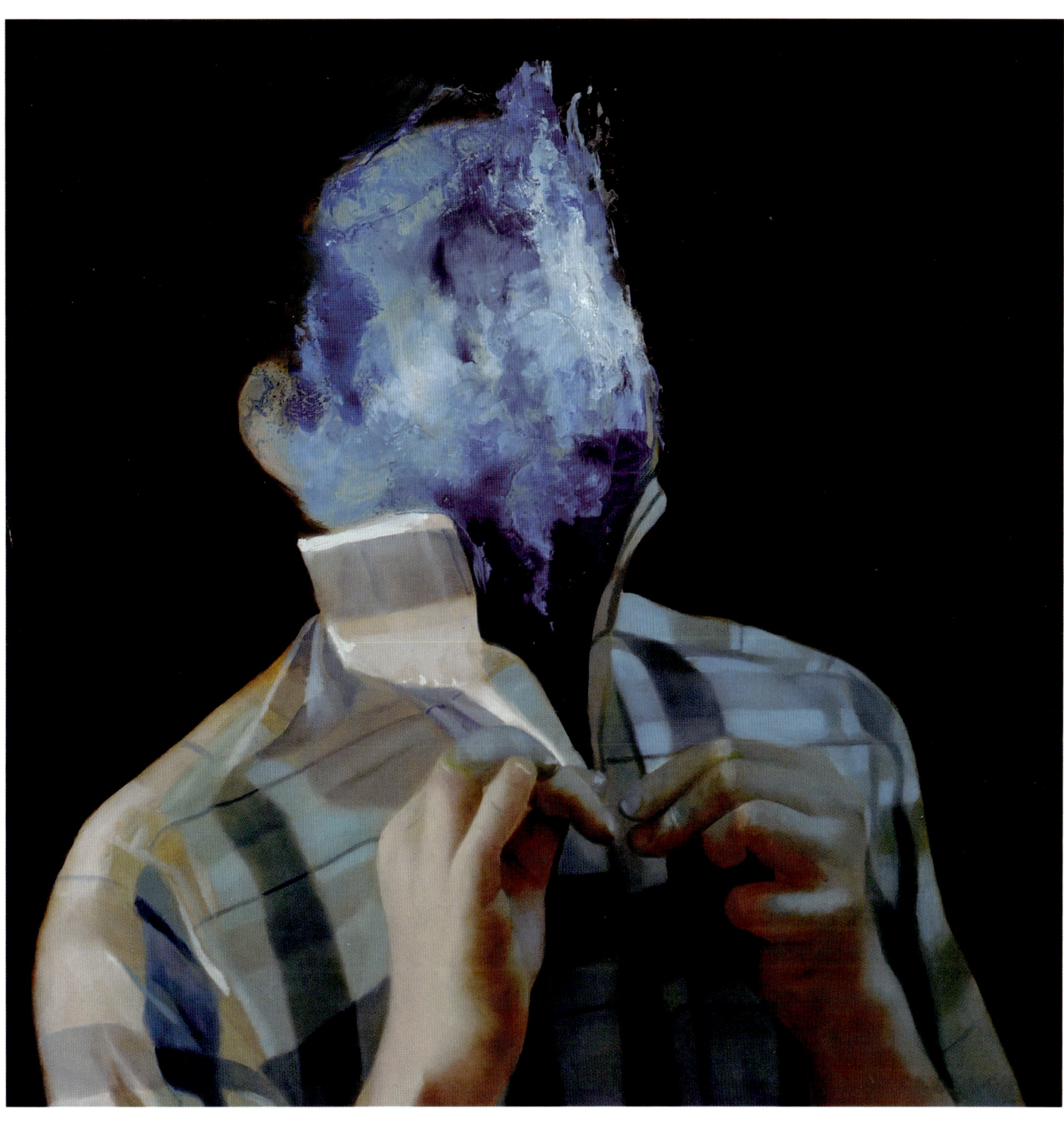

Jean-Paul Mallozzi. *So It Begins*, 2016.
Oil on cradled wood panel: 16 × 16 inches.

MEREDITH MARSONE

Lives and Works in: Blenheim, New Zealand
Education: Bachelor of MediaArts, major in painting,
Waikato Institute of Technology
Selected Collections: Waikato Trust Collection, Wallace Collection
Representation: Corey Helford Gallery, Los Angeles

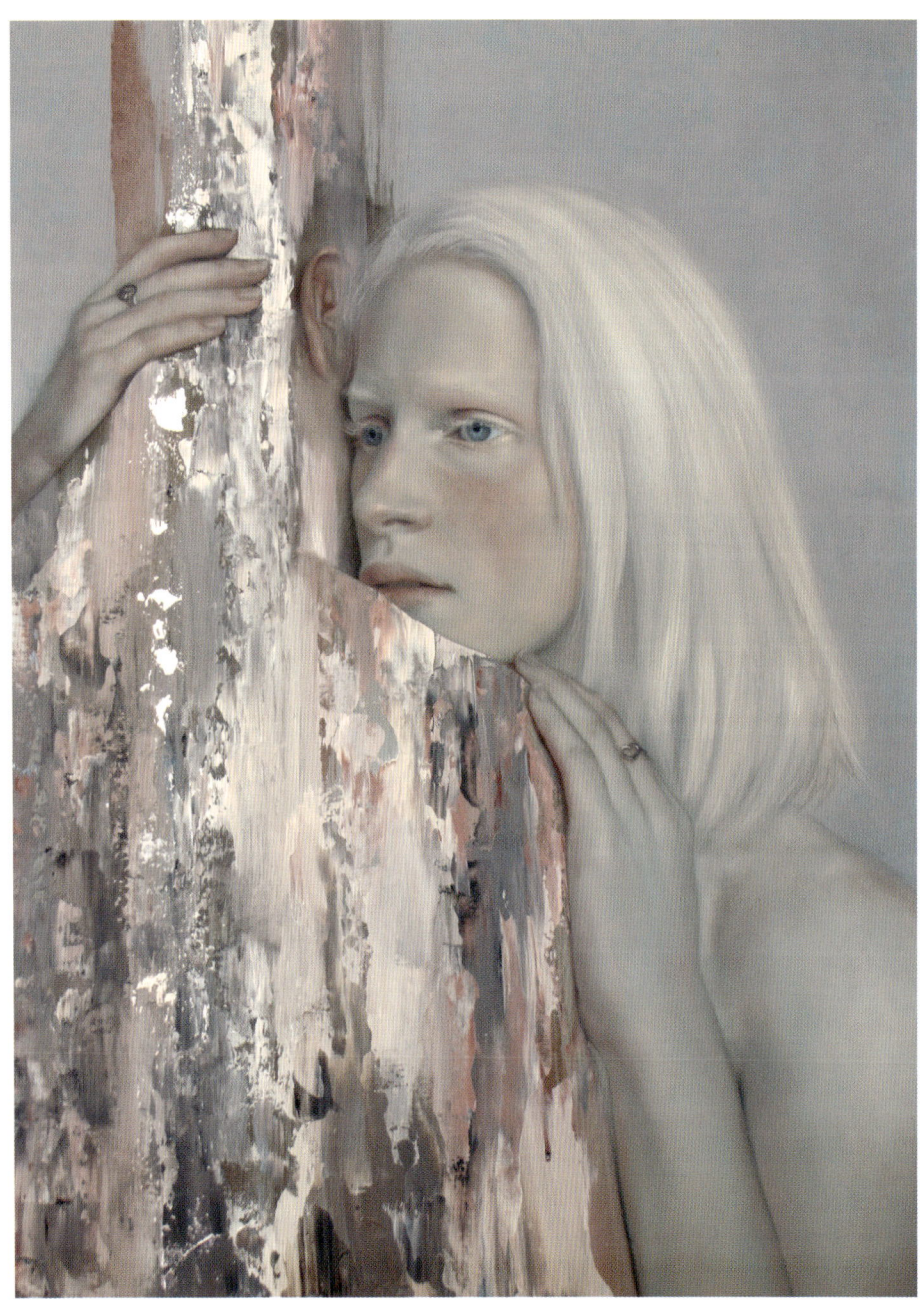

I create figurative paintings infused with the human condition.

How and why does your work disrupt or deviate from traditional realism?

I'm interested in techniques that infuse my work with meaning and emotion without having to incorporate a lot of superfluous pictorial elements. I want people to connect with my work on an emotional level. The combination of realistic figures with an abstract element that unites either the figure to the surroundings or represents another figure creates an entry point for the viewer to find or create meaning. I have my own stories and influences within each painting, but equally important is what the viewer sees and feels looking at the painting. The communication of emotion and experience in a painting is a subjective task and one I will continue to pursue until my last brushstroke.

How has your work evolved and developed over time?

When I first began using oils, I was obsessed with mastering the traditional techniques and methods and so developed an approach that best measured the progression of my skills in realistic figurative painting. Over time, as I became increasingly confident with my materials, I began wanting to push the medium further and experiment with an alternative way to communicate what I was seeing. Combining realism with an abstract component became my new language. It's an effective way to convey the form as well as an emotive quality that is difficult to capture in a purely realistic rendering.

What are some of the influences that have shaped your work?

Early on, my main influences were Klimt and Schiele, and some might say they can see this in my work today, even though it's not a conscious intention. Klimt's work in particular I found so compelling; it must have just seeped into my artistic bones somehow. After seeing a retrospective of his work in Paris in 2007, my work was forever changed. The experience of seeing his work up close and en masse is something I will always treasure. I came home from that trip with a renewed enthusiasm and confidence that to this day hasn't left me.

Mention something interesting about your life and background.

I spent my early working career as an exhibitions designer for museums and galleries in New Zealand until 2007, when I became a full-time artist. But I've always juggled my painting career with being a mother. My children, from eldest to youngest, span fourteen years!

Meredith Marsone. *Loveloss II,* 2015.
Oil and silver leaf on board: 15.7 × 11.8 inches.

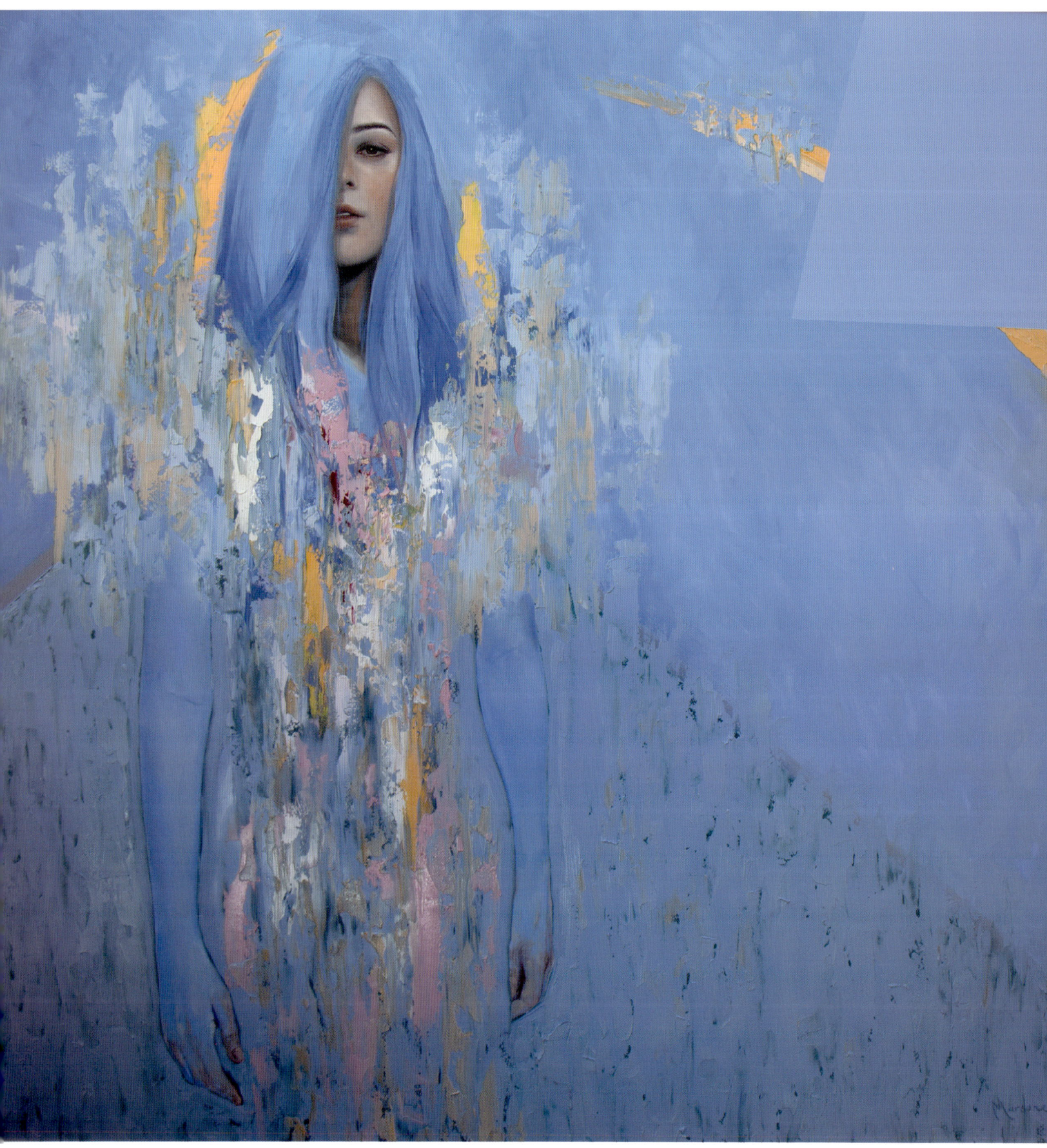

Meredith Marsone. *Blue Woman*, 2017.
Oil on panel: 47.2 × 47.2 inches.

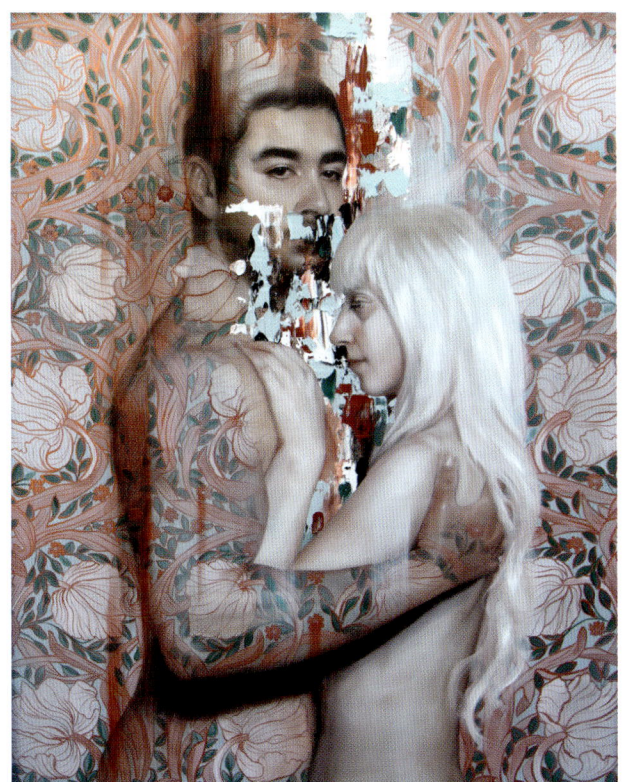

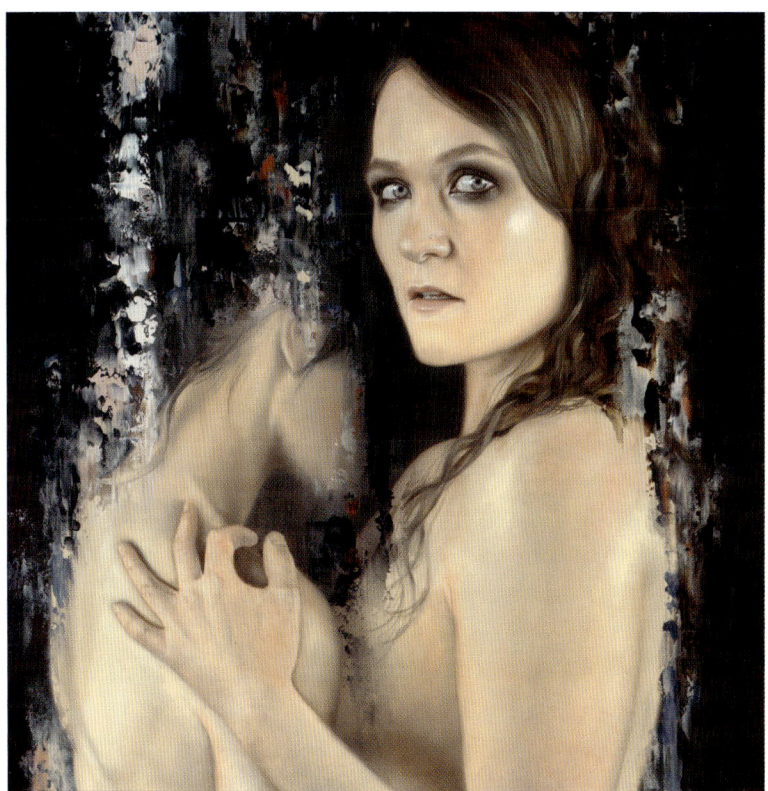

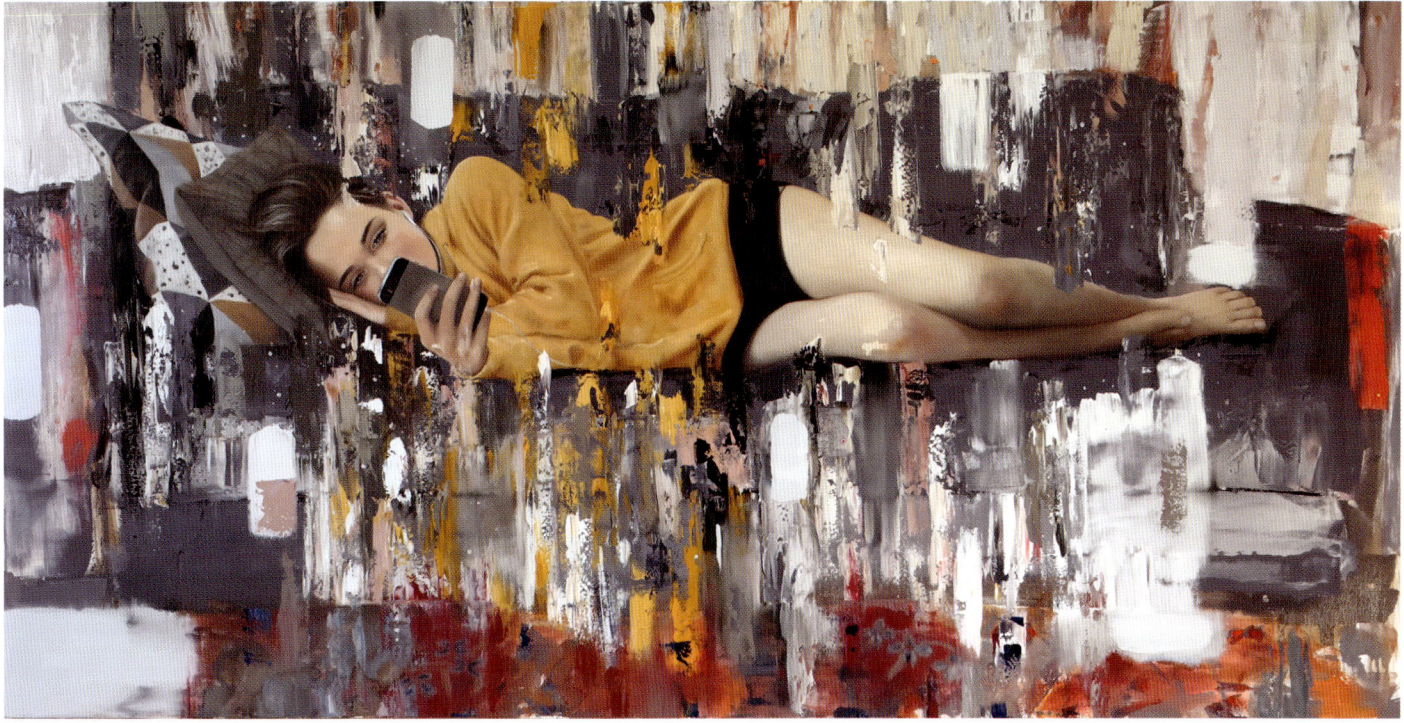

Top left: Meredith Marsone. *Loveloss—Surrender,*
2018. Oil on board: 19.7 × 15.7 inches.

Top right: Meredith Marsone. *Lovers,* 2016.
Oil on canvas: 19.7 × 19.7 inches.

Meredith Marsone. *Lost Generation,* 2018.
Oil on canvas: 70.8 × 35.4 inches.

JOHN WENTZ

Lives and Works in: Paris
Education: Academy of Art University
Selected Collections: Hyatt Regency Hotel, San Francisco
Representation: Hashimoto Contemporary, San Francisco

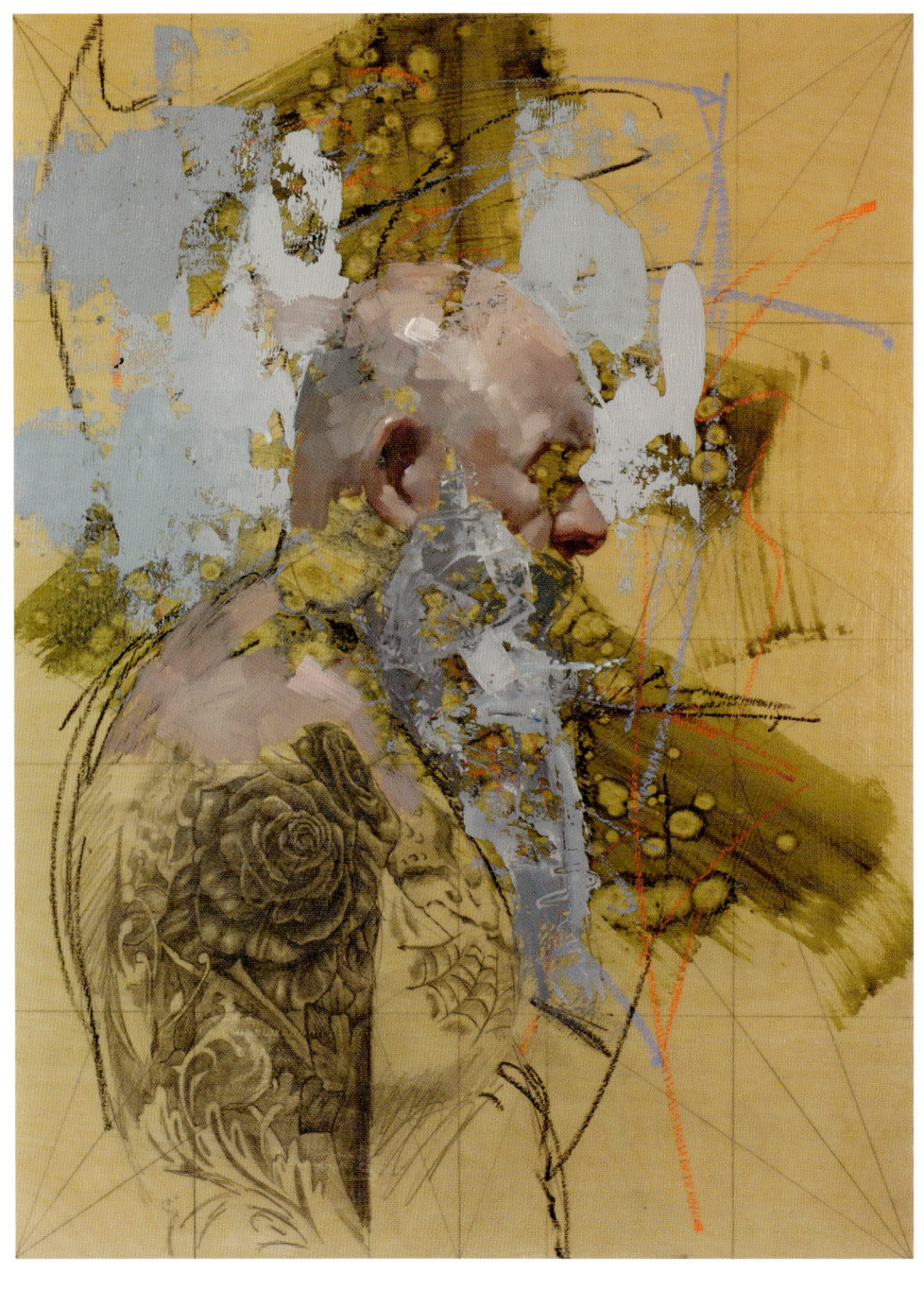

My work is slowly creeping toward abstraction.

How and why does your work disrupt or deviate from traditional realism?

I try to work more with stylization, exaggeration, and abstraction. Traditional realism has steered more and more toward mimetics. I think that is due in part to photography, but also just to this ever-growing notion that realism means just as it is seen. For me, expression and emotion are in stylizing and exaggerating the figure, be it to a small or great extent. With regard to surface, I try to destroy the image, or basically leave parts unknown to engage with the viewer. I'm interested in how the brain perceives an image. So, it's basically pareidolia. But what I find really fascinating is within that, there is a large room for emotion.

How has your work evolved and developed over time?

In a sense, I feel it has become more abstract. That is, I'm more interested in marks, design, and emotion than I am in realistically depicting an object. I've also become increasingly fascinated with texture. With a world so inundated with photography, I really strive to differentiate the surface of a painting from that of a photograph. Texture, to me, is like the fourth dimension of painting.

What are some of the influences that have shaped your work?

The biggest influence on my work has been the lectures of neuroscientist V. S. Ramachandran. He has developed some fascinating theories on exaggeration and abstraction on art and how it affects the human brain. I first saw him in a great documentary by BBC, *How Art Made the World*. His lectures are all on YouTube and, in my opinion, are a must-see for artists.

Mention something interesting about your life and background.

My most encouraging teacher was in the sixth grade. I used to draw through every lesson, and instead of punishing me she fostered my art by getting the school to allow me to design everything for the annual Christmas play. I've never forgotten that and it still encourages me.

My work is slowly creeping toward abstraction.

John Wentz. *Imprint #78*, 2015.
Oil on canvas: 18 × 24 inches.

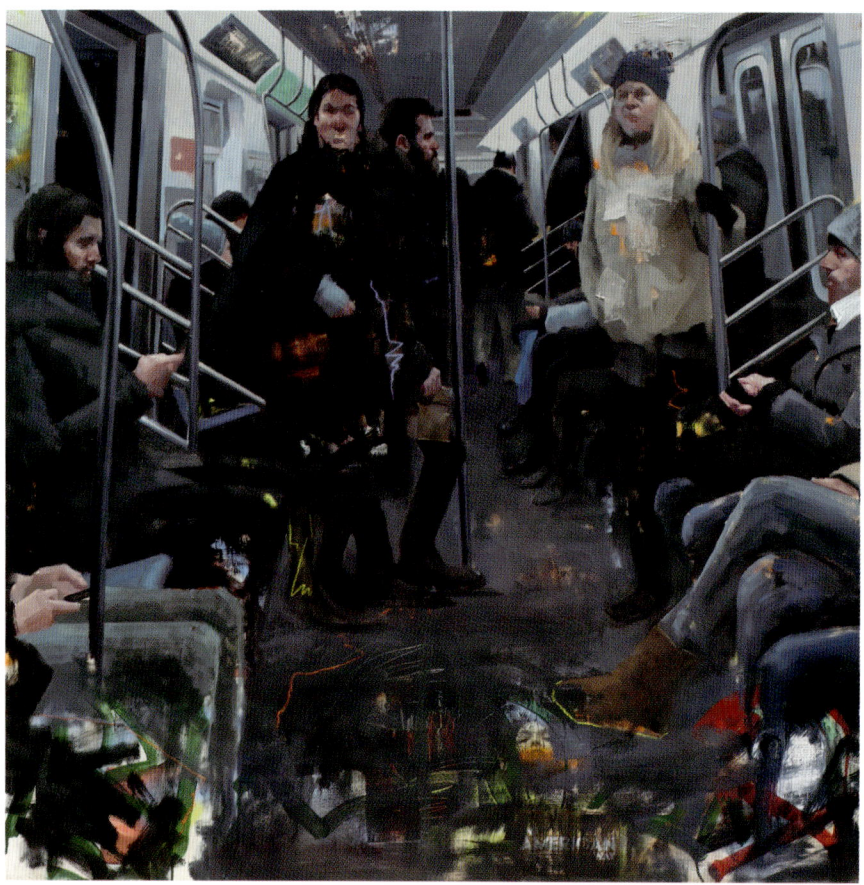

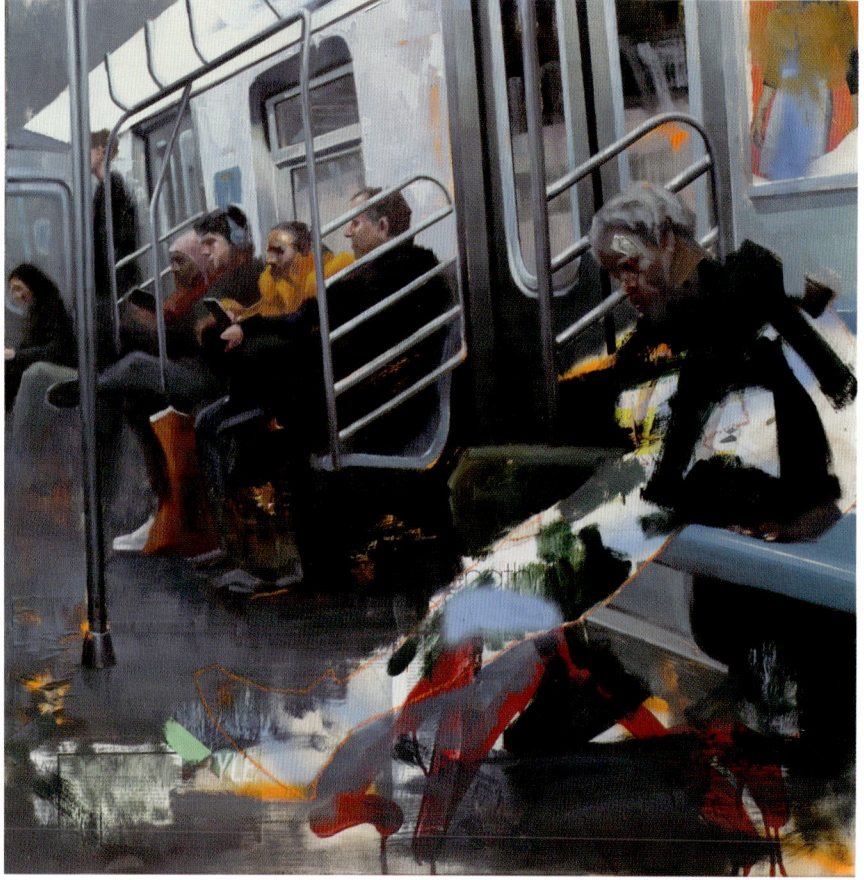

John Wentz. *Time and Pills, Let's Waste a Year,* 2017.
Oil on canvas: 60 × 60 inches.

John Wentz. *Unsure These Passing Days Won't
Try to Leave,* 2017.
Oil on canvas: 36 × 36 inches.

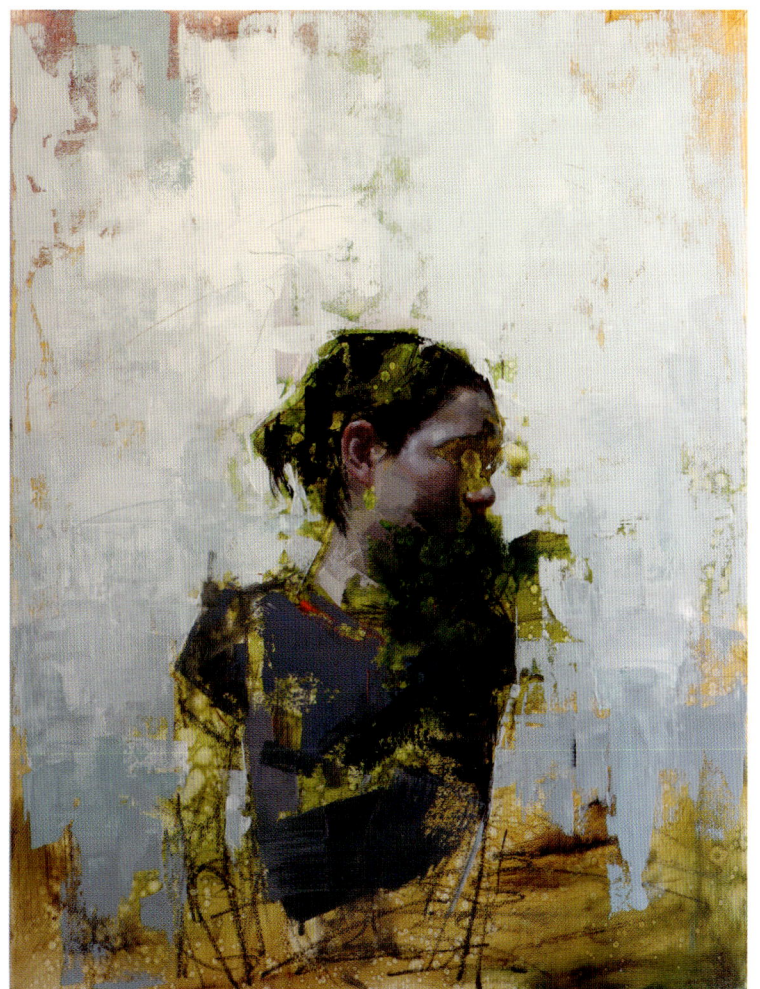 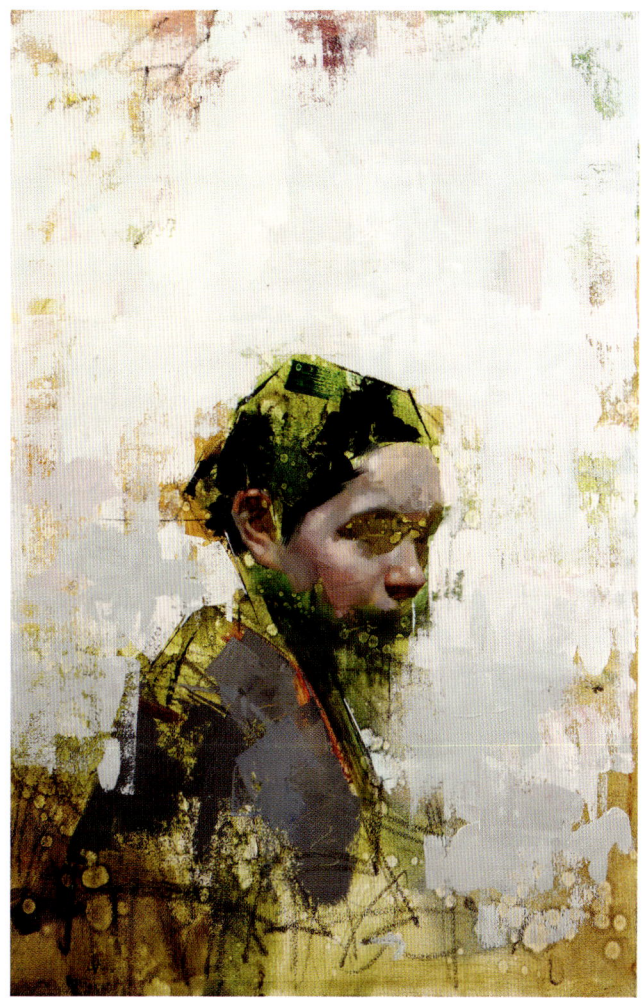

John Wentz. *Imprint #8,* 2015.
Oil on canvas: 35.5 × 27 inches.

John Wentz. *Imprint #1,* 2015.
Oil on canvas: 30 × 20 inches.

ZACK
ZDRALE

Lives and Works in: Madison, Wisconsin
Education: University of Wisconsin–Madison;
Academy of Art University, San Francisco
Representation: Abend Gallery, Denver, Colorado

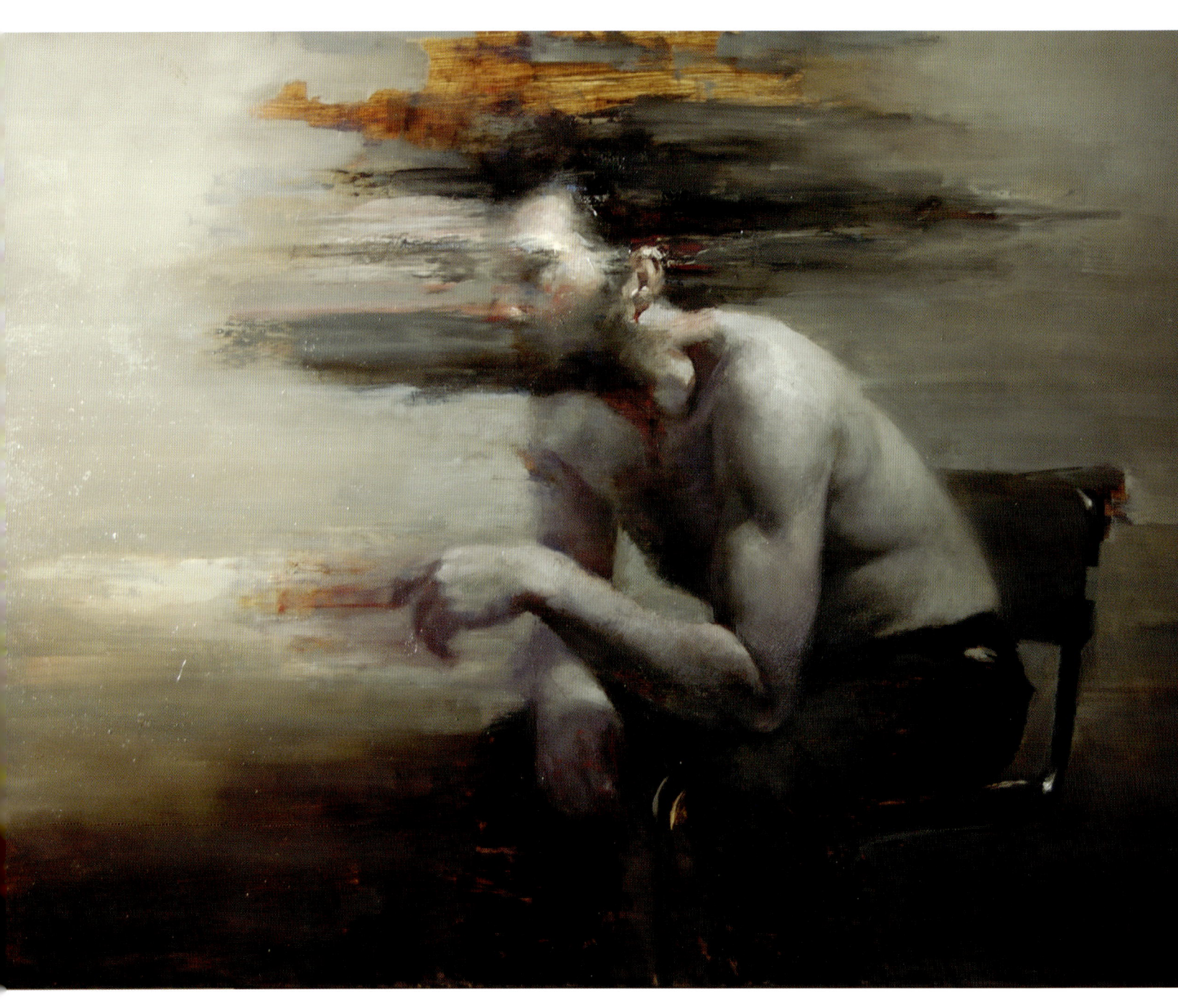

My works depict the stillness that occurs after an unexpected bang.

How and why does your work disrupt or deviate from traditional realism?

I've taken passages of traditionally rendered figures and smashed them, breaking the illusion of form in space. I want to show the paint doing things that only paint can do. I force the paint to conform to my drawing and then allow it to have its own voice.

How has your work evolved and developed over time?

My work has always been figurative, beginning with simple compositions and moody descriptions of light on form. The early work was very cathartic and necessary. Once I had moved past my early impulses, it became less exciting to compose the paintings this way. I began smashing the figure, breaking the rendering of form that I had clung to. It was self-destructive and liberating. I wanted to see action in the paint, and this was the climax of violence in my work. From there I've tried to retain the energy, freedom, and brute force while being less dark. I'm after what feels right rather than strictly what is correct.

What are some of the influences that have shaped your work?

Seventeenth-century masters, nineteenth-century academic painting, baroque, tonalists (particularly Innes and Whistler), Jacob Collins, Steven Assael, Alex Kanevsky, Phil Hale, Ann Gale, Antonio Lopez Garcia, Jenny Saville, Mark Tennant (particularly the evolution of his work), loud vamping music . . . Music plays a bigger role than I think I am aware of. Also, whatever book I'm currently reading seems to influence my perception of the world around me. How I react to this can help to shape my work, or at least how I physically paint it.

Mention something interesting about your life and background.

I had a large brain tumor that has had a profound impact on my work and life.

Zack Zdrale. *Dissociation III,* 2016.
Oil on panel: 24 × 18 inches.

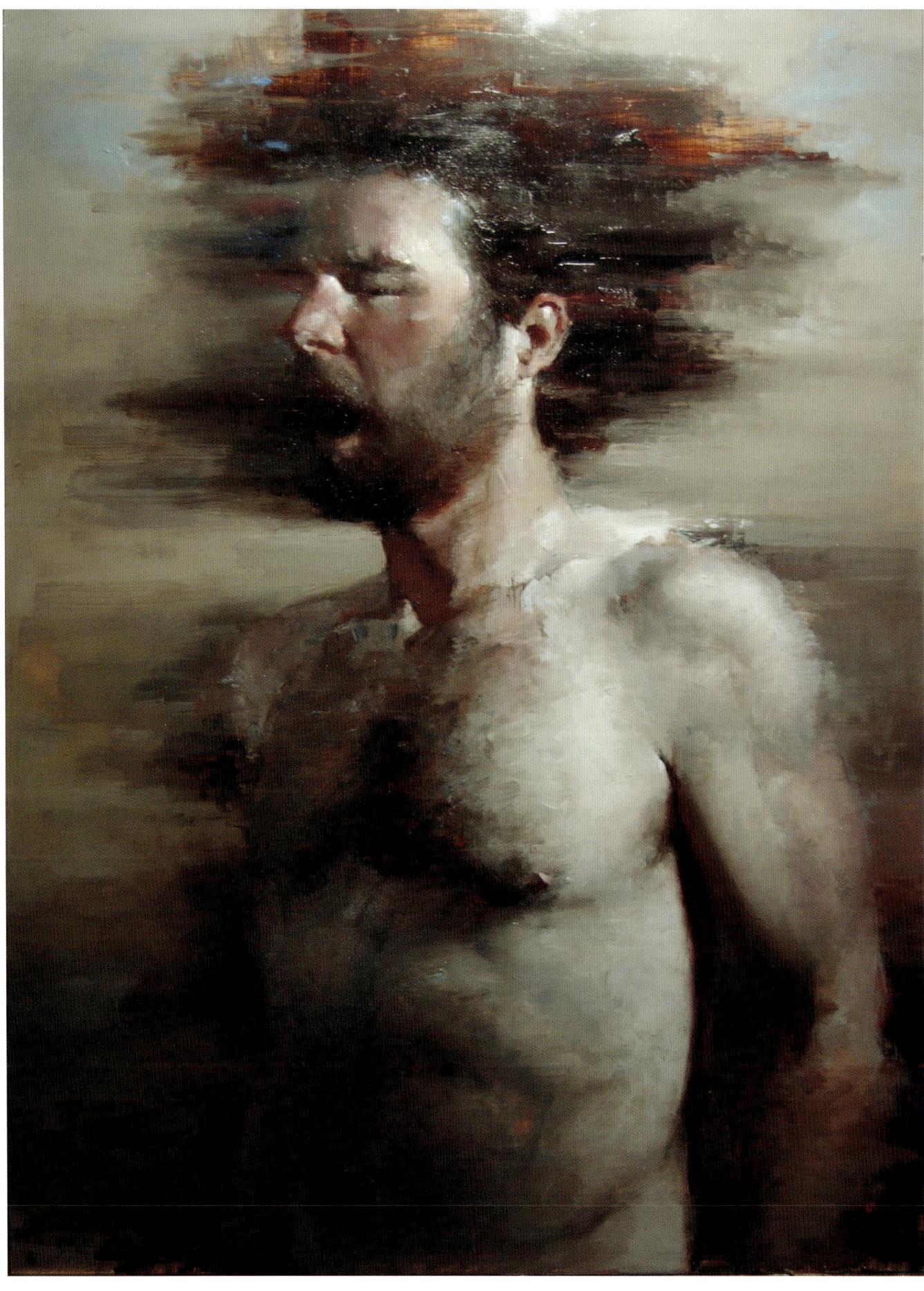

Zack Zdrale. *Dissociation*, 2016.
Oil on panel: 24 × 18 inches.

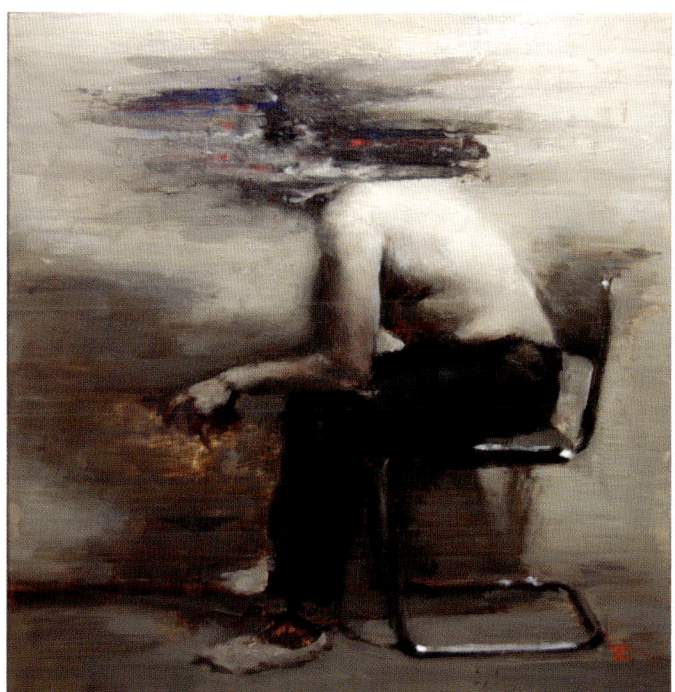

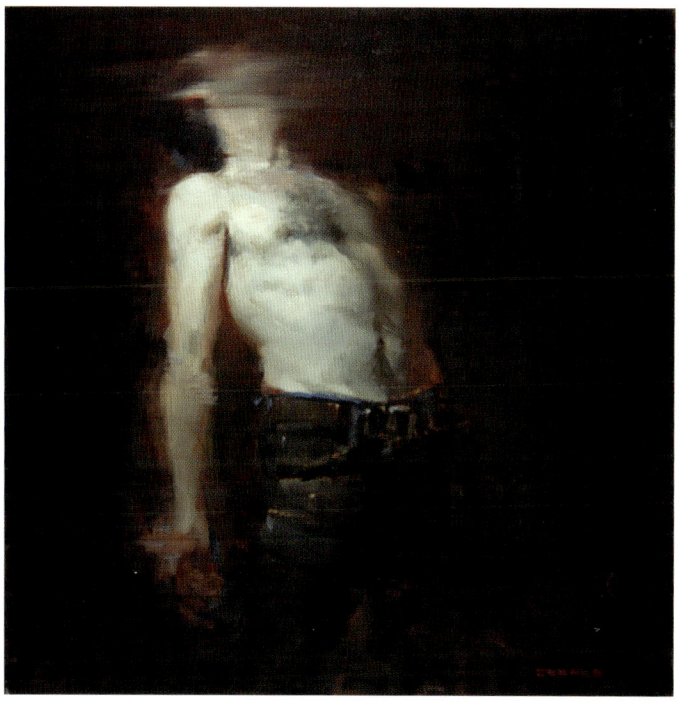

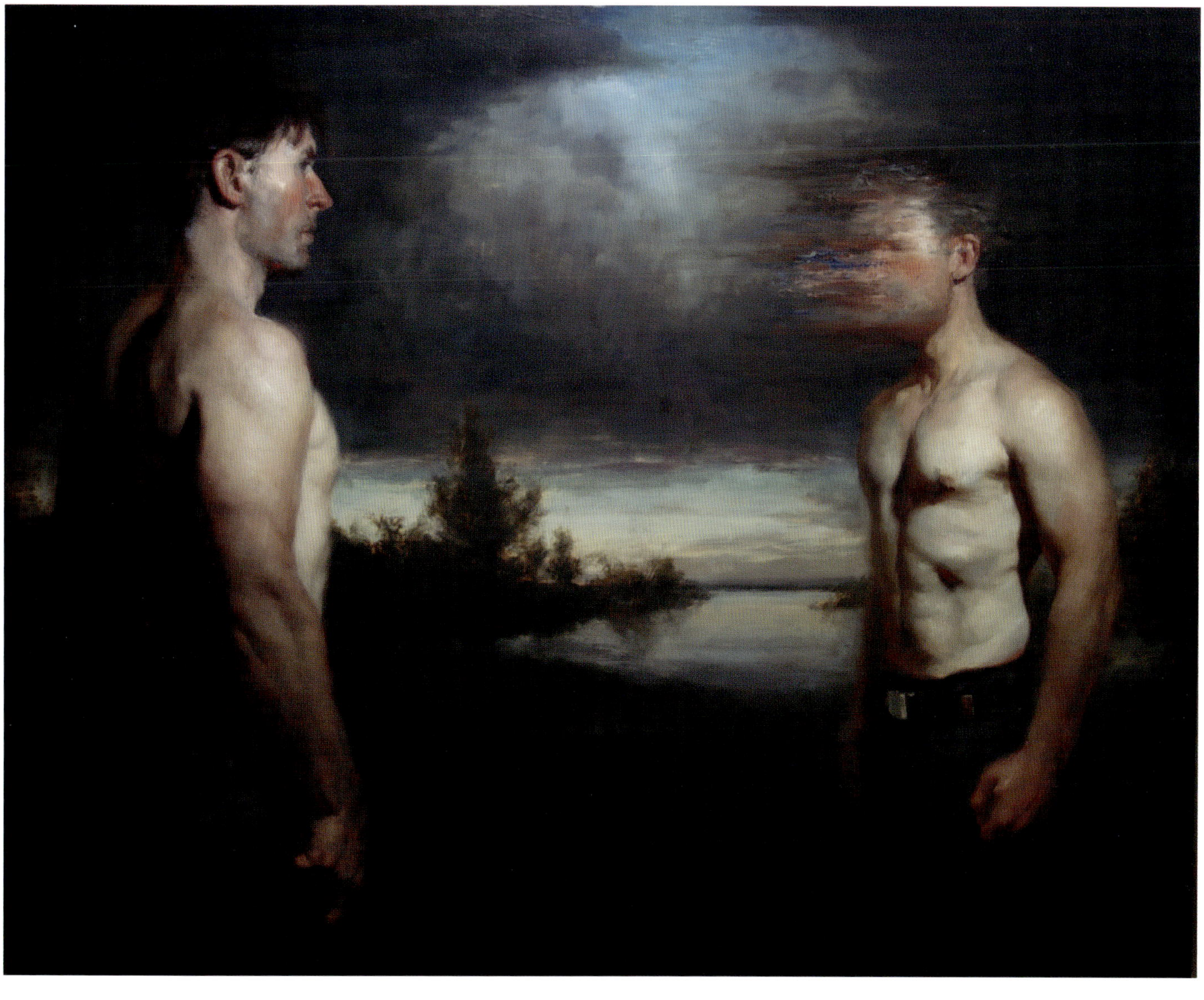

Top left: Zack Zdrale. *Dissociation II*, 2016.
Oil on panel: 6 × 6 inches.

Top right: Zack Zdrale. *N.G.*, 2016.
Oil on panel: 12 × 12 inches.

Zack Zdrale. *Reflect 2*, 2016.
Oil on panel: 24 × 30 inches.

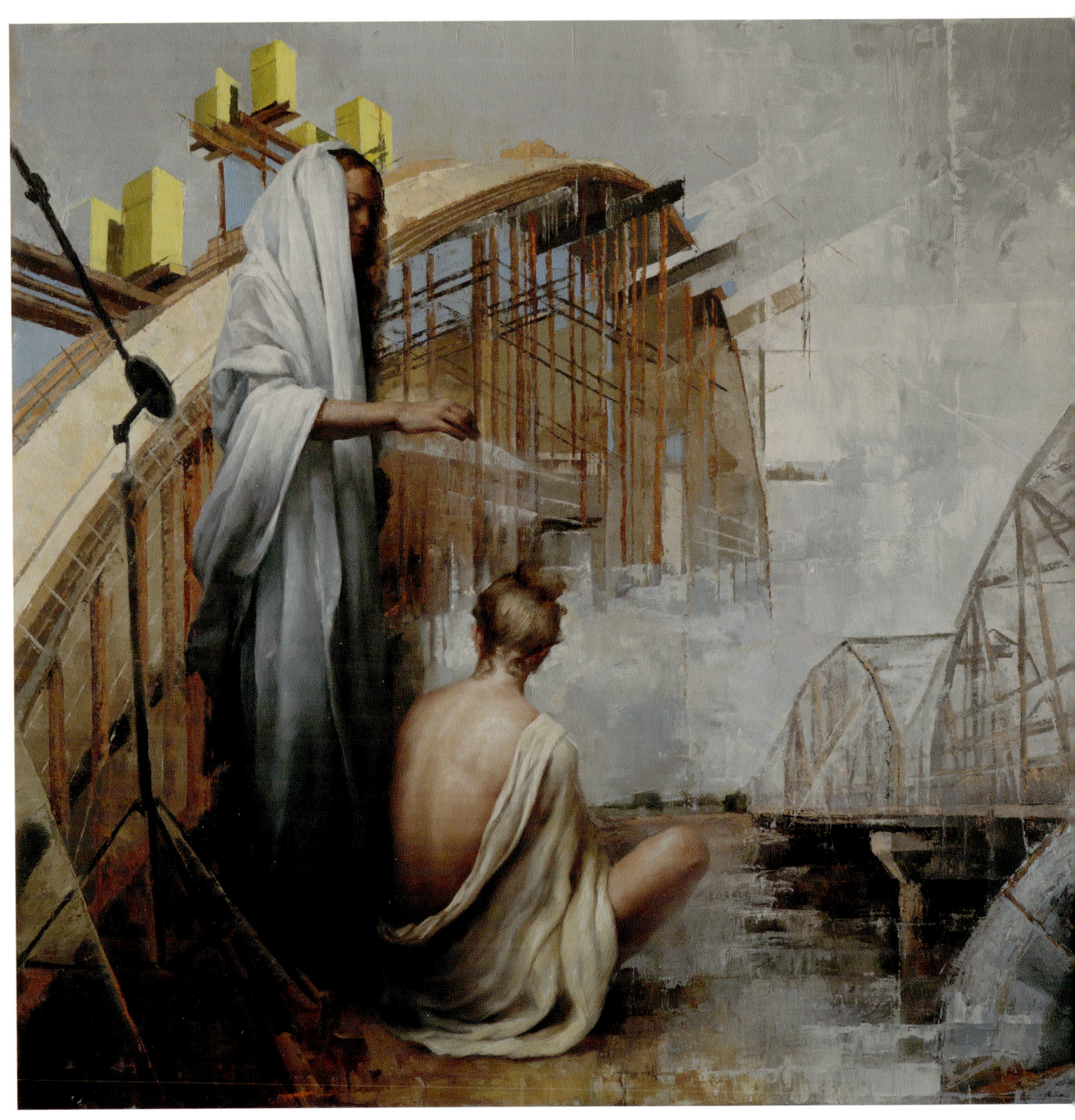

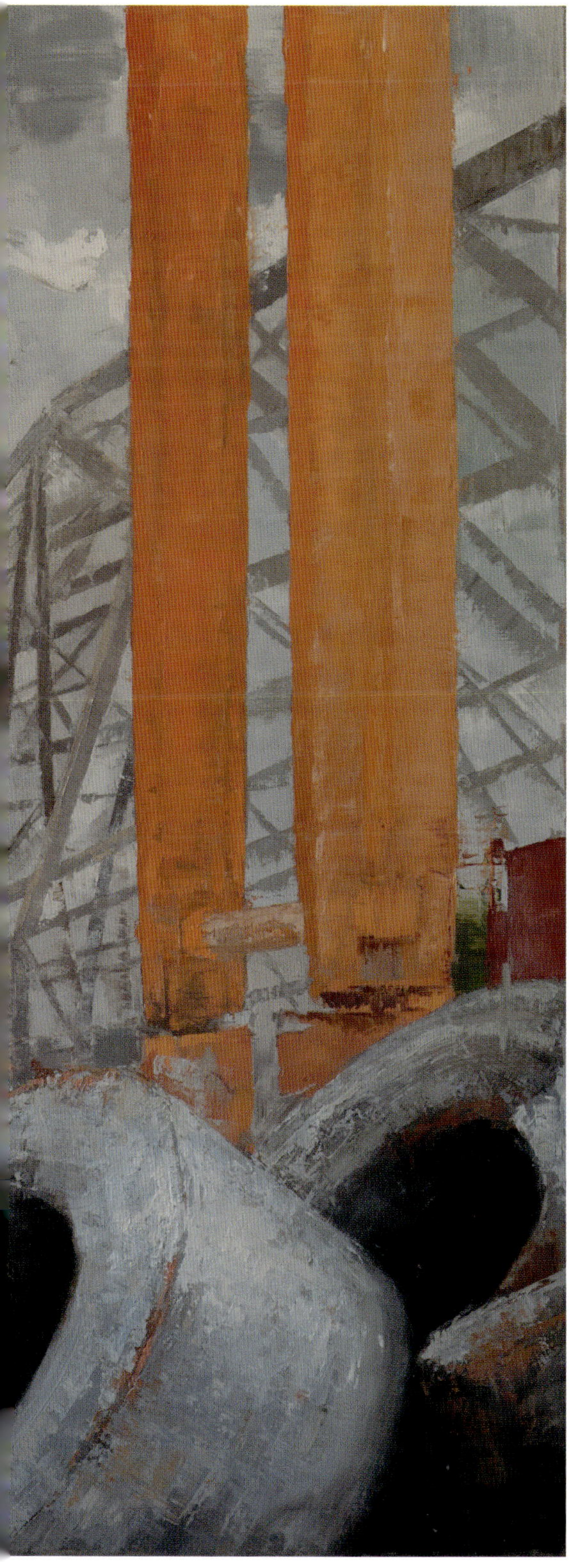

Maria Kreyn. *Even Here II*, 2016. Oil on canvas: 40 × 60 inches.

Myths and Visions

It's hard for me to conceptualize the category of traditional realism, or realism at all. Perhaps all realism is disrupted realism: a mediated, filtered version of our physical vision, emotional landscape, and personal mythscape.

—Maria Kreyn

When the poetic and the personal merge, the result can be a sense of universal connection and revelation. Painting images that both evoke reality and break from it allows artists to take their own lives toward the mythic. When the work is dreamlike there may be psychological suggestions—as in surrealism—but also conscious narratives that tell stories that are not literally possible. Similarly, in a time when religion is both prevalent and receding, painting has the ability to generate visions that foster meaningful conversations between the secular and the spiritual.

RADU BELCIN

MIA BERGERON

KAREN KAAPCKE

STANKA KORDIC

MARIA KREYN

ALYSSA MONKS

LOU ROS

RADU BELCIN

Lives and Works in: Brasov, Romania

Education: National University of Arts, Bucharest

Selected Collections: Numerous private collections

Representation: Galerie Martin Mertens, Berlin; Galerie Valerie Delaunay, Paris

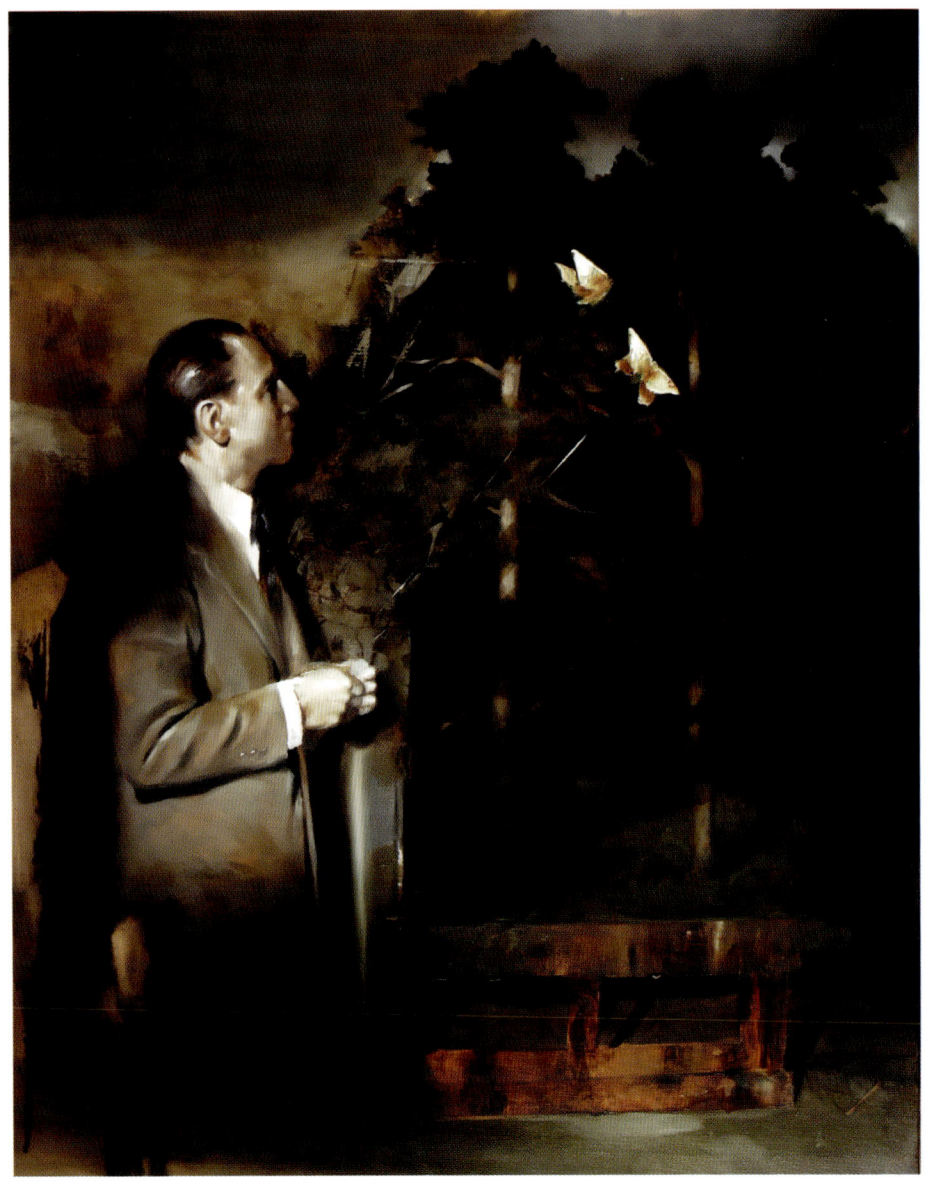

In my works I try to create a poetic universe where viewers are taken out of their mundane reality and thrown into unexpected situations and scenarios.

How and why does your work disrupt or deviate from traditional realism?

Painting is the most suitable language for me to express my thoughts and ideas. My intention is not to show raw reality—like a camera—but to construct the concepts of my works behind the curtains of reality. I see realism in painting as a tool that I can use only to create scenarios for my future works. I take elements from my personal environment and endow them with new meanings, creating symbols that complete the grammar of my painting.

When I begin a new painting, the main element that I work with is the action that's taking place behind the visual elements: that which is not actually represented, but only felt or perceived. Later, I focus on the importance of adding a title that offers significant clues that can aid in interpreting the work.

How has your work evolved and developed over time?

My work has developed in a way that parallels my own life experiences. Over time my awareness and my understanding of the world has grown, and that growth is naturally reflected in my work. The process is slow and hard to explain: it's like a snowflake that's becoming bigger and bigger by adding new layers all the time. When I look back at my earlier works, I see what's missing and I understand where I was at that point in time.

What are some of the influences that have shaped your work?

During my childhood I was very impressed by traditional paintings, including Flemish works from the fifteenth and sixteenth centuries, Spanish baroque works (and their chiaroscuro), and by the clarity of the German Renaissance paintings like those by Cranach, whose images I studied in my parents' library. That was the beginning of my art journey, and it still is the core of it. In time, I gradually absorbed these images and moved toward greater complexity, but I still feel their early influence.

Mention something interesting about your life or background.

My life occupies the spaces between the reality that surrounds me and the fictional realities that I create. It's a dreamlike existence that I want to experience and retain as much as I possibly can.

Radu Belcin. *Learning to Fly*, 2014.
Oil on linen: 39.4 × 31.5 inches.

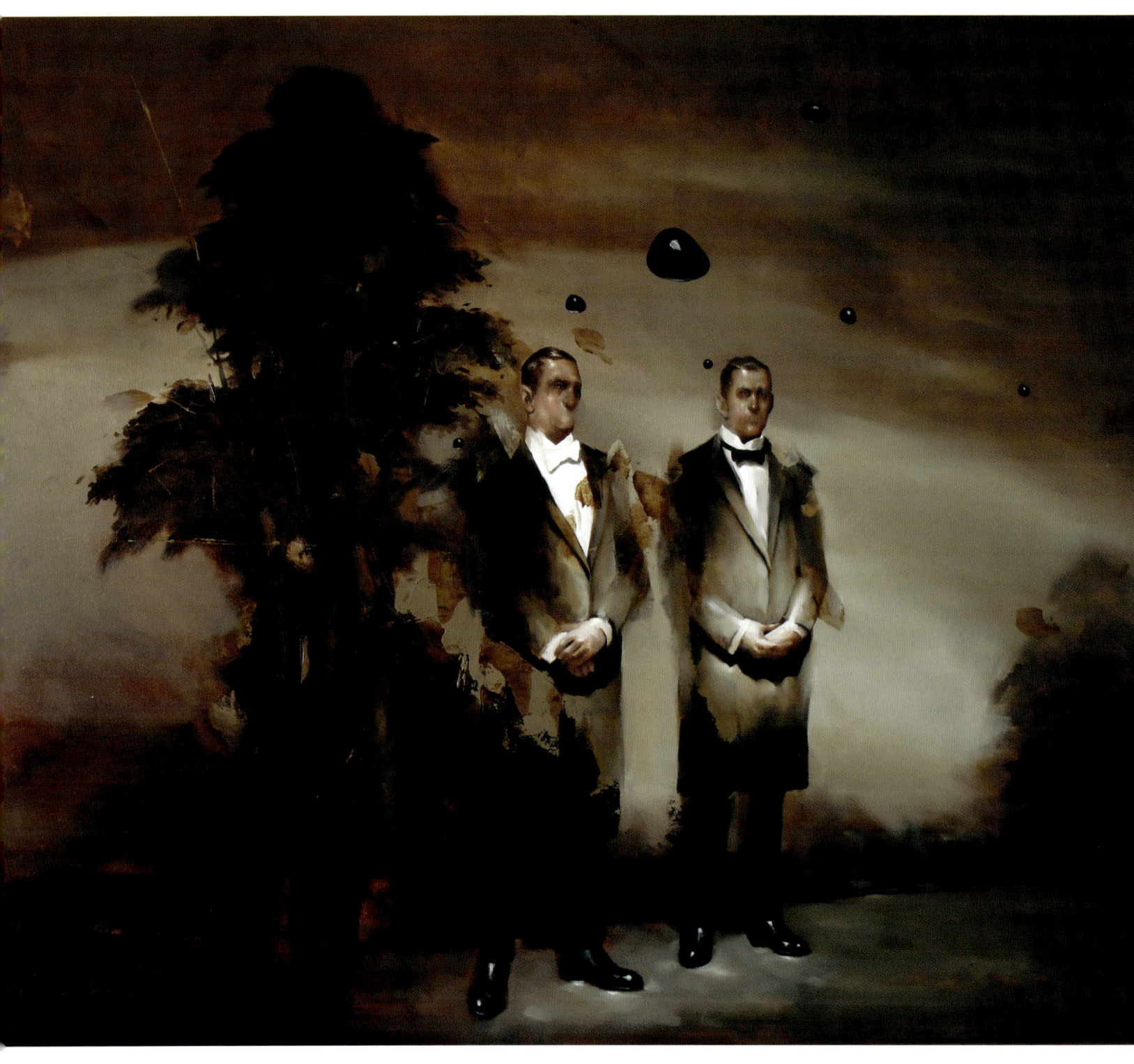

Radu Belcin. *Vanished into Time,* 2014.
Oil on linen: 47.2 × 55.9 inches.

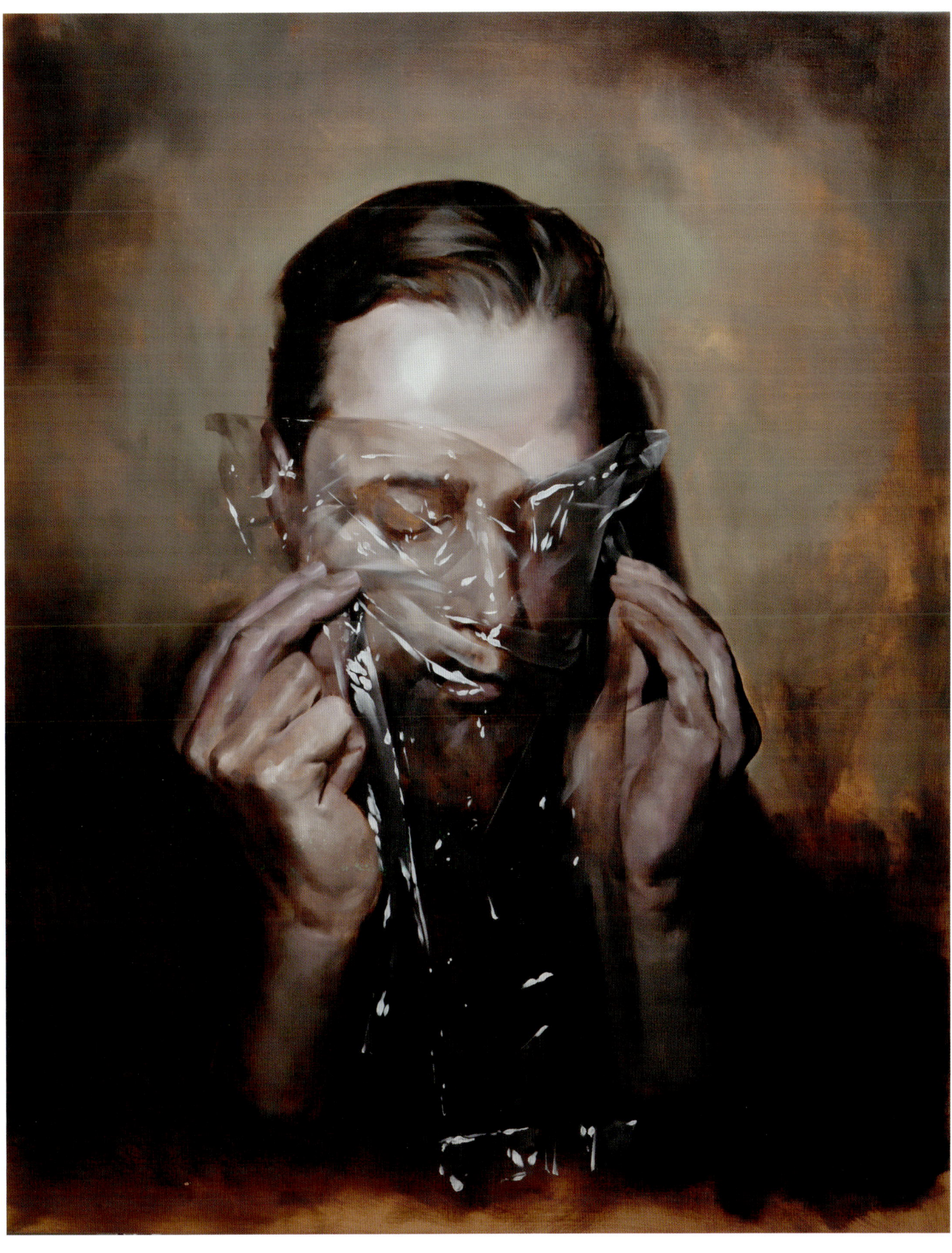

Radu Belcin. *Find Me Where I'm Hiding,* 2015.
Oil on linen: 55.9 × 44.9 inches.

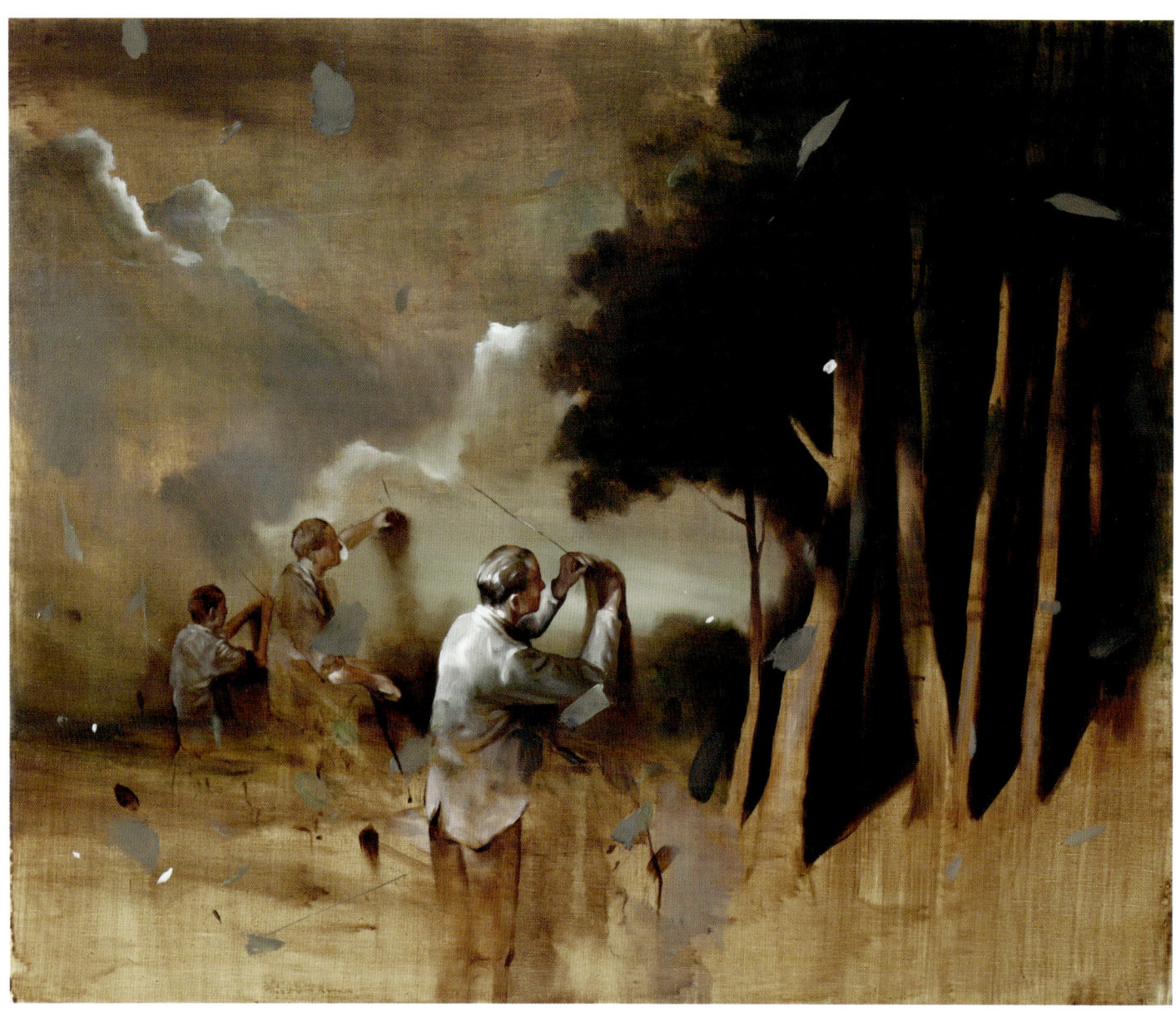

Radu Belcin. *Lessons for Catching Memories,* 2015.
Oil on linen: 24.8 × 28.7 inches.

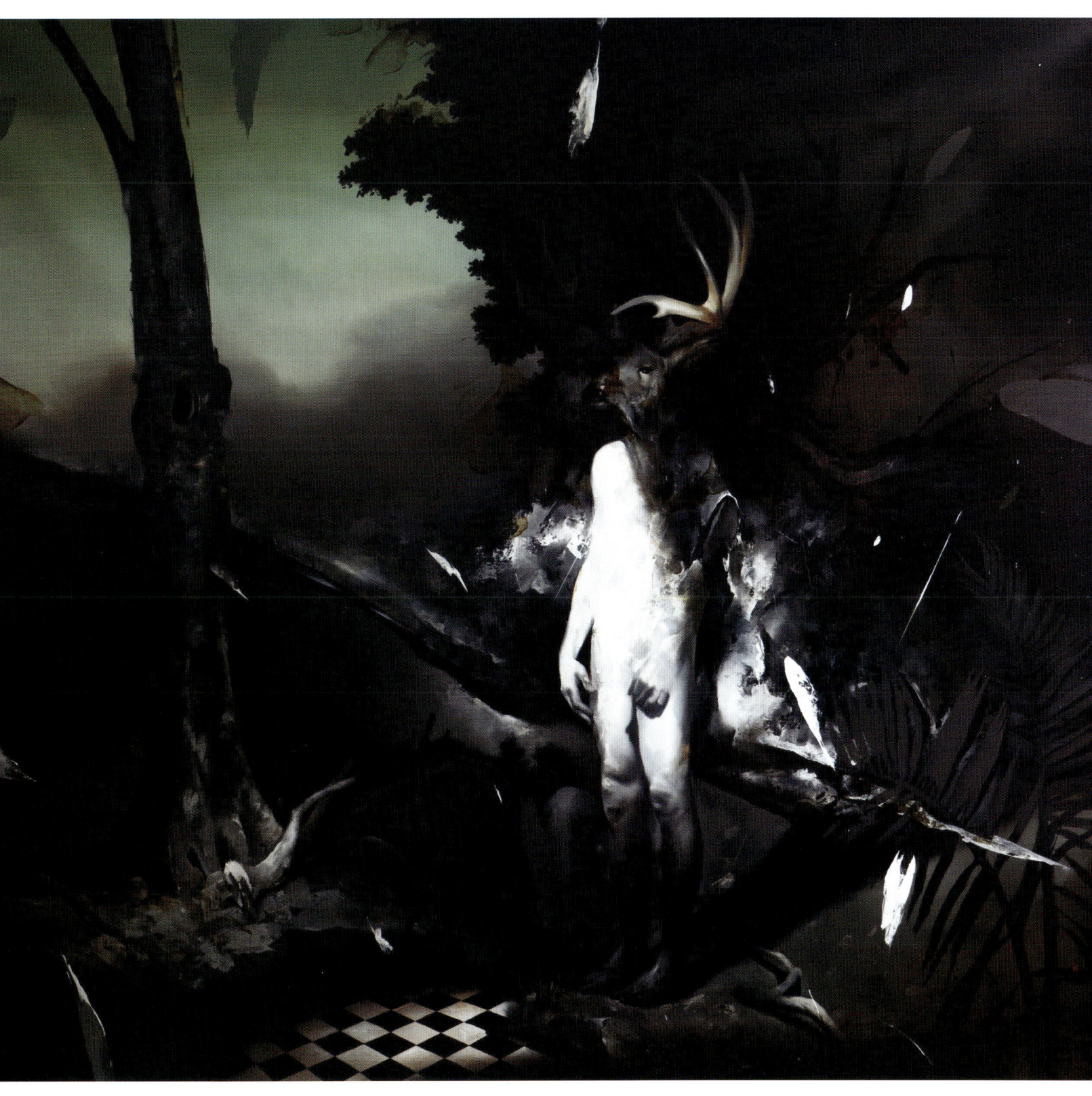

Radu Belcin. *Nightfall,* 2016.
Oil on linen: 66.9 × 74.8 inches.

MIA
BERGERON

Lives and Works in: Chattanooga, Tennessee

Education: Rhode Island School of Design;

Charles H. Cecil Studio, Florence, Italy

Selected Collections: The Bennett Collection, the Dial Collection

Representation: Robert Lange Studios, Charleston,

South Carolina

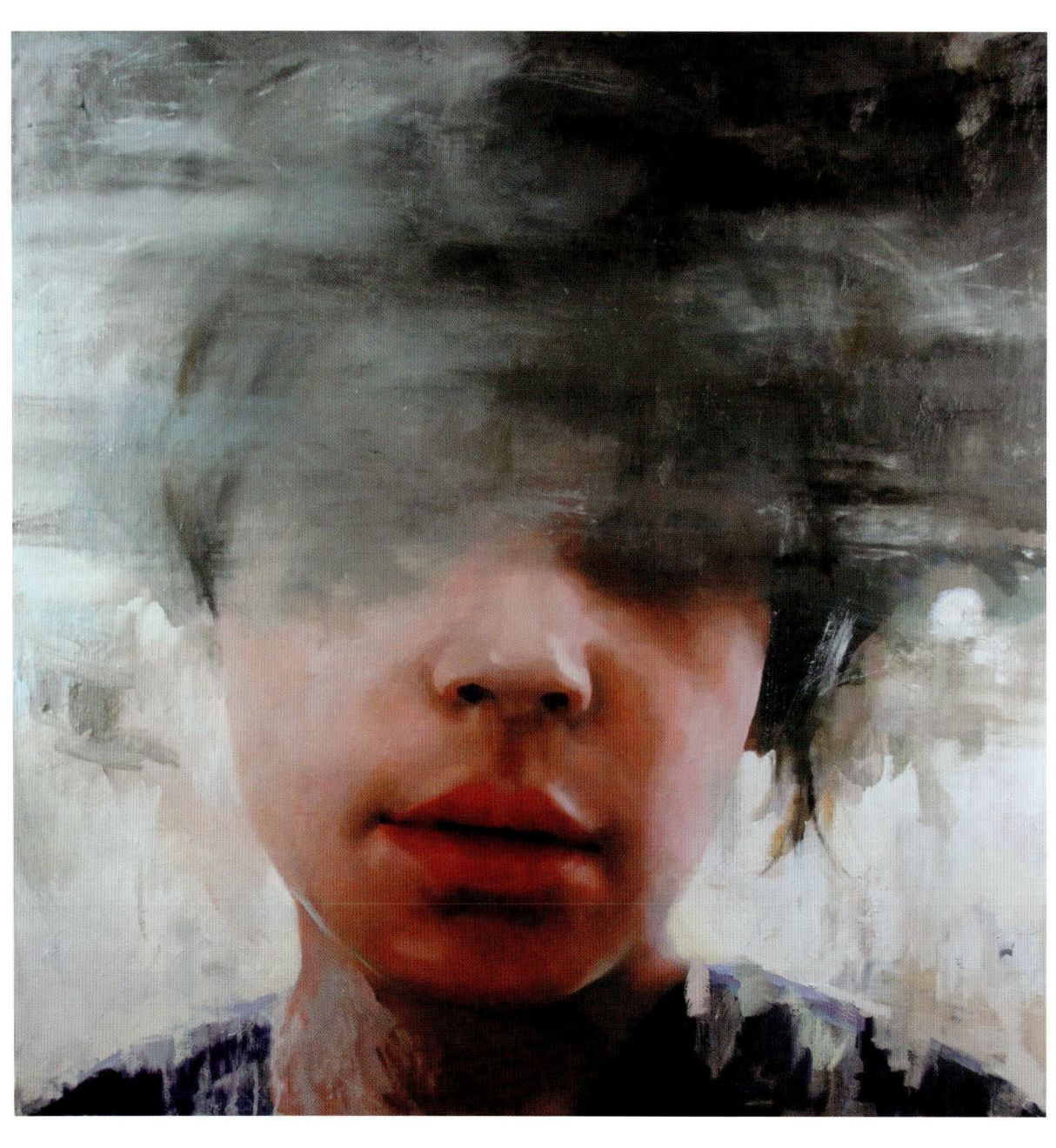

*My paintings depict the introspective
wanderings of my eyes and mind.*

**How and why does your work disrupt
or deviate from traditional realism?**

Traditional realism today seems to uphold clarity as one of its main strategies for engaging viewers. Realism also seems to value just how much it can say, often focusing on technique to portray a vision or story. I believe my work deviates from this idea in that I often seek to camouflage the details and story, sometimes obliterating them altogether. My goal is rarely to simply employ technique or achieve clarity. For me, painting is a strange back and forth—a conversation—in which the work in progress sometimes tells me what needs to be said and what needs to go unsaid.

**How has your work evolved and
developed over time?**

I was trained as a realist portraitist in Italy between 2002 and 2005. Although I had some of the best technical training available, I knew I would drop much of it in order to satisfy my own questions about expression. I feel my work has evolved considerably since then, both in terms of narrative and in how I am actually stating these ideas. My method of working has also evolved. Originally I worked to say something in a painting as clearly as I knew how. Today most of my paintings are questions that sometimes I ask successfully, while failing valiantly at other times.

**What are some of the influences
that have shaped your work?**

My work has been shaped by watching nature and also by observing my own life, the lives of my peers, and my place in history as a figurative female painter working today.

**Mention something interesting
about your life or background.**

I grew up speaking French as a first language until I was about six years old. My parents are both French Canadians, and before they switched entirely into an English-speaking life, our home was a small oasis of Québécois French.

Mia Bergeron. *Loss*, 2013.
Oil on panel: 40 × 40 inches.

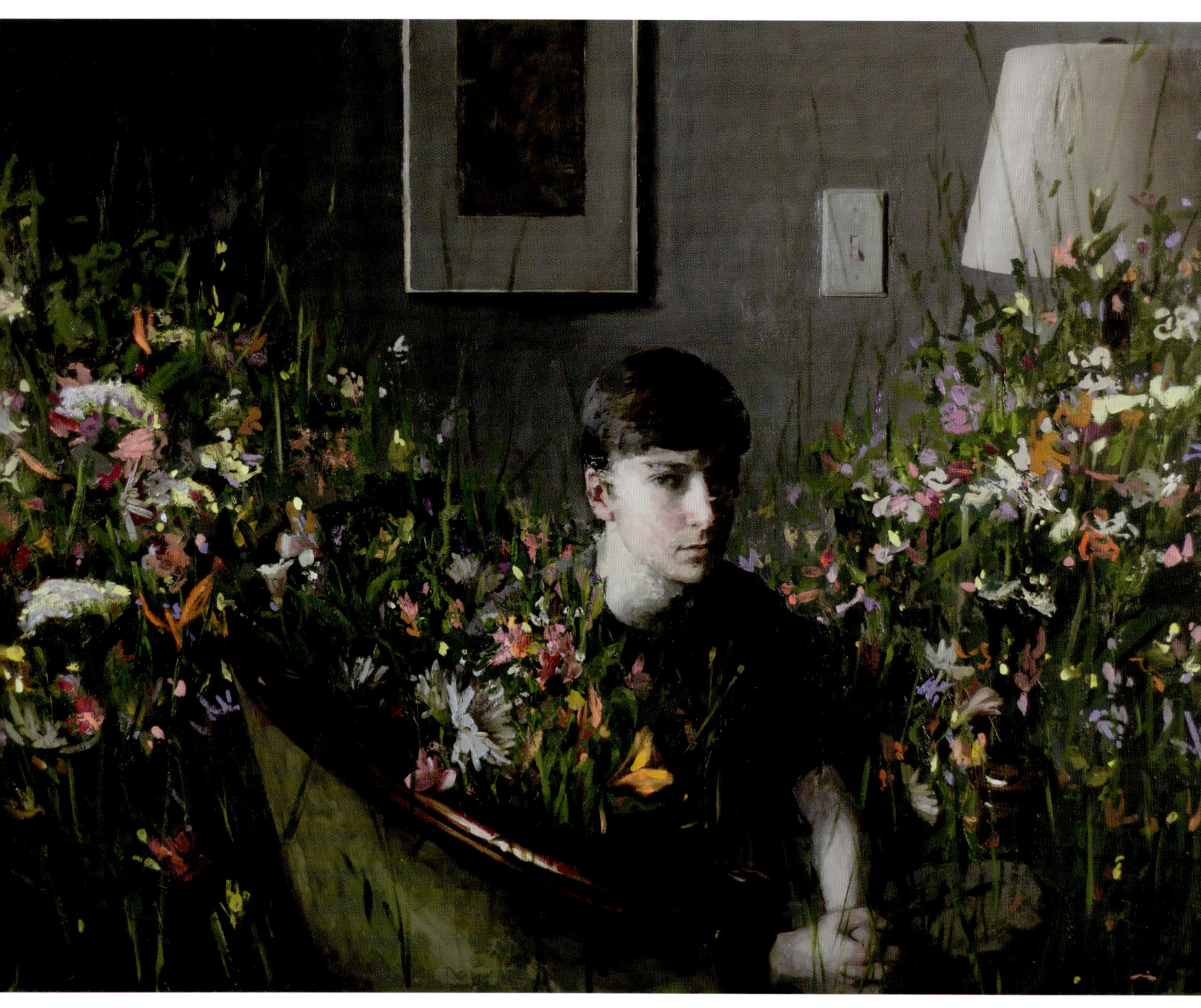

Mia Bergeron. *Outside In*, 2017.
Oil on aluminum: 48 × 36 inches.

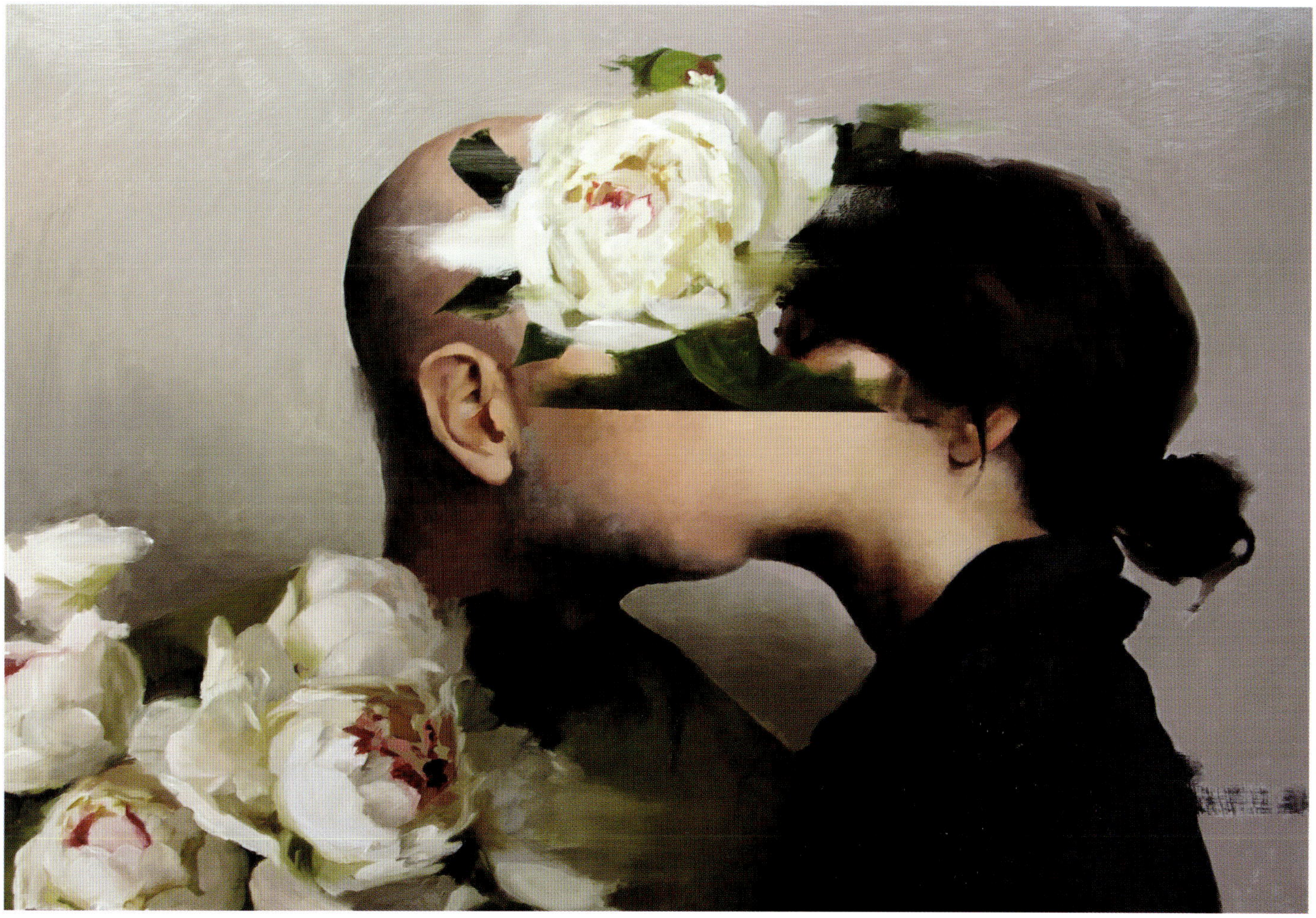

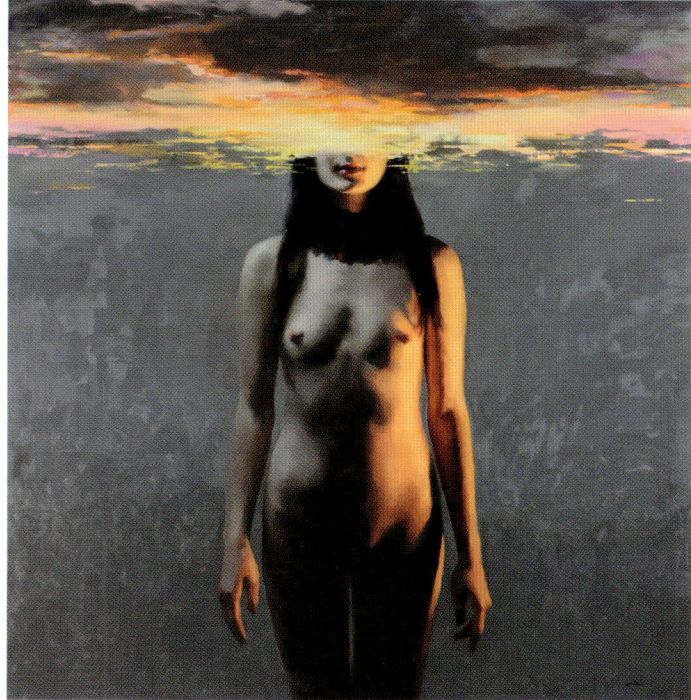

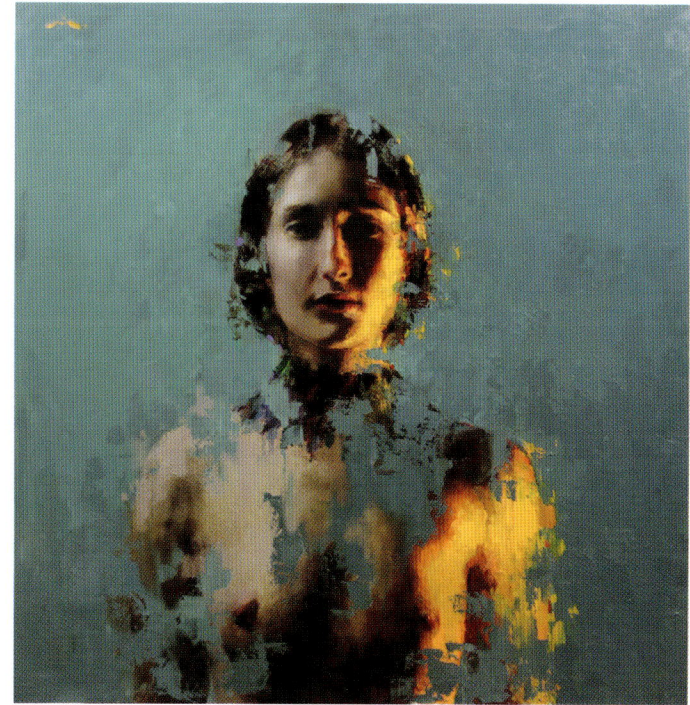

Top: Mia Bergeron. *Sanctuary*, 2016.
Oil on panel: 13.5 × 20 inches.

Mia Bergeron. *The Truce*, 2016.
Oil on panel: 40 × 40 inches.

Mia Bergeron. *Resolved*, 2015.
Oil on panel: 24 × 24 inches.

KAREN KAAPCKE

Lives and Works in: New York

Education: MA in philosophy, SUNY Binghamton, New York; Art Students League, New York

Selected Collections: Private collections in the United States and overseas

Representation: The Artist Study, Southampton, New York

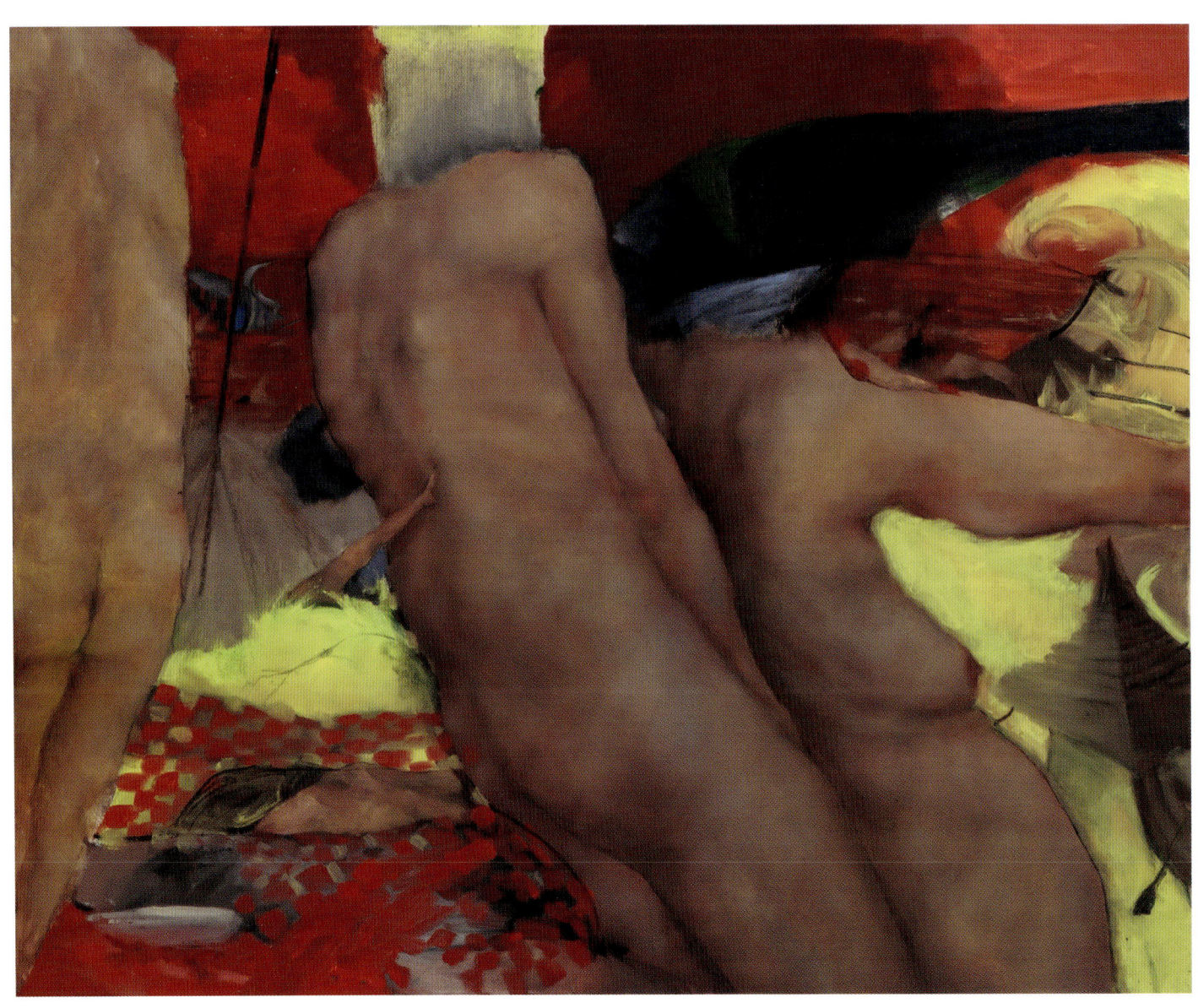

I use my training in classical figuration to create metaphorical works, mainly from memory and imagination.

How and why does your work disrupt or deviate from traditional realism?

While still working observationally, I noticed that I was able to retrieve memories or recall dreams when I was very focused, and I used this practice to begin two important series of paintings. One series featured images of my mother—who died when I was younger—while another depicted a young boy who was very close to our family and who died suddenly. Working on these two series opened up the realization that painting is, essentially, a bringing to presence of absence, more than a reproduction of presence. I began to think about visual ideas as opposed to verbal/literal ideas, of "aesthetic correctness" instead of or along with "anatomical correctness," which allows for the presentation of a nonverbal, deeper truth. The majority of my work is now done from memory and imagination. I see the space in the painting functioning as a visual language: the elements in the painting, being knowable, being "correct" when they need to be, become part of the language.

How has your work evolved and developed over time?

I initially studied classical technique and abstraction, but after a trip to Madrid—where I viewed the works of Velásquez, Goya, and other Spanish masters—I became recommitted to figuration. I started working from live models, but that was never quite enough. I was always trying to work in other elements to say more. Then, after struggling with this new approach, I returned to working from life.

Then my son's dear friend died. I knew that if I was to paint anything, it needed to be this boy. I realized that painting is about absence—there is no verisimilitude other than to the necessary visual story—and in my work I can now do whatever it takes.

What are some of the influences that have shaped your work?

Rodin and Michelangelo jump-started my work. I am currently looking at a lot of early Renaissance painting, Enguerrand Quarton and Della Francesca. I like Diebenkorn, Guston, and Giacometti. I value Kiki Smith for her serious play and like several recent figurative artists: Lucien Freud and Paula Rego in particular. Joan Mitchell and Robert Ryman have been important abstract artists for me. Another big influence was the artist Sidney Goodman. Toward the end of my studies I saw his work in a gallery, and it knocked me off my feet. I am also influenced by poetry.

Mention something interesting about your life and background.

I fully intended to pursue my philosophy studies through the PhD level; however, while getting my MA, I for the first time developed issues with writing and took to drawing instead, when after seeing a book of Rodin's work in the library on a break I sensed immediate truth in his work.

Karen Kaapcke. *Elle Capitaine,* 2018.
Oil on panel: 24 × 30 inches.

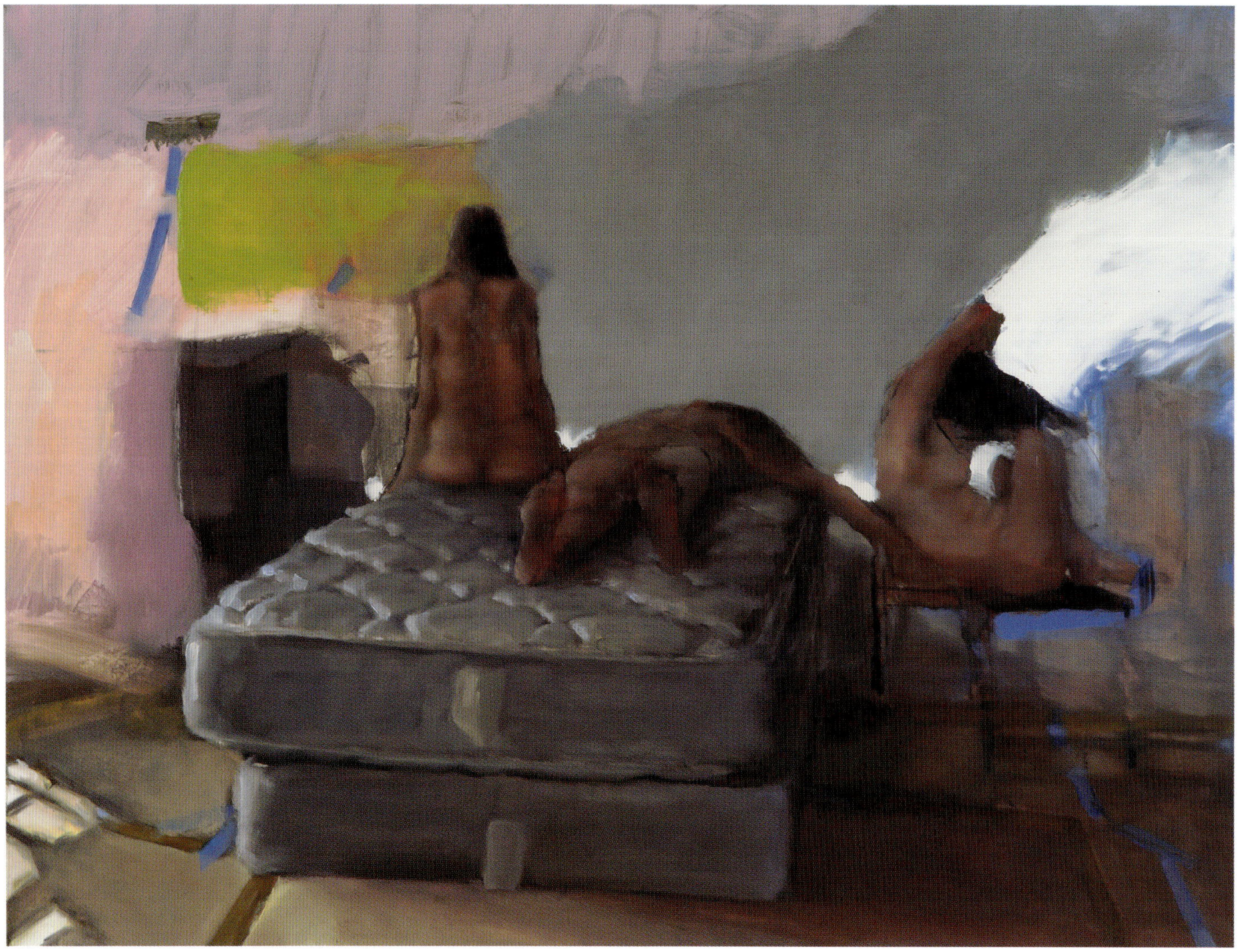

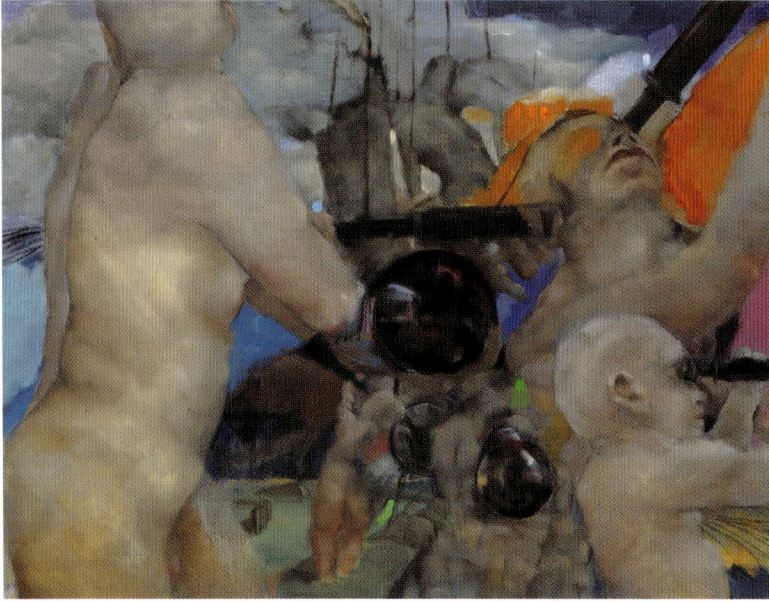

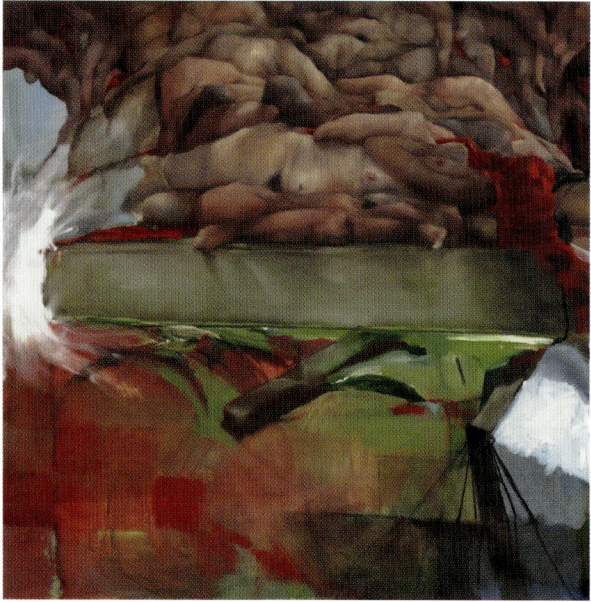

Top: Karen Kaapcke. *Mourning (Grief I)*, 2015.
Oil on linen: 18 × 24 inches.

Karen Kaapcke. *Oculus*, 2017–18.
Oil on canvas: 18 × 24 inches.

Karen Kaapcke. *Raft III (Moored)*, 2018.
Oil on canvas: 36 × 36 inches.

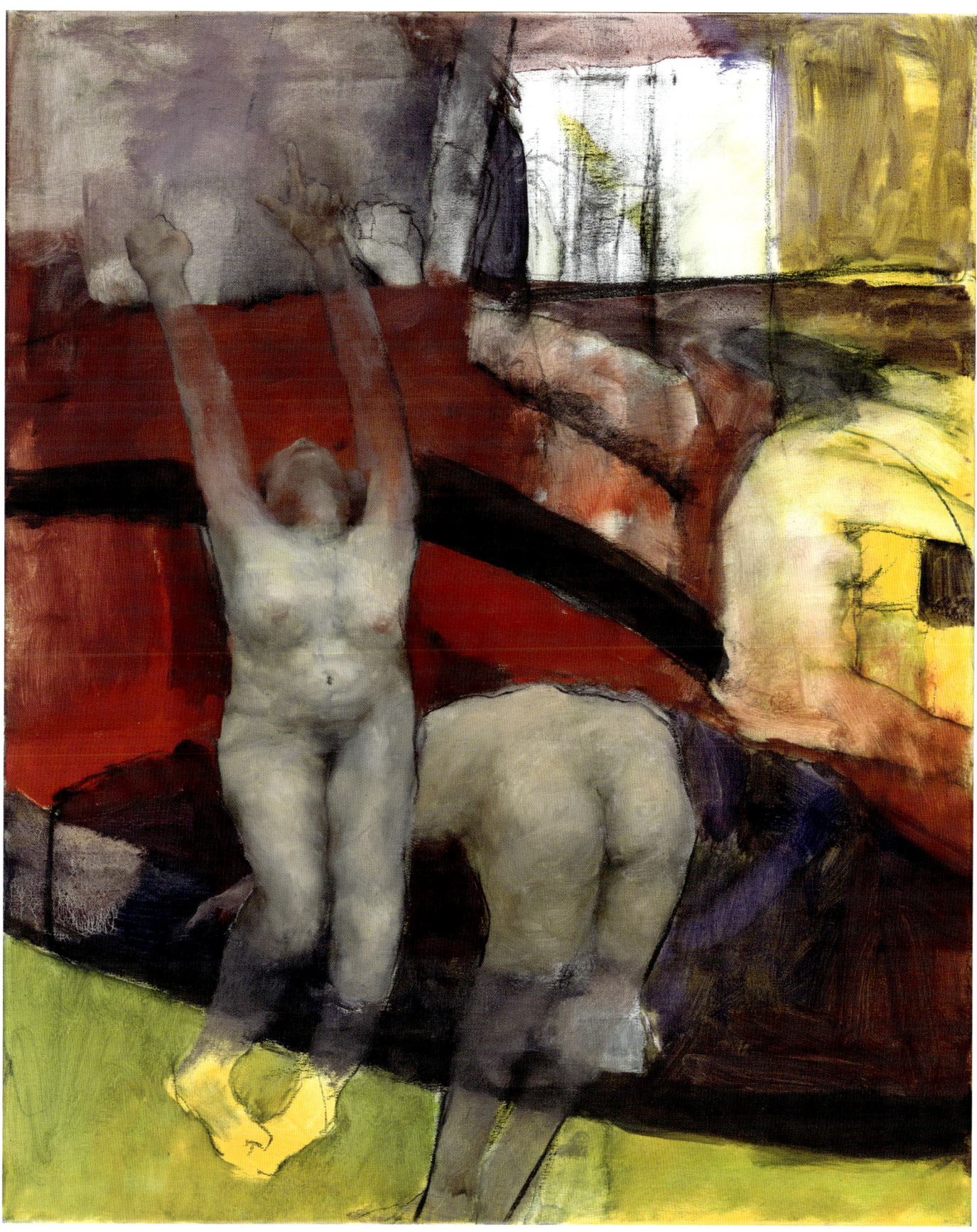

Karen Kaapcke. *Duet,* 2017.
Oil on linen: 23.6 × 19.7 inches.

STANKA KORDIC

Lives and Works in: Cleveland, Ohio
Education: The Cleveland Institute of Art
Collections: Cleveland Clinic, Key Bank (Cleveland), Simone and Oliver d'Oelsnitz (London)
Representation: Stanek Gallery, Philadelphia

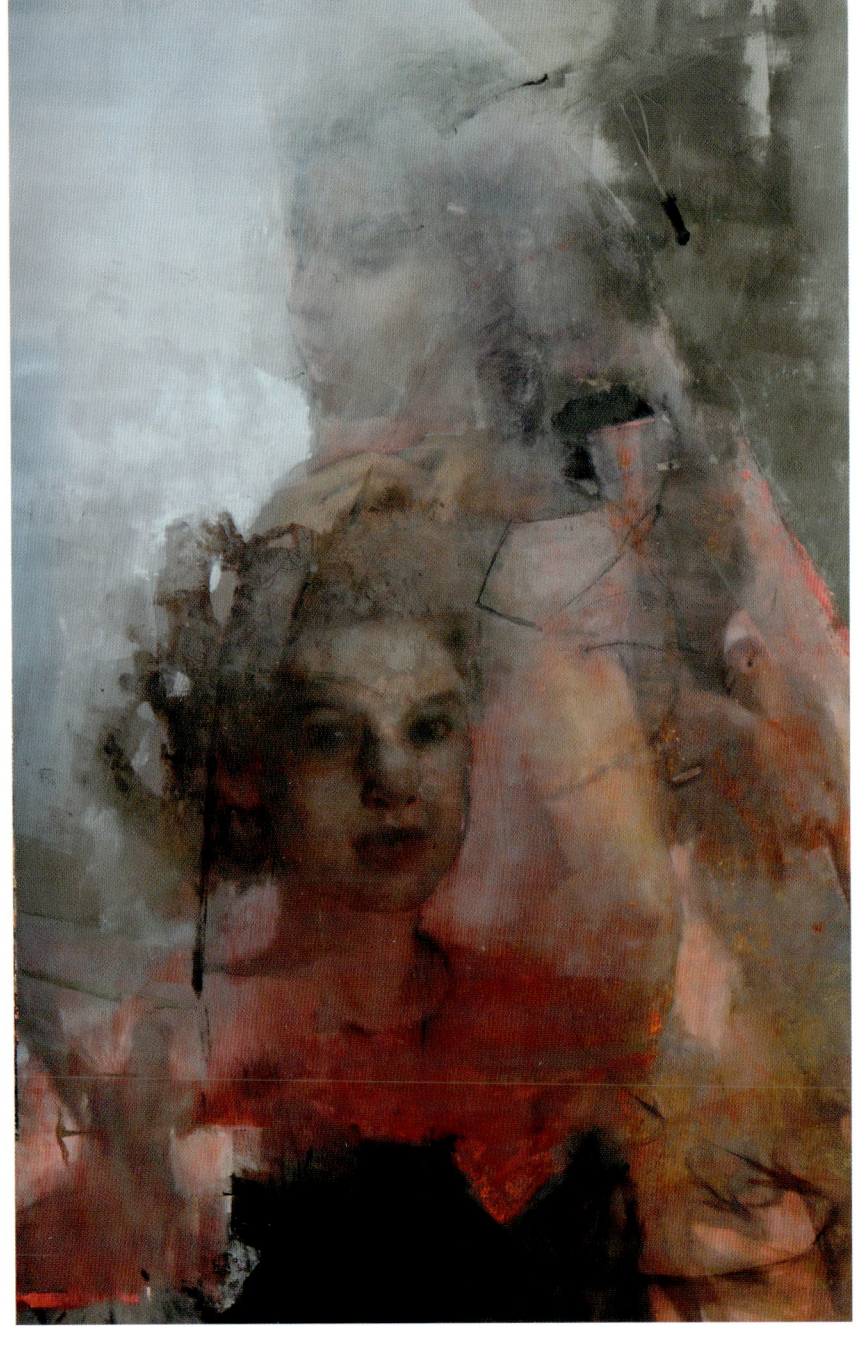

My paintings present a layered conversation of what is felt, observed, and revealed through the boundaries that figurative representation provides.

How and why does your work disrupt or deviate from traditional realism?

They start from straight-up realism as far as the figure goes in the first layer, with no conceptual thoughts as far as what I hope to achieve. I am primarily process driven. However, my time working with the model does affect things. I prefer using photos of that shoot, in order to better access my memory in bits and pieces on an emotional level, as well for the occasional logistics reasons. That particular human has an impact on the work, even though their exterior likeness may often change.

Then comes life with all its complexities and how that filters through me energetically. What and if anything gets "disrupted" is dependent on the moment and how I feel it. Each pass on the painting is different. Completion is agreed upon from not only a place of balance designwise, but from that intuitive space, using whatever means to get there. But that too can change. I have often removed the final varnish and come back to the piece after some time. It drives me batty but has frequently been a positive result.

How has your work evolved and developed over time?

My traditional methods began shifting when my curiosity about what paint can do took over. I became fascinated with the idea of using nontraditional tools for mark making. The concerns I had about accuracy moved to that intuitive place, where realism is not my primary goal anymore. The story of the paint has become more important to me than the initial inspiration the image triggered.

What are some of the influences that have shaped your work?

My curious nature. My stubborn nature. Time spent in museums during college. A history of drawings (starting from childhood) featuring females as power figures. My recent need to "color outside the lines," which was lying dormant in me for a looong time (I was educated by Catholic nuns . . . LOL).

My early morning yoga practice. A good work ethic. Persistence. My introverted personality. Keeping journals. Time outdoors without gadgets. A strong support system of family and friends.

Mention something interesting about your life and background.

Both of my brothers are artists too, and my parents have no idea from whom it sprang . . . they were simple Croatian farmers from Herzegovina.

I almost became someone's terrible secretary until a little nun veered my course to art when I was fifteen. She needed to convince my parents that this was a good thing.

Stanka Kordic. *See the Light without Looking,* 2016.
Oil on panel: 36 × 24 inches.

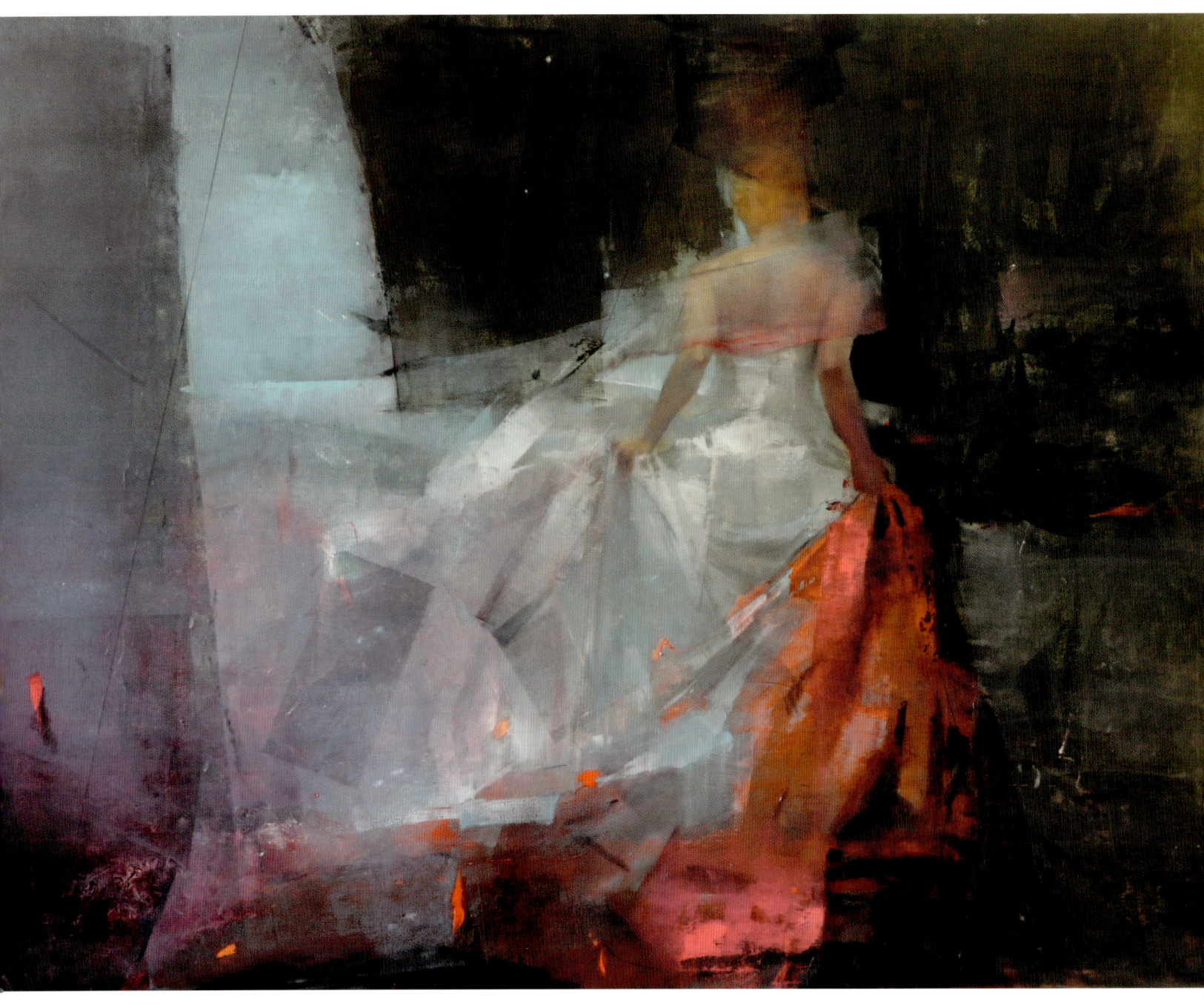

Stanka Kordic. *Bridges Turn #1,* 2017.
Oil on birch panel: 36 × 48 inches.

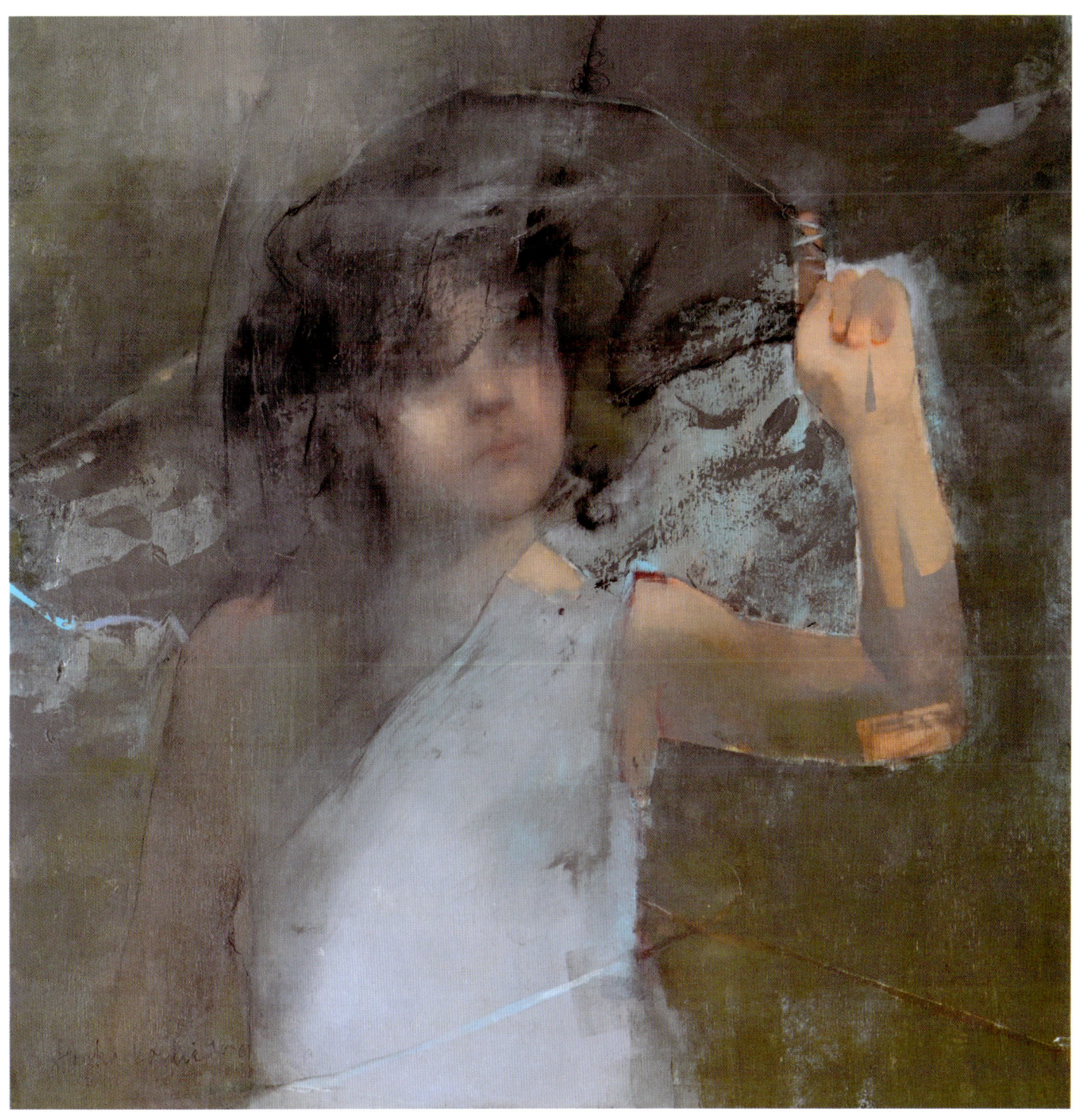

Stanka Kordic. *Caught*, 2016.
Oil on birch panel: 24 × 24 inches.

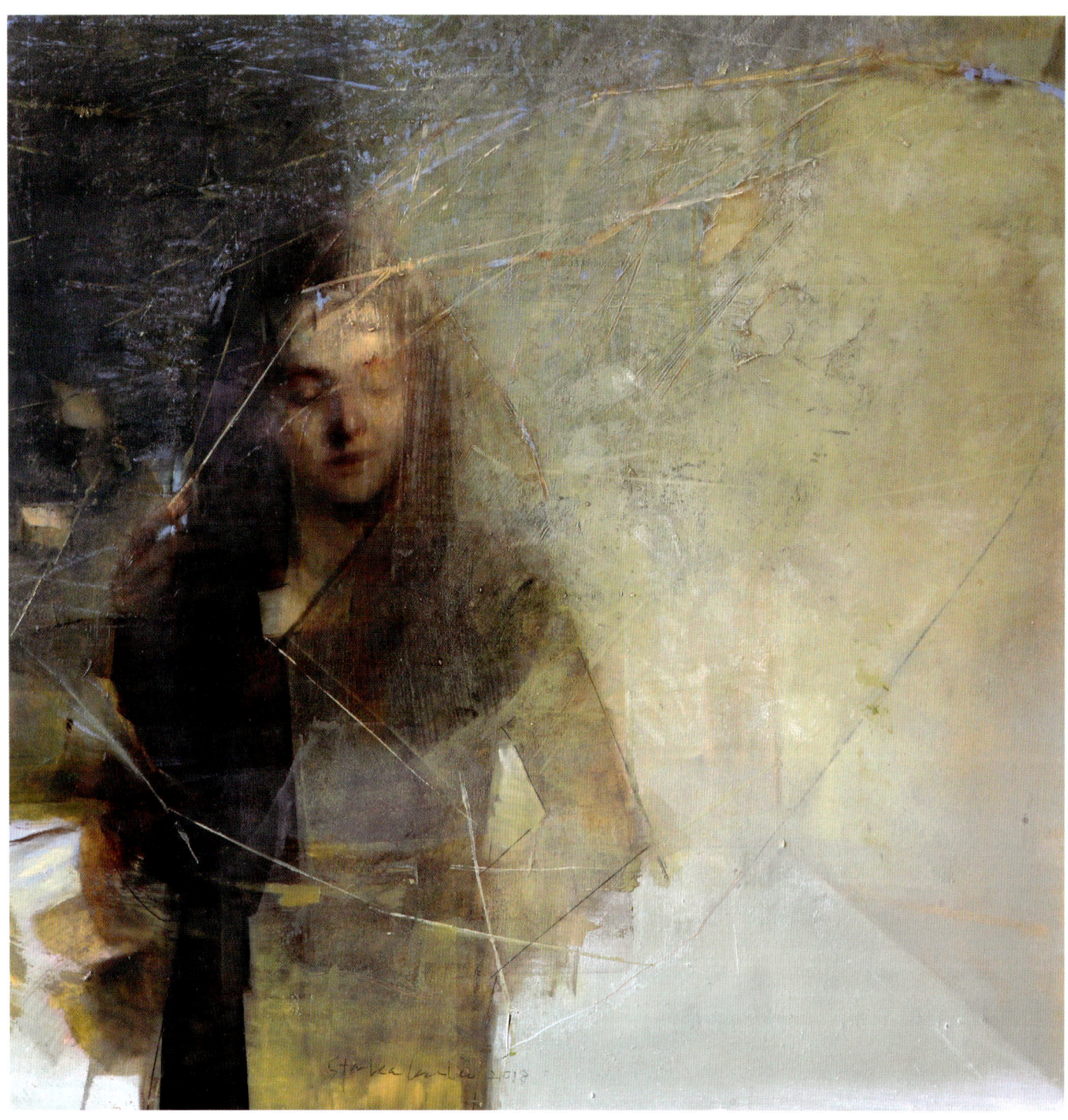

Stanka Kordic. *Discernment,* 2018.
Oil on birch panel: 36 × 36 inches.

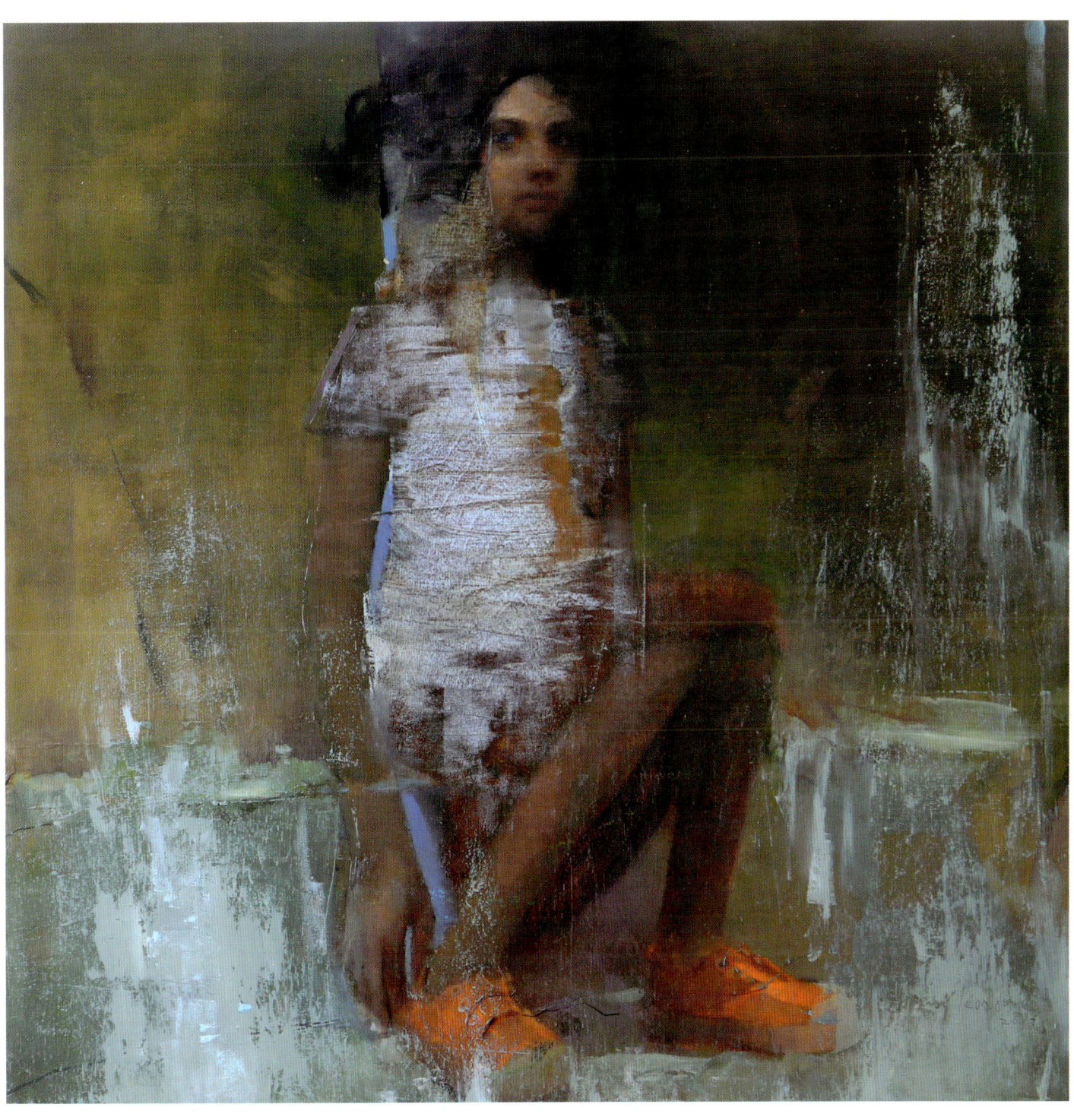

Stanka Kordic. *Surge,* 2017.
Oil on birch panel: 30 × 30 inches.

MARIA KREYN

Lives and Works in: Brooklyn, New York
Education: Math/philosophy, University of Chicago

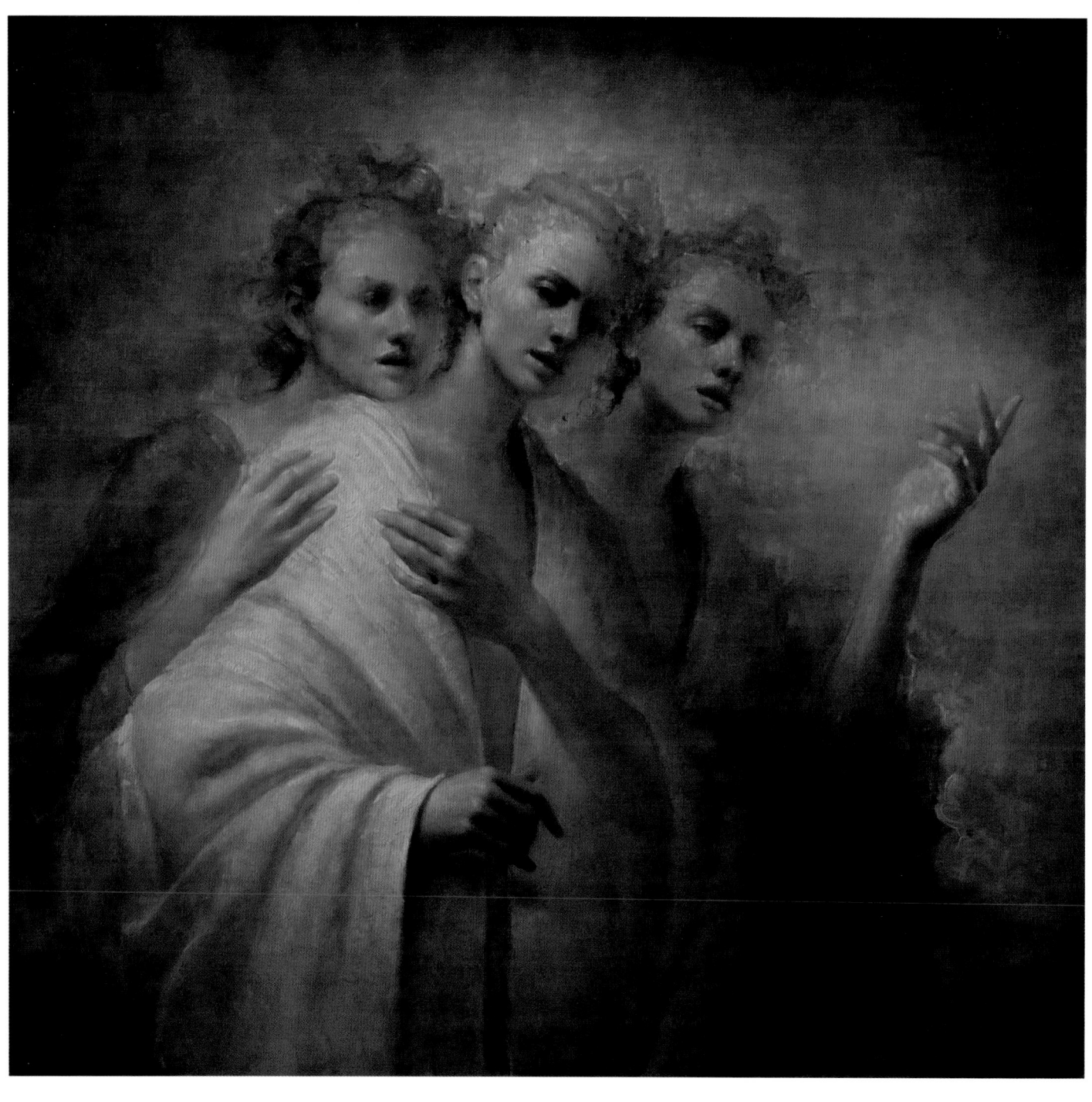

I want you to feel moved.

How and why does your work disrupt or deviate from traditional realism?

It's hard for me to conceptualize the category of traditional realism, or realism at all. Perhaps all realism is disrupted realism: a mediated, filtered version of our physical vision, emotional landscape, and personal mythscape. The boundary of the concept "realism" is fuzzy at best and serves art history more than it serves art or the artist. It implies the notion of represented things to look like the things in the world. But this boundary is so ill defined, and now even the science of perception would corroborate its lack of clarity.

My paintings rely on illusionistic space, and also on contradicting it. They rely on representation of people and objects, yet also on cognitive dissonance. I use the visual language of allegory, but I scramble the symbolic order, begging of the viewer to "read" the image, but leaving the narrative forever open ended.

How has your work evolved and developed over time?

At first, illusionistic space was my main concern, and I privileged it in terms of how I understood painting or art at large. Over time I've become more interested in the way the oil paint simply sits on the canvas, and in its often-erratic physics. Though my images are largely depictions or interpretations of what one might see in the world, I have come to define my compositions not only by the what, but by the how—by the sensuality, structure, and architecture of the paint itself on the surface, capitalizing on randomness and abstraction to aid in revealing a familiar form.

What are some of the influences that have shaped your work?

I use the visual language of the baroque and filter it through my own experience in the world to make my work. A combination of citation, mash-up, personal reference, and abstractly encoded personal philosophy and mythology all collide in my painting. I'm inspired by Masaccio, Caravaggio, Rodin, Neo Rauch, Michel Borremans, and David Altmejd, and the list goes on. In all of what has shaped me, I find both a gentleness and a violence, a deep sensitivity somehow coupled with intensity, or even aggression. I love complex, moving work that signals at once both destruction and rebirth.

Mention something interesting about your life and background.

I come from a family of polymaths, and my education has been fairly diverse. I dabbled in math and philosophy at university, and the ideas gleaned there ultimately informed my painting practice, which was mostly self-guided as I did not attend art school.

Maria Kreyn. *Ghosts*, 2011.
Oil on canvas: 44 × 22 inches.

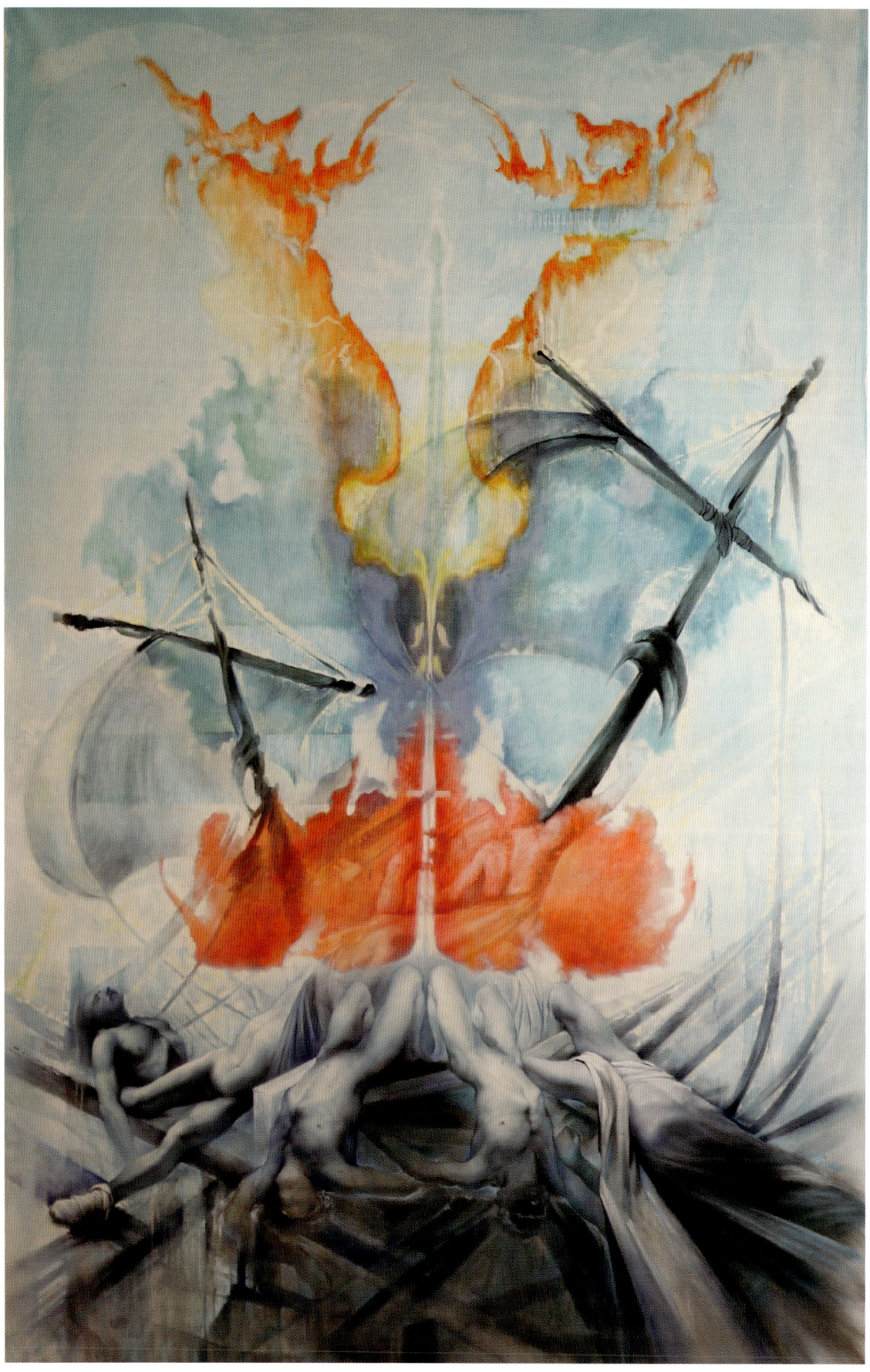

Maria Kreyn. *Cartography*, 2014.
Oil on canvas: 68 × 102 inches.

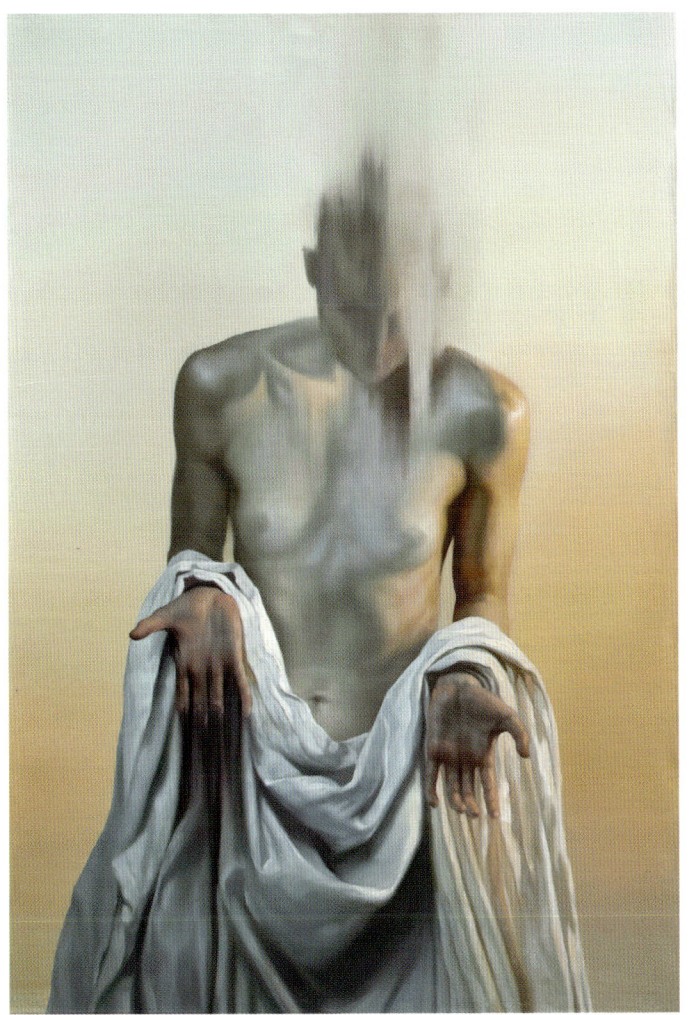

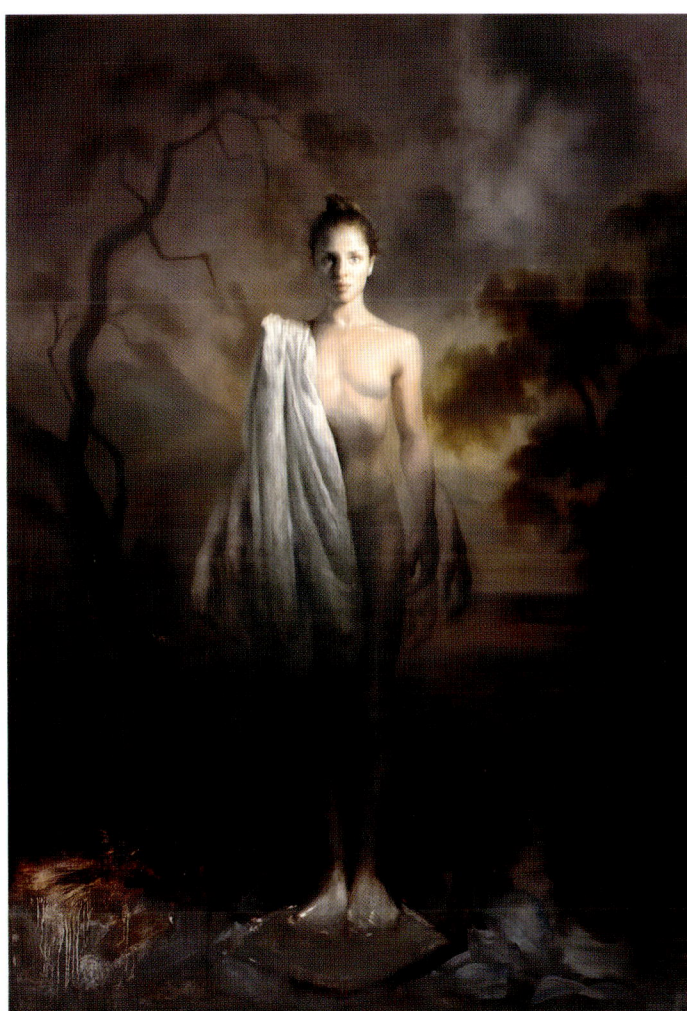

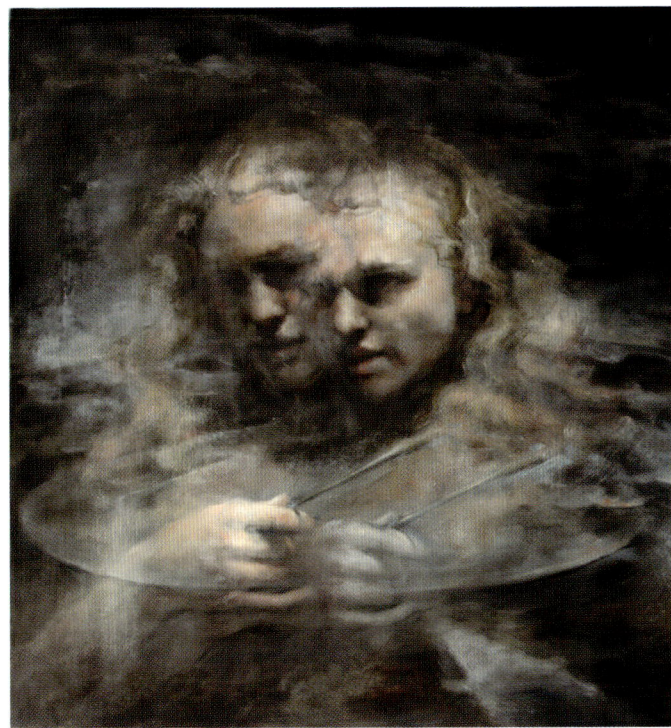

Maria Kreyn. *The Sieve*, 2018.
Oil on canvas: 42 × 60 inches.

Maria Kreyn. *The Solipsist*, 2018.
Oil on canvas: 42 × 60 inches.

Maria Kreyn. *Double Vision 1*, 2010.
Oil on canvas: 26 × 26 inches.

ALYSSA MONKS

Lives and Works in: Brooklyn, New York
Education: BA, Boston College; MFA, New York Academy of Art
Selected Collections: Seavest Foundation; Eric Fischl; Steven Bennet; Luciano Benetton; the Center for Contemporary Art, Bedminster, New Jersey; Savannah College of Art & Design Museum of Art; Howard Tullman; Fullerton College
Representation: Forum Gallery, New York

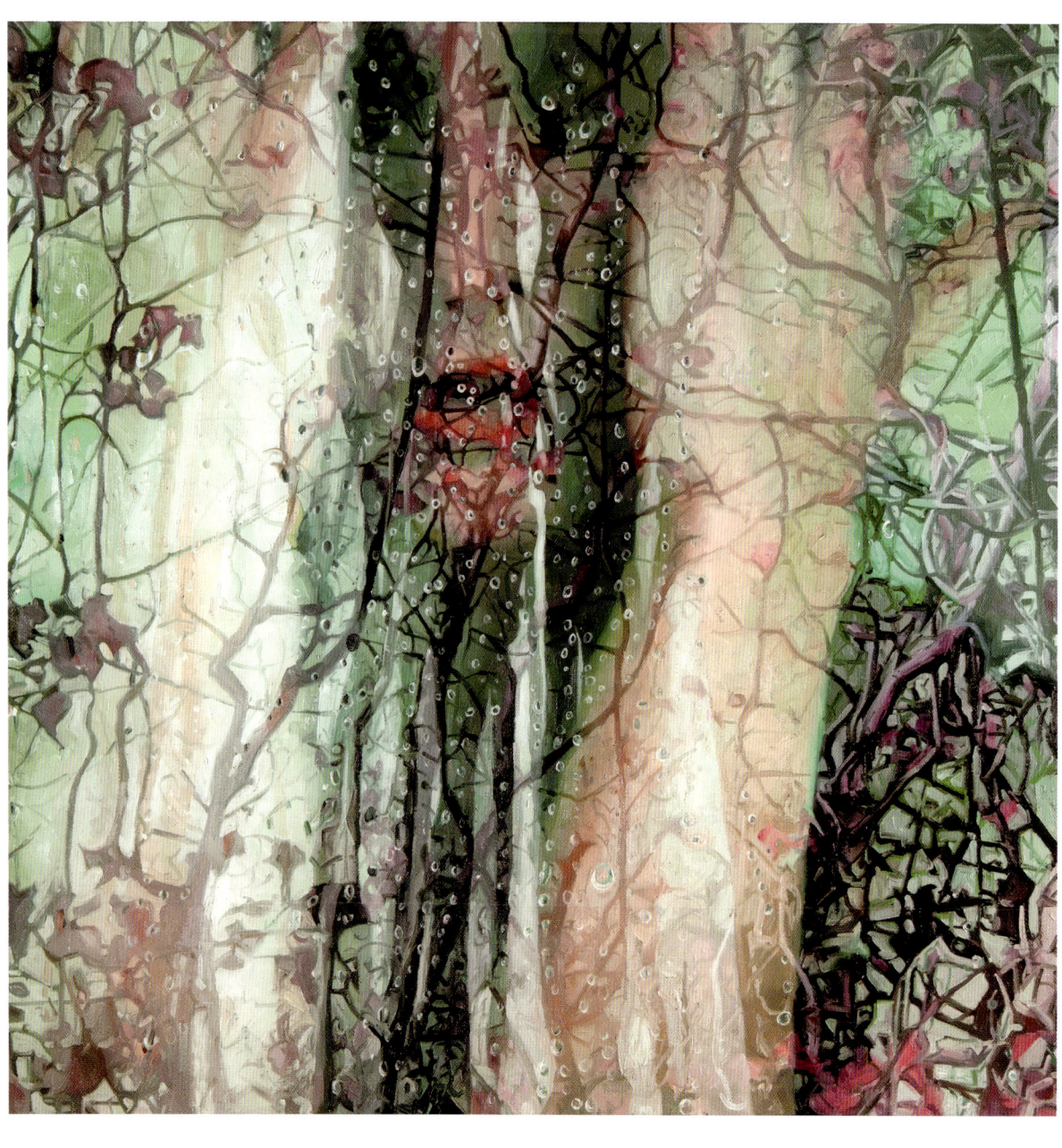

My works are realistic paintings
of abstract moments.

How and why does your work disrupt or deviate from traditional realism?

I went pretty far down the rabbit hole of realism at the New York Academy and for a few years post, after struggling for years to make paintings look real and what I thought was "serious." After getting to a certain point that felt "real" enough, I became attracted to experimenting with an *abstracted* reality, using different filters such as textured glass, plastic, water, steam, etc., to obfuscate the body and portrait. I found this to be actually a more effective way of presenting and exploring the "real" as it left so much open for the mind to connect to emotionally and cerebrally.

After ten years of that, I began to "layer realities," using landscape as a transparent "filter." Now I am pushing that further and inventing a color palette that is not of this world but is hopefully psychologically charged. I am no longer interested in a mimetic copy of reality as I once was, but rather I want to evoke the emotional and psychological experience of my subject as authentically and viscerally and as memorably as possible.

How has your work evolved and developed over time?

In addition to what I described above, my paint quality has evolved over time as well. As my images became less tied to reality, more surface texture appeared, getting more experimental over time, less predictable. There is less of a focus on rendering overall, less control, and more surprise and getting lost. I am curious about invention, rather than imitating reality.

What are some of the influences that have shaped your work?

In addition to the works of Egon Schiele, Gustav Klimt, Vincent Desiderio, Jenny Saville, and many other painters too numerous to name, I have often been influenced by film in terms of color and composition and how they work together to create a psychological impact and intrigue. The mystery that David Lynch creates in his films, using color as a character and simple composition, I find comparable to recent works such as in *The Handmaid's Tale*. The rawness of Nan Goldin's and Philip Lorca di Corcia's photography has also been impactful to me. Sally Mann's confrontational photography, and the experimentation in her later work, inspires me as well. The music and poetry of badass feminist musicians like Ani DiFranco and Natalie Merchant, the #MeToo movement, and all the brave women who have come forward to share their stories. And, of course, likely the biggest influence on me has been the humbling and grounding experience my mother's illness and death, through which the lessons of acceptance and presence of Buddhist teachings and meditation ushered me.

Mention something interesting about your life and background.

I am the youngest of eight kids, with six brothers between my sister and me. I started painting when I was eight. It helped me create a world of my own, and it became a very effective coping strategy and outlet throughout my formative years. I studied quite a bit of psychology in my college years, always fascinated and a little unsettled by the human psyche.

Alyssa Monks. *Tangled*, 2018.
Oil on linen: 30 × 30 inches.

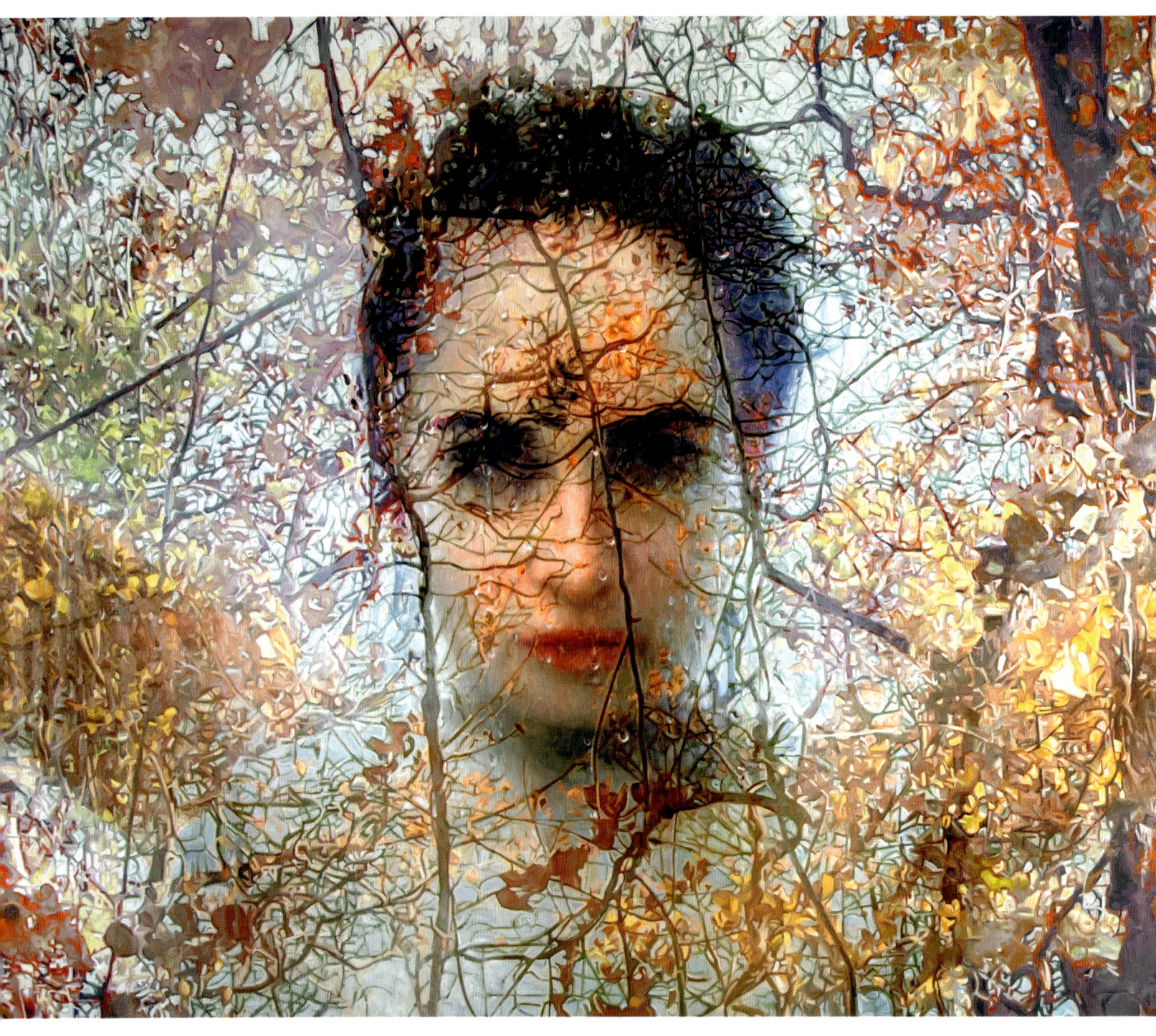

Alyssa Monks. *Elpis*, 2018.
Oil on linen: 68 × 86 inches.

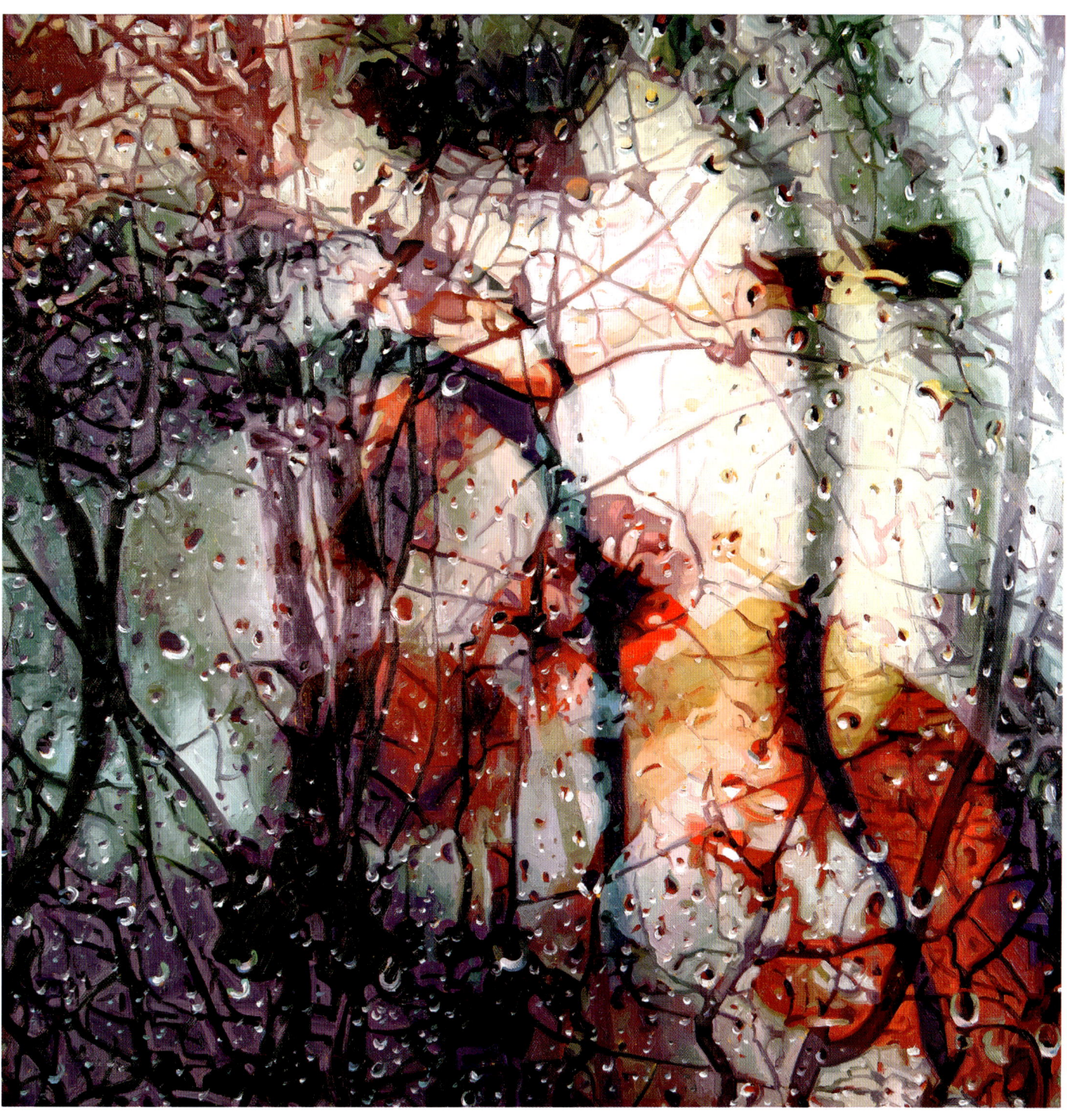

Alyssa Monks. *Mired,* 2018.
Oil on linen: 30 × 30 inches.

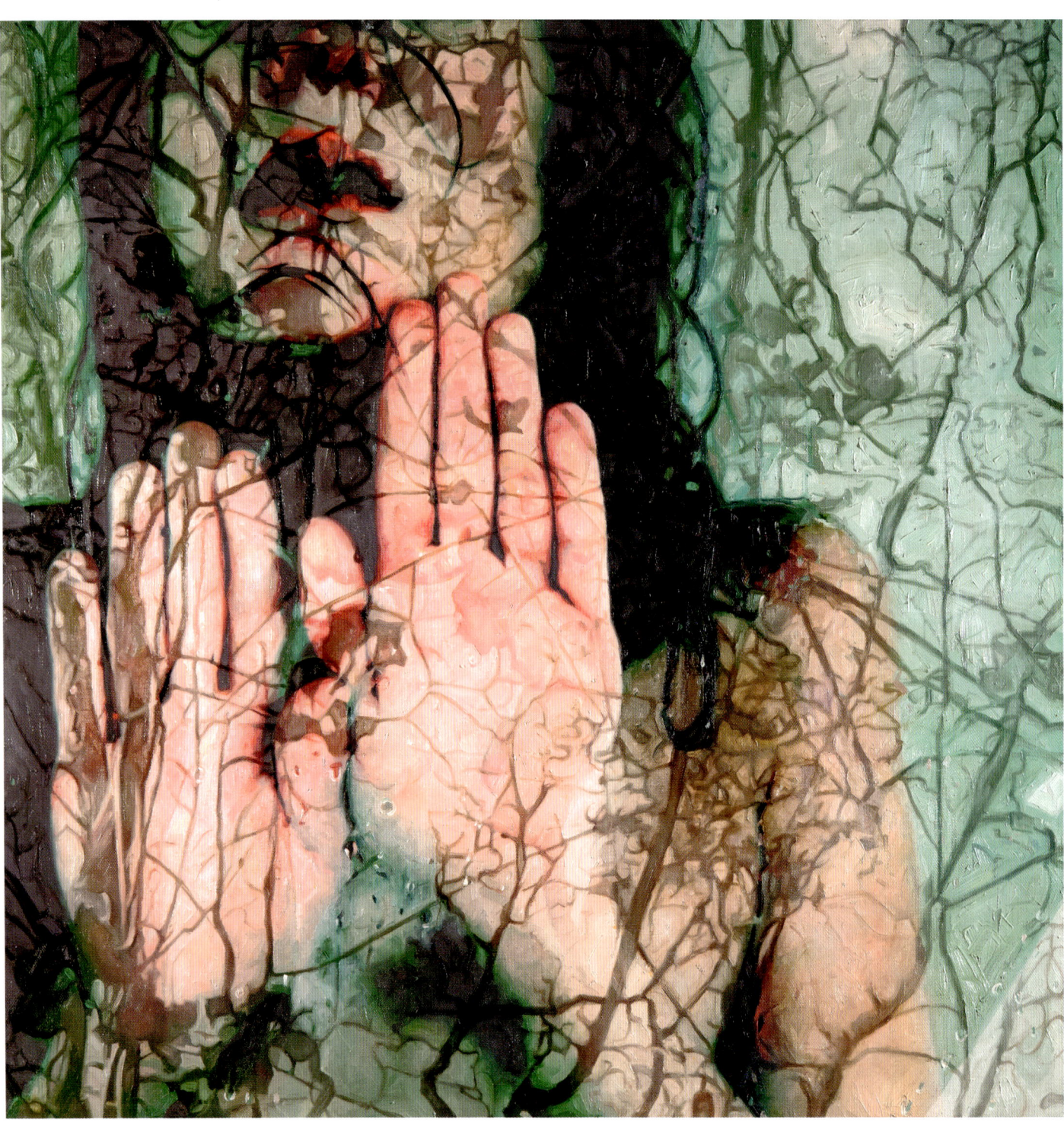

Alyssa Monks. *I Said No,* 2018.
Oil on linen: 36 × 36 inches.

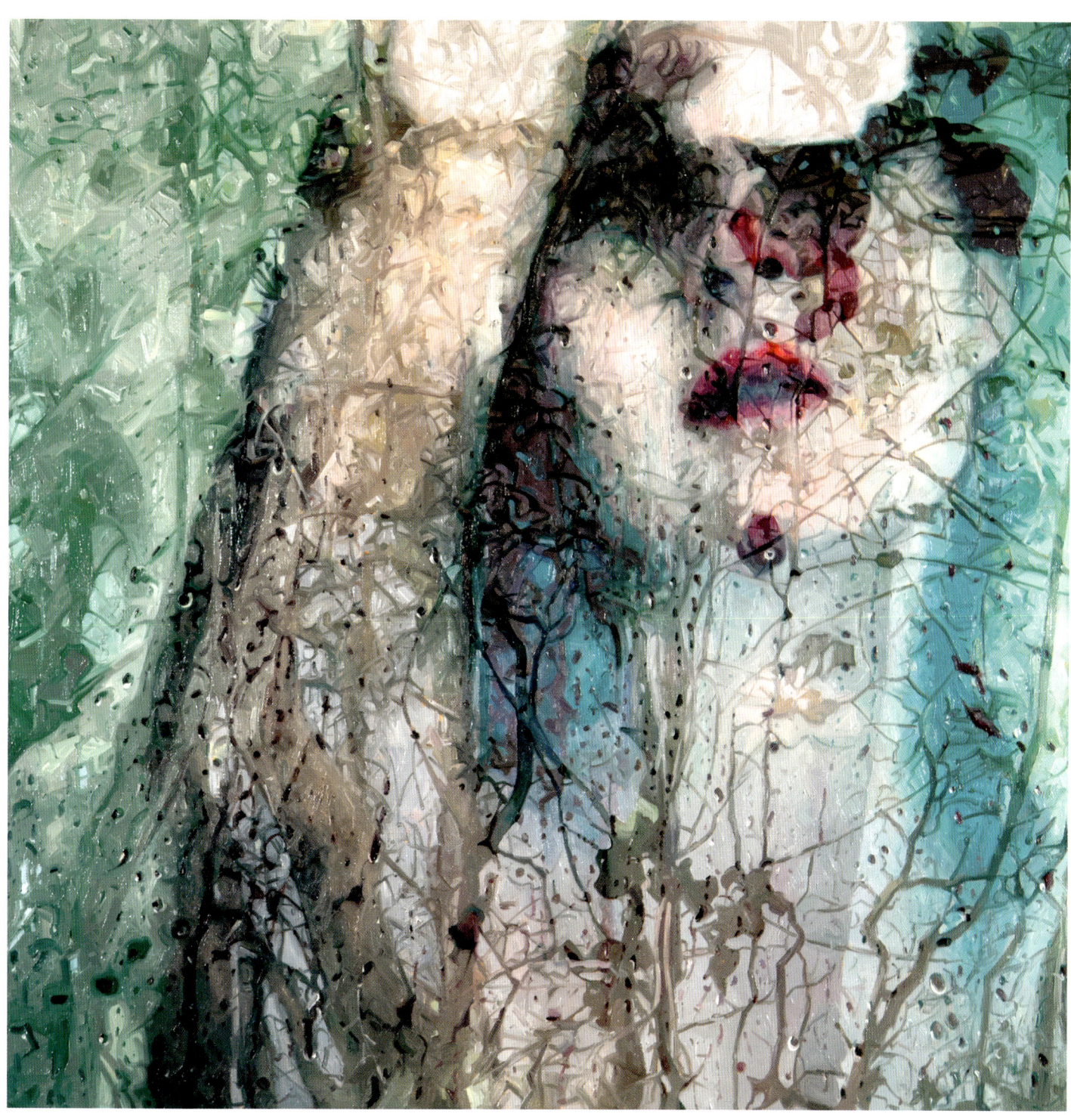

Alyssa Monks. *Wanting*, 2018.
Oil on linen: 40 × 40 inches.

LOU ROS

Lives and Works in: Paris
Selected Collections: Taittinger, Fleuriot
Representation: Dolby Chadwick Gallery, San Francisco

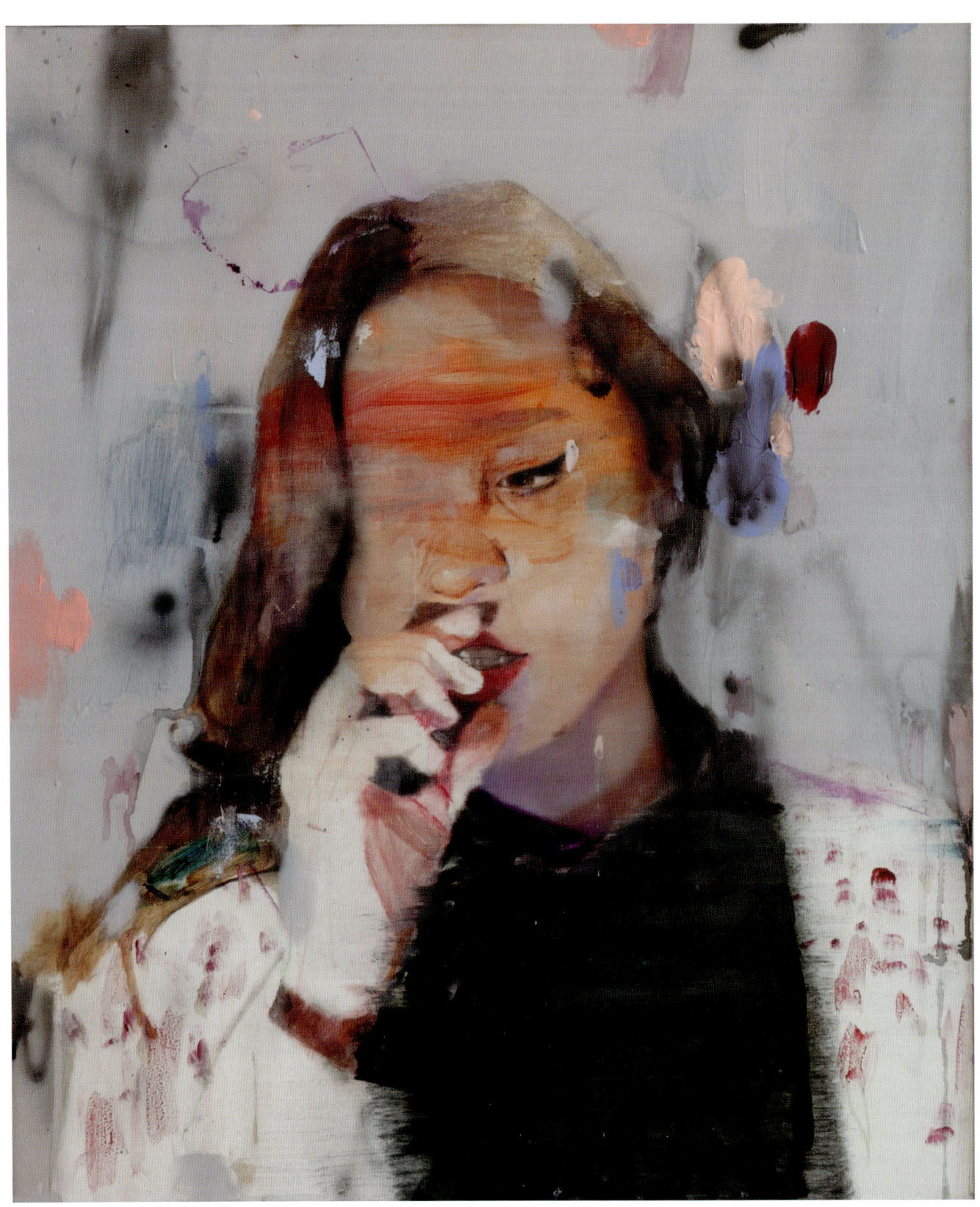

I search for the moment where a hint is enough to suggest a structure that interests me, leaving the imagination open at the moment when a scene is starting to appear. Then, I try to know when to stop before saying too much.

How and why does your work disrupt or deviate from traditional realism?

I often say that it's important for viewers to be able to construct, imagine, and complete their own image of a painting. That is why I would say my work deviates from traditional realism. It's because not everything in my work is fully realized. Some parts of my images are abstracted—changed from what I see—or even left unpainted. A part of my process initially trying to stay close to reality and then trying to go somewhere else.

How has your work evolved and developed over time?

I really think my work is evolving in a less realistic way. I'm trying to keep only the mood of the painting itself and let that do the job instead of the technique and the ability to fool the eye and the brain with a perfect realization of what one might say is a realistic painting. I'm not saying that realistic paintings only fool the eye, I simply mean that it's not what I am trying to do anymore. At the beginning I was worried that my collectors were looking for technique and the ability to paint something "well." After fifteen years of painting I would say that I am really using painting as a form of searching, rather than just concerning myself with the finished result.

What are some of the influences that have shaped your work?

It's funny because at first I was really influenced by the paintings of an artist that wasn't really described as a painter. It was Marcel Duchamp. I was really in admiration looking at his paintings. Then a big influence was the work of Francis Bacon; it was really a long time looking at his paintings, and still now I am really still crazy about his work. I think it's important at the beginning to admire some paintings, and it can influence your work for some time. But it's really a big step to be able to go forward and try to do your own research in the world of painting.

Mention something interesting about your life and background.

Well, if I can be honest: when I was a child I wasn't really hoping to be a painter. I didn't know what to do later in life. I was not particularly talented in drawing, but it's really something you can work on with practicing. So, everything is possible even if you don't know what you want to do at the beginning!

Lou Ros. *GP2*, 2016.
Acrylic, oil, and pastel on canvas: 22 × 18 inches.

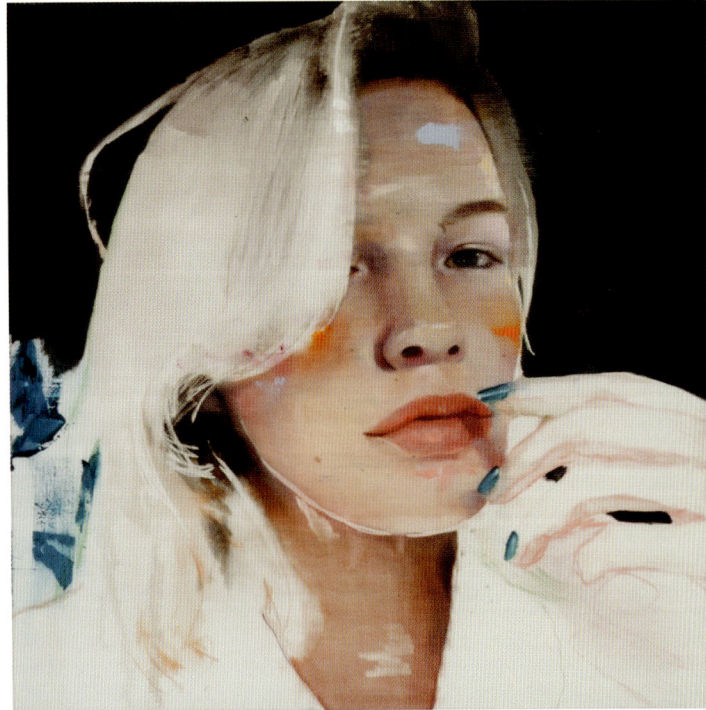

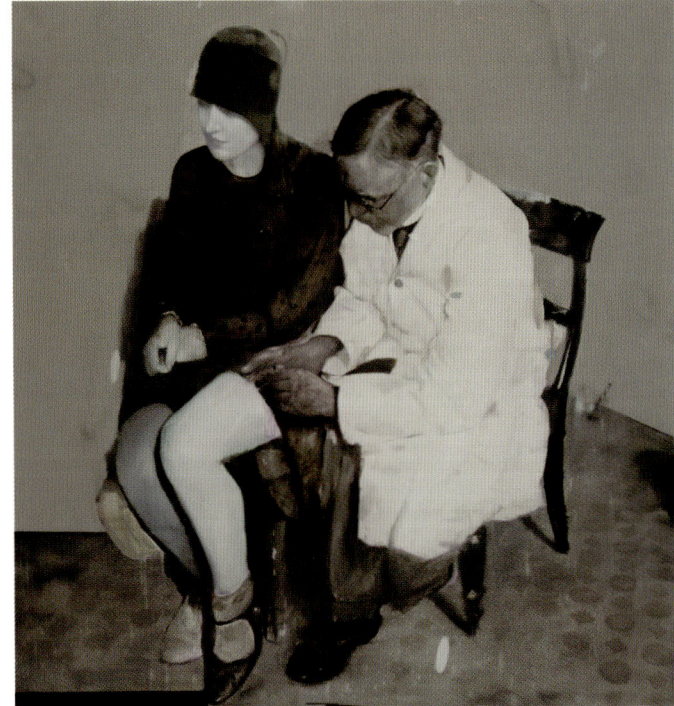

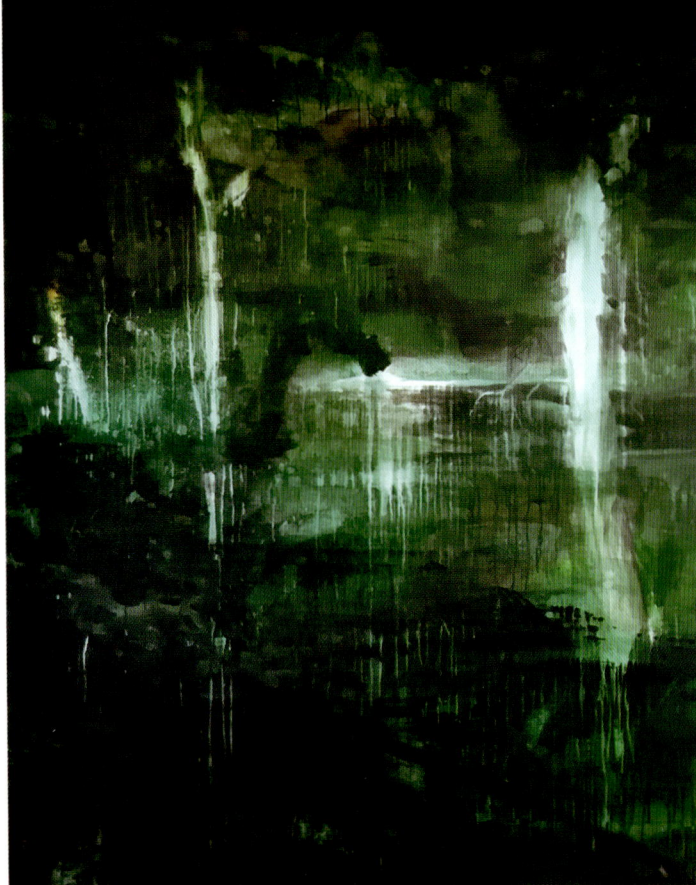

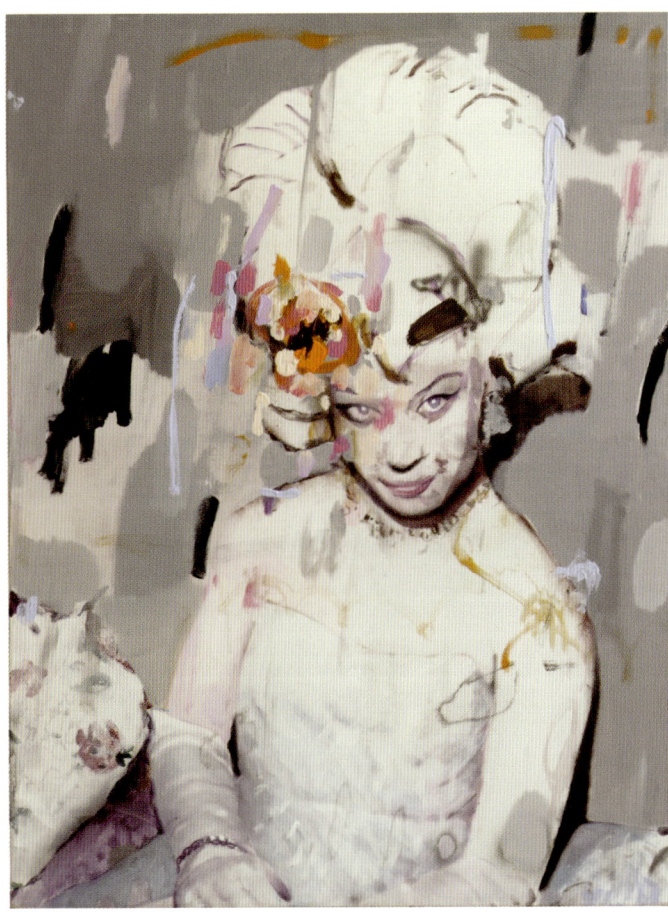

Lou Ros. *SR2*, 2015.
Acrylic, oil, and pastel on canvas: 20 × 20 inches.

Lou Ros. *No Man's Land #4*, 2016.
Acrylic, oil, and pastel on canvas: 79 × 63 inches.

Lou Ros. *The Doctor*, 2016.
Acrylic, oil, and pastel on canvas: 60 × 60 inches.

Lou Ros. *INC 10*, 2016.
Acrylic, oil, and pastel on canvas: 25.75 × 20 inches.

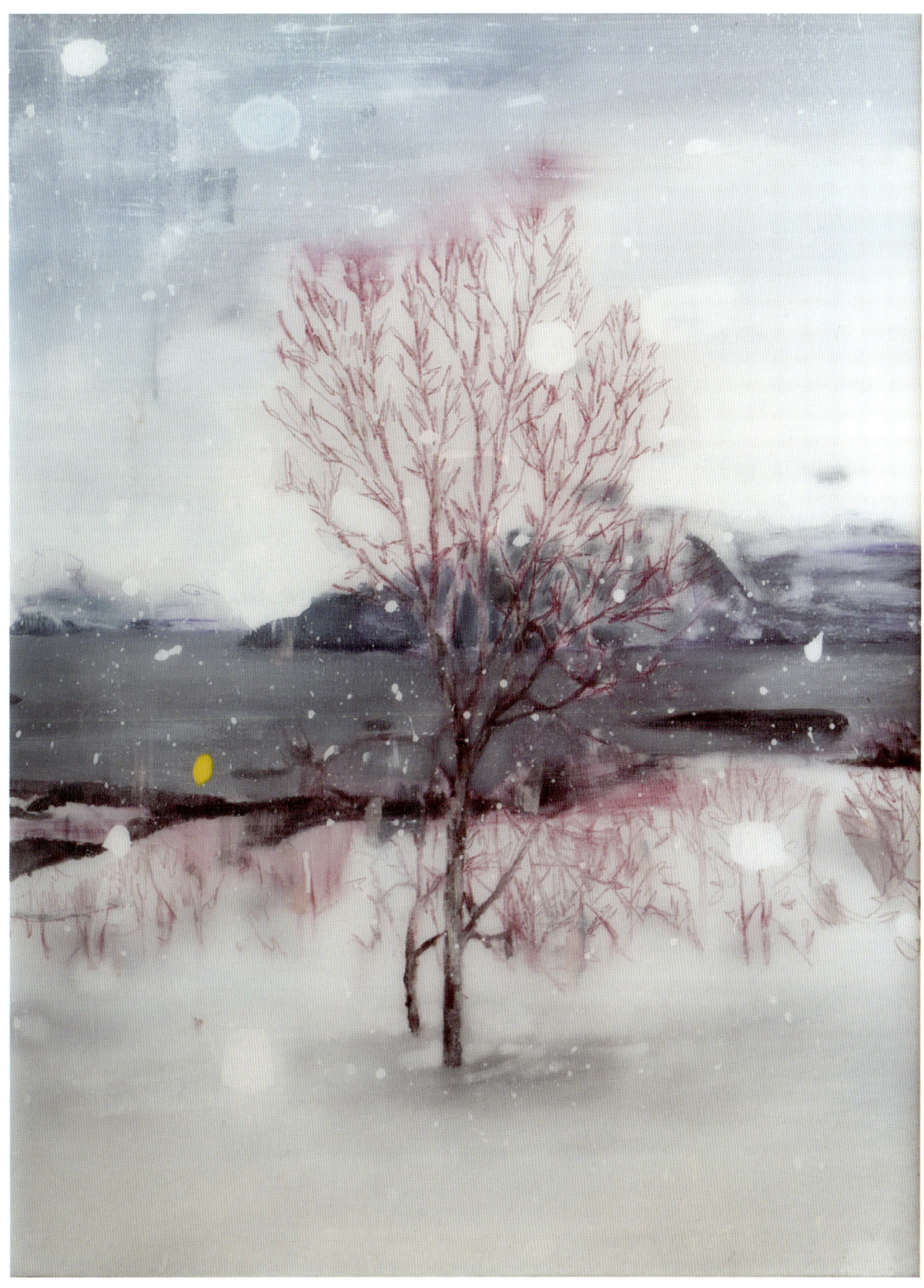

Lou Ros. *La Carte*, 2016.
Acrylic, oil, pastel, and resin on canvas
mounted on wood: 47.25 × 36.5 inches.

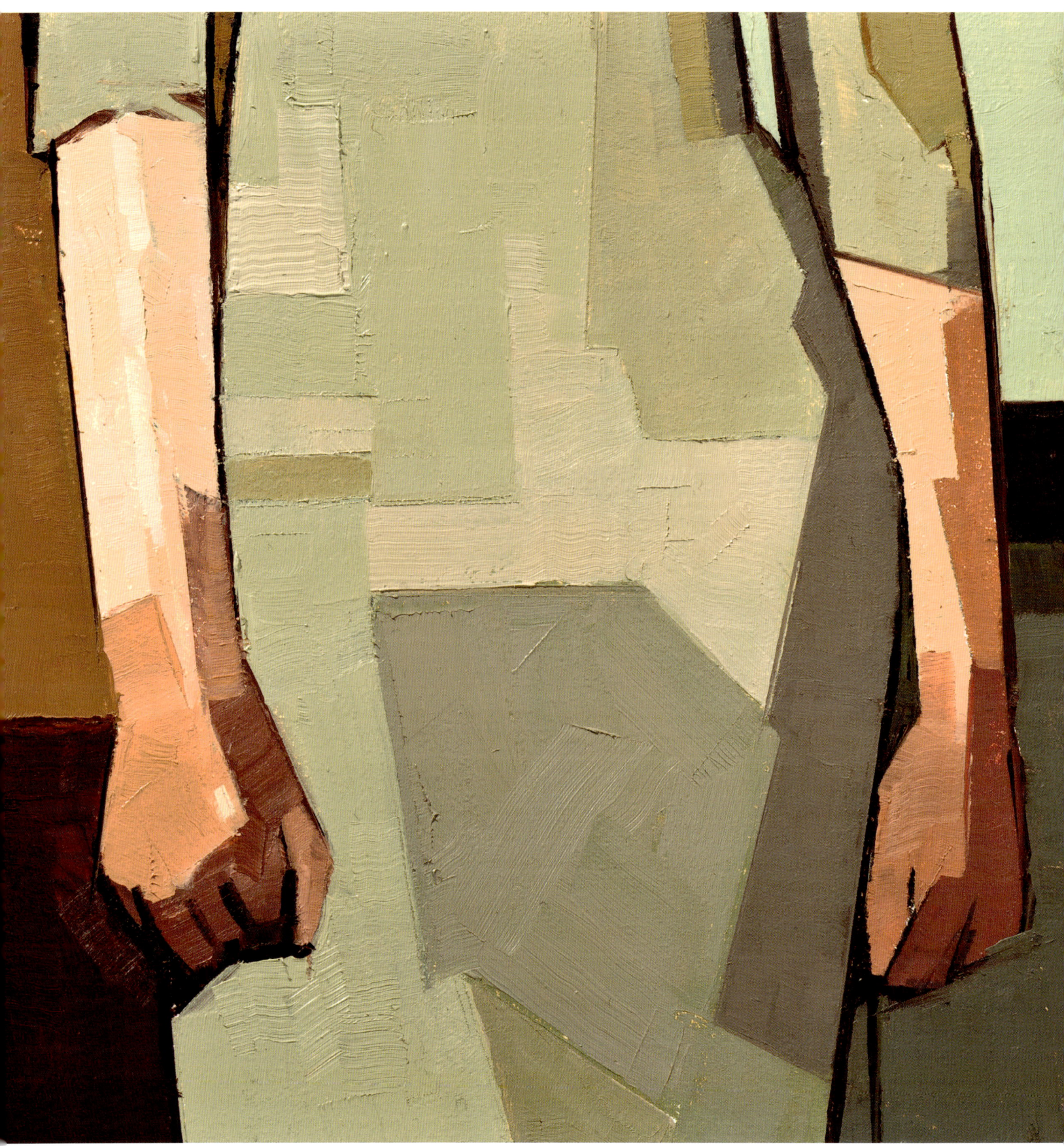

Patterns, Planes, and Formations

I am leaning toward translating the motif into geometric shapes.

—Catherine Kehoe

Breaking down the space and illusory structure of painting was one of the great projects of modern art, especially for the cubists. Now, with the resurgence of painters who are reclaiming the skills of representation, there seems to be a fresh interest in structure. Breaking imagery into planes and patterns can emphasize the abstract nature of illusion (and of painting itself) while also facilitating visual clarification or complication; it can go either way. There is a lovely tension possible between seeing the world and interweaving it with new orders and rhythms.

JAMES BLAND

RYAN BRADLEY

ZOEY FRANK

CATHERINE KEHOE

AIDEN KRINGEN

JOSHUA MEYER

STEPHANIE PIERCE

DORIAN VALLEJO

Catherine Kehoe. *After Uglow,* 2018.
Oil on panel: 5 × 5 inches.

JAMES BLAND

Lives and Works in: Canterbury, United Kingdom
Education: Canterbury Christchurch University
Selected Collections: The Ruth Borchard Collection
Representation: The John Natsoulas Gallery, California

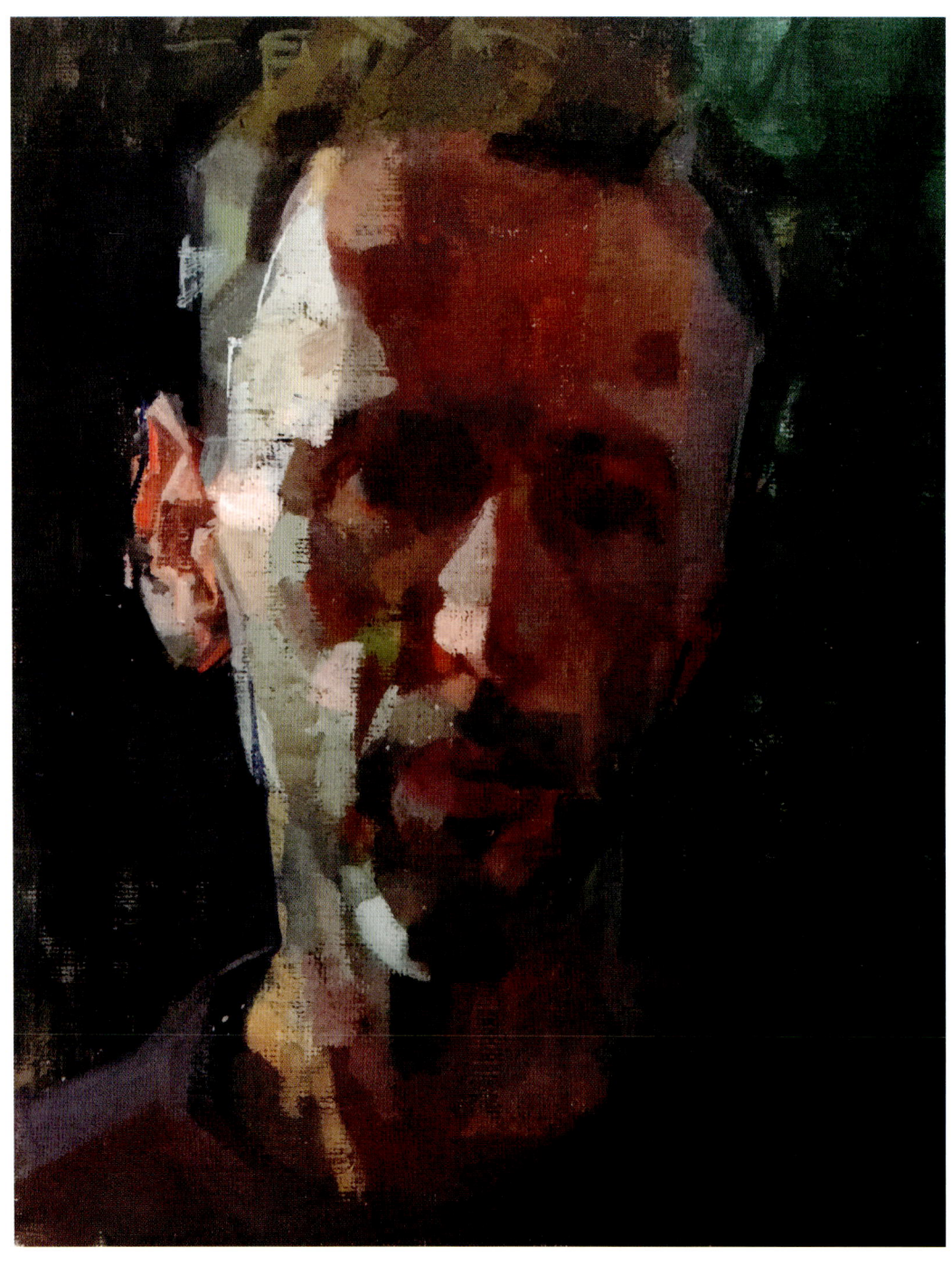

For me, each painting is a journey of discovery. Realism is just one aspect of what I enjoy about making art.

How and why does your work disrupt or deviate from traditional realism?

I don't think of myself as a realist. I like having a connection to something I can see when I paint, but I'm always painting more about ideas and feelings than appearances; I try to abstract from reality just what supports the idea and helps me to feel its significance emotionally and physically. If I painted with the aim of achieving realism, I think I'd get lost in the pileup of visual facts. A lot of improvisation happens between hitting on an idea and painting about it, sometimes involving the destruction of the whole image, or the removal of some central part of the motif, so the destruction of the image is also quite often a feature of my work.

How has your work evolved and developed over time?

I've always been most engaged when painting from life, but it's become less central to my painting. When I stopped being so concerned about accuracy (about five years ago), I found that it increased the range of things I could do. I started working with multiple layers of paint and discovered that I enjoyed reconciling contradictions of style and spatial depth within one painting. I found that I had to respond differently to my work: I couldn't judge rightness any longer in terms of accuracy—I had to think more about how the painting actually felt in order to find a way forward. This was and is quite scary, but it has opened up all kinds of possibilities.

What are some of the influences that have shaped your work?

My formal art training was influenced by the leading figures of the Slade School, such as Euan Uglow and William Coldstream. I love late medieval / early Renaissance Italian art; for example, the paintings of Giotto in Padua, where I lived for a year after graduating. Nature, reading, and music are big influences too, but memories, especially those of childhood, are the main source of inspiration.

Mention something interesting about your life or background.

At thirteen I had surgery for the scoliosis that was twisting my spine as I grew. The outcomes have been very good (as a student I used to row), and the treatment was entirely free thanks to the National Health Service.

James Bland. *Self-Portrait,* 2018.
Oil on canvas: 13.8 × 15.7 inches.

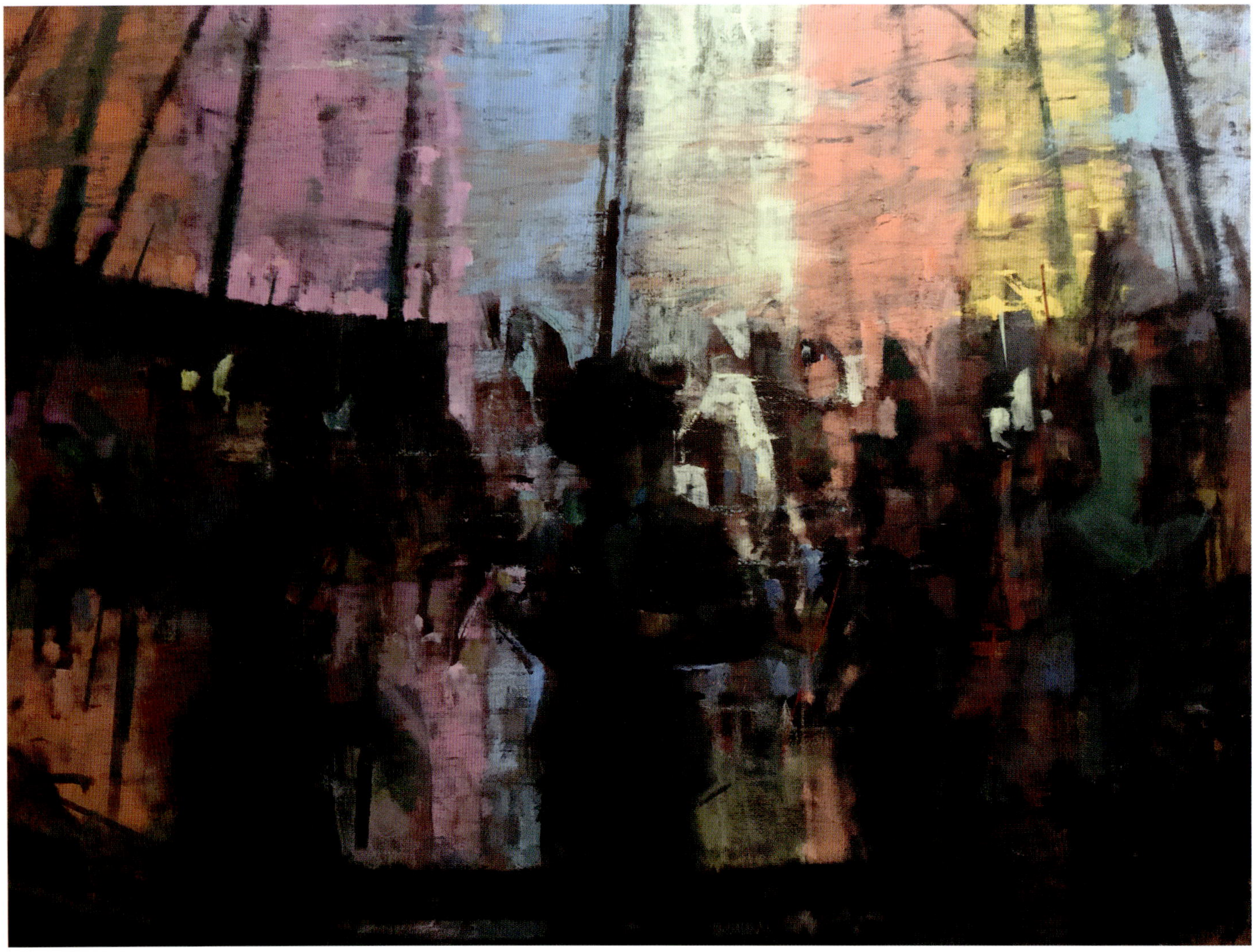

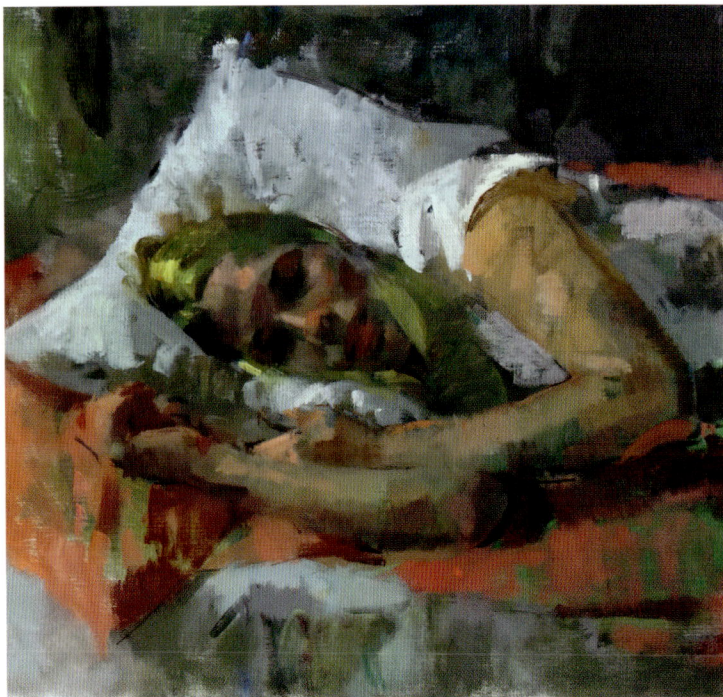

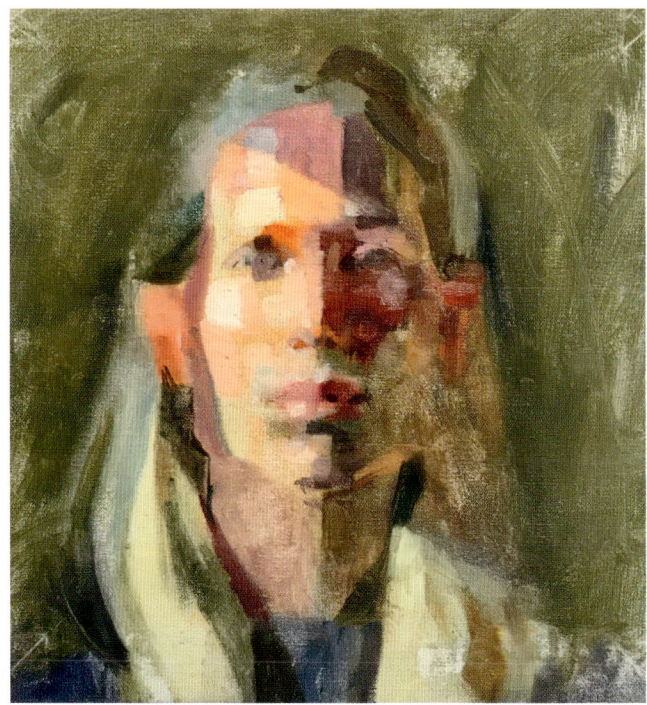

Top: James Bland. *Carousel No. 5*, 2018. Oil on canvas: 27.5 × 43.3 inches.

James Bland. *Fiona Reclining*, 2017. Oil on canvas: 19.7 × 21.6 inches.

James Bland. *Fiona in Sunlight*, 2017. Oil on canvas: 14.9 × 15.7 inches.

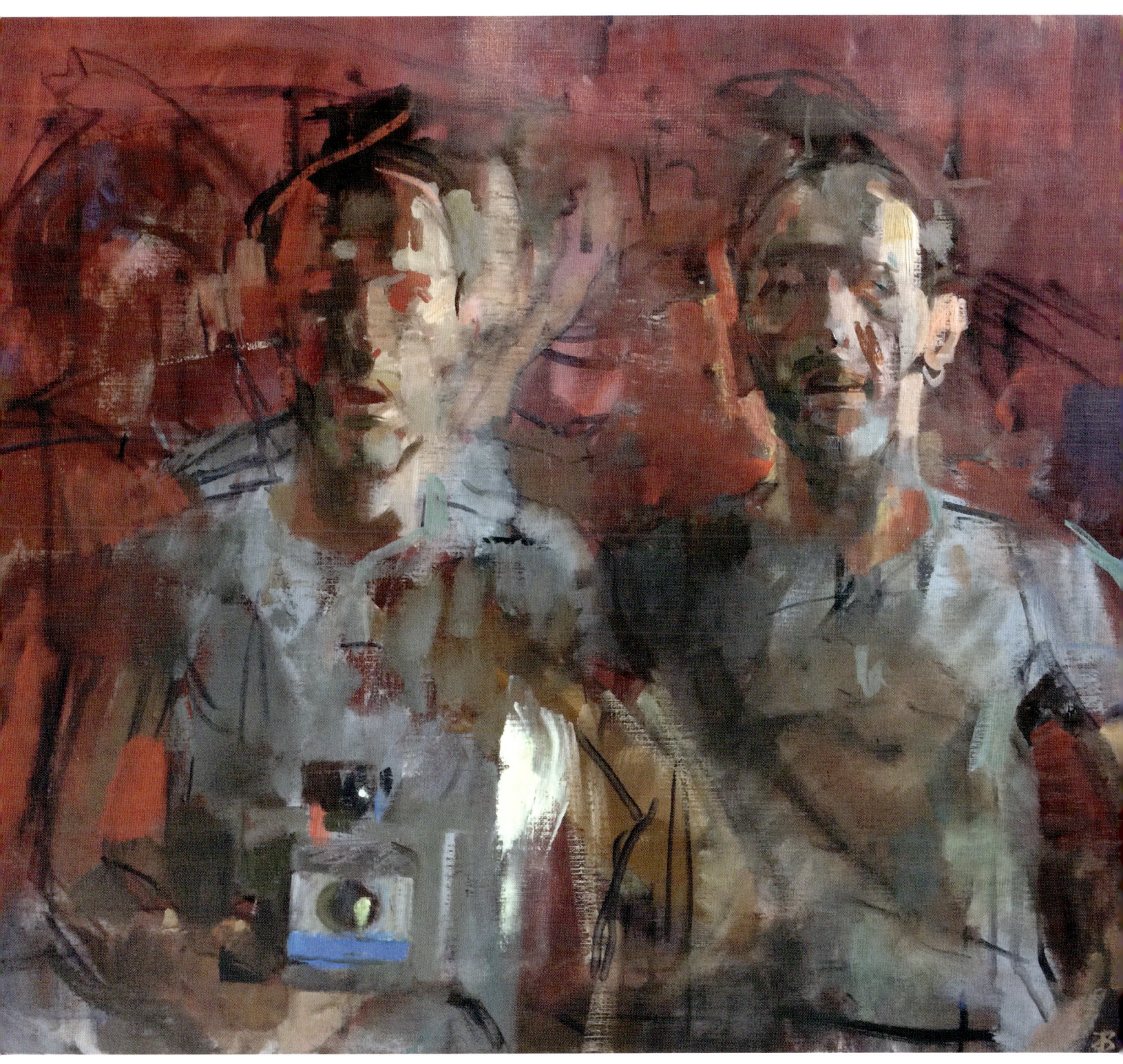

James Bland. *The Photographers*, 2017.
Oil on canvas: 23.6 × 27.5 inches.

RYAN BRADLEY

Lives and Works in: New York
Education: BFA, Maryland Institute College of Art;
MFA, School of Visual Arts
Representation: Gallery Henoch, New York

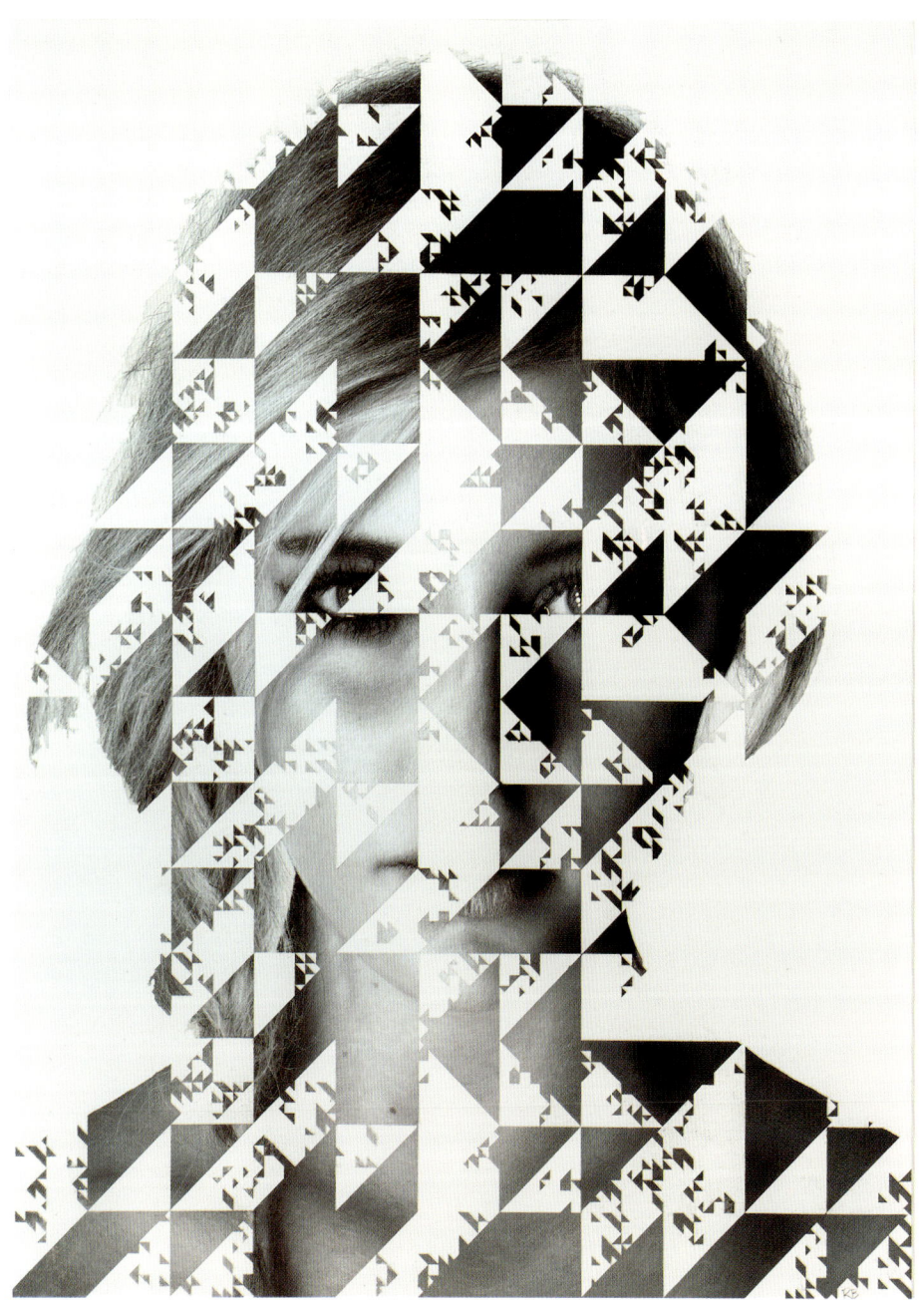

My work pushes the boundaries between the recognizable and the abstract through the insertion of complex patterns.

How and why does your work disrupt or deviate from traditional realism?

I am interested in the phenomenon called *pareidolia*, which causes our minds to recognize familiar patterns where none exist. We have a desire to recognize faces and other familiar forms when only visual fragments are available. My work plays against this instinct, breaking down the figure and pushing the boundaries between the recognizable and the abstract.

Each of my portraits is carved away using a complex matrix of patterns and voids. These ornaments overlap, interlace, invert, mirror, and subtract from one another, each creating distinct interpretations of the original form. By emphasizing specific features through the absence of others, these compositions challenge our ability to detect and perceive the face. Since I work in series, each painting serves as a singular element in a complex puzzle. Each image informs the next, and what is absent in one is readily apparent in the next. Seen together, these components form a complete and coherent image.

How has your work evolved and developed over time?

While in graduate school I started thinking about the idea that patterns themselves don't have to be rigid or stagnant; they can also be mobile and portray movement. Patterns can also freely move and include both dispersions and swarms.

I have always been enamored of the additive/subtractive design process. The idea that what is unsaid/absent is just as important, if not more, than what is readily available. I am a realist painter who has very little interest in traditional realism. Instead, the story that I am trying to tell is much less about the portrait than it is about the abstraction and void. Over time I attempted to reduce the figure down to the barest of fundamental elements. As part of these experiments I created a portrait with its right eye removed, and then made another in which that eye was the only component. I wanted to know if viewers would be able to complete this visual puzzle in their minds.

What are some of the influences that have shaped your work?

I am interested in every facet of design and am enamored of all carefully considered aesthetics. Textile design continues to be my main source for inspiration. I am also heavily influenced by the elaborate ornamentation of Victorian floral motifs and baroque design and am interested in a re-interpretation of traditional/classical ideals into a progressive manner.

My current series, titled Fabienne I–V, was developed as a system of successional tessellations; puzzling hard-edged geometric forms loosely inspired by Anni Alber's etching *Second Movement IV, 1978.*

Mention something interesting about your life or background.

I suffer from an eye condition known as keratoconus, a bulging of the cornea that causes severe distortion and the ghosting of images. Essentially, several single images sit on top of and circulate around one another, blurring the overall object being viewed. Because of my failing eyesight, I am forced to work very close to the image I am working on. I can see relatively well extremely close up, though I often must go over mistakes and smears caused by my nose rubbing against my paper as I work.

Ryan Bradley. *Untitled (Fabienne 1),* 2018.
Pastel on Arches paper: 24.5 × 18 inches.

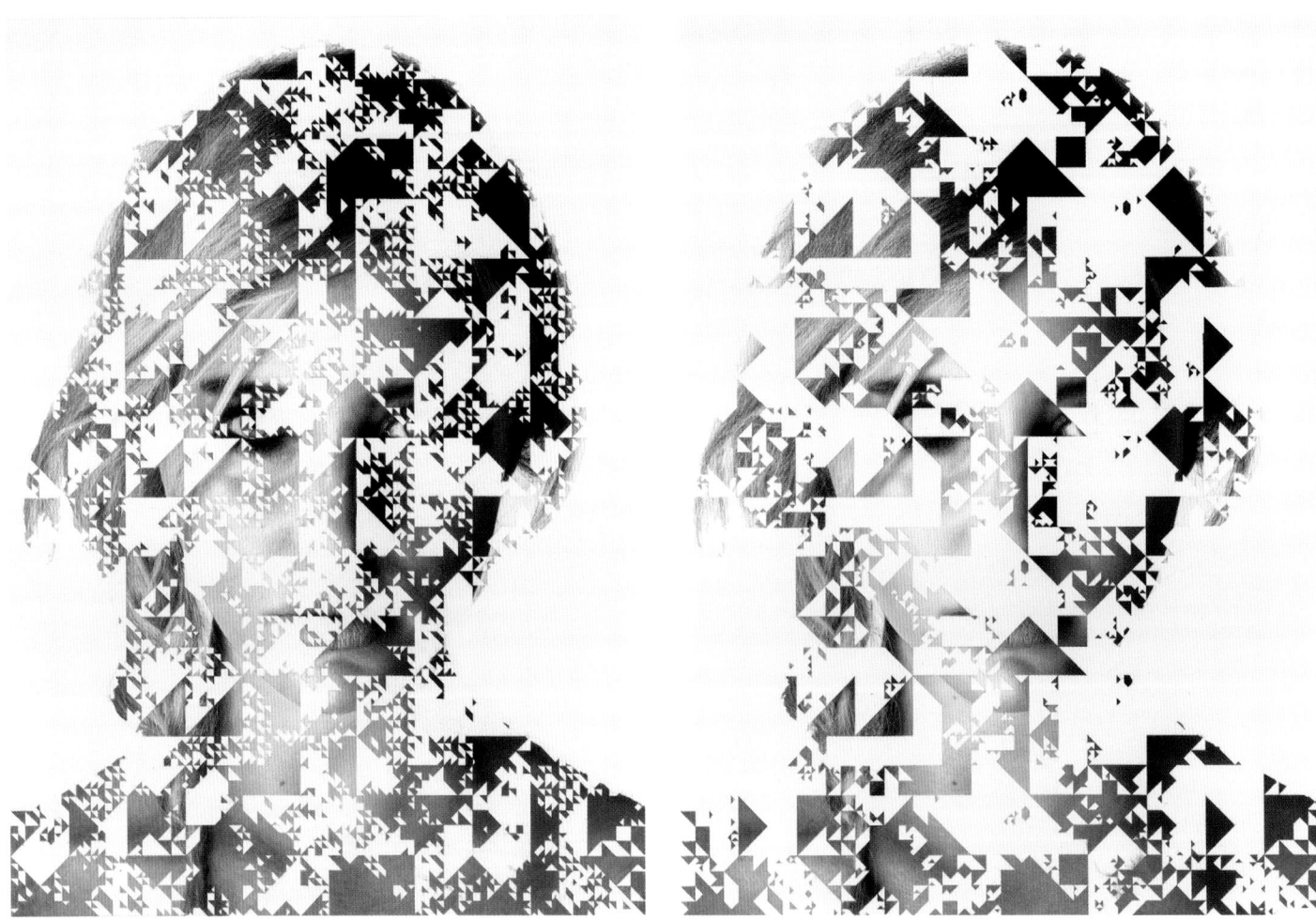

Ryan Bradley. *Untitled (Fabienne 2)*, 2017.
Pastel on Arches paper: 24.5 × 18 inches.

Ryan Bradley. *Untitled (Fabienne 3)*, 2018.
Pastel on Arches paper: 24.5 × 18 inches.

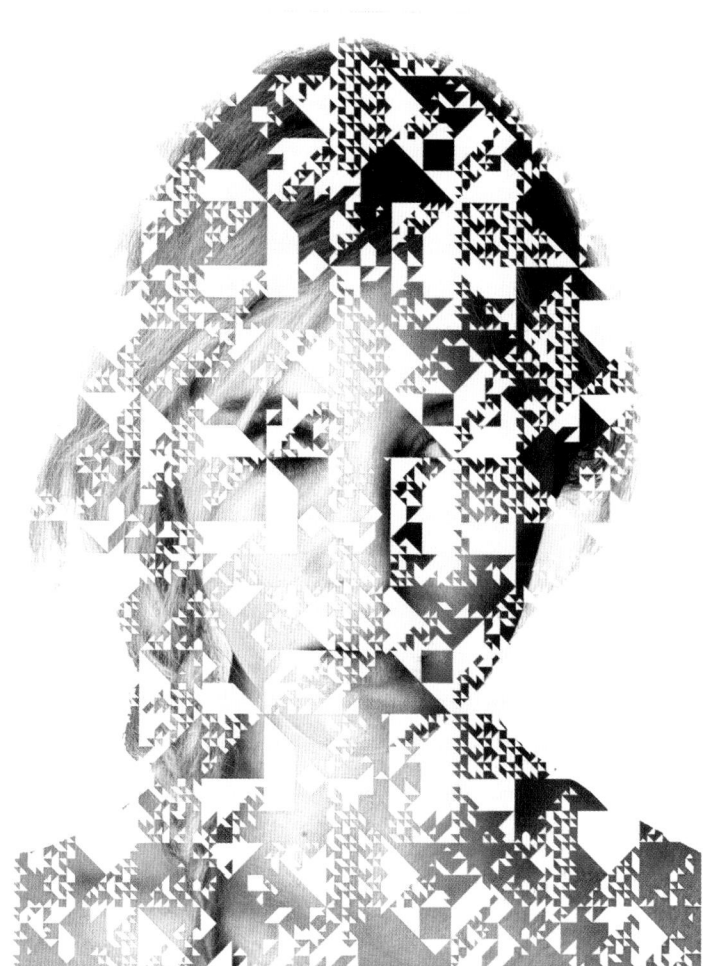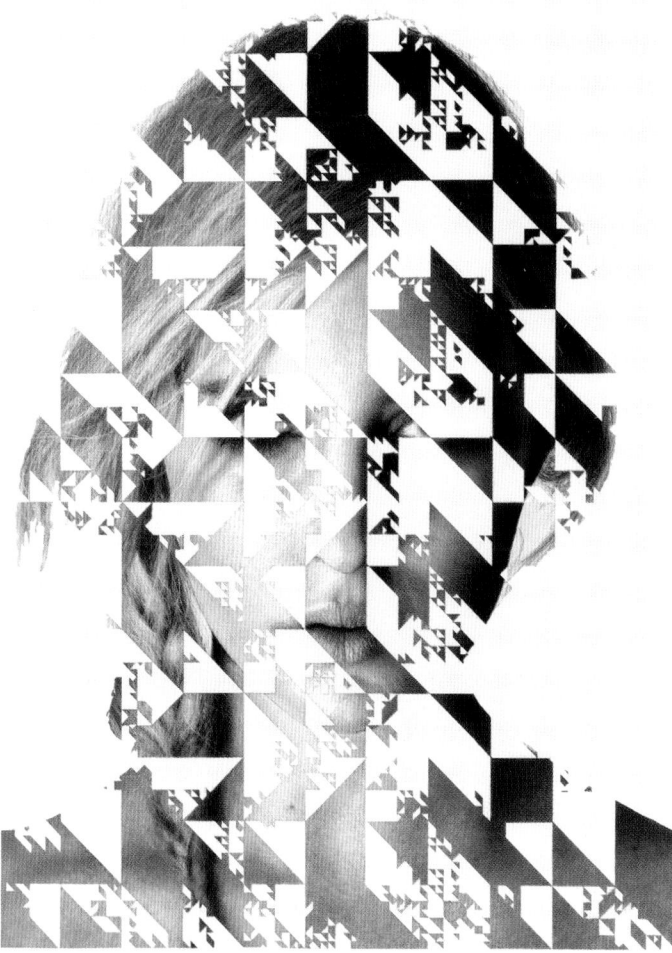

Ryan Bradley. *Untitled (Fabienne 4),* 2014.
Pastel on Arches paper: 24.5 × 18 inches.

Ryan Bradley. *Untitled (Fabienne 5),* 2015.
Pastel on Arches paper: 24.5 × 18 inches.

ZOEY FRANK

Lives and Works in: Loveland, Colorado
Education: MFA, Laguna College of Art and Design
Selected Collections: Bennett Collection
Representation: Galerie Mokum, Amsterdam

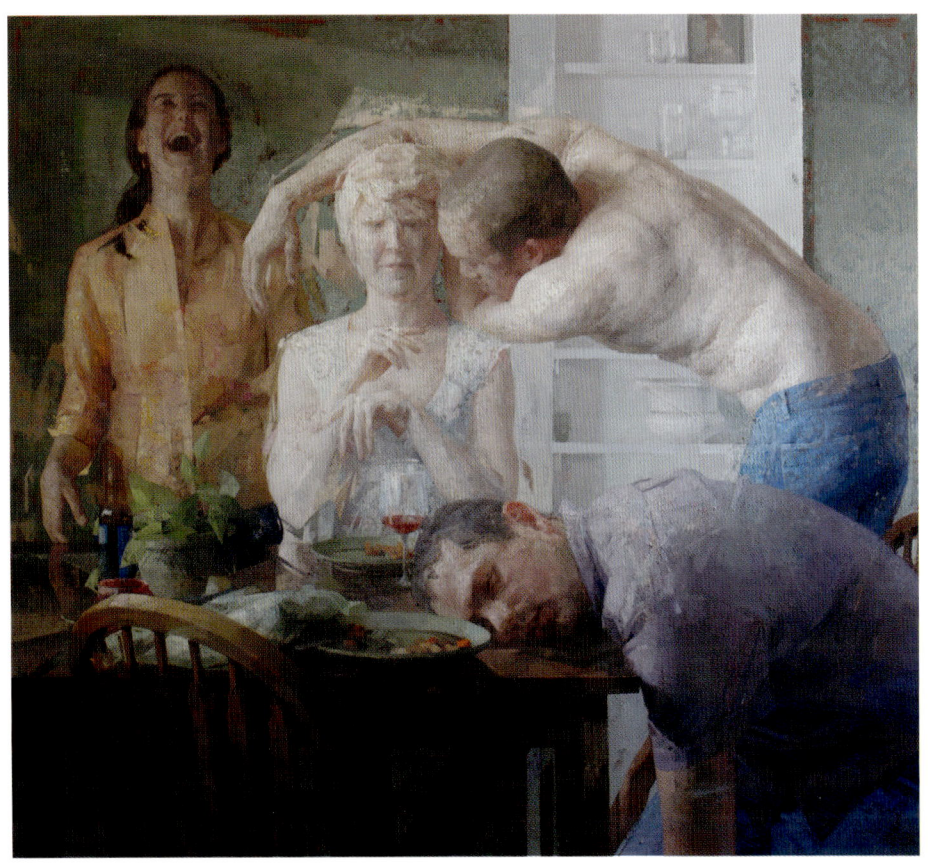

I make use of traditional painting skills, gained in an atelier program, to make paintings that experiment with pictorial space, abstraction, and time.

Zoey Frank. *Dinner Party*, 2017.
Oil on linen: 54 × 60 inches.

How and why does your work disrupt or deviate from traditional realism?

I'm interested in the element of time and change in my paintings. I've recently been allowing previous states of the painting to show through and complicate the surface of the work. This is incredibly liberating. As I'm working, I make drastic changes to the motif and repaint entire sections of the painting. The result feels more genuine and lived-in for me than is the case when I meticulously plan out a composition. I'm able to be more spontaneous and responsive in the act of painting. I can let something emerge between me and the material.

As compositional problems come up, I've also started to use arbitrary planes of color rather than objects to resolve them. This frees me up even more to make intuitive changes while I'm painting. And I like how representational objects can be held within a value and color structure that isn't directly tied to the objects themselves.

How has your work evolved and developed over time?

I began my studies with a classical atelier training in order to gain a foundation of traditional painting skills. Since then my work has been motivated by a series of formal experiments that have broken open that training. In a way, these experiments have tracked the history of modernism: I've experimented with ways of incorporating time into my paintings, with different approaches to color composition, with different ways of representing pictorial space, with multiple or fractured perspectives, and with abstraction. I want to make work that is rooted in the history of art but that isn't nostalgic—work that is made now, in the present, where I am. For me this can't only be about contemporary subject matter; it has to be about the structure and form of how the painting is made.

What are some of the influences that have shaped your work?

My initial interest in painting was the work from the High Renaissance and the baroque. Lately I've been looking farther back at early Greco-Roman frescoes, Giotto and Piero della Francesca, on the one hand, and farther forward to Cézanne, Braque, De Kooning, Joan Mitchell, on the other.

I also increasingly find myself influenced by digital media. I make use of found images from the internet and sometimes construct digital collages of photographs when planning out the composition of a painting.

Our current political moment has affected how I depict women in my work. I'm unwilling to paint female nudes now in a way that seems sensual or seductive. And I've striven to be more inclusive in my choice of models and subjects.

Mention something interesting about your life and background.

My work generally comes out of my surroundings and my everyday life. I use family and friends as models for my paintings. Lately, I've painted mundane objects like deli sandwiches, bottles of mouthwash, microwaves, and washing machines. These objects have no special interest for me. They're cheap and mass produced. But I like working with them because they're objects that are not just for display, that we're engaged with physically, and that we handle and use in our everyday life. I'm able to paint them in a way that is tactile and that emphasizes the way we interact with them. It's a more engaged, personal way of looking at the world.

Overleaf: Zoey Frank. *Wedding*, 2018.
Oil on linen: 96 × 140 inches.

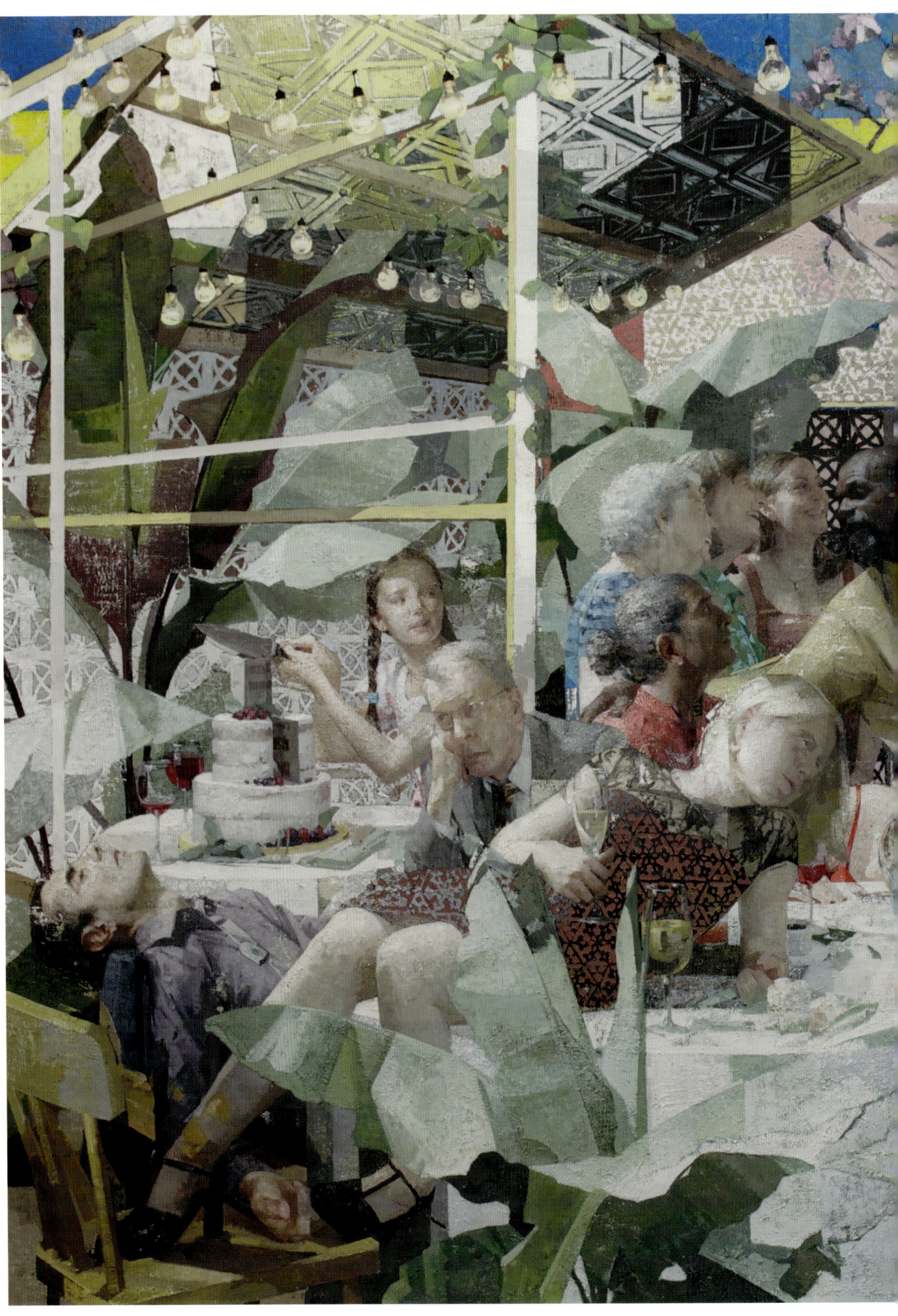

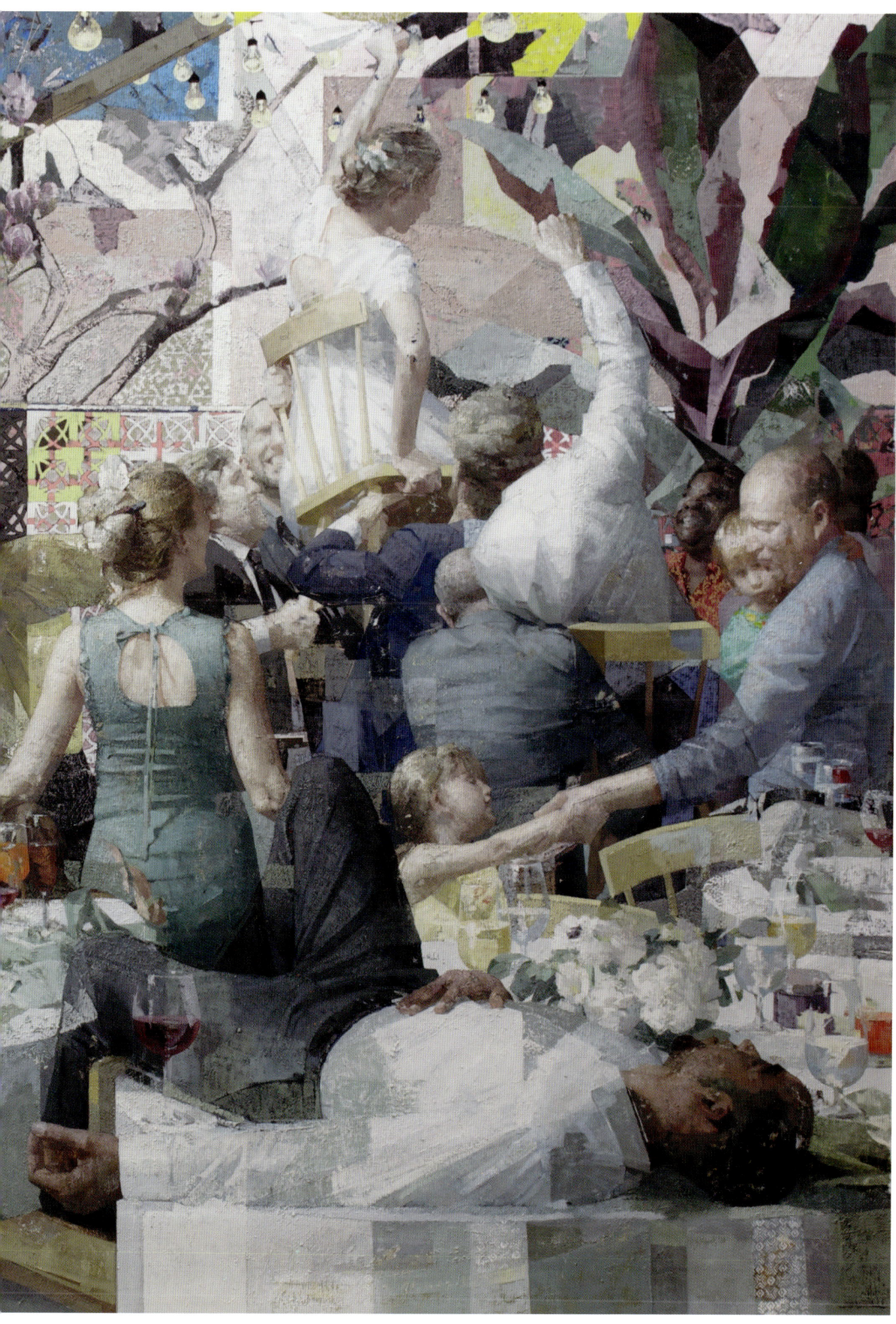

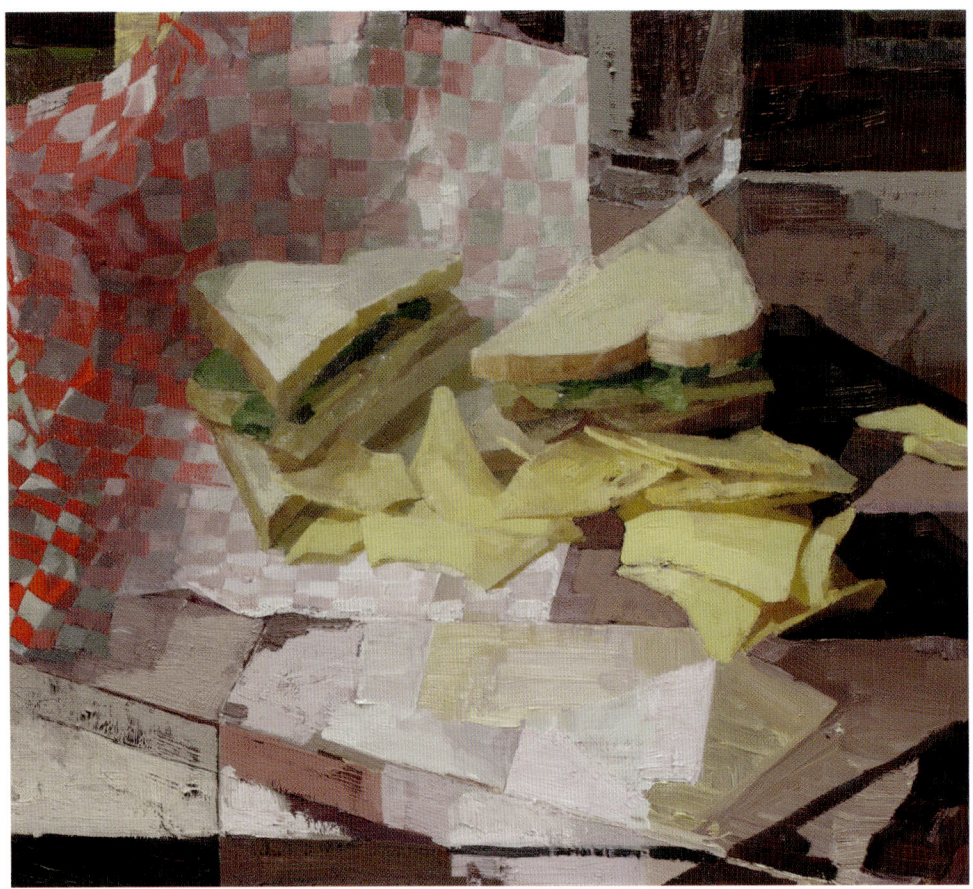

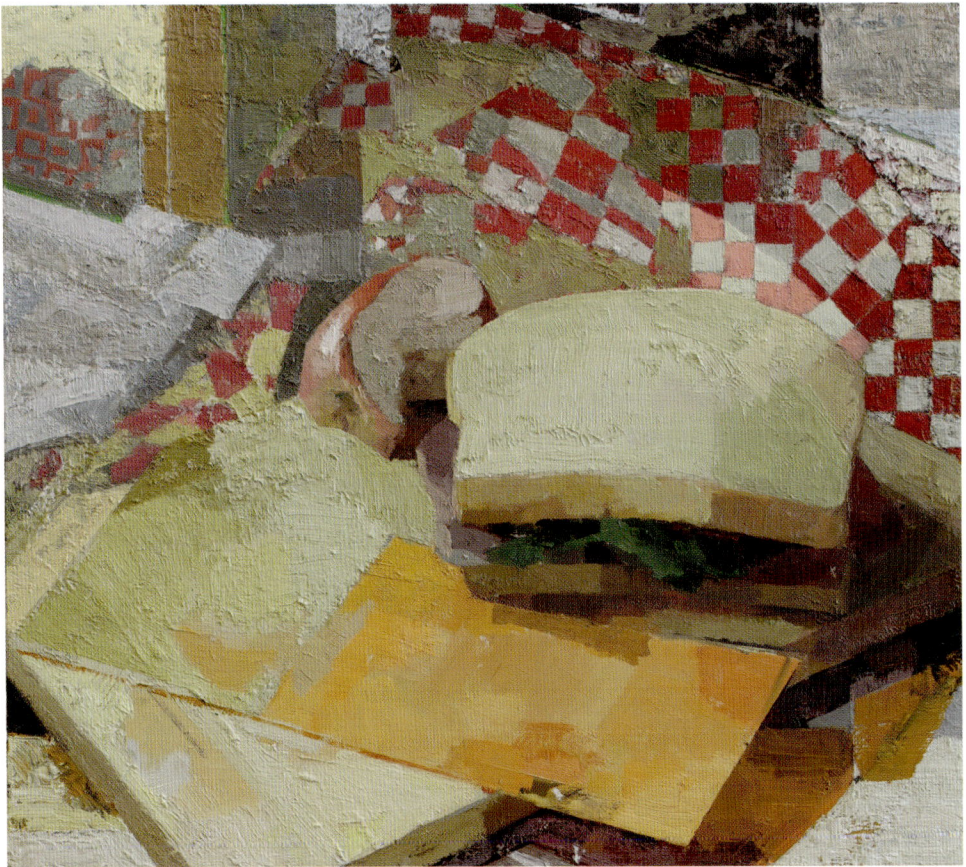

Zoey Frank. *Sandwich #7*, 2018.
Oil on panel: 14 × 16 inches.

Zoey Frank. *Sandwich #13*, 2018.
Oil on panel: 14 × 16 inches.

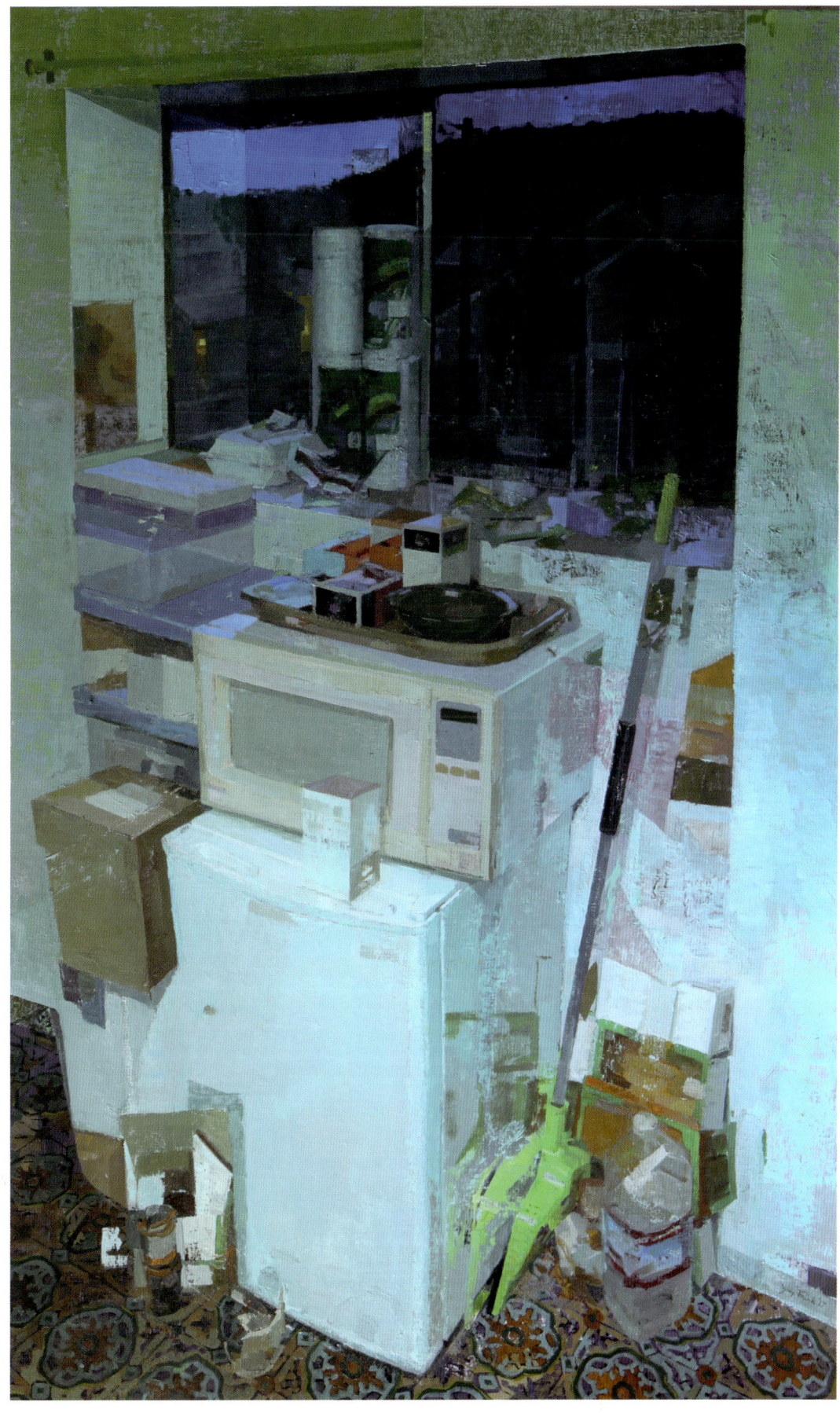

Zoey Frank. *Window at Night,* 2017.
Oil on linen on panel: 61 × 38 inches.

CATHERINE KEHOE

Lives and Works in: Rehoboth, Massachusetts
Education: BFA in painting, Massachusetts College of Art and Design; MFA in painting, Boston University School of Visual Arts
Representation: Howard Yezerski Gallery, Boston

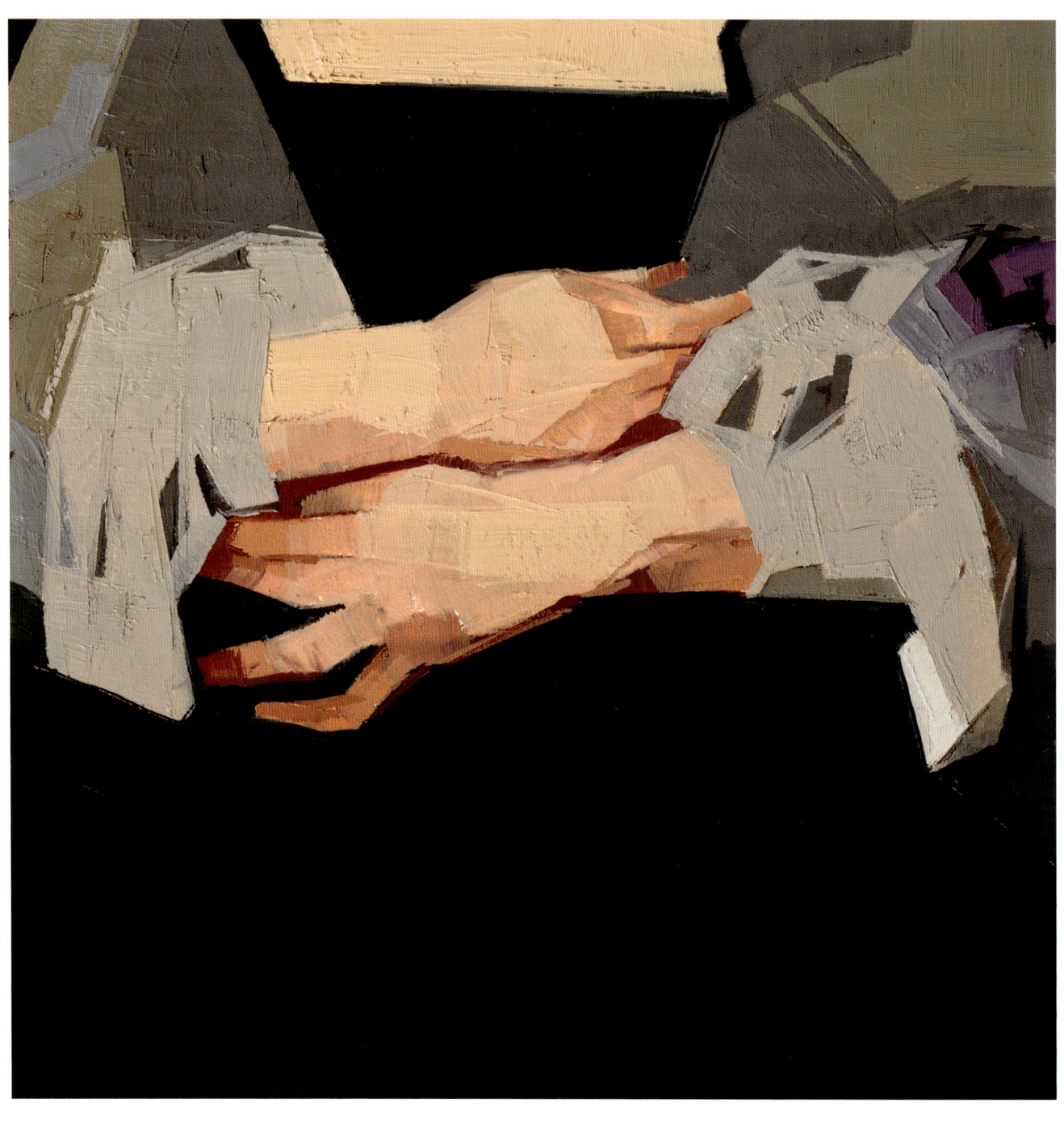

I follow my interests wherever they lead.

How and why does your work disrupt or deviate from traditional realism?

I never liked the word "realism" and do not identify as a realist painter, disruptive or otherwise. I start with a subject that is before my eyes and respond to it in paint. Mostly I remain true to what is there, only to discover how odd and surprising the appearance of things becomes when one puts aside the kind of seeing that helps us navigate in the world. There is another kind of seeing that kicks in when I am painting. It is less about things and more about the surprising relationships between things.

How has your work evolved and developed over time?

When I began studying painting, I sought control and mastery over the nearly unfathomable medium. I was able to describe things but had a difficult time relating one thing to another in space. I also sought pictorial stability—this showed itself in centrally focused, symmetrical compositions. As I learned to get paint to do my bidding, I developed a taste for complexity and high contrast in my paintings. Lately my paintings are less about description and more about making a design within a rectangle. I am leaning toward translating the motif into geometric shapes.

What are some of the influences that have shaped your work?

There are so many. When I was in graduate school my paintings were criticized for their fuzzy, all-purpose paint application. Graham Nickson, a visiting artist, introduced me to the work of Euan Uglow. The clarity of his paintings opened new possibilities for me.

Through social media I have discovered the work of my contemporaries, whose work is personal and risk taking: Ruth Miller, Susan Lichtman, Jennifer Pochinski, Amy Mahnick, to name a few.

Mention something interesting about your life and background.

I grew up in a home where art, culture, and higher education were unknown. My mother went as far as the seventh grade. My father graduated high school. He robbed a bank when I was six years old. My father's sister, Muriel, put me through art school.

I follow my interests wherever they lead.

Catherine Kehoe. *After Rubens,* 2018.
Oil on panel: 5 × 5 inches.

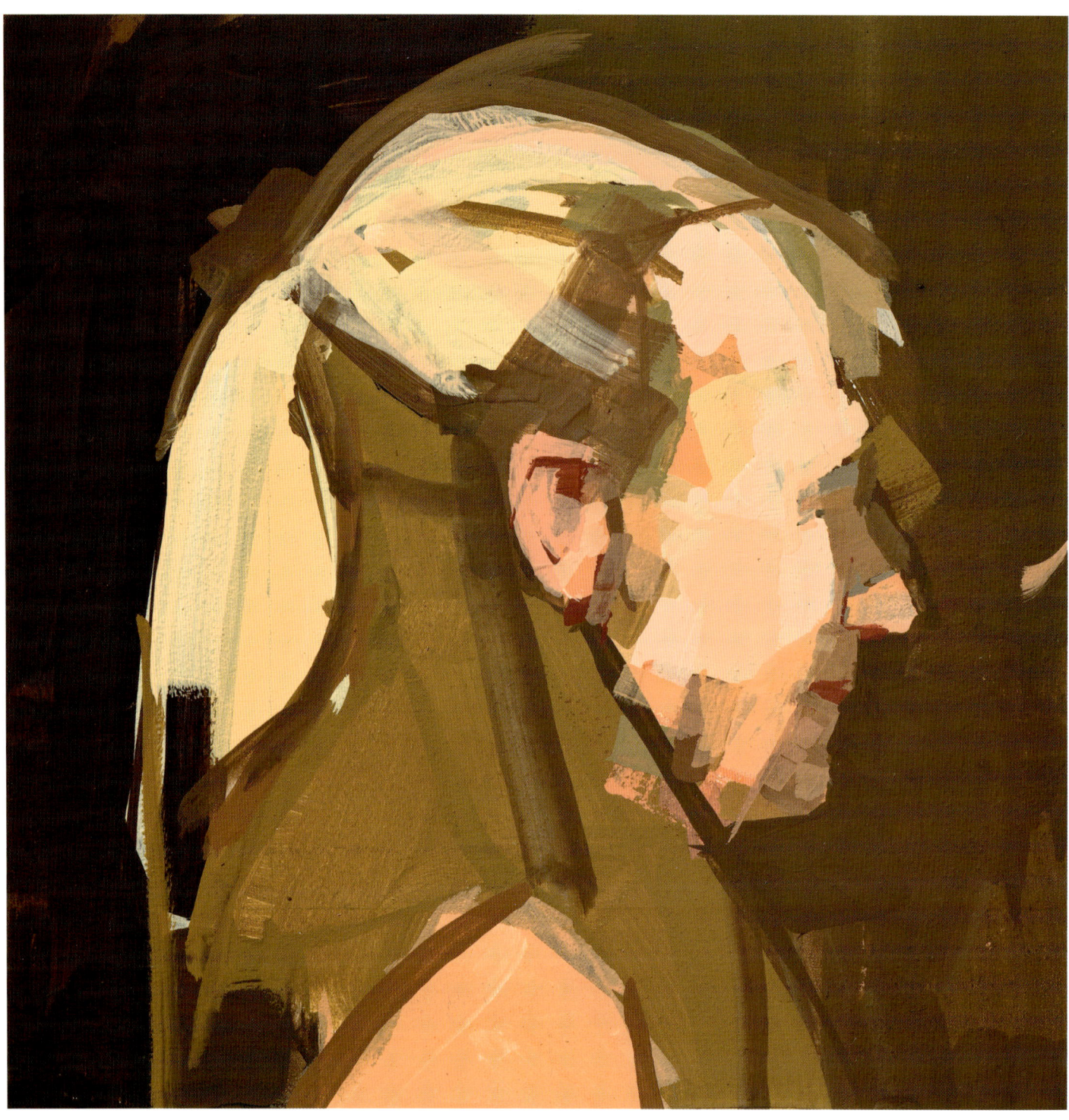

Catherine Kehoe. *Andrea Profile*, 2018.
Acrylic gouache on panel: 6 × 6 inches.

Opposite, top: Catherine Kehoe. *Dark Days*,
2018. Oil on panel: 5 × 5 inches.

Opposite, bottom: Catherine Kehoe.
Glimmer, 2018. Oil on panel: 6 × 6 inches.

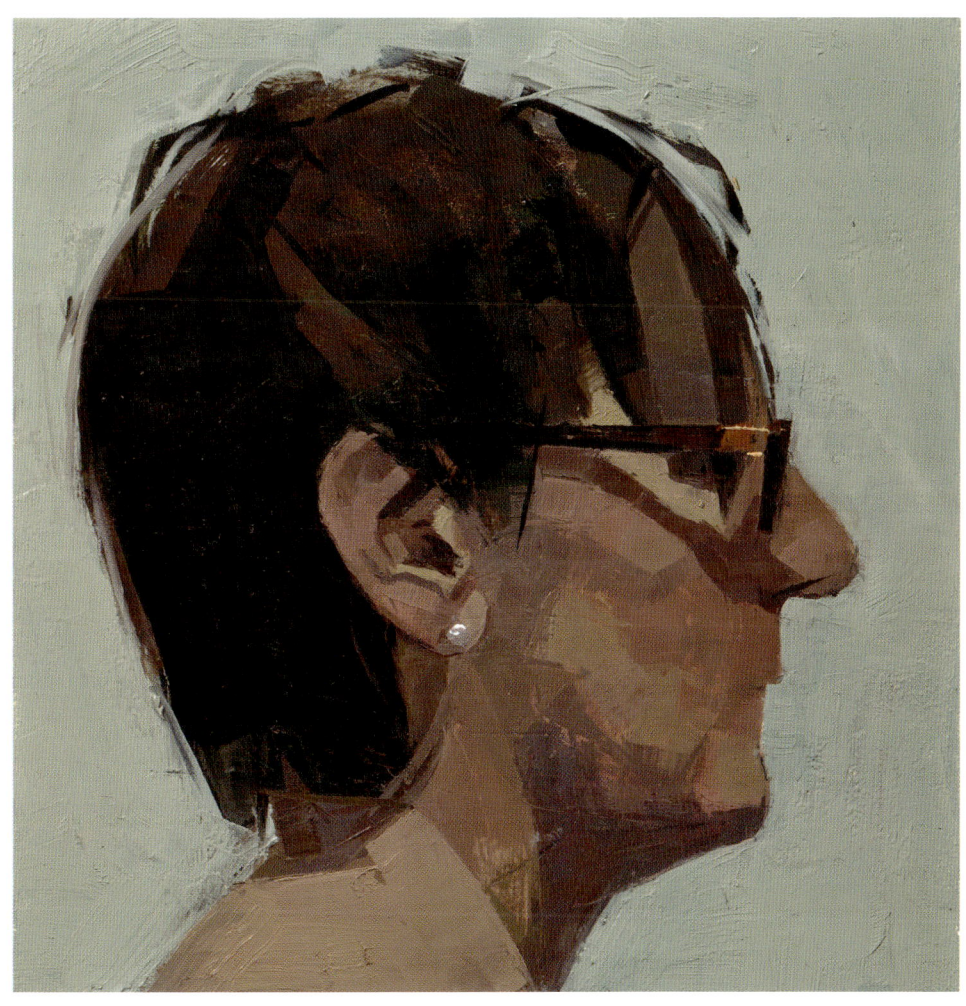

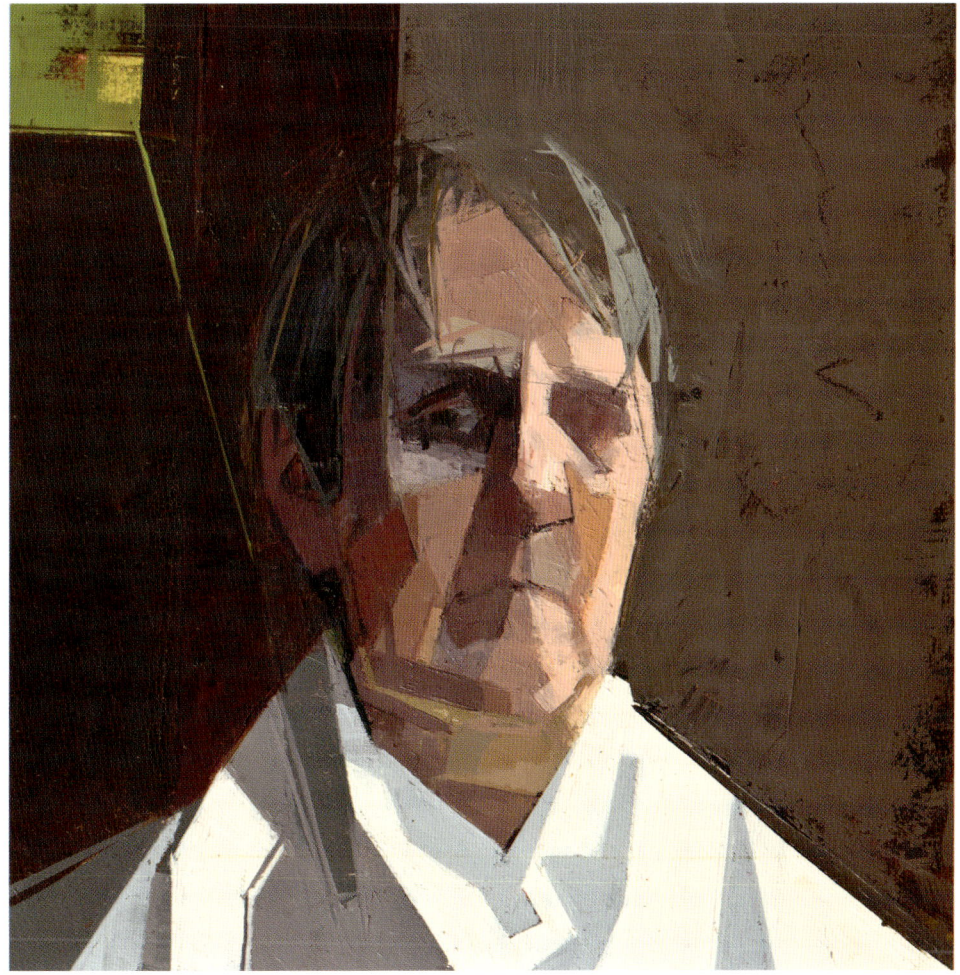

AIDEN KRINGEN

Lives and Works in: Sonoma County, California
Education: Santa Rosa Junior College
Representation: Chris Winfield Gallery, Carmel, California

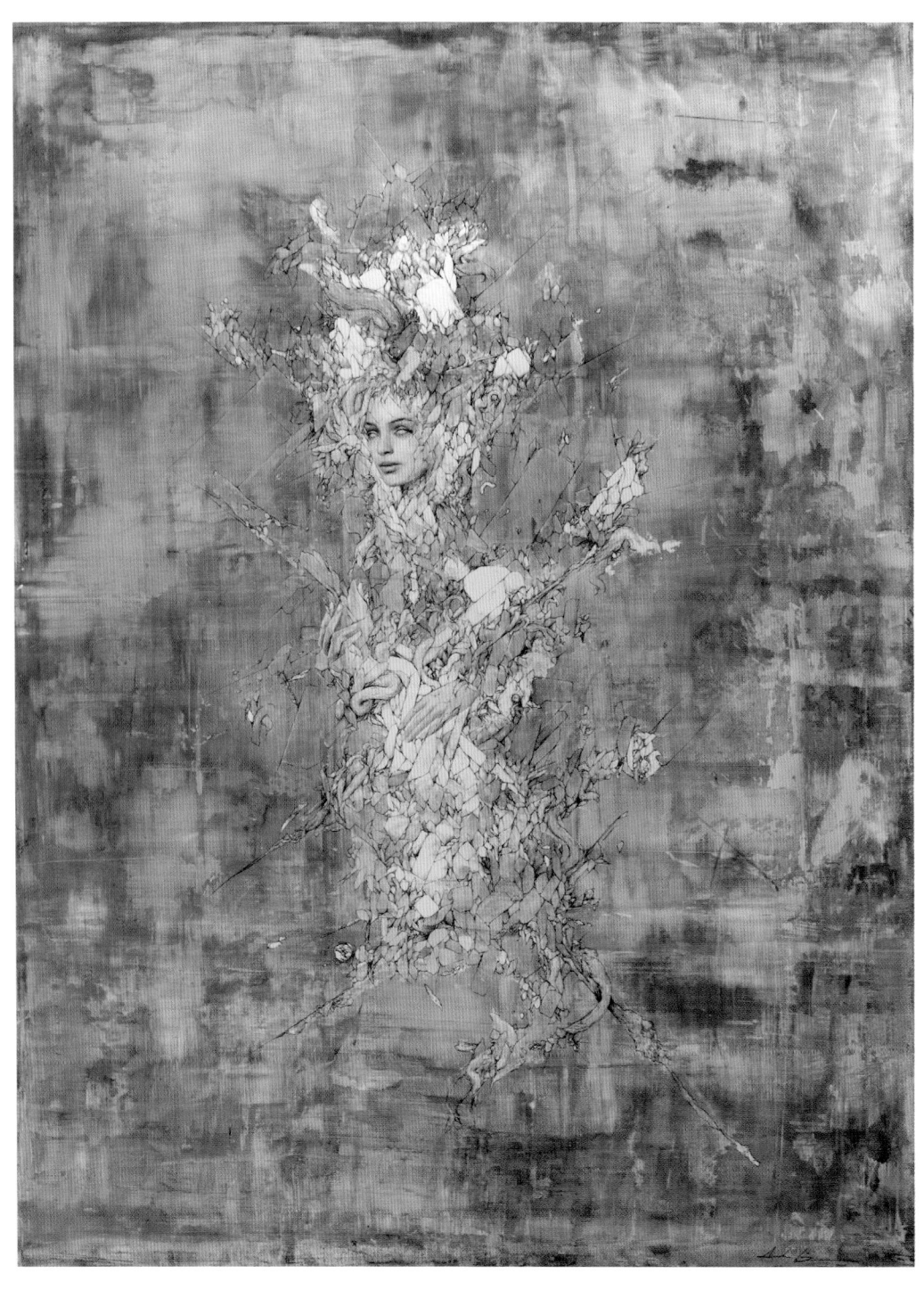

*I strive for beauty through controlling
and organizing chaos.*

**How and why does your work disrupt
or deviate from traditional realism?**

I've always had an interest in traditional realism, but within my work, I've strived to pare it down and reassemble it along a geometric framework that fits within a modern context. For me, the process of painting a portrait or figure involves balancing between reality and abstraction, down to each single feature of the face or hand. I dissect the figure using line work, dividing between tone and texture, and then reconnect the pieces along invisible planes throughout the painting. My goal as an artist is to encapsulate idealized beauty through a cracked or broken lens. I feel as though I have a respect for the pure and beautiful human essence while accepting that it is imperfect, and therefore depict it through fractured line work.

**How has your work evolved and
developed over time?**

When first developing the process of fracturing the human form, my line work was heavier and the pieces of the figures seemed to be isolated from the figure itself. My early work was also darker in content. Since becoming a father, I've made a choice to see more of the subtle beauty in life, and this has reflected itself in my work. I have worked to refine and perfect the "pieces" that define my figures by paying more attention to the details. Over time, I've been able to bring the planes of color and shape "closer" together within each painting.

**What are some of the influences
that have shaped your work?**

I've always been influenced by artists that work large and with confidence. I was first inspired by the careers of Jean-Michel Basquiat and Keith Haring, and their bold work compelled me to paint and develop my own unique vision. I then grew to appreciate the abstract expressionists, such as Franz Kline and Cy Twombly. From a young age, I was constantly being introduced to edgy and interesting work in my home life. And when I met my wife, she acquainted me with her own artistic interests and another world of traditional beauty through classical artworks.

**Mention something interesting
about your life and background.**

At age six, I was struck by a foul ball at a Dodgers game. The doctors said that my head had taken a significant blow to the left hemisphere of the brain, which controls language. It took two years to recover, after many speech therapy classes and struggling in school.

Aiden Kringen. *Seraph 1*, 2018.
Acrylic, gold leaf and mixed media on canvas:
48 × 36 inches.

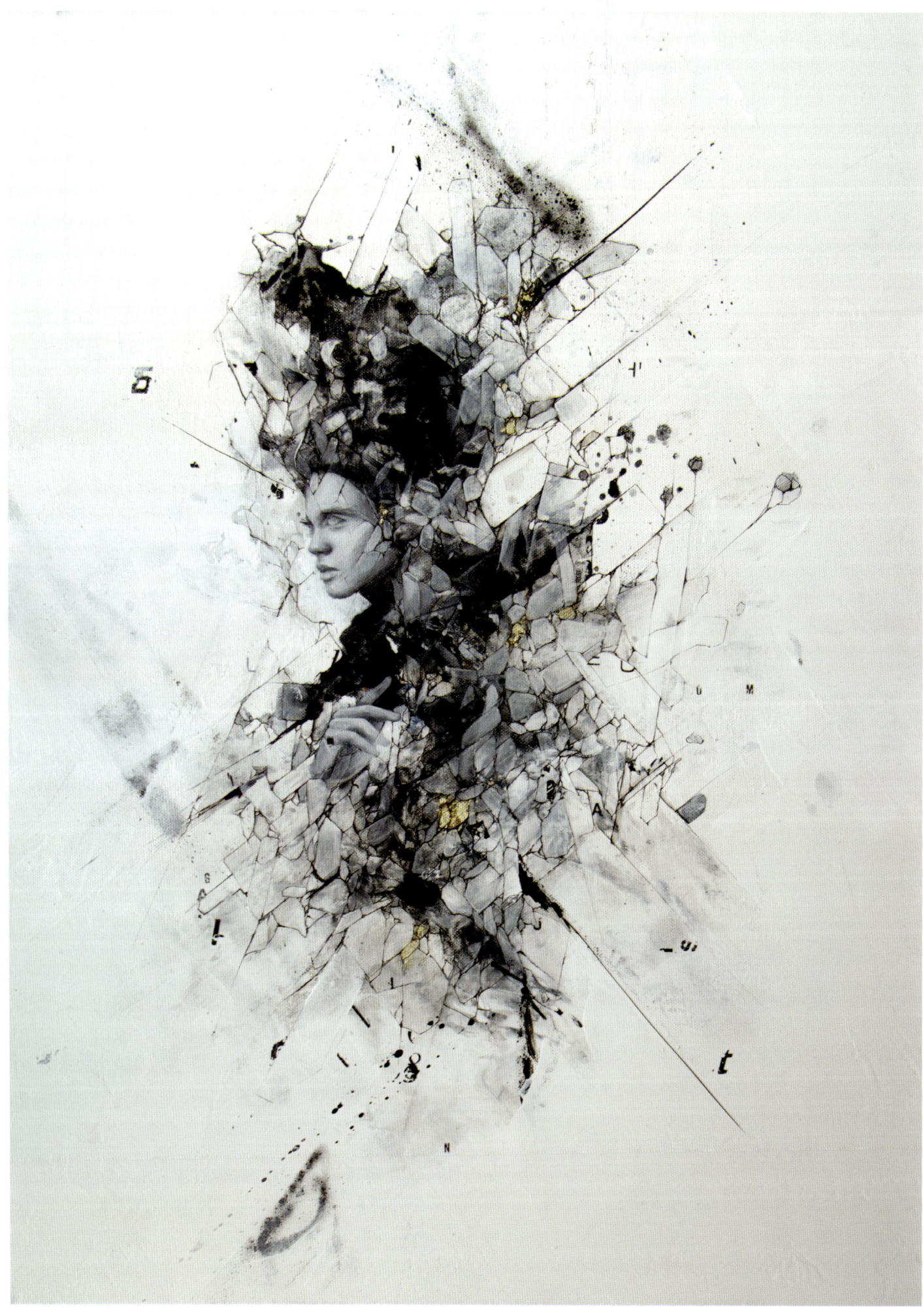

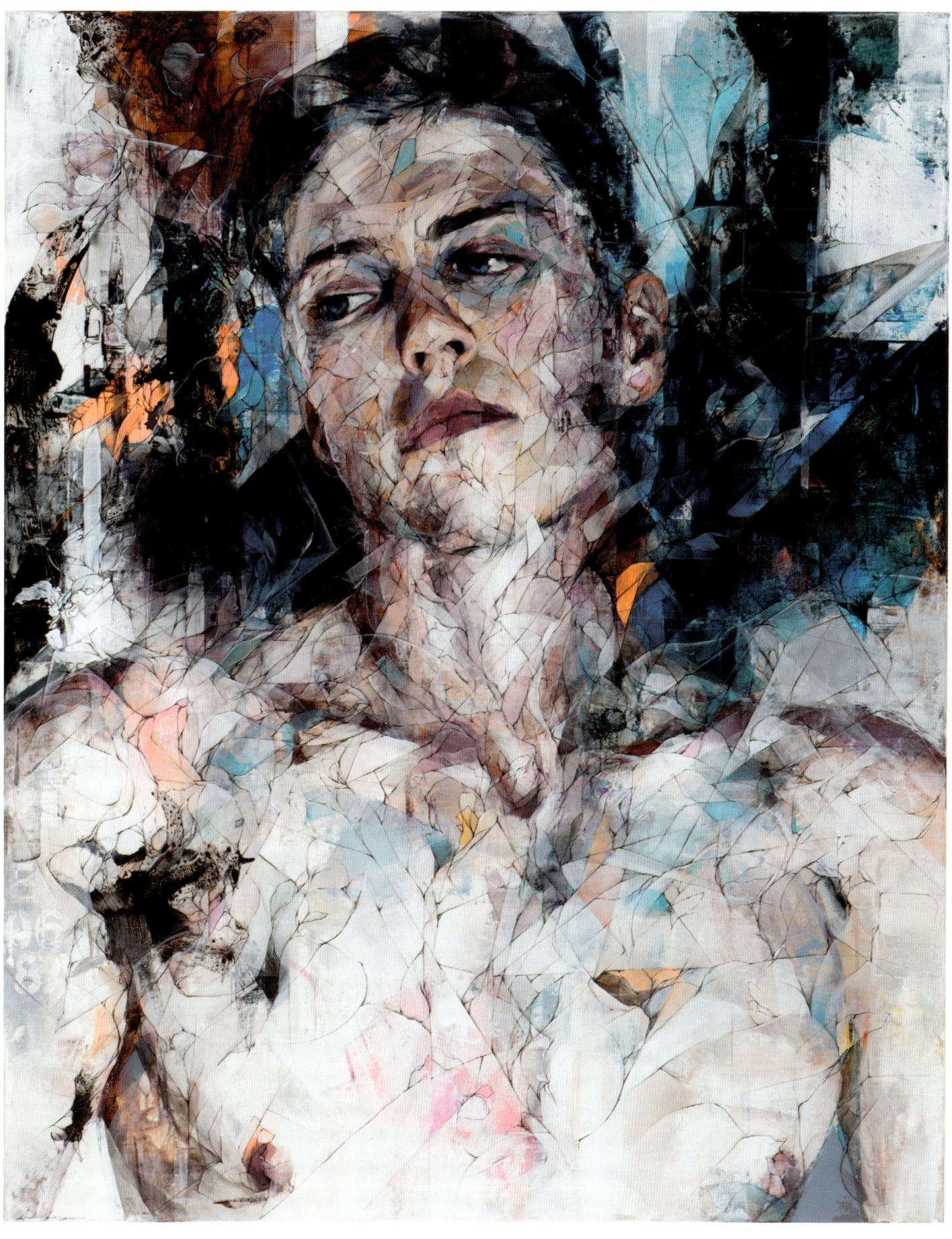

Aiden Kringen. *Seraph 4*, 2018.
Acrylic, gold leaf and mixed media on canvas:
24 × 18 inches.

Aiden Kringen. *Mind's Eye*, 2018.
Acrylic and mixed media on canvas: 60 × 48 inches.

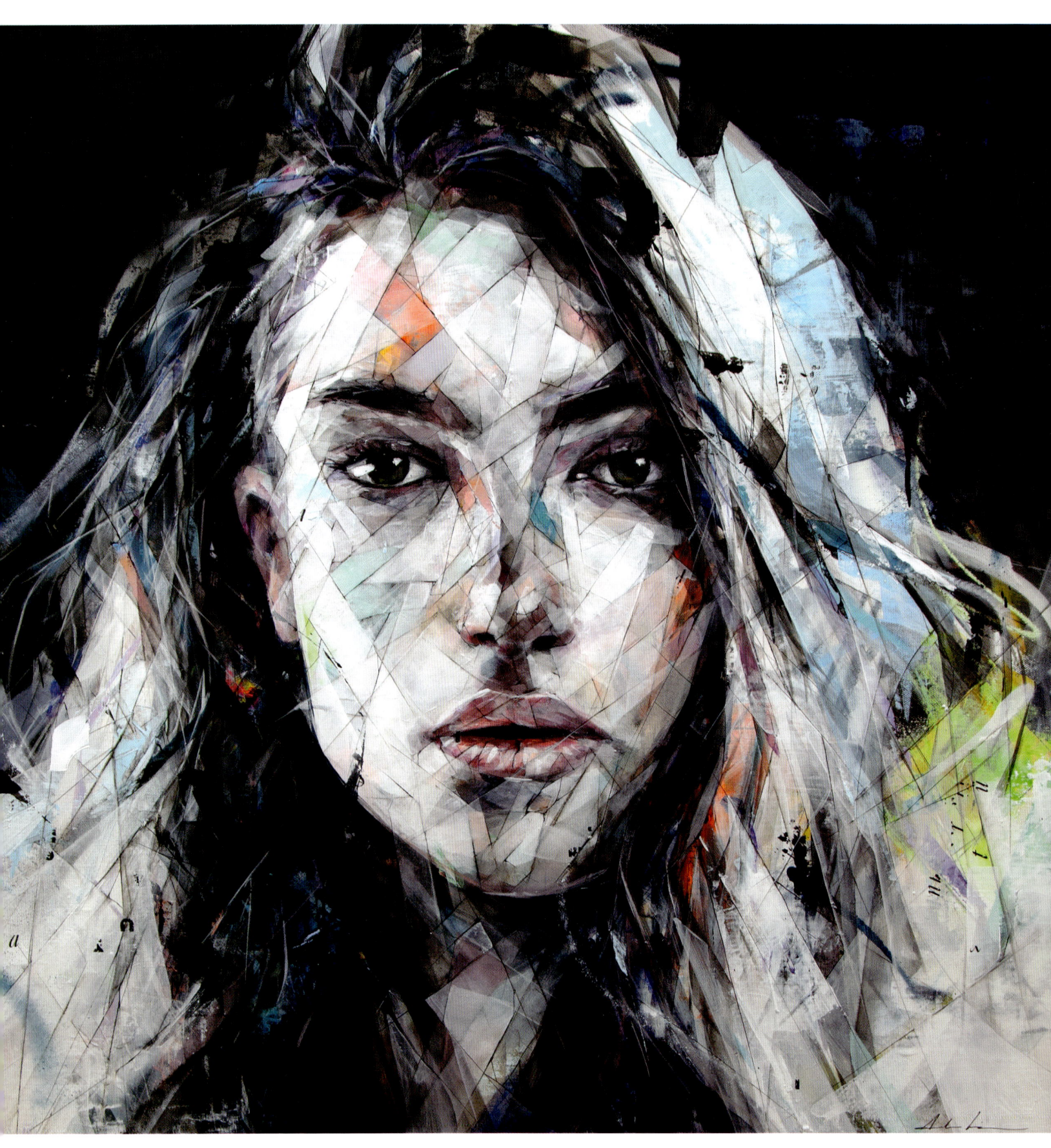

Aiden Kringen. *Emanate*, 2018.
Acrylic and mixed media on canvas:
30 × 30 inches.

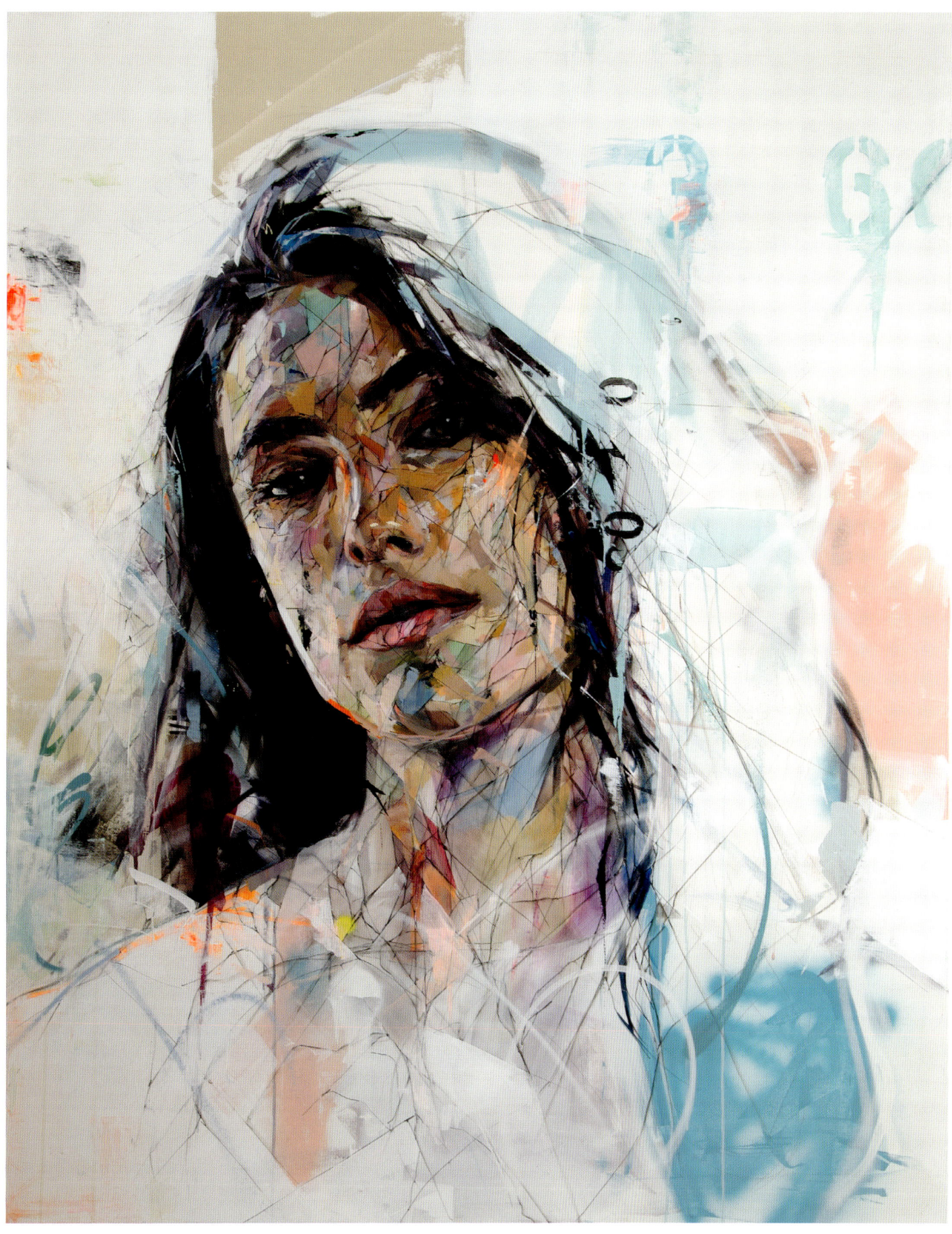

Aiden Kringen. *Intimation*, 2018.
Acrylic and mixed media on canvas:
60 × 48 inches.

JOSHUA MEYER

Lives and Works in: Cambridge, Massachusetts
Education: Yale University
Selected Collections: Public and private collections around
the world, including Hebrew College, Boston
Representation: Dolby Chadwick Gallery, San Francisco;
Lyons Wier Gallery, New York

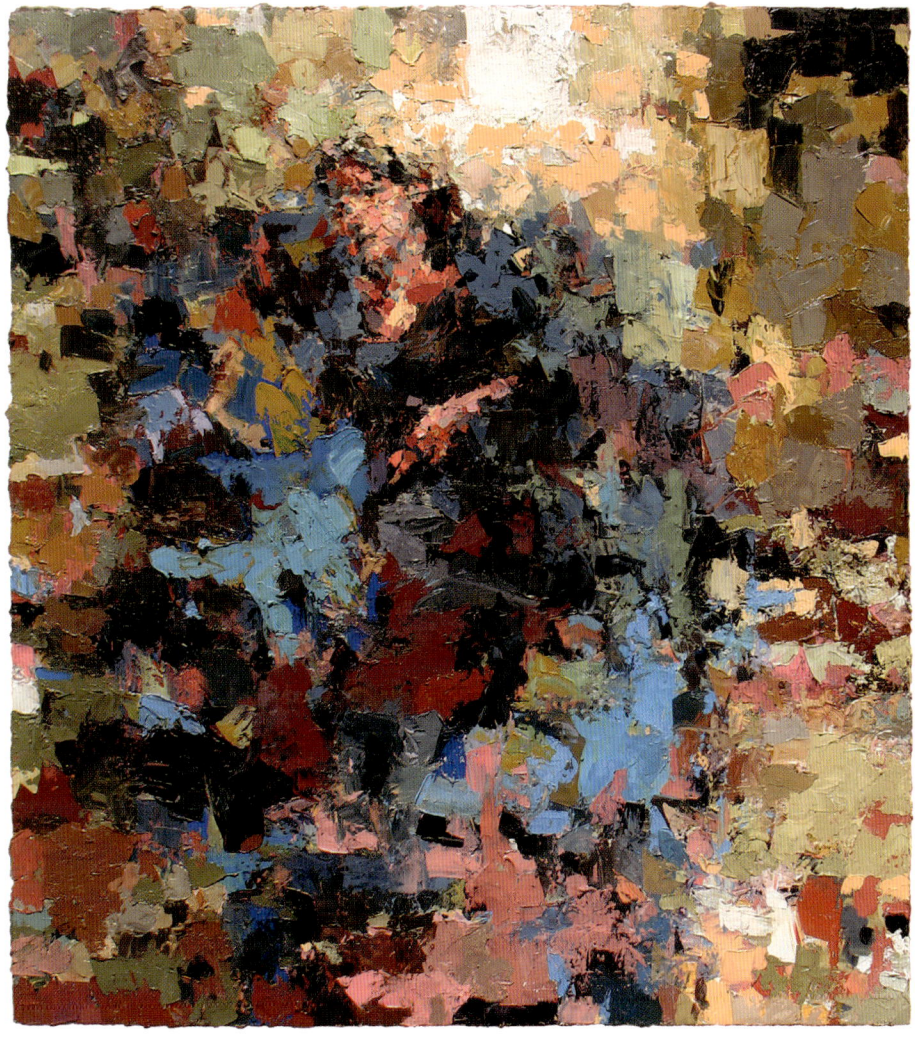

*My paintings are built
up by layering paint, so
that when you look at
the overlapping marks,
you see the days and
the months pass as the
people hide or emerge.*

Joshua Meyer. *Wild Blue Yonder,* 2010.
Oil on canvas: 38 × 42 inches.

How and why does your work disrupt or deviate from traditional realism?

A realist has to be fundamentally distrustful. That is the job of an artist: I am a questioner of reality. Without a healthy dose of skepticism, art will never reflect the world with any degree of honesty. My paintings show a process of searching. I'm not interested in fooling your eyes. Instead, I want to describe my relationship to the world.

I paint from life and I paint friends and family members. Over the weeks and months that it takes to finish a painting, lots of ideas and facts accrue. The paintings become physically thick. I am compelled by the facts that I see, but I distrust them. Different colors and forms emerge and compete. Facts contradict each other, and layers of paint accumulate on the canvas as a result of the struggle.

I want someone who approaches the painting to feel what it is like to make a painting, and to feel the struggle to understand and to see the world. It would be disingenuous if I left you with a harmoniously contoured image, because it took me so much more to get there. These paintings allow you to see when I pause and think.

I like a little dissonance. Art should be hard to pin down, and I am at my best when the pictures are unstable—unresolved in a way that demands that you, the viewer, play an active role.

How has your work evolved and developed over time?

My earliest paintings from my first few years out of Yale looked much more conventionally realistic. I painted with barely visible brushstrokes, and I was deeply indebted to Velásquez and Zurbarán and even Freud.

But—and I know this is a complicated distinction—I discovered that I was making paintings that looked like reality, instead of paintings that actually reflected the world around me. So I threw away my paintbrushes in an attempt to force myself to create a new vocabulary for my art. My paintings immediately changed. By leaving my process open and visible, the paintings can contain—just as a person can—many overlapping ideas and stories. It is hard to know a person until you see these aspects and impulses begin to weave together.

What are some of the influences that have shaped your work?

So many painters have helped me grapple with the world, from Giacometti and Frank Auerbach to Antonio Lopez Garcia. But poets are the artists most responsible for shaping the way I approach realism. The brilliant Polish poet Wislawa Szymborska, who wrote "The Joy of Writing," and A. R. Ammons are able to simultaneously describe and translate the world around them. Wallace Stevens is often with me in the studio. More than anyone else, he goes directly at the motives for metaphor and the disjunction between art and reality. I cannot stop rereading "Prologues to What Is Possible."

Mention something interesting about your life and background.

In kindergarten my teacher yelled at me for writing with a yellow crayon. I was really upset—and I don't know why anyone let her work with kids—but that was the first time I wanted to be an artist. These days I use yellow as much as my heart desires.

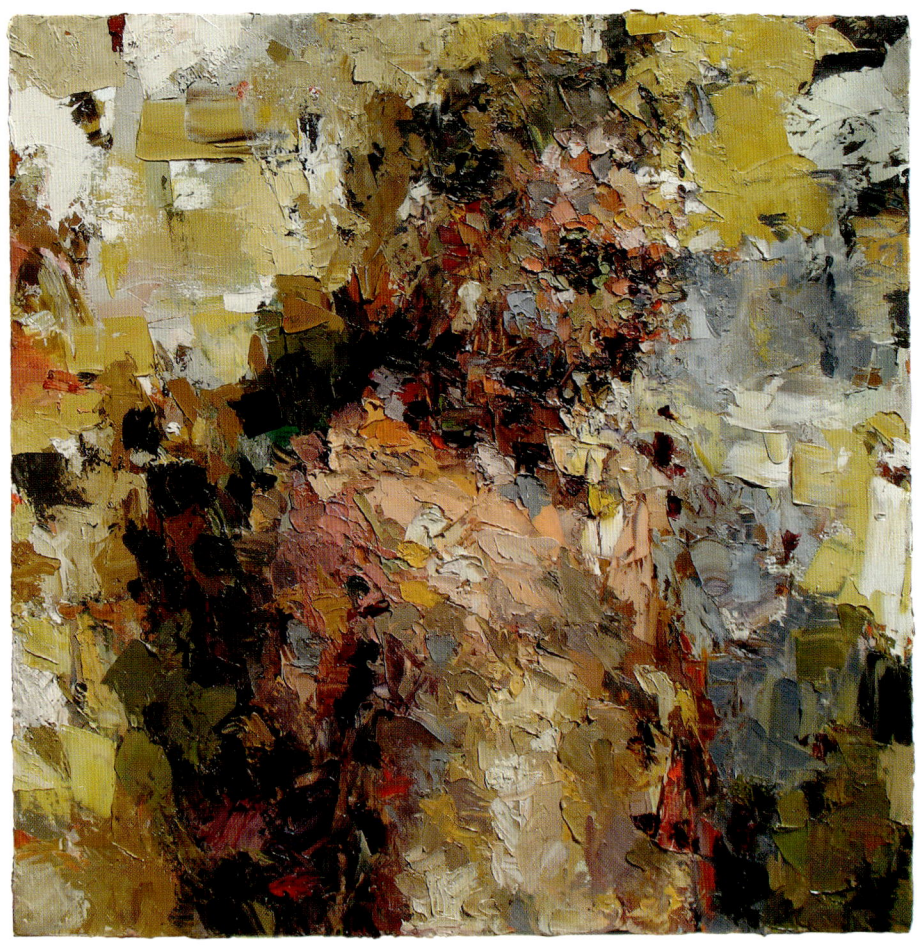

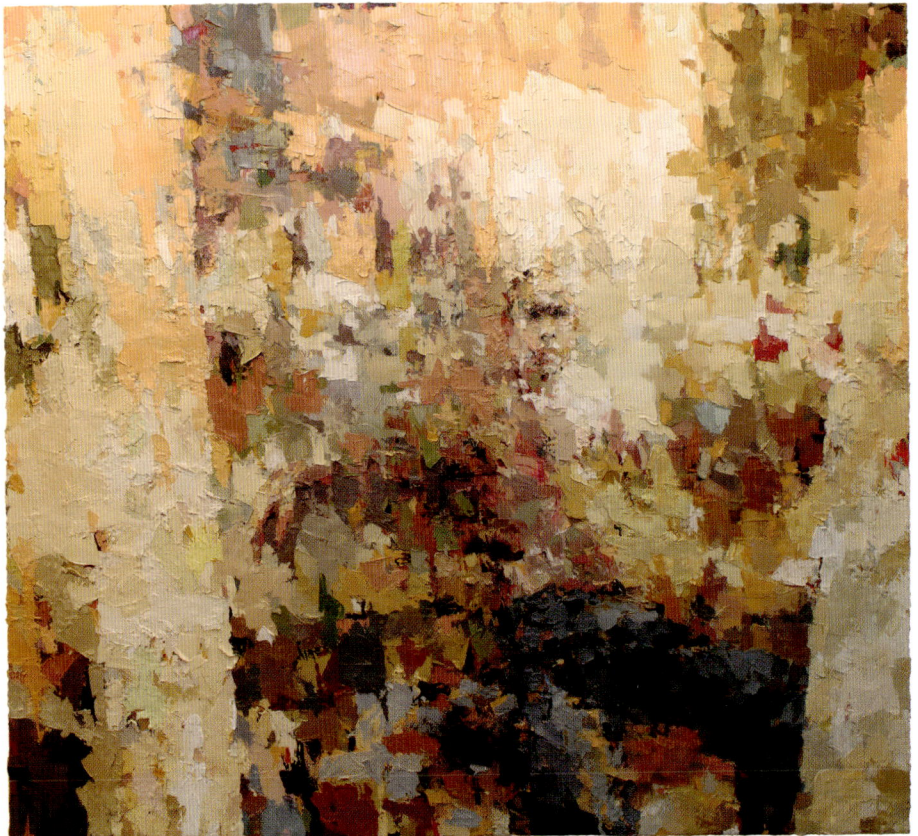

Joshua Meyer. *Accidents That Always Happen,* 2009.   Joshua Meyer. *Hide,* 2011.
Oil on canvas: 24 × 24 inches.   Oil on board: 48 × 43 inches.

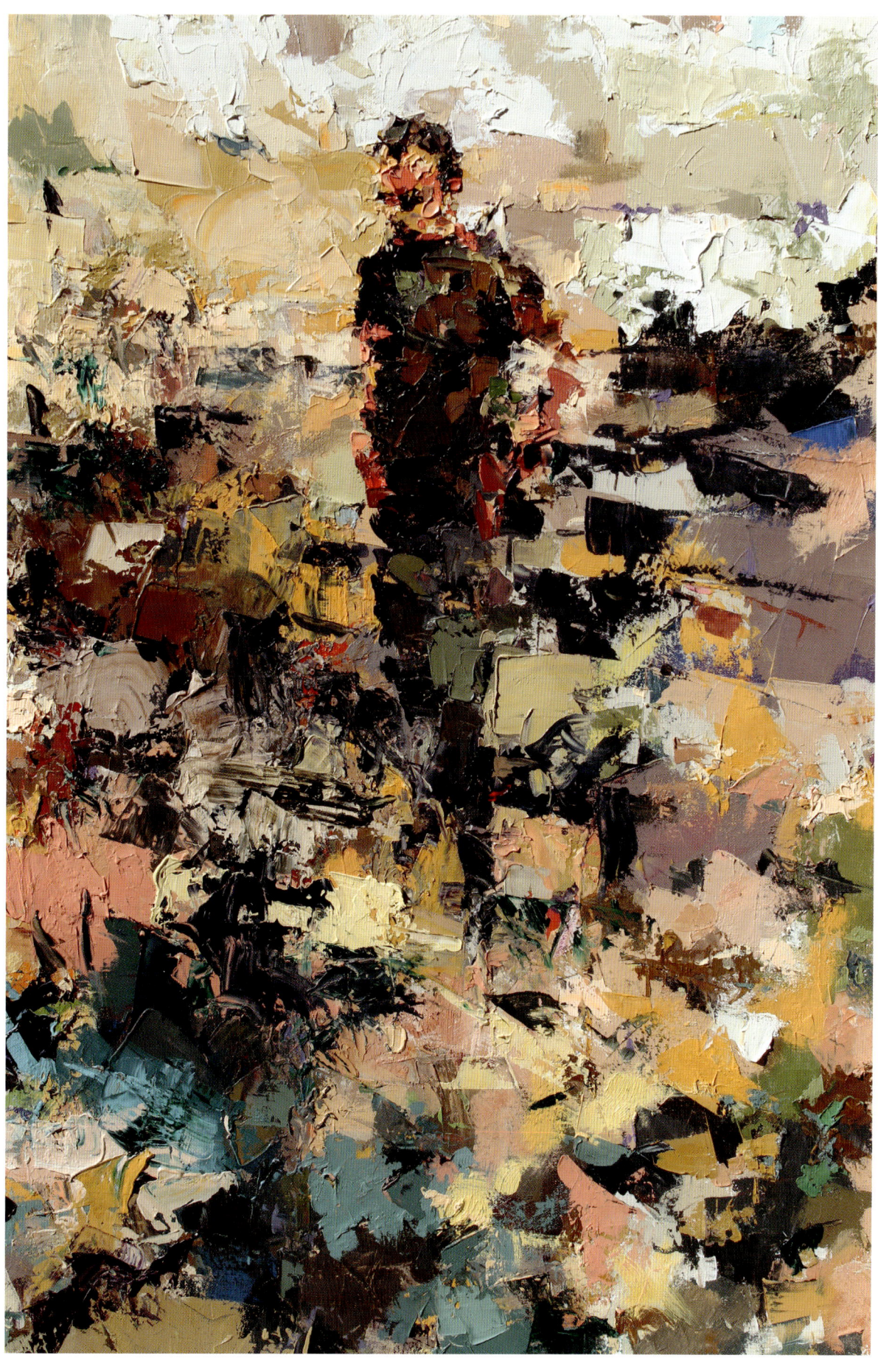

Joshua Meyer. *The Grinding Water and
Gasping Wind*, 2017.
Oil on canvas: 40 × 36 inches.

Overleaf: Joshua Meyer. *Many Distances*, 2017.
Oil on canvas: 48 × 36 inches.

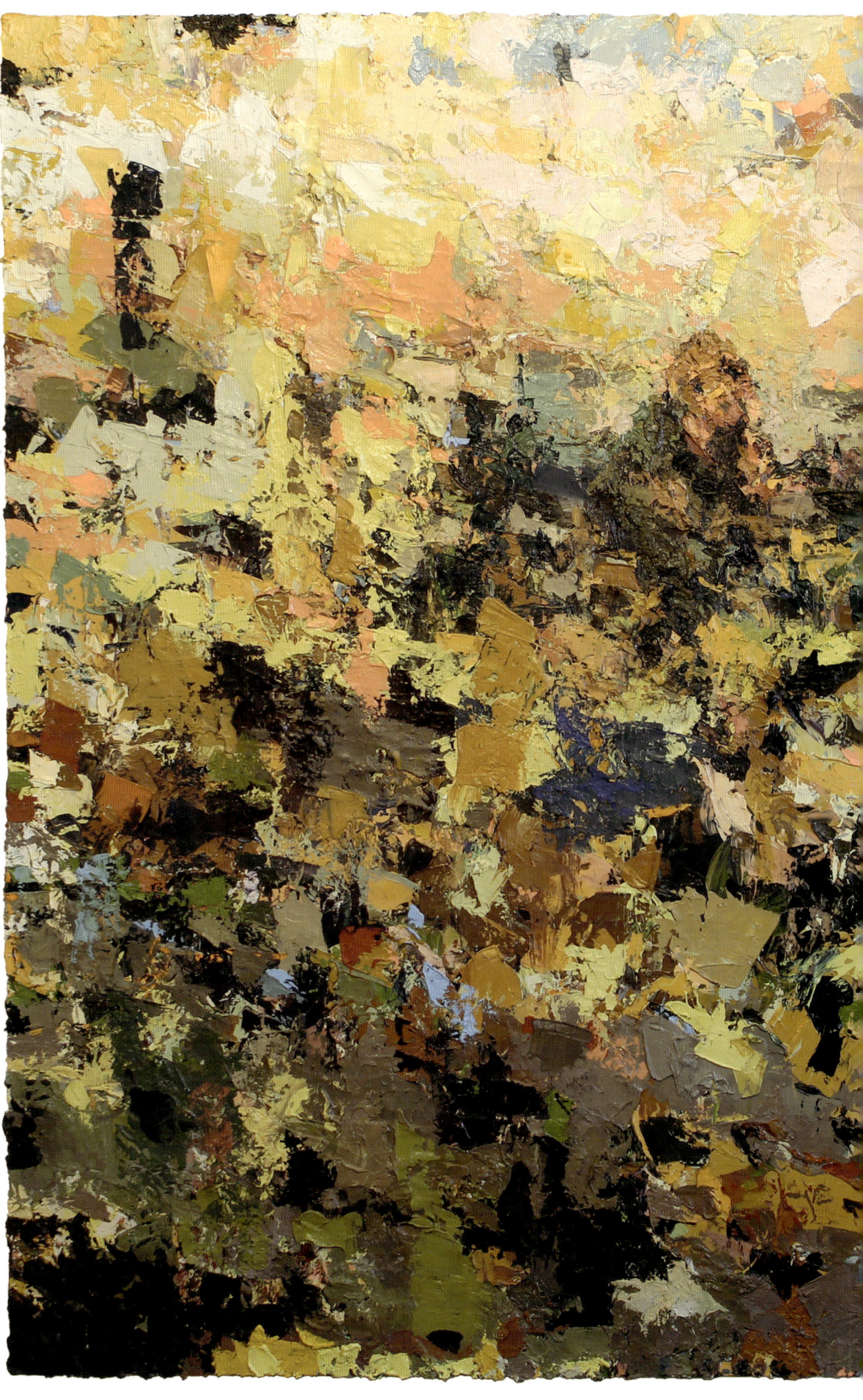

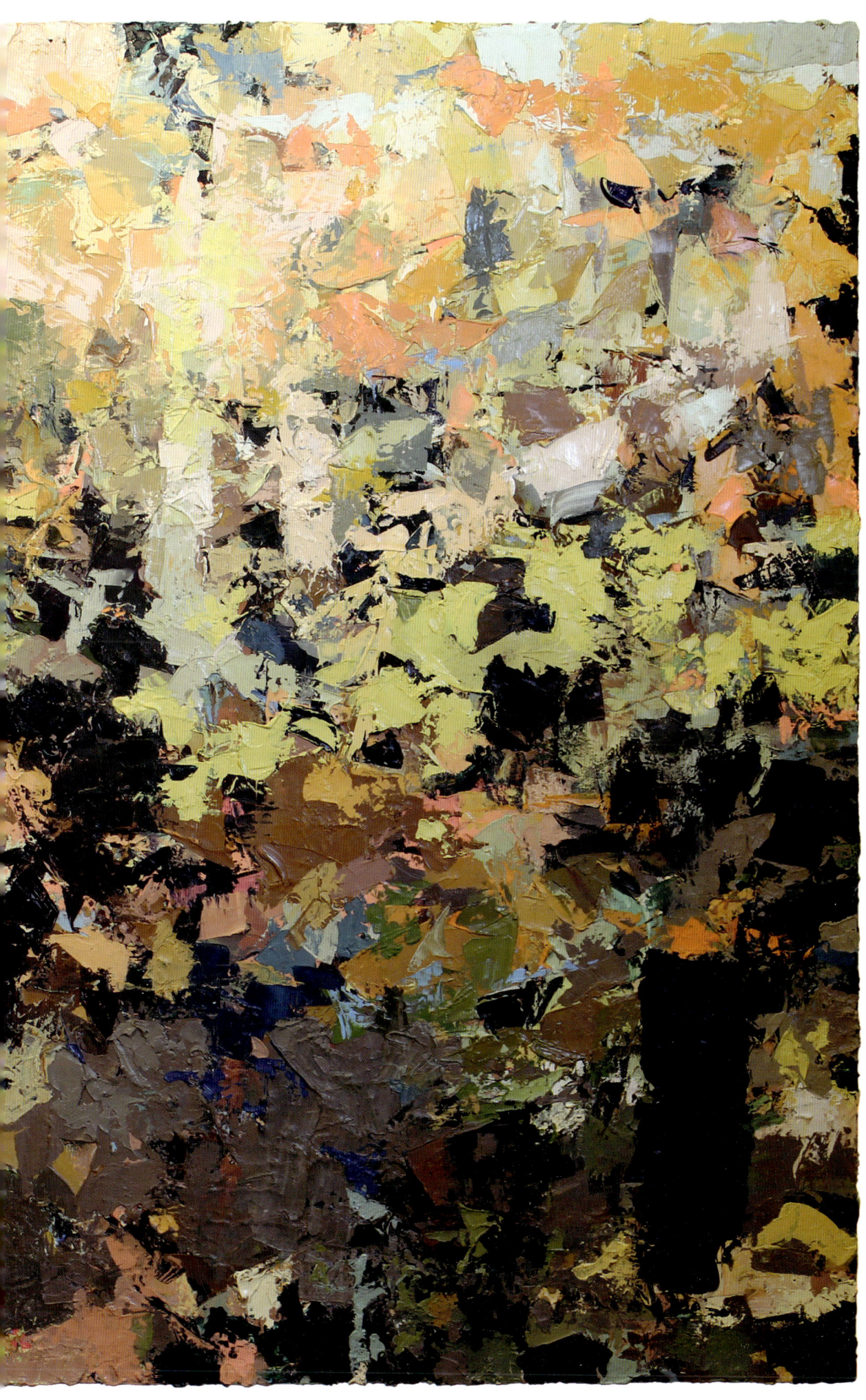

STEPHANIE PIERCE

Lives and Works in: Brooklyn, New York
Education: BFA, the Art Institute of Boston; MFA,
University of Washington, Seattle
Selected Collections: William Dreyfus, Kisco, New York; Wellington
Management, Boston; the Museum of Fine Arts, Boston
Representation: Steven Harvey Fine Art Projects, New York

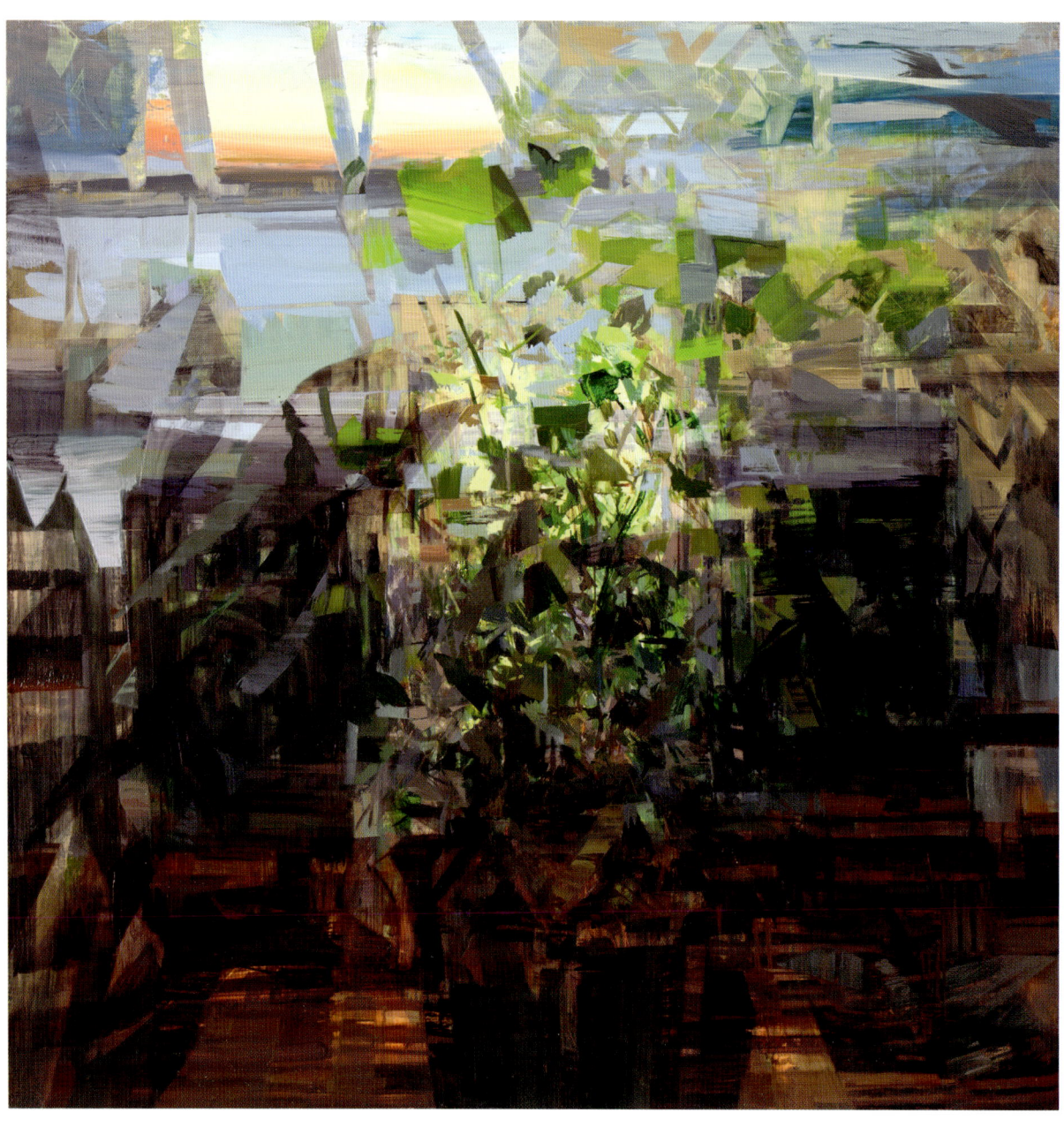

I strive to remain open to phenomenal experience, perception, and time, and to getting lost inside it.

How and why does your work disrupt or deviate from traditional realism?

It depends on which tradition of realism is being referred to. I make observation-based paintings that explore interrelationships between light, time, and perception and how things evolve as they are reconsidered over time. The paintings are a record of ongoing transitions, rather than a seamless illusion of a single moment. The paintings are concrete statements that convey transition and offer multiple readings of what is seen.

How has your work evolved and developed over time?

I've lost the sense of expectation about what my paintings are going to look like. I work to unfamiliarize things that I'm looking at until there's a kind of hallucinatory sense of all-at-once-ness and realization of time transitions in the paintings. My process has slowed down a lot; the paintings may take up to a year to complete and span several seasons. They've increasingly become more intensely layered.

What are some of the influences that have shaped your work?

I've always been mesmerized by the movement of shapes of light sweeping through a room, and was trying to paint moving things long before art school. Some influences on my work have been Cézanne, cubism, Antonio Lopez Garcia, and ideas related to perception and experience. As a student I gravitated toward artists whose work conveyed a sense of flux or seemed unfixed. De Kooning was an early love, and specific works by Picasso: a drypoint of Marie Therese and his linocuts, especially the portrait after Cranach. During undergrad at Yale Norfolk I once met Gideon Bok, whose work was a revelation to me. The dissonance and unraveling heard in some punk bands like Hüsker Dü and so many other punk bands have also been influential on how I think about painting.

Mention something interesting about your life and background.

I was liberated as a teenager by painting (thanks to my first mentor, Bill Hicks) and punk music. Painting and the DIY community have been central in my life ever since. I've lived all over the country in many different kinds of places, and I'm interested in them all.

Stephanie Pierce. *Searcher,* 2018.
Oil on linen: 20 × 20 inches.

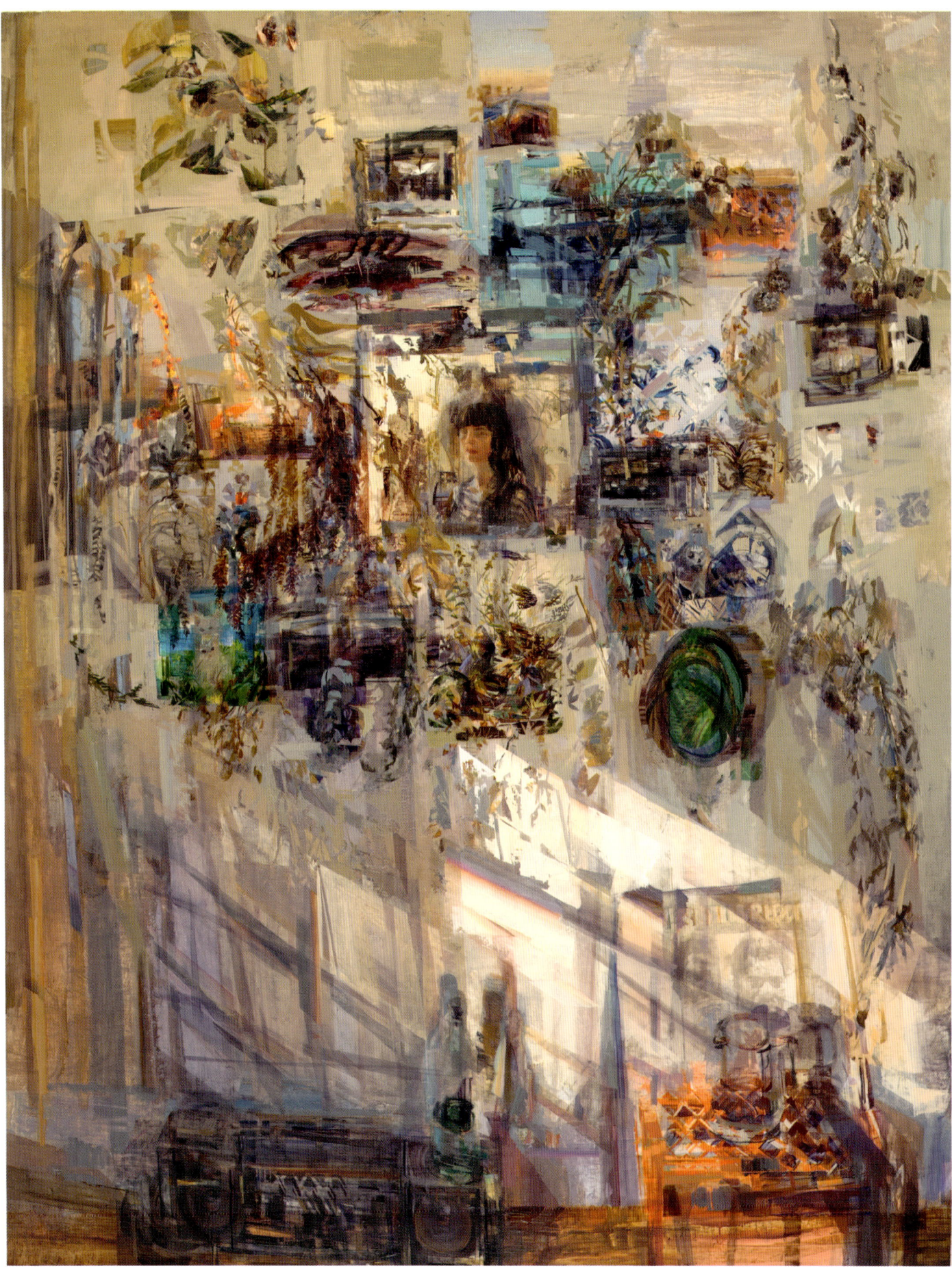

Stephanie Pierce. *I, Cloud,* 2018.
Oil on linen: 64 × 50 inches.

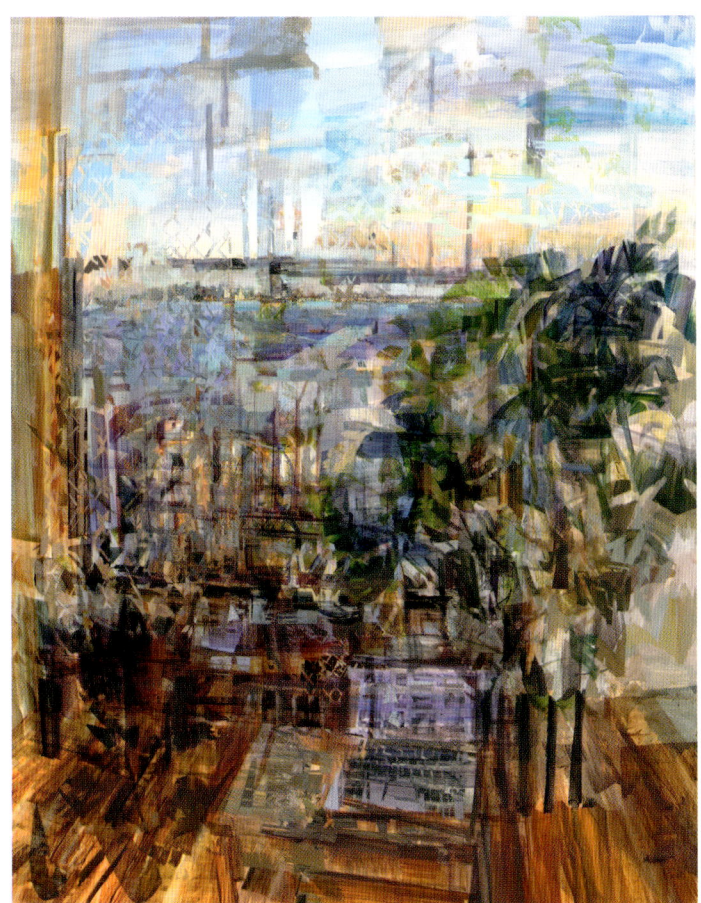

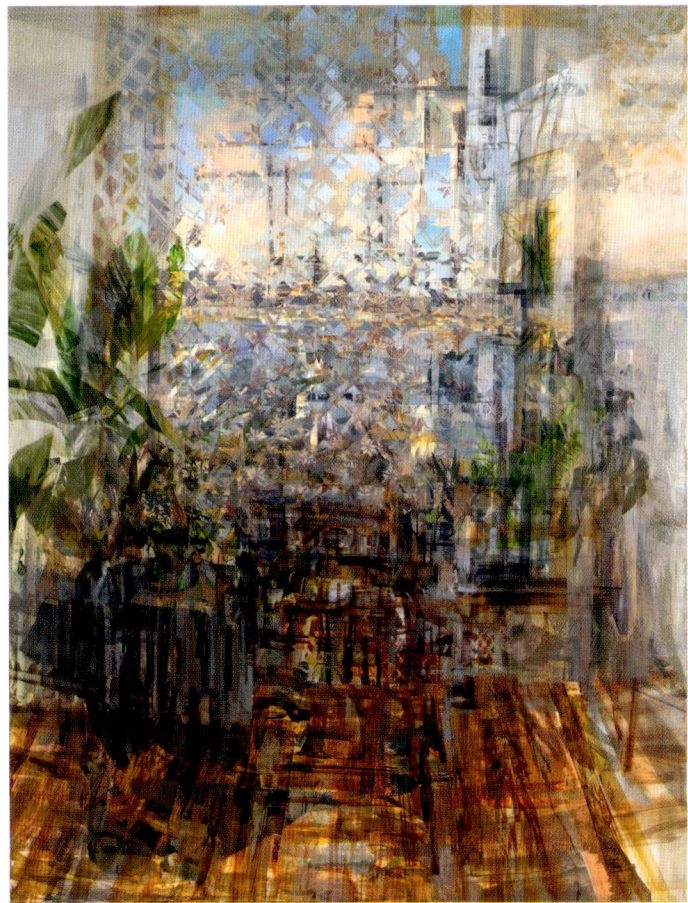

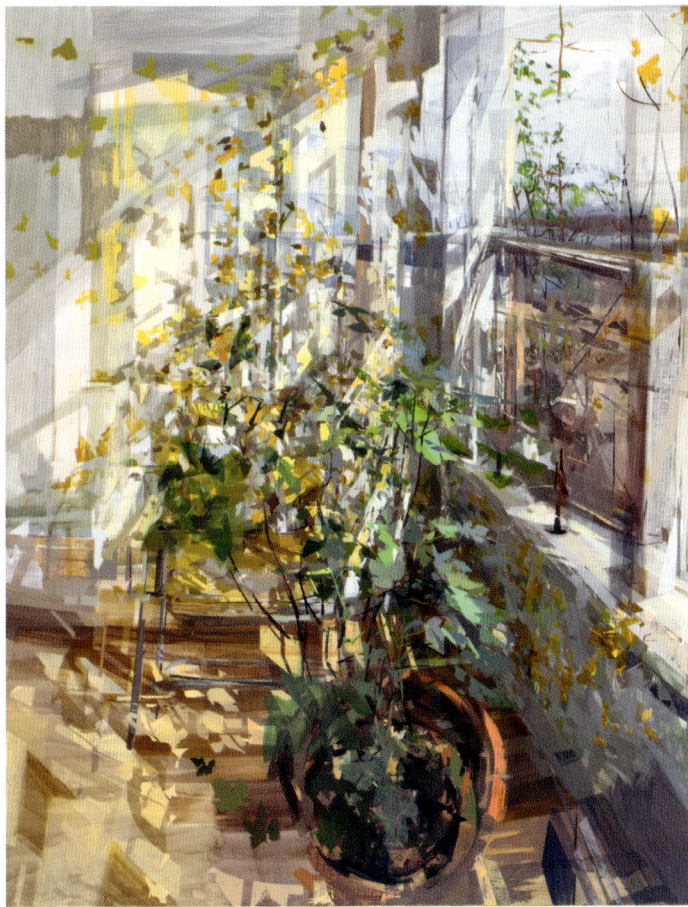

Top left: Stephanie Pierce. *Diamond Light*, 2018. Oil on linen: 64 × 50 inches.

Top right: Stephanie Pierce. *Voyager*, 2016. Oil on linen: 64 × 50 inches.

Stephanie Pierce. *Radiant Welter*, 2013. Oil on canvas: 64 × 50 inches.

DORIAN VALLEJO

Lives and Works in: Easton, Pennsylvania
Education: School of Visual Arts, New York
Selected Collections: Private
Representation: Rehs Gallery, New York

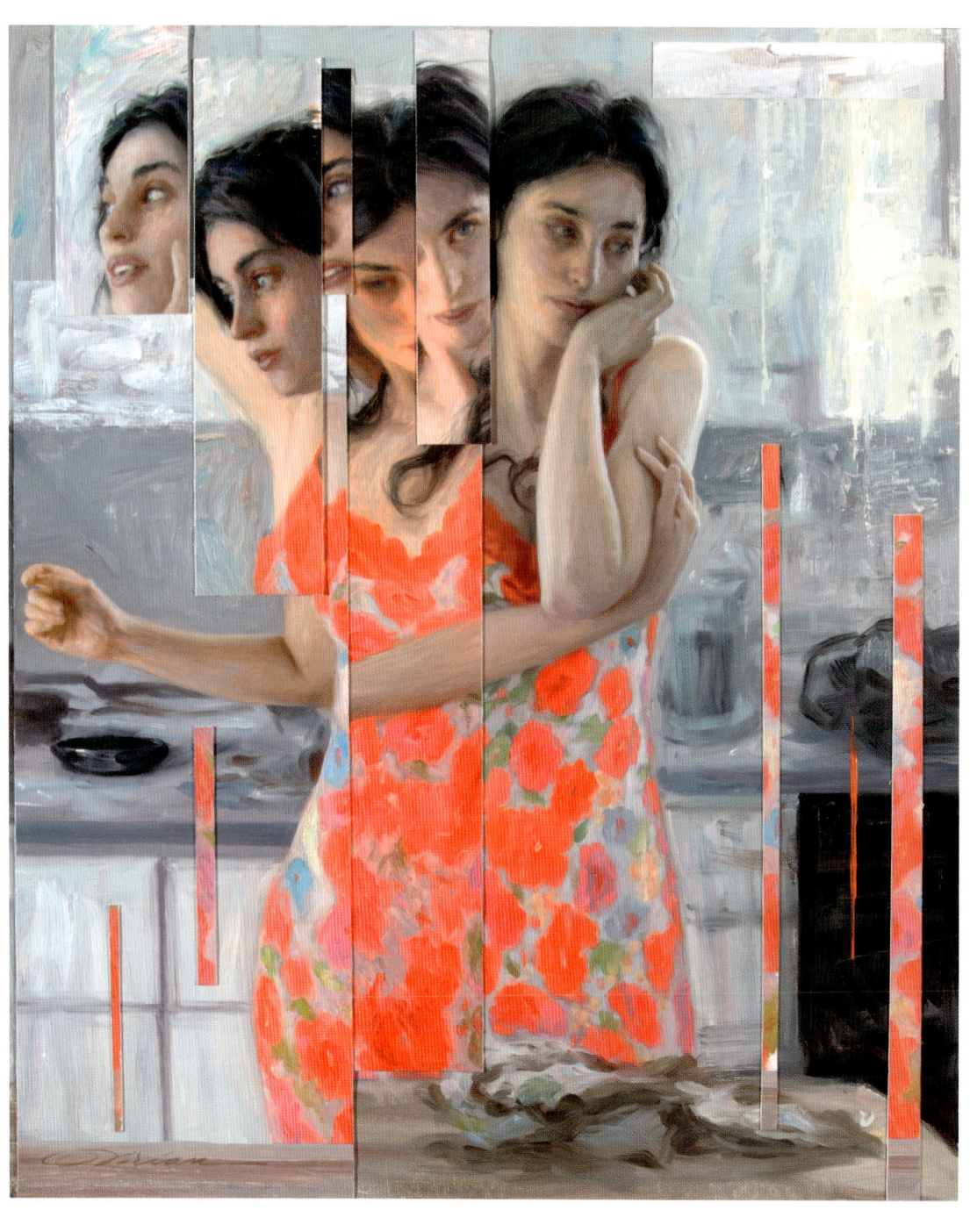

My paintings and drawings are a type of romantic realism; they are an optimistic, inquisitive, poetic response to life, for which I hold a deep reverence.

How and why does your work disrupt or deviate from traditional realism?

One of the most salient aspects of the artistic process for me is the freedom to experiment. Without question, my sentiments regarding the history of art lie squarely with the tradition of realism, as first developed by the ancient Greeks. Perhaps it's precisely for that reason that I choose to challenge my most cherished values by engaging abstraction. The intention in mining new territory was specifically to depart from traditional representation, in pursuit of a symbolic narrative. Not necessarily to disrupt anything I hold dear, but in order to genuinely ascertain whether I might add another way of sharing what I understand as the human experience.

How has your work evolved and developed over time?

When my first artistic ambitions began to emerge, I made a promise to myself that I would sincerely work to make my current attempt better than the previous one. This has never been difficult because I've always been able to see room for improvement. It has indicated to me when it was necessary to change directions, as my interests have expanded and kept me excited about the process. I wouldn't say that I was fearful when I was younger, but over time I've become more willing to be reckless with my experiments.

What are some of the influences that have shaped your work?

My earliest influences were gleaned from a steady diet of comics, sci-fi/fantasy movies, and the artistic environment my parents cultivated in our home. While attending art school I became enthralled by the purity of working directly from life, and it became a major part of the way I work and think about art. After school I found the writing of Joseph Campbell and several philosophers, which helped to shape much of the internal dialog that would eventually make itself apparent in my experimental paintings and drawings.

Mention something interesting about your life and background.

Almost all aspects of my life are related to my experience as an artist. I never need a break from art. Food, exercise, reading, home, relationships, etc. are all part of a set of values carefully considered within my choice as an artist.

Dorian Vallejo. *The Clarity of Thought*, 2016. Oil on panel: 22 × 26 inches.

Overleaf: Dorian Vallejo. *Composition of Thought,* 2016. Oil on paper: 9 × 12 inches.

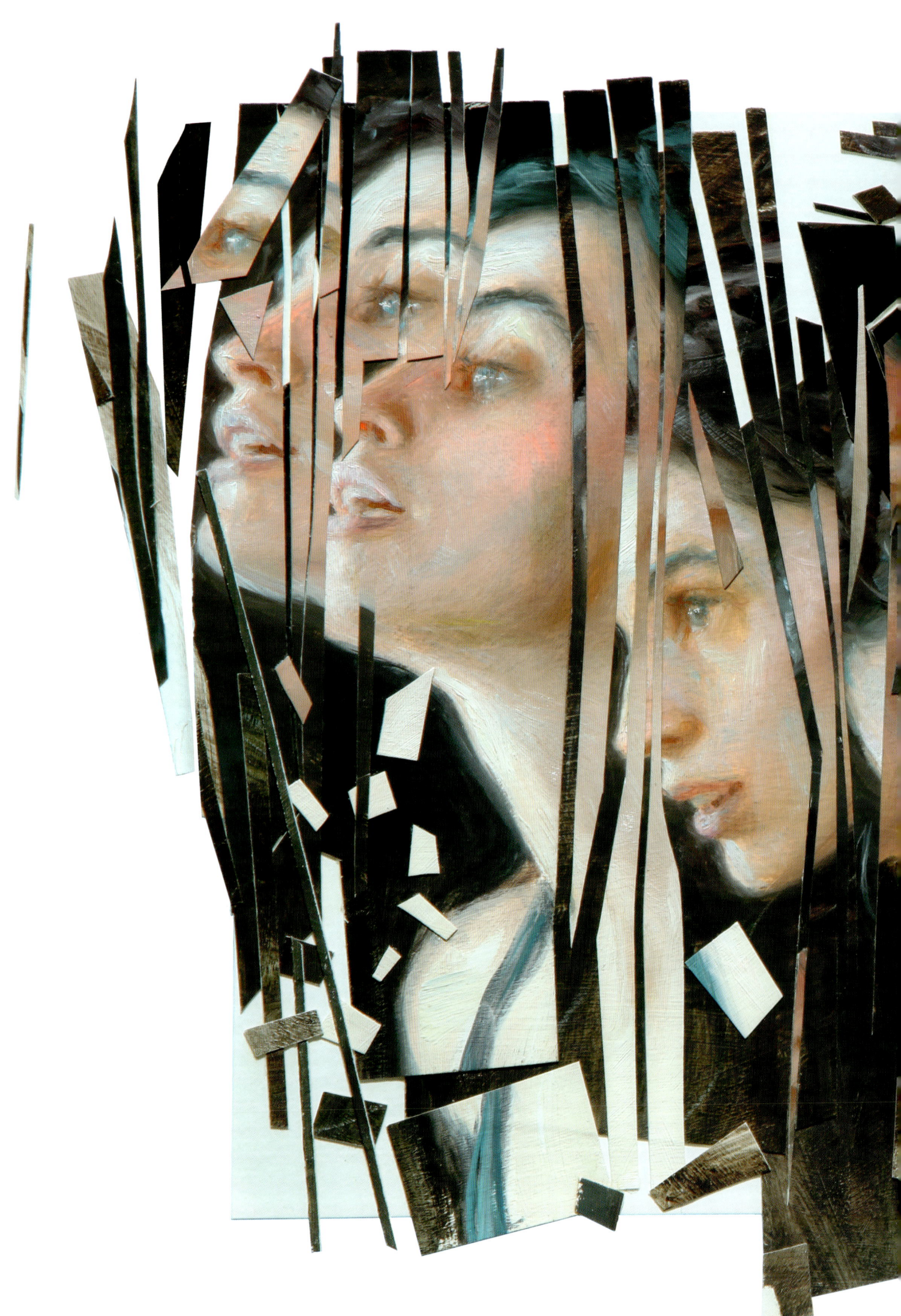

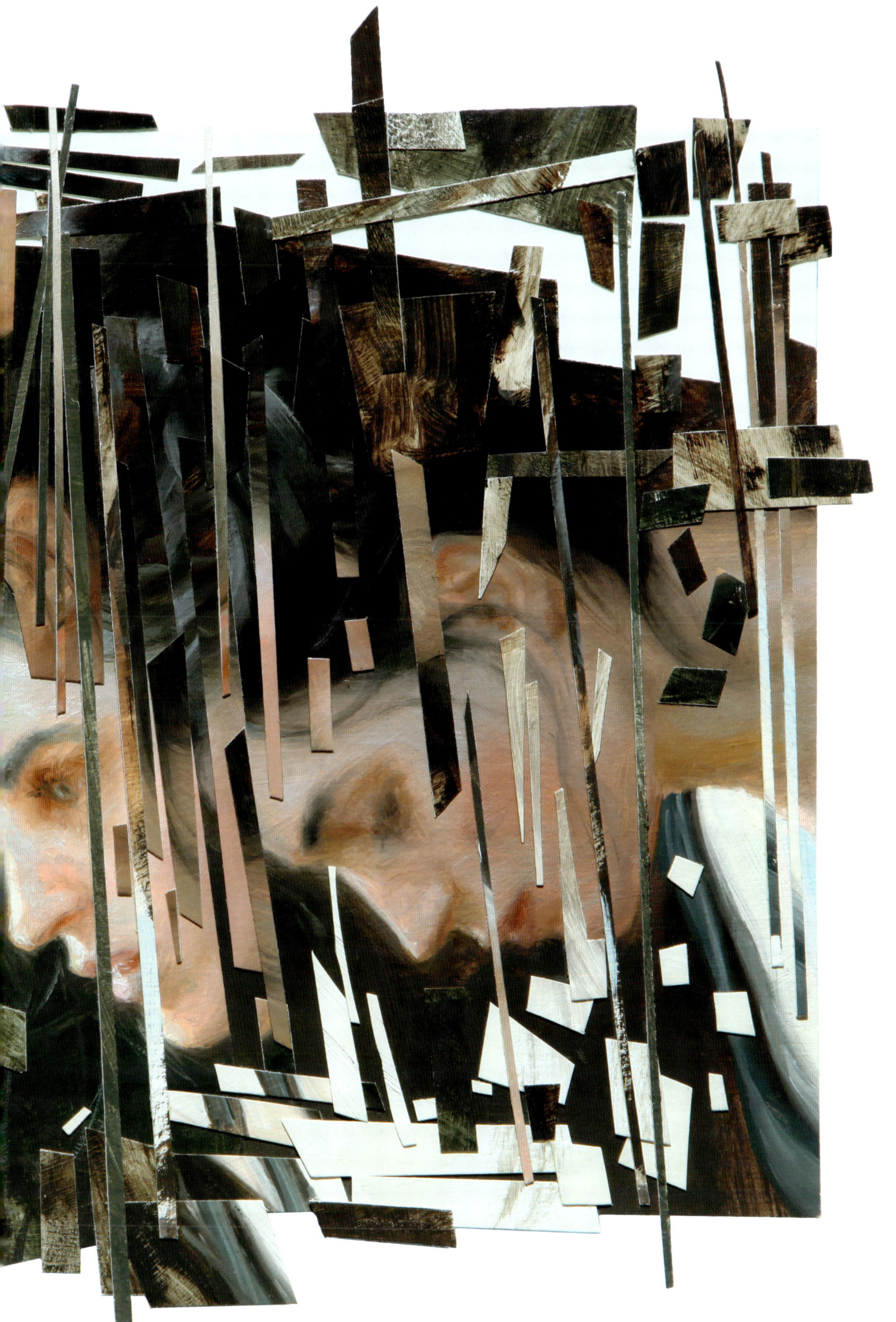

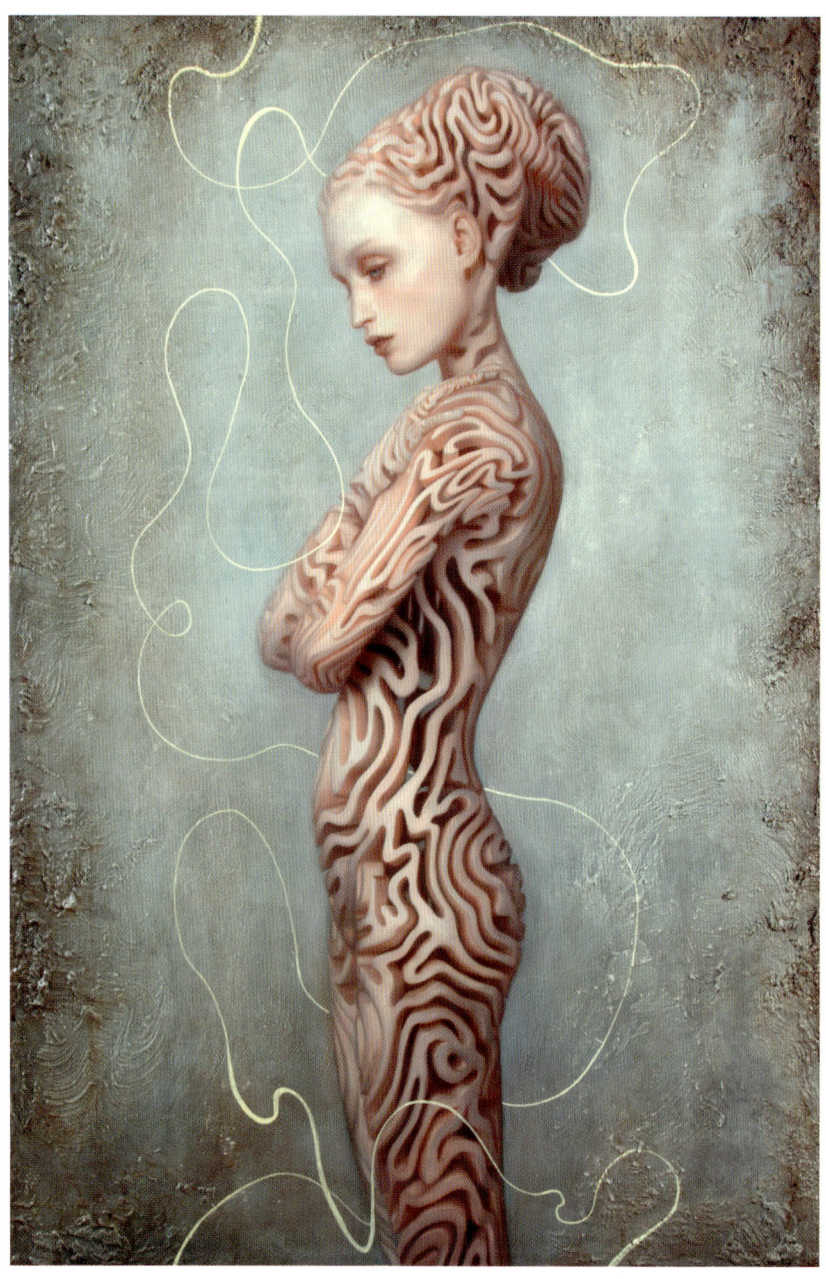

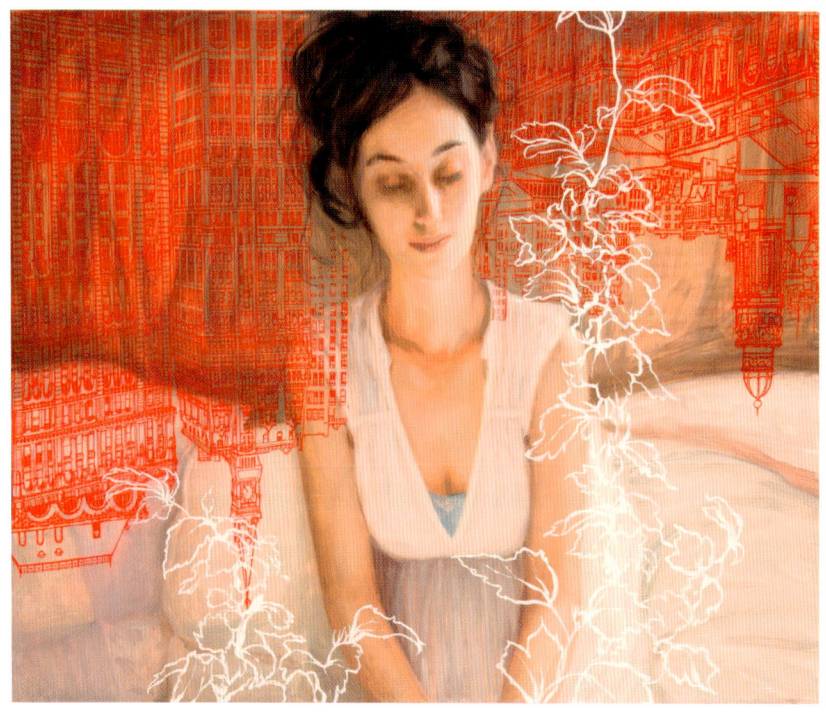

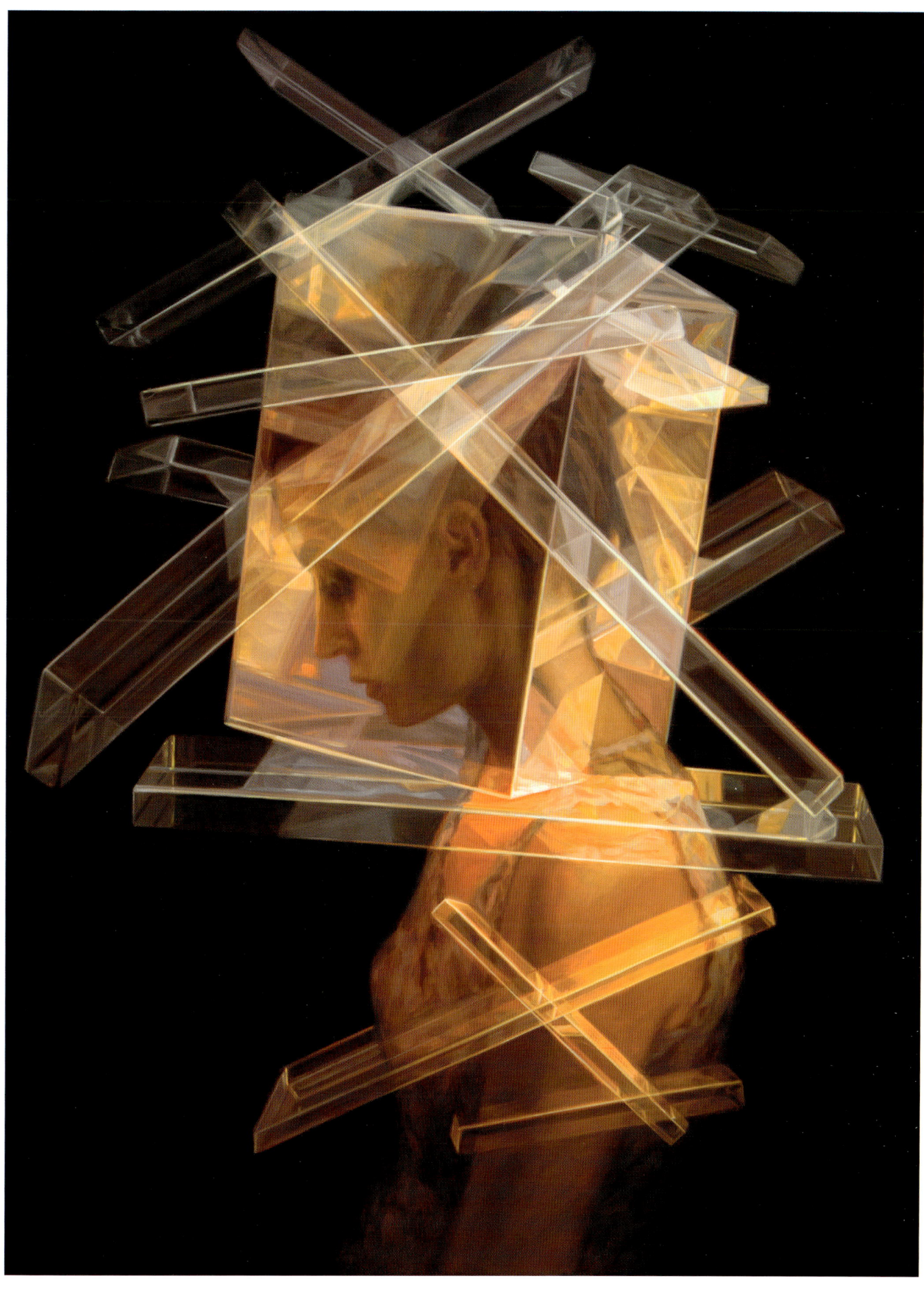

Dorian Vallejo. *Passages,* 2016.
Oil on panel: 24 × 36 inches.

Dorian Vallejo. *Remembrance of Clarity,* 2016.
Oil on panel: 20 × 24 inches.

Dorian Vallejo. *Reflections,* 2016.
Oil on panel: 18 × 24 inches.

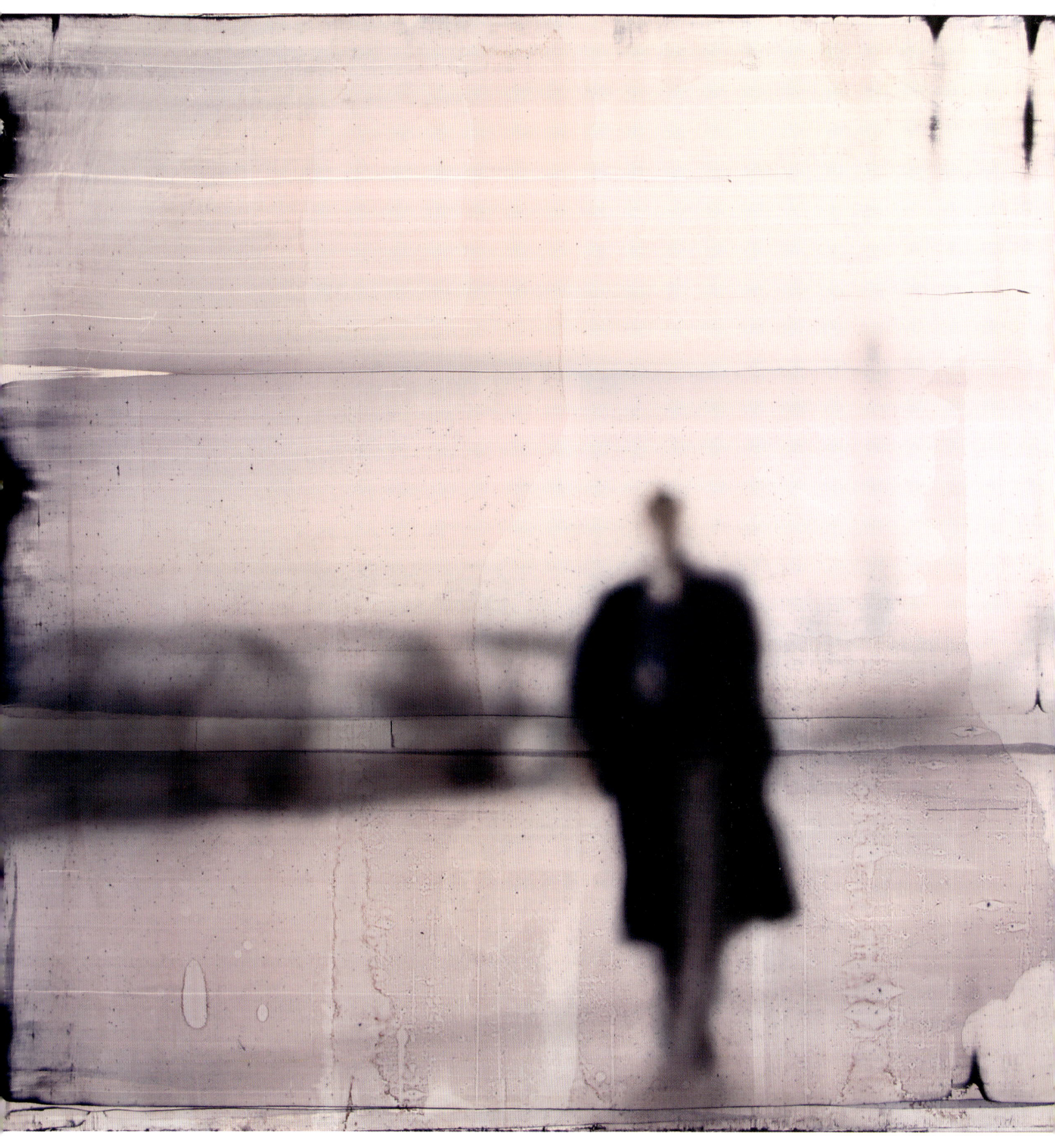

Between Painting and Photography

Richter's overpainted photographs had a big effect on me. They challenged any clear notions I had about what "abstract" and "representational" meant.

—Wendelin Wohlgemuth

There isn't a painter alive today who hasn't grown up in a world saturated by photographs, film, and video. The familiarity and omnipresence of these images have made them part of culture, and of memory. The question of what to do with these images (and the memories of them) challenges the current generation of painters. Finding ways to merge, intermingle, and call up photographic imagery with a brush is a paradoxical and challenging task.

Wendelin Wohlgemuth. *Man with Lighthouse,* 2018. Oil on panel: 31.4 × 31.4 inches.

COLIN CHILLAG

GAGE OPDENBROUW

ADAM VINSON

WENDELIN WOHLGEMUTH

COLIN CHILLAG

Lives and Works in: Phoenix, Arizona

Education: San Francisco Art Institute

Selected Collections: Arizona State University Art Museum, Tempe; Scottsdale Museum of Contemporary Art, Scottsdale, Arizona; University of Arizona Art Museum, Tucson

Representation: Elizabeth Houston Gallery, New York

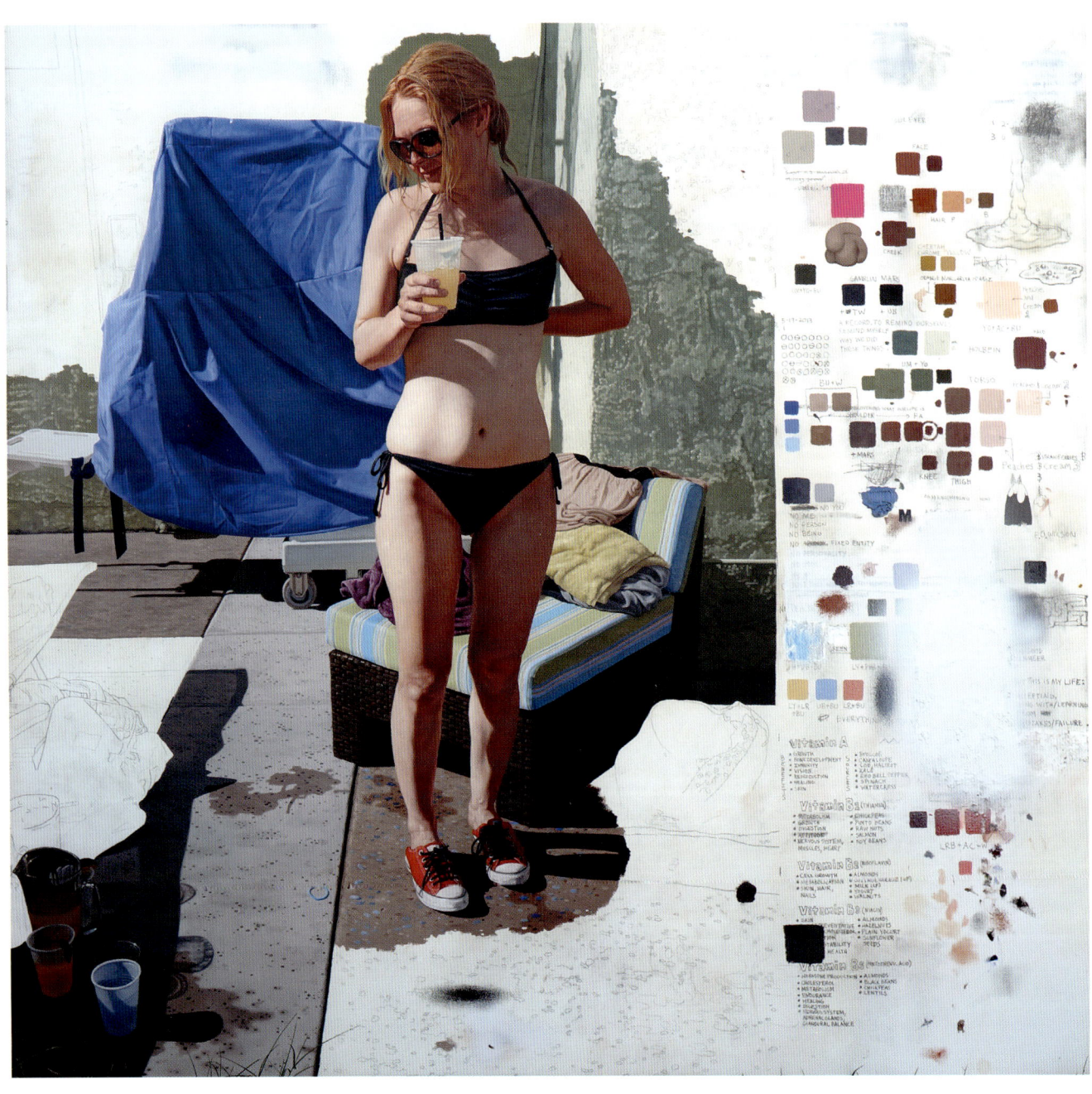

It would be very difficult to describe my work in a single sentence, given the range and general disparity of my styles, subjects, and intentions.

How and why does your work disrupt or deviate from traditional realism?

As a young artist, realism was one among many different genres of painting that I explored; my earlier work tended toward a pluralistic approach to painting. At a certain point, however, realism became my sole focus. For a time I pursued a very stripped-down and minimal form of realist painting, which was intended to be devoid of all formal or conceptual exaggeration or embellishment. There was nothing fantastic or romantic in these works, and I also wanted to remove everything in relation to narrative in favor of what I felt was a purely observation-based way of painting. It was this process of intense and sustained focus and close observation of everyday reality that appealed most to me.

How has your work evolved and developed over time?

During this exploration I was confronted with what seemed like an intractable contradiction between what I considered to be this most honest and straightforward way of painting and the highly illusionistic and somewhat deceptive method of depicting material reality. This is why I developed a paradoxical view of realist painting in my work. My solution to this dilemma—if it can be called that—was to reveal as much of the painting process as possible. So, many of the works during this period have a "half-finished" look that reveals a portion of the underlying pencil sketch and various states of completion, as well as other markers of the process, like color swatches, palette mixtures and scrapings, and notes to self regarding the process. I was happy for a time with having achieved a way of working that felt symbolically meaningful in its process and physicality and that had achieved what felt like a degree of parity between what was being depicted and the process by which it was being depicted.

What are some of the influences that have shaped your work?

One notable influence on my work that relates significantly to my realist work is meditation. My meditation practice is spotty at best these days, but for a number of years I was very involved with it, and I think the practice of present-time awareness had a direct impact on how I paint to this day.

Mention something interesting about your life or background.

One of the many jobs I've held over the years was as a long-haul truck driver.

Colin Chillag. *Poolside Jenna*, 2014.
Oil on canvas: 54 × 64 inches.

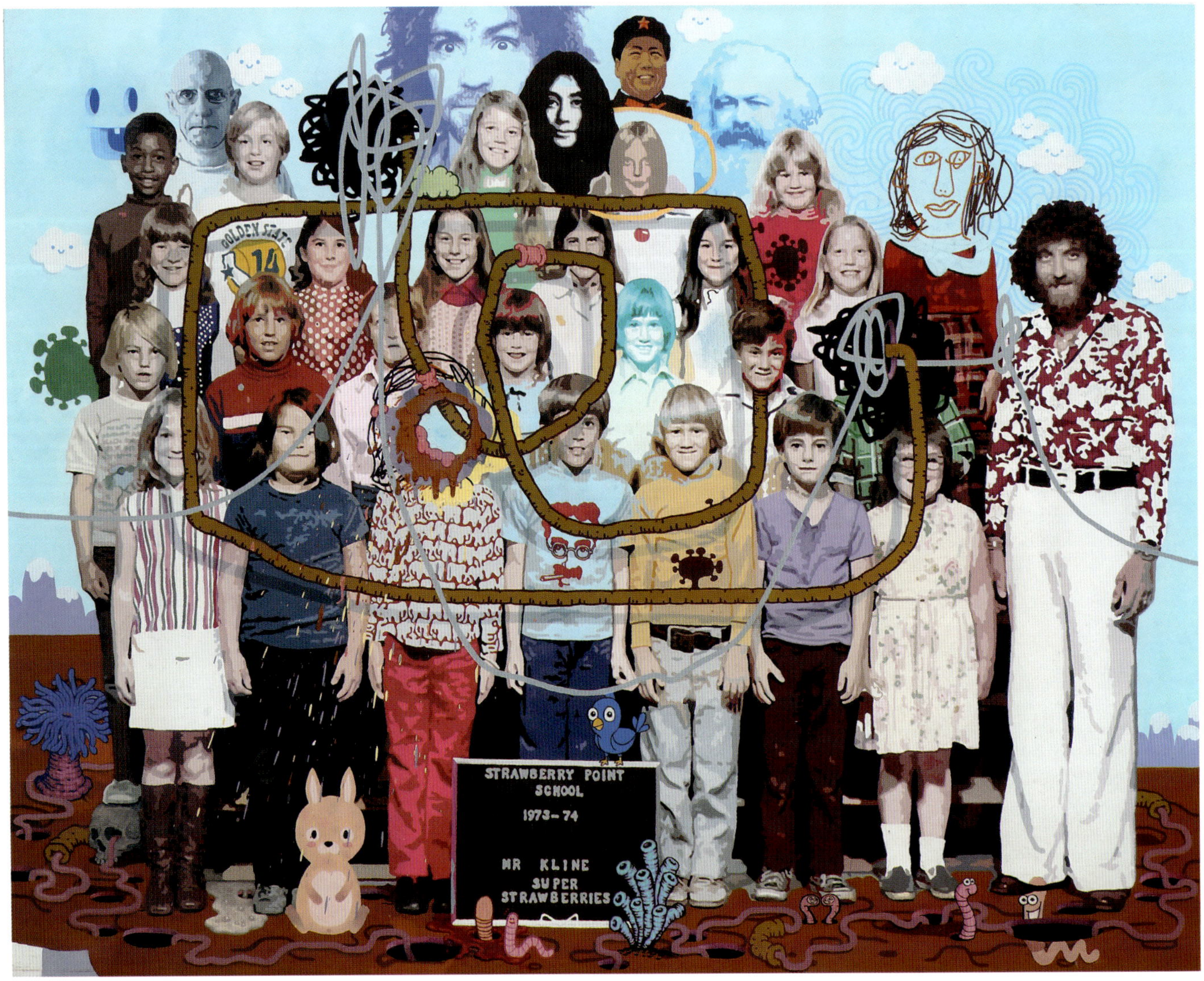

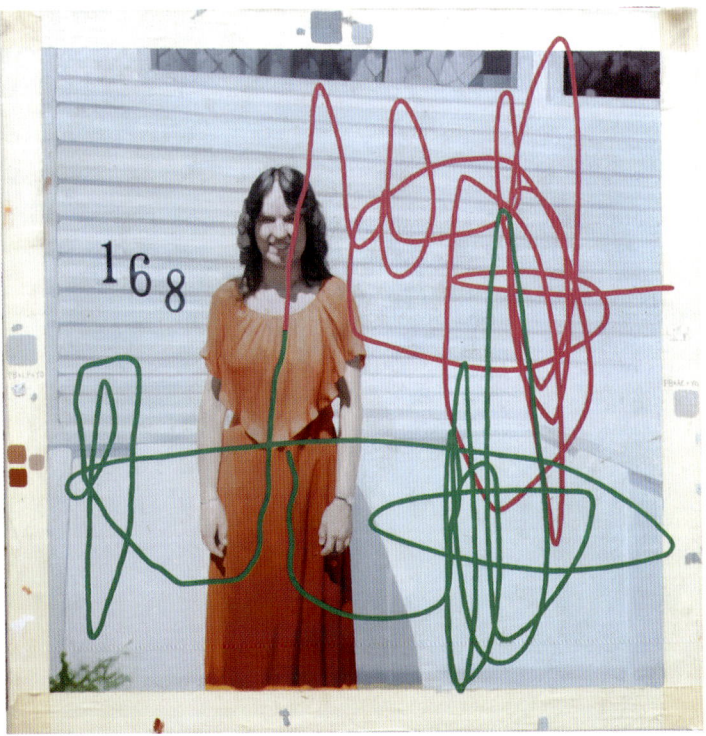

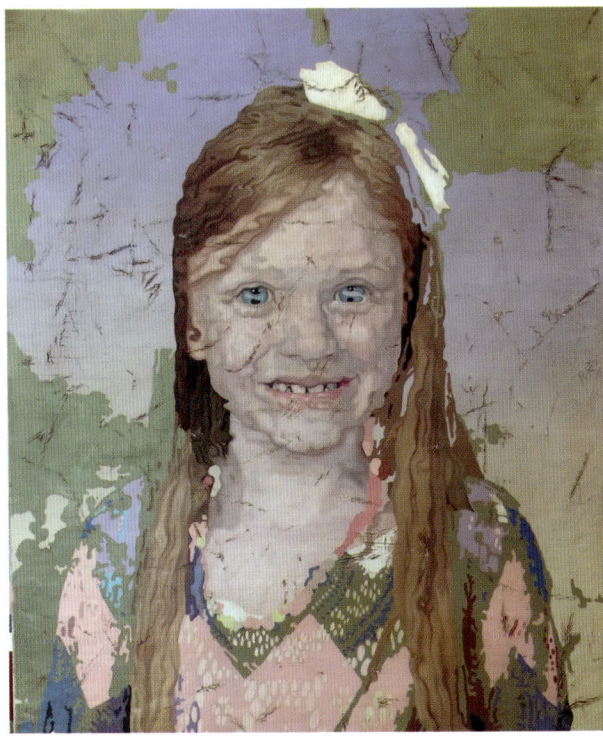

Top: Colin Chillag. *Class Snuggle*, 2017.
Oil on canvas: 54 × 68 inches.

Colin Chillag. *Punctum 5*, 2018.
Oil on canvas: 24 × 24 inches.

Colin Chillag. *Portrait of a Girl 5*, 2018.
Oil on canvas: 18 × 24 inches.

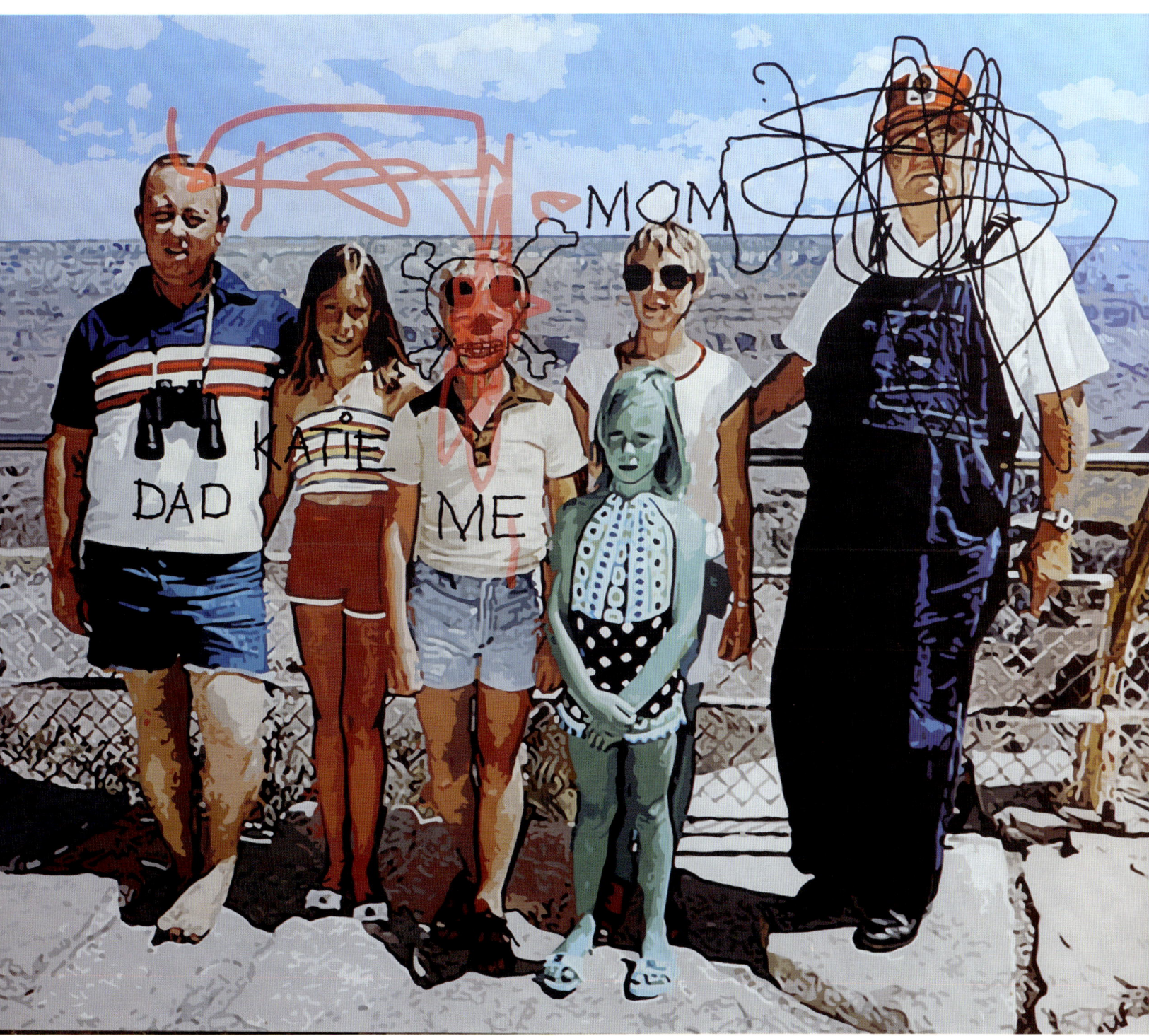

Colin Chillag. *Family Portrait 1 (Grand Canyon)*, 2017–18.
Oil on canvas: 60 × 72 inches.

GAGE OPDENBROUW

Lives and Works in: Oakland, California
Education: BFA, Academy of Art College, San Francisco
Selected Collections: Friends and artists across the US
Representation: John Natsoulas Gallery, Davis, California

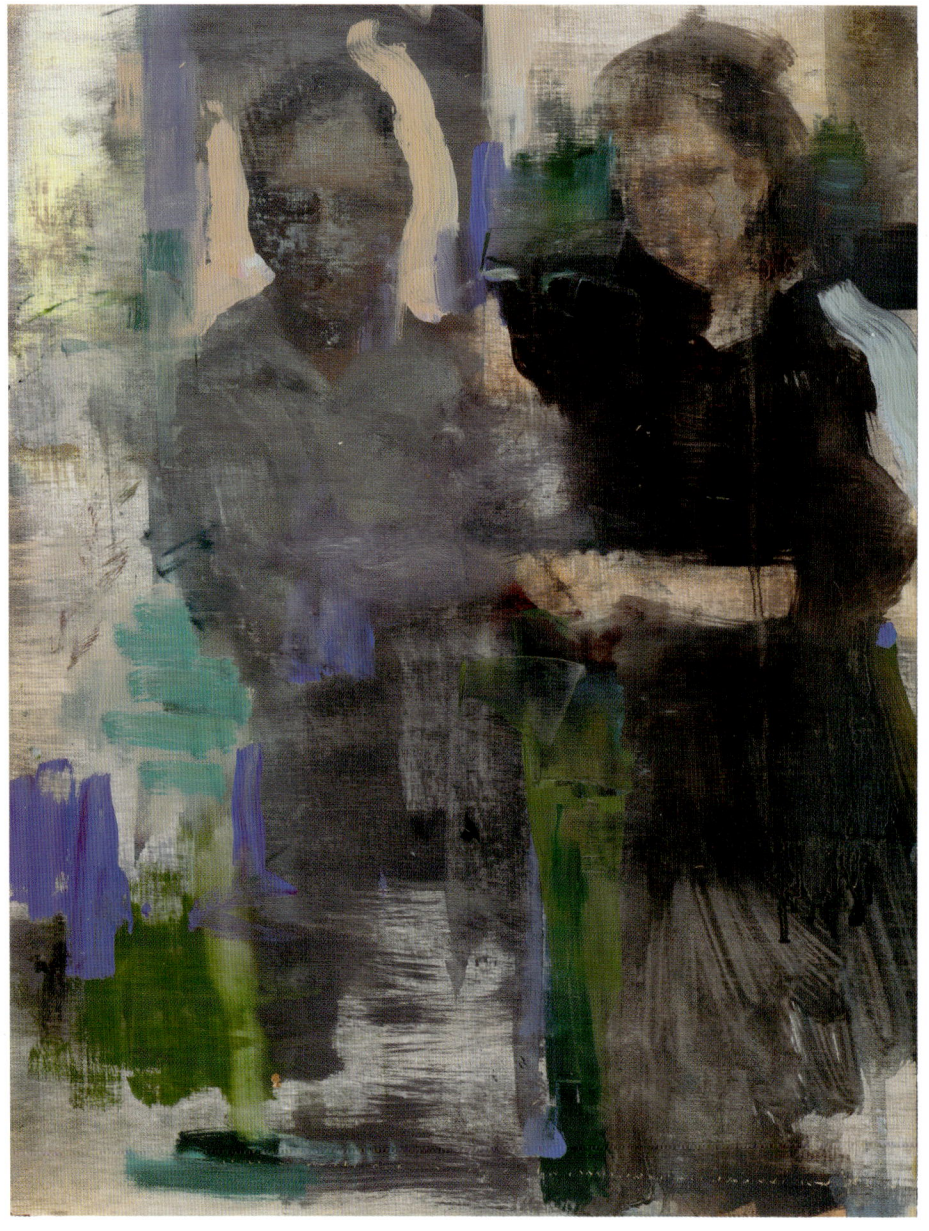

I would like these paintings to be achingly full and rich, lush and beautiful, and yet on the verge of disintegrating, solid and palpable, ephemeral and transient. They are ultimately a meditation on time and universal themes like light and shadow, presence and absence, love and loss.

Gage Opdenbrouw. *Fading Couple,* 2016.
Oil on panel: 16 × 20 inches.

How and why does your work disrupt or deviate from traditional realism?

I've often found artists who are very invested in the idea of "realism" to be a bit reactionary and angry. The term has never meant much to me, and, in fact, as I learned to paint, I found that often as one approached "realism" in terms of "finish," the poetry in the painting began to die. My goal is not to depict a single moment photographically rendered, but rather to show a compression of moments and observations condensed into a single image. Disruption is not a goal but rather a means of editing. Like a time-lapse photo but made by hand, with plenty of wrong turns and driving into the ditch, torn apart in moments of doubt, and pasted back together again, with notes scribbled on it.

I am influenced by many kinds of painting, and those that approach perceptual fidelity to appearances are only one set of influences. I welcome changing light, changing thoughts, and drastic changes into my process. I'm after a realism of atmosphere, of feeling, a realism of experience that goes beyond replicating outward appearances.

How has your work evolved and developed over time?

In some ways I think my work has developed from a sort of emotional realism, early on, driven by feeling and, frankly, angst, to focusing more on the quiet joys of humble subjects. Light, time, the development of the painting itself, color, paint, abstraction—these are all things that have grown more and more important to me. So in one way it could be characterized as a shift away from the dramatic to the quiet, or better yet a realization that there is plenty of depth and resonance in small, everyday things, and attention is all that is needed. I've also shifted pretty consistently to a modest or often even intimate scale for my paintings. One constant that has remained the ultimate driving force is a concern with color and light, atmosphere and space. I consider my painting from a more meditative angle than an overtly emotive one these days, and yet it is my hope that the paintings are still rich with feeling.

What are some of the influences that have shaped your work?

Nature, wilderness, hiking. Direct observation. DIY ethics. Meditation. Yoga. Buddhist philosophy. Transience/impermanence. Books, lots of books. Music, lyrics . . . Mary Oliver. Philip Larkin. Poetry in general. Punk rock. The paintings of others, of course. There's definitely a romantic vein in my work, in the sense of, say, Freidrich or Turner, or late Inness. Anselm Keifer. Manet, Vuillard, Bonnard. Morandi. Giacometti. Cézanne. Likewise, I love plenty of AbEx painters, like Joan Mitchell, Franz Kline, De Kooning, Rothko, Motherwell. The scrupulous attention of painters like Andrew Wyeth, Antonio Lopez Garcia, Euan Uglow, I find very inspiring, although I am much less patient and more impulsive and likely to improvise. The Bay Area Figurative painters, of course: Diebenkorn, David Park, Elmer Bischoff, Paul Wonner were fantastic. Edwin Dickinson. Bellows. I also love Agnes Martin, certain Ad Reinhardt paintings, a lot of traditional Asian painting. Reduction is good; meaningful simplicity is a goal worth striving for.

Mention something interesting about your life and background.

I was born in Silicon Valley—the land of gadgets—in 1977. I have somehow evolved into a quiet and nature-focused person who doesn't like watching TV or playing with gadgets, hates computers, and is basically a friendly recluse who is happiest with a dog, a bass, and a paintbrush close at hand. At forty-one I still don't know how to tie a necktie without a little help and am mostly proud of that.

Overleaf: Gage Opdenbrouw. *August Nude,* 2015–16. Oil on panel: 20 × 30 inches.

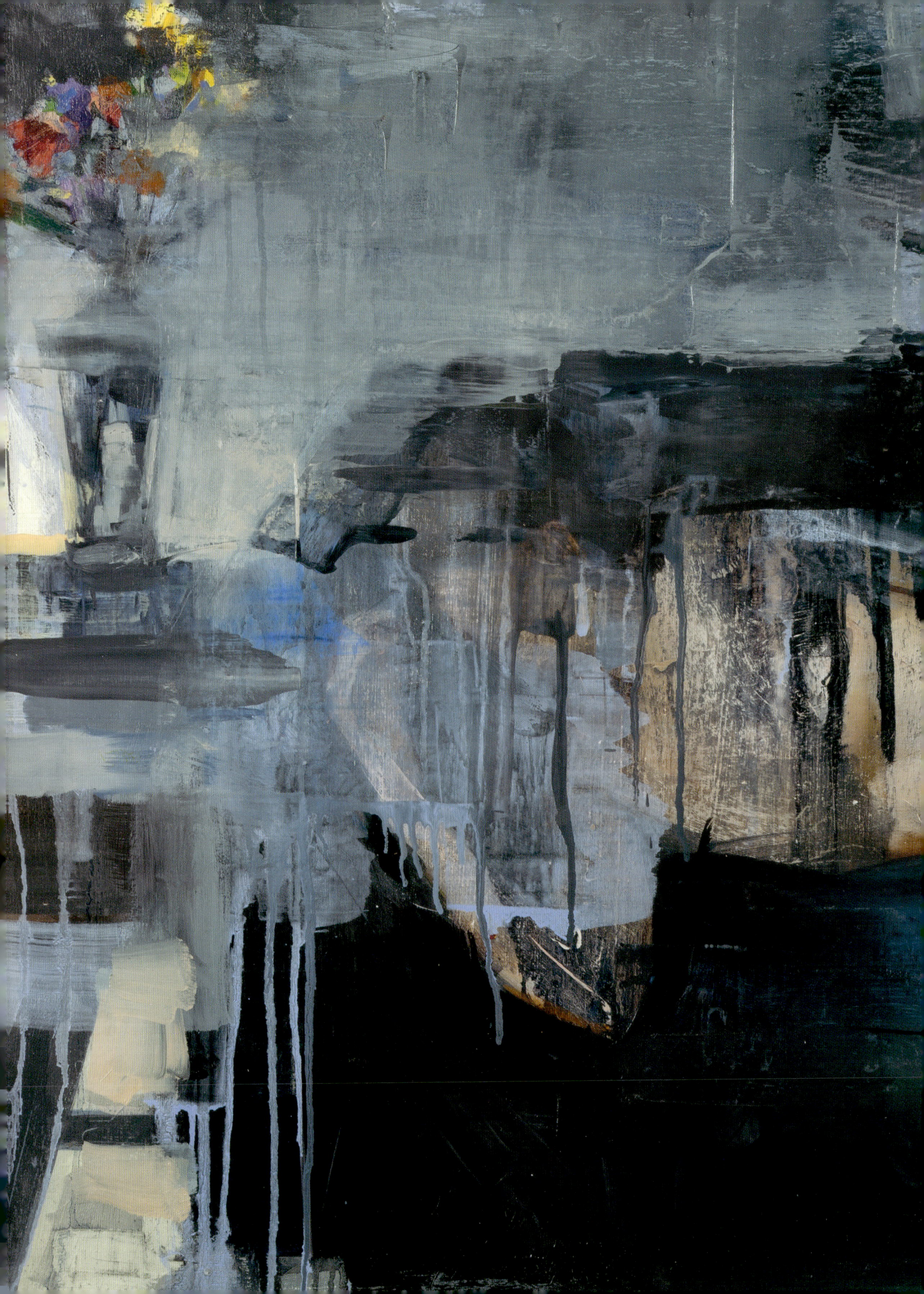

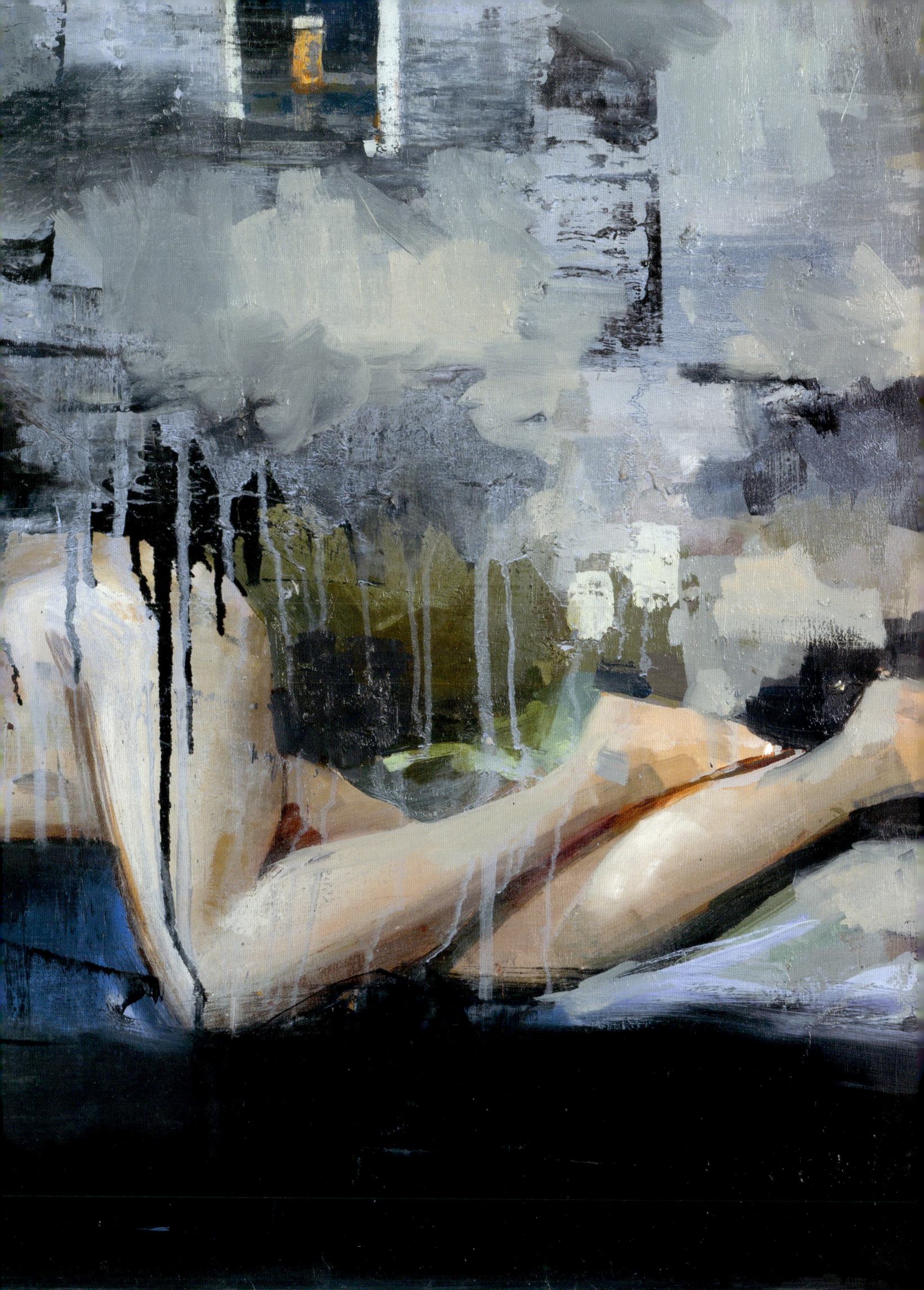

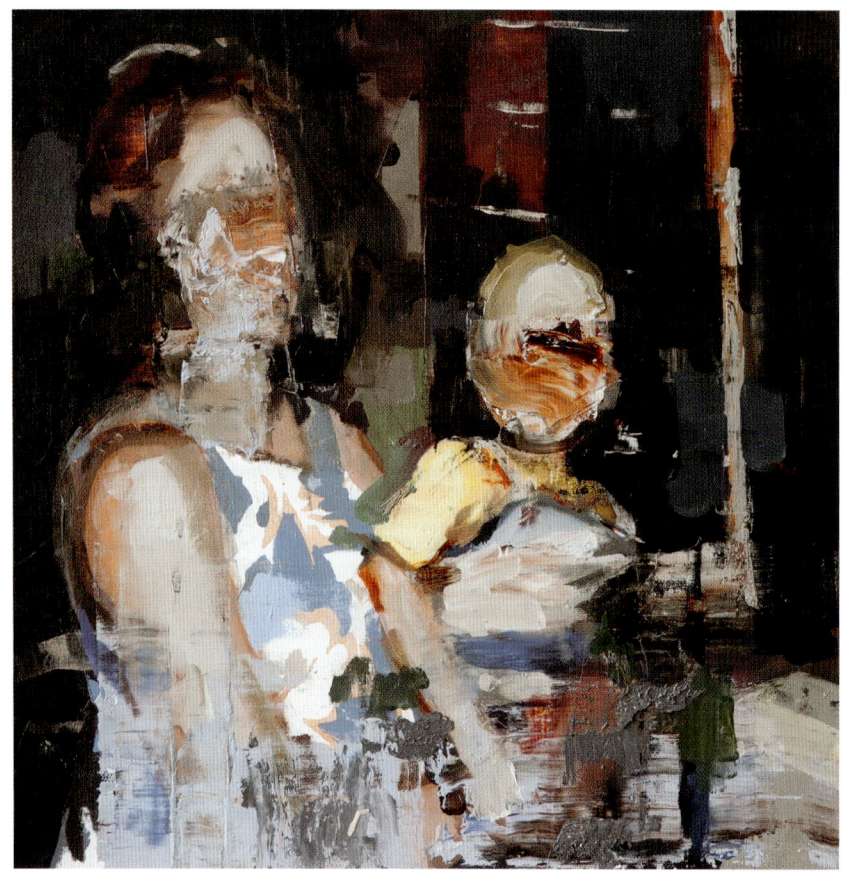

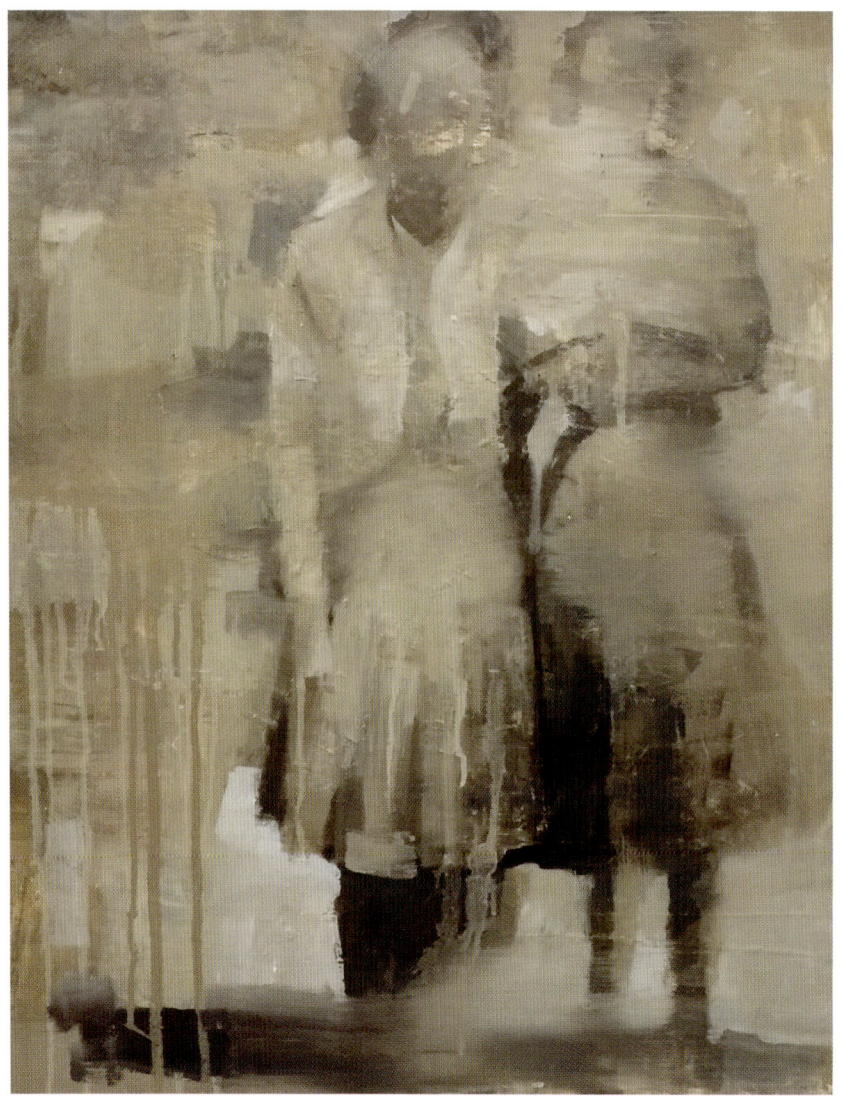

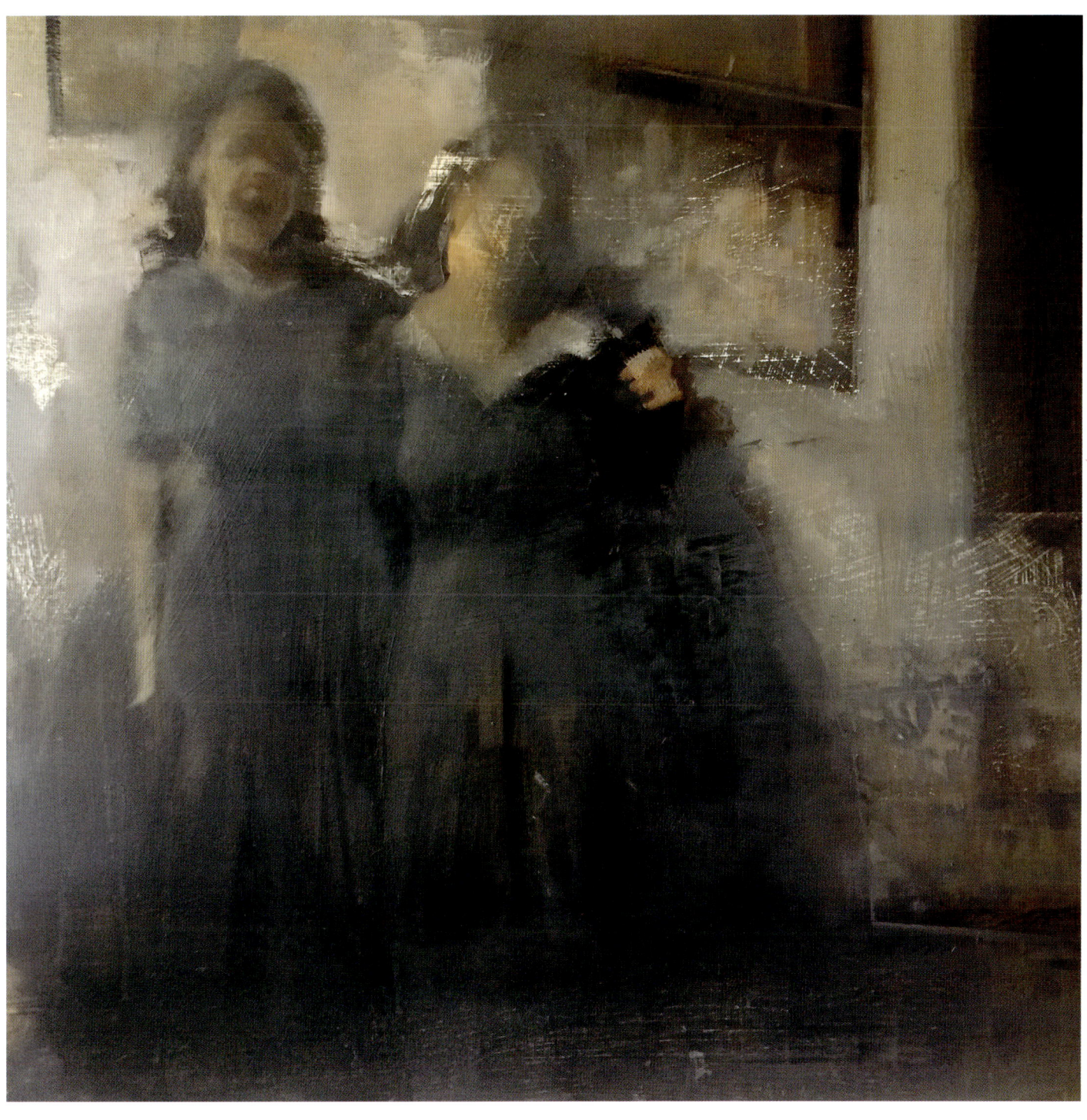

Gage Opdenbrouw. *Untitled*, 1979, 2015.
Oil on panel: 14 × 14 inches.

Gage Opdenbrouw. *Fading*, 2016.
Oil on panel: 16 × 20 inches.

Gage Opdenbrouw. *Sing Out, Sing Out*, 2015–16.
Oil on panel: 24 × 24 inches.

ADAM VINSON

Lives and Works in: Philadelphia

Education: The Waichulis Studio, Pennsylvania Academy of the Fine Arts

Representation: Arcadia Contemporary, Pasadena, California

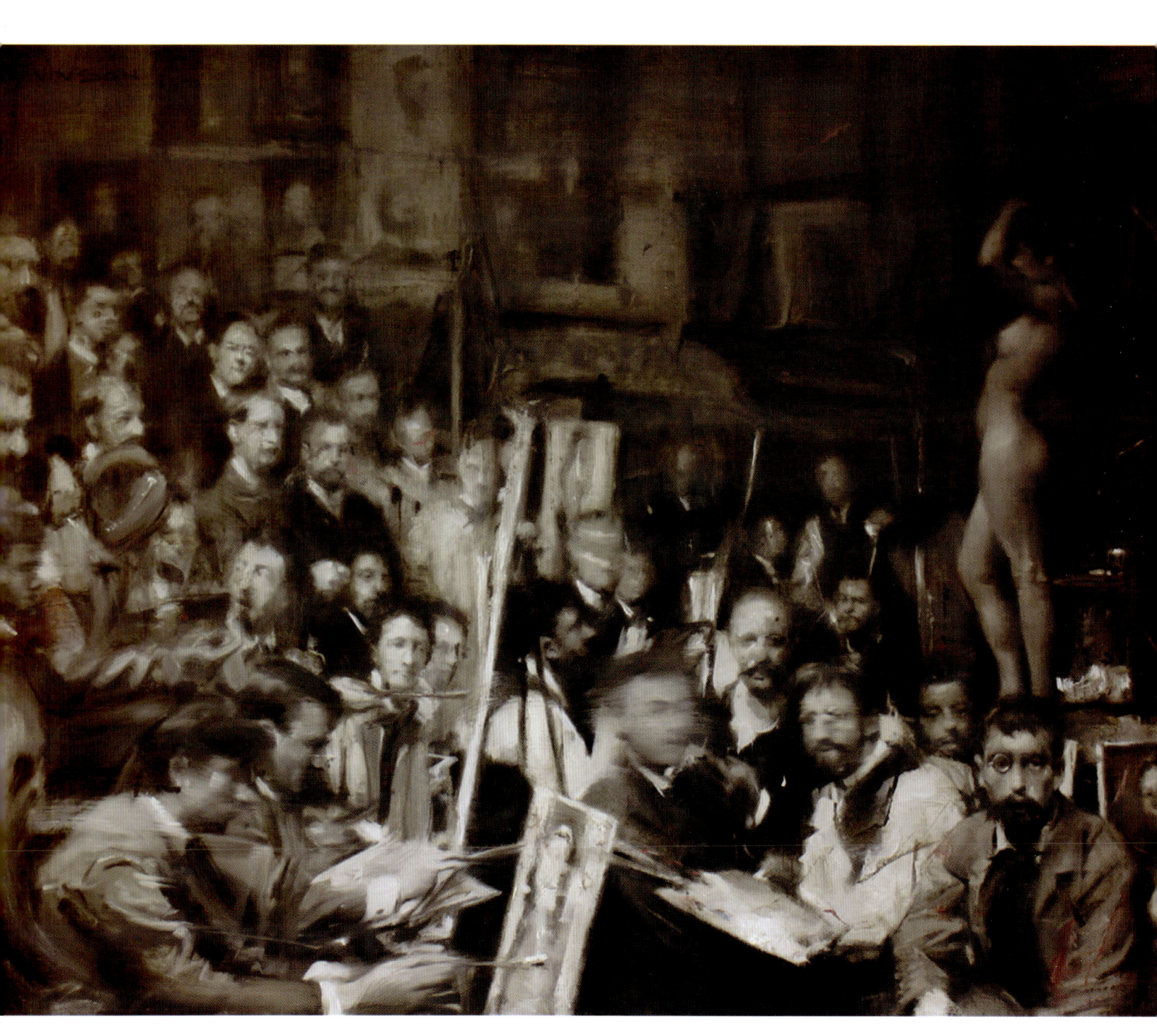

I see myself as an invasive weed in life's garden, cultivated by a quixotic and feckless pursuit of the unattainable.

How and why does your work disrupt or deviate from traditional realism?

In terms of the Western academic tradition, I'm not sure that it deviates at all. My most recent approach to painting is more emotive, exploratory, and expressive than that of my earlier oeuvre, which focused heavily on technical accuracy and meticulous execution.

How has your work evolved and developed over time?

These days, I care less about achieving a level of verisimilitude that is visually deceitful in spite of the nature of the materials, or technically impressive for its own sake, and more about inspiriting the painting by conceding to the materials and process more organically. The craft of painting does not necessarily produce the poetry of painting, but it is the poetry of painting that now primarily influences my craft.

What are some of the influences that have shaped your work?

[Intentionally left blank]

Mention something interesting about your life and background.

I'm an art school dropout, a uselessly astute music enthusiast, and an ultra-marathoner. I have a twin sister (thankfully, for her sake, we are not identical).

Adam Vinson. *Captive Audience,* 2018.
Oil on panel: 16 × 20 inches.

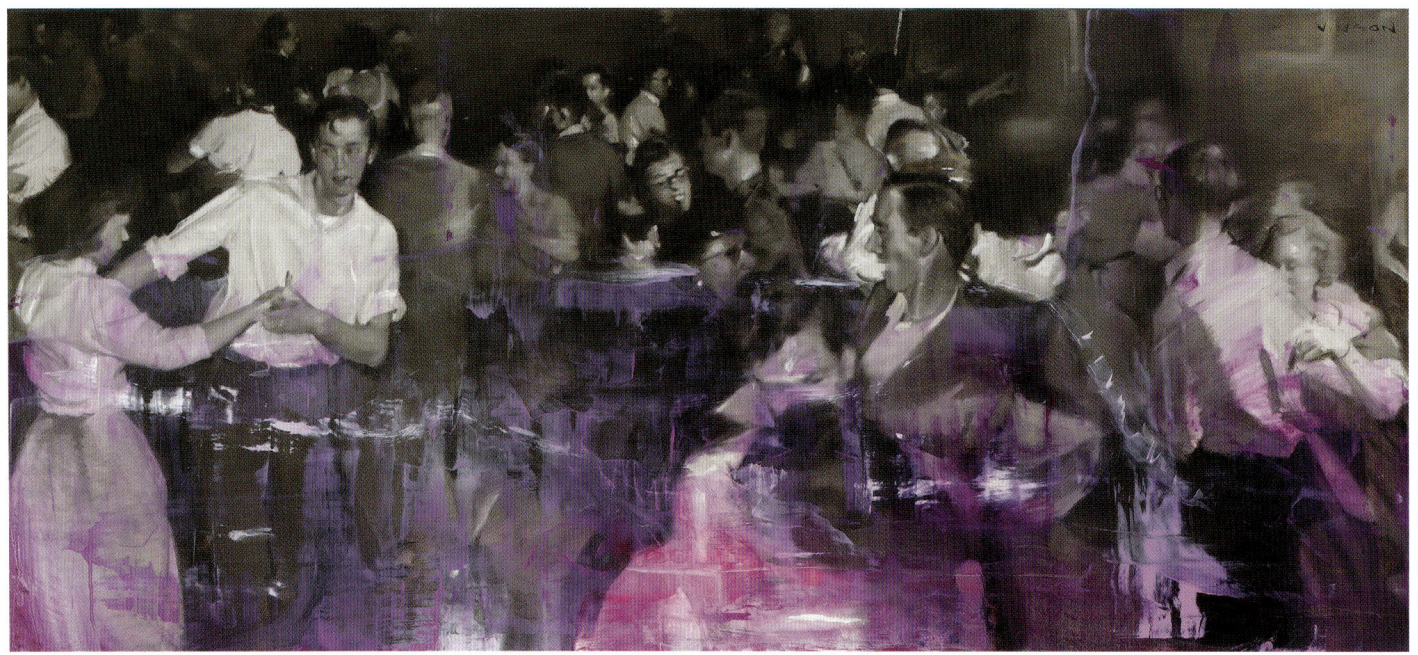

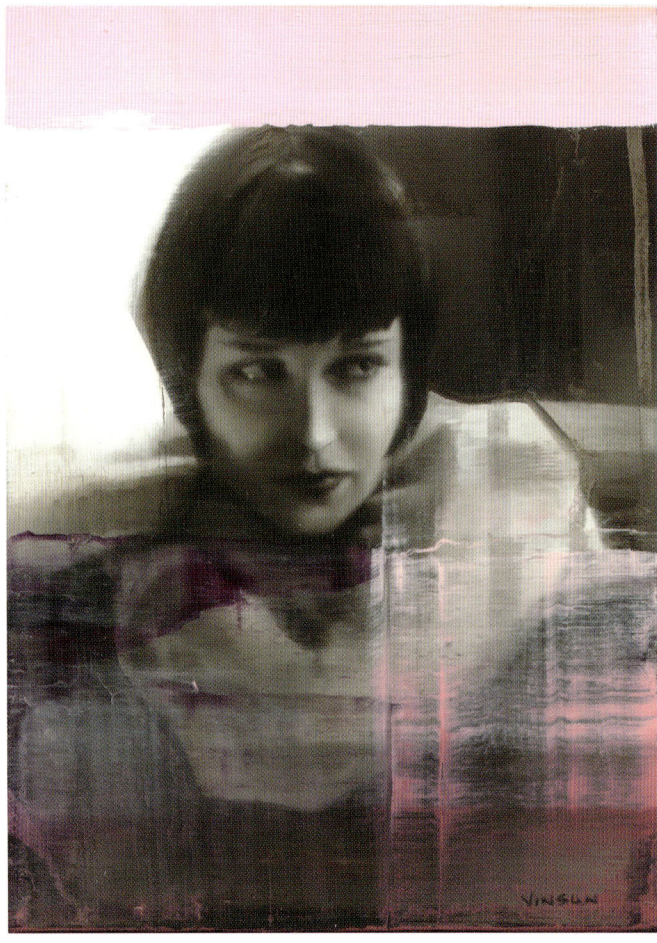

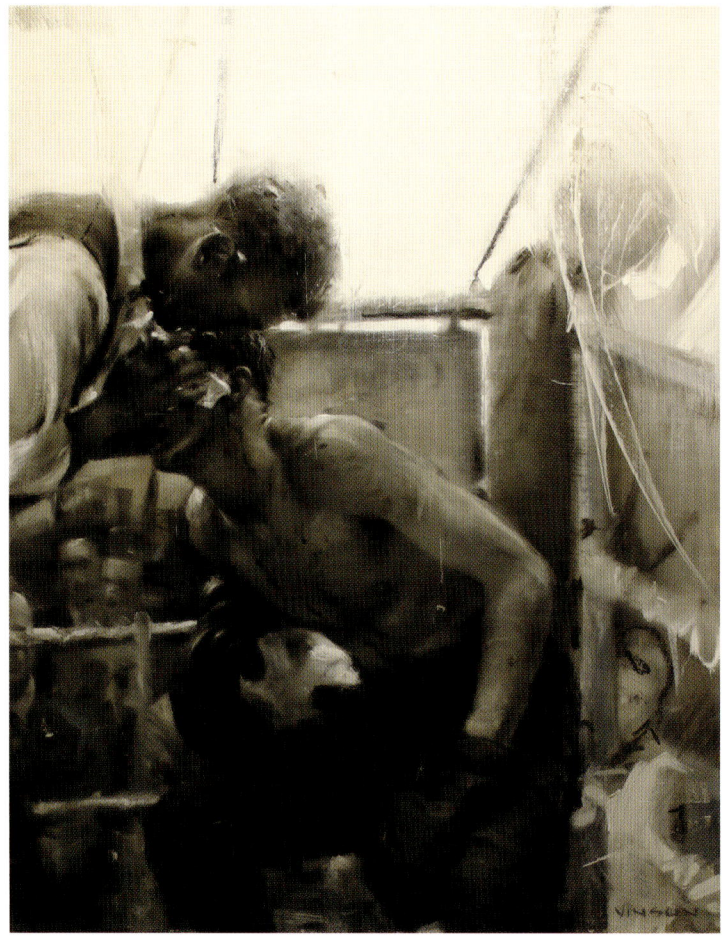

Adam Vinson. *Do Si Do to Midnight*, 2017.
Oil on panel: 24 × 54 inches.

Adam Vinson. *Minx in Pink*, 2017.
Oil on panel: 8 × 6 inches.

Adam Vinson. *The Reminders*, 2018.
Oil on panel: 20 × 16 inches.

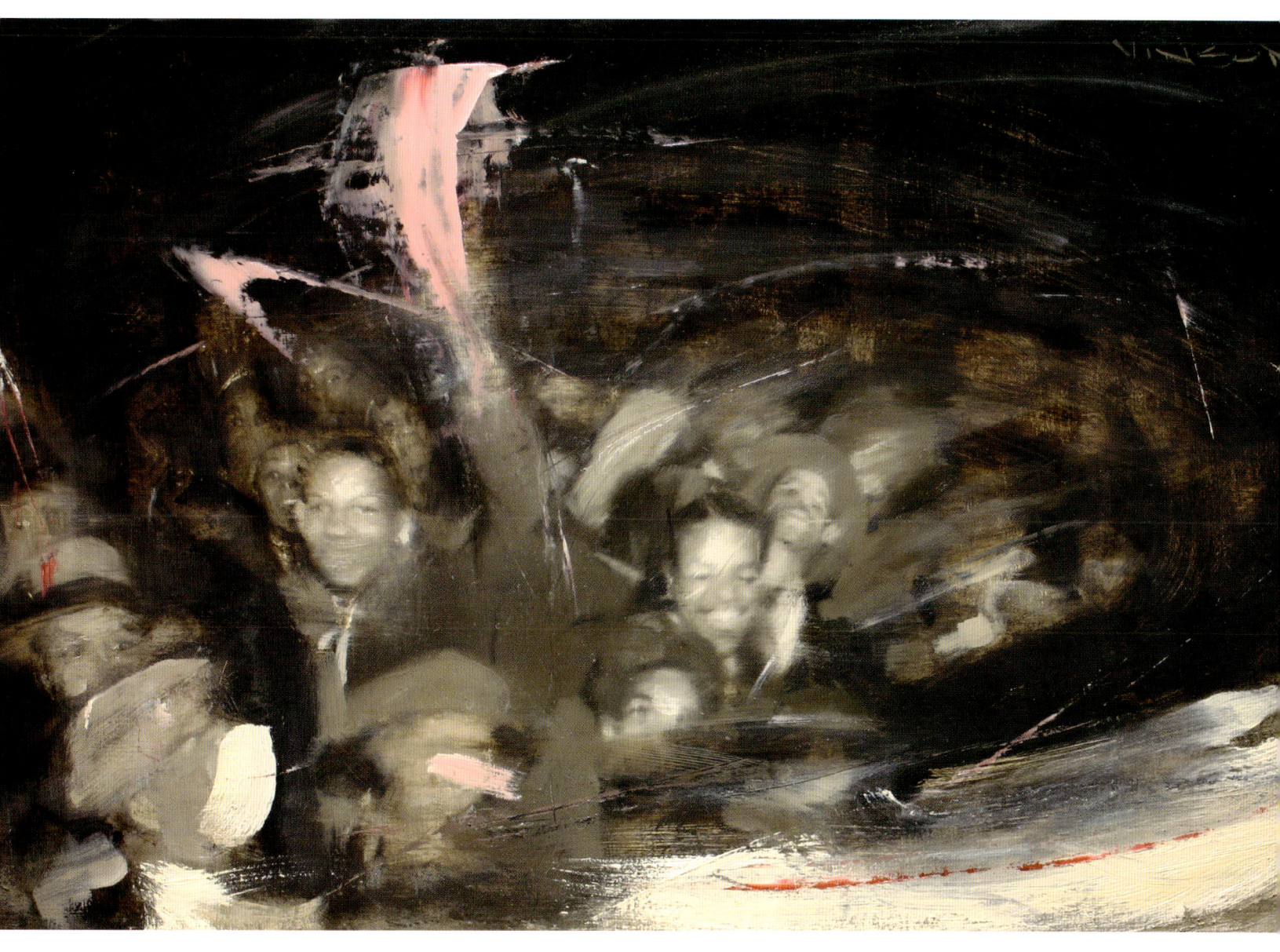

Adam Vinson. *Plenum*, 2018.
Oil on panel: 8 × 12 inches.

WENDELIN WOHLGEMUTH

Lives and Works in: Berlin
Education: Western Washington University
Representation: Galerie Guido Romero Pierini, Paris

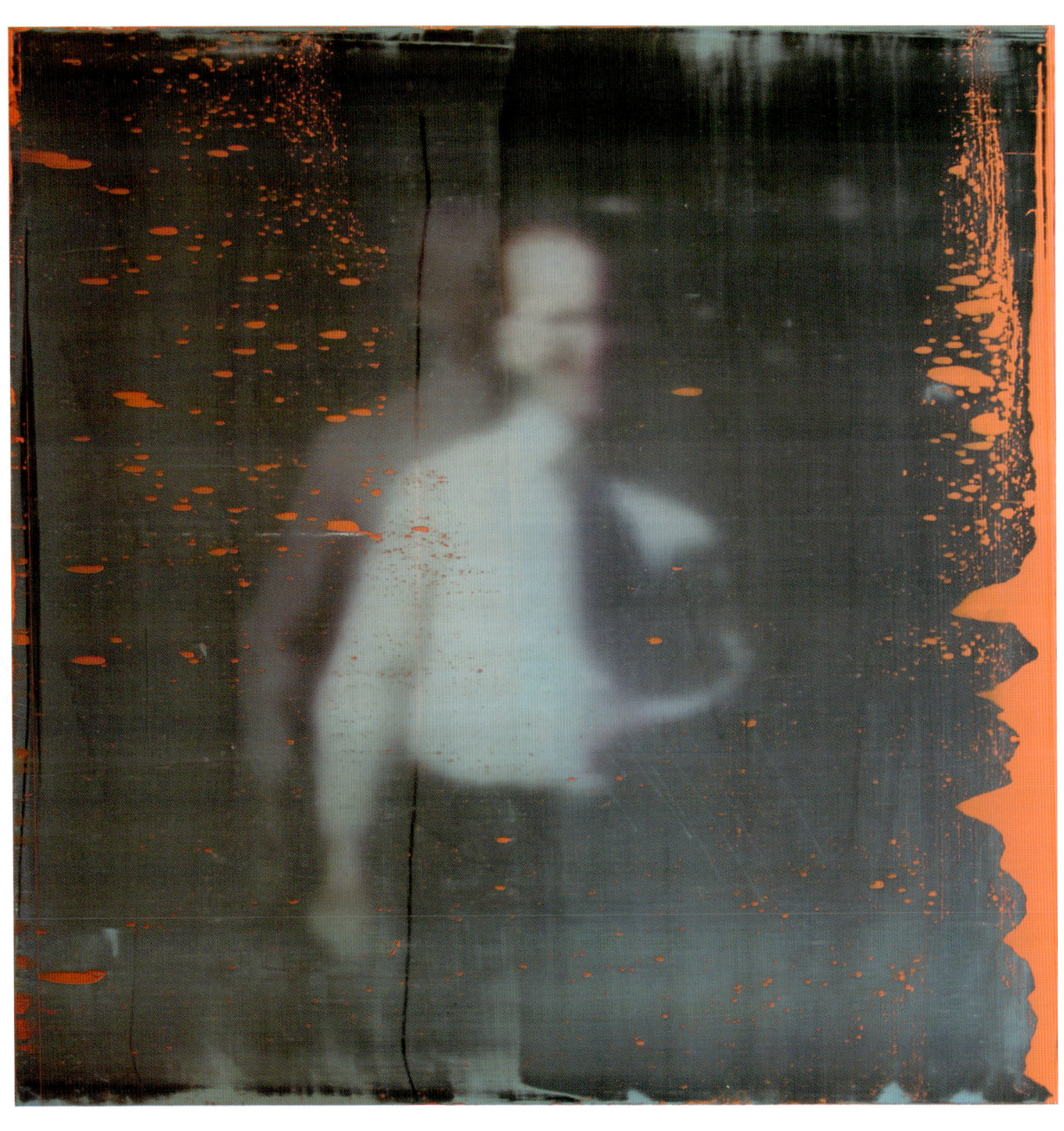

*My paintings present a shared memory
of human existence while exploring the
paradoxical visual properties of oil paint.*

How does your work disrupt or deviate from traditional realism?

From a technical standpoint, my work deviates from traditional realism in two major ways: first, my reference photos are often heavily distorted due to the manner in which the image was captured (mainly screenshots from low-resolution 35 mm video archives that I find online). Second, I apply textures, marks, and color glazes on top of the representational image in successive layers, using squeegees and other nontraditional tools.

How has your work evolved and developed over time?

I was initially attracted to a manner of painting where one disrupts the representational image via a process of building and destroying forms on top of one another in a very interactive manner. But I've since developed a way of working where the representational and disruptive aspects exist on different visual planes. But I have still retained interest in the visual tension between paint's two main functions: both as a virtual medium that allows one to view another object and as a purely physical substance. It is this visual paradox that interests me most.

What are some of the influences that have shaped your work?

Gerhard Richter's overpainted photographs had a big effect on me. They challenged any clear notions I had about what "abstract" and "representational" meant. They made it clear that a blob of color and a photograph are both equally representational and abstract all at once. More of my earliest inspirations include Sigmar Polke and Robert Rauschenberg and their use of texture alongside manipulated photography in their paintings. I draw a lot of my aesthetic inspiration from alternative photographic techniques such as photo transfers that I experimented with in art school. But now I find oil paint is the perfect medium for exploring all of these visual ideas.

Mention something interesting about your life and background.

I am a dual citizen of both the US and Germany.

Wendelin Wohlgemuth. *Boy Outside,* 2017.
Oil on panel: 16 × 16 inches.

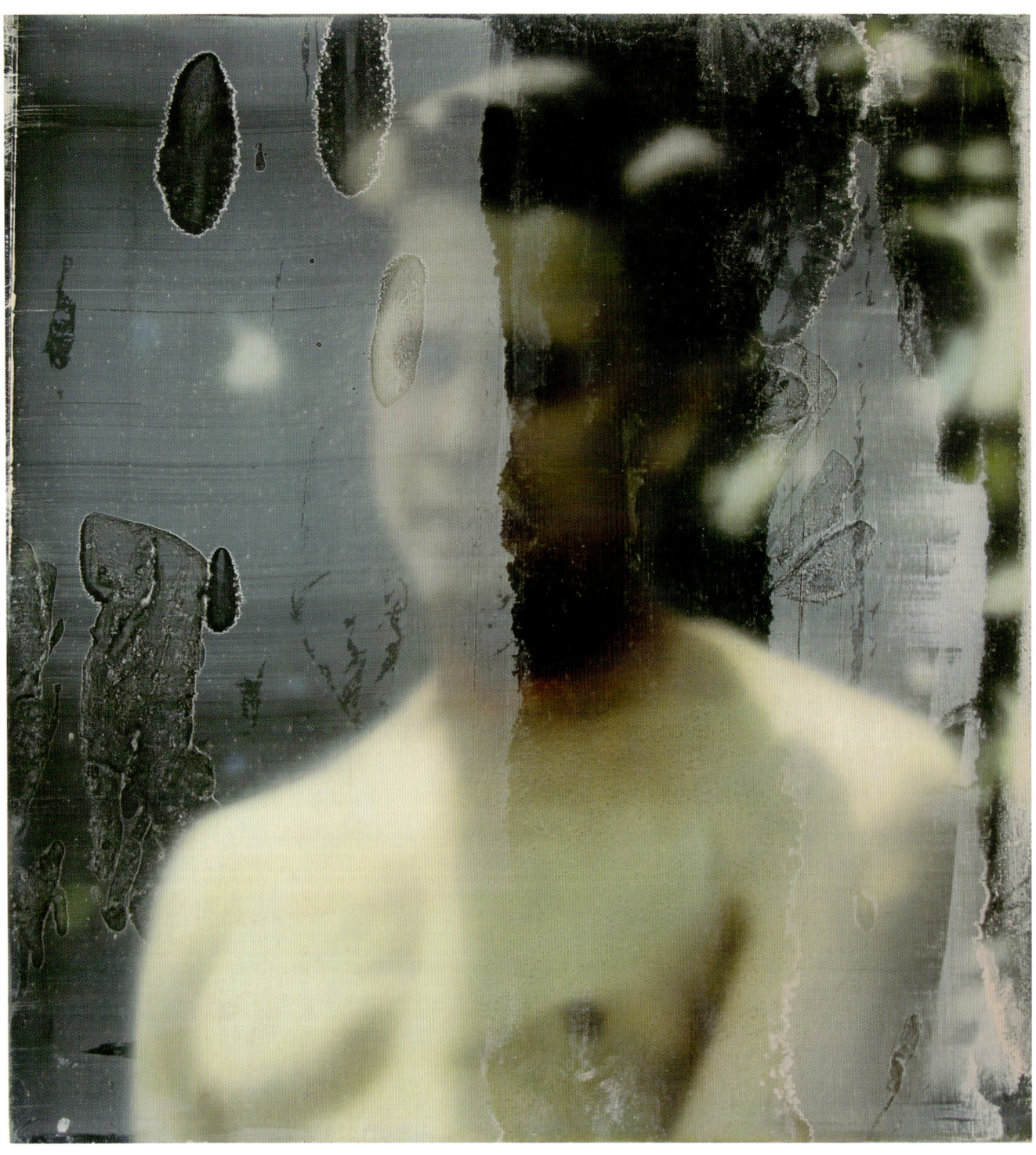

Wendelin Wohlgemuth. *Man by the Lake,* 2018.
Oil on panel: 17.7 × 18.8 inches.

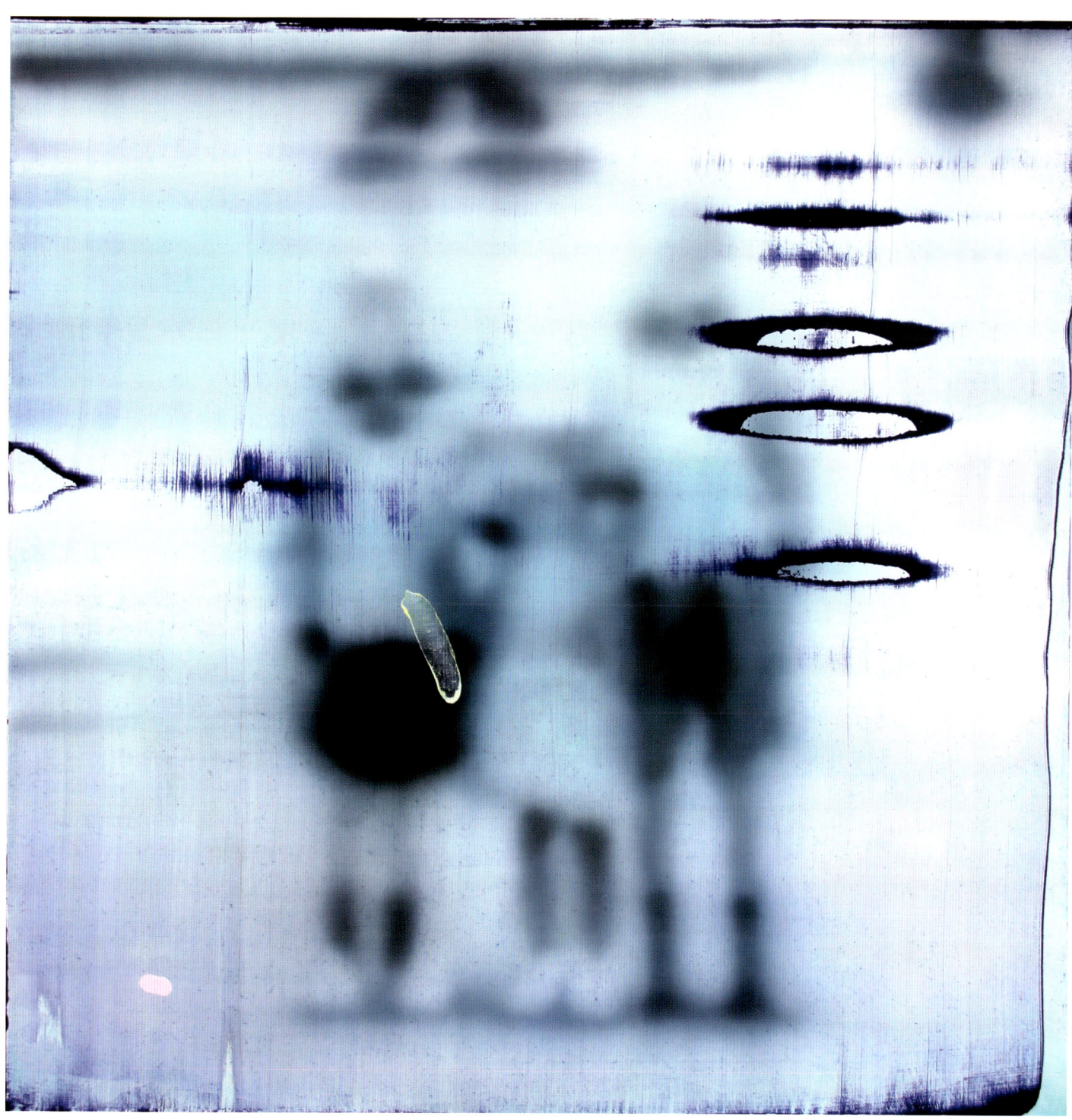

Wendelin Wohlgemuth. *Siblings,* 2017.
Oil on panel: 20 × 20 inches.

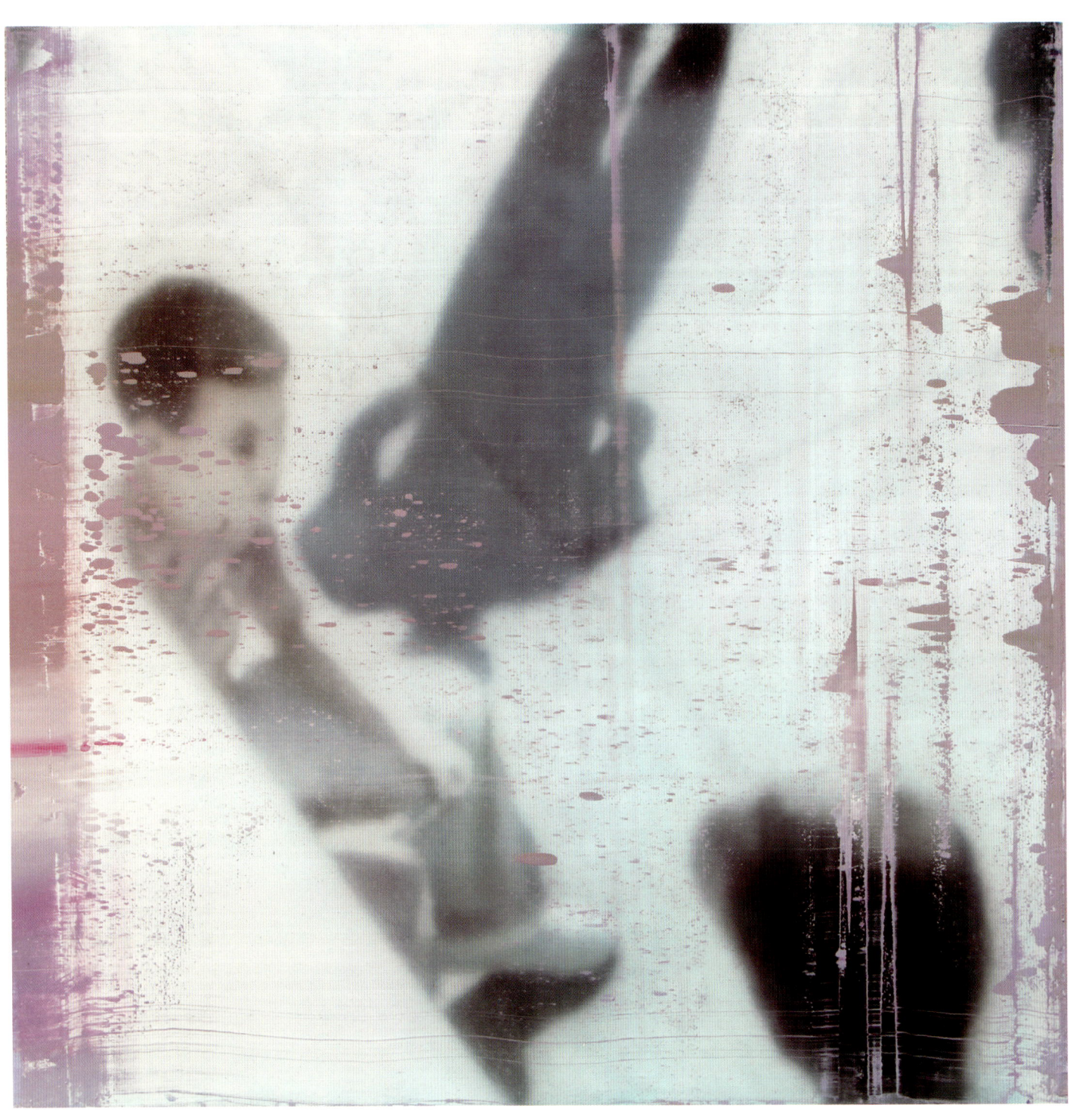

Wendelin Wohlgemuth. *View X*, 2018.
Oil on panel: 20 × 20 inches.